Lord Dufferin, Ireland and the British Empire, c. 1820–1900

This book explores the life and career of Frederick Temple Hamilton-Temple-Blackwood, 1st Marquess of Dufferin and Ava (1826–1902). Dufferin was a landowner in Ulster, an urbane diplomat, literary sensation, courtier, politician, colonial governor, collector, son, husband and father. The book draws on episodes from Dufferin's career to link the landowning and aristocratic culture he was born into with his experience of governing across the British Empire, in Canada, Egypt, Syria and India. This book argues that there was a defined conception of aristocratic governance and purpose that infused the political and imperial world, and was based on two elements: the inheritance and management of a landed estate, and a well-defined sense of 'rule by the best'. It identifies a particular kind of atmosphere of empire and aristocracy, one that was riven with tensions and angst, as those who saw themselves as the hereditary leaders of Britain and Ireland were challenged by a rising democracy and, in Ireland, by a powerful new definition of what Irishness was. It offers a new perspective on both empire and aristocracy in the nineteenth century, and will appeal to a broad scholarly audience and the wider public.

Annie Tindley is Professor of British and Irish Rural History at Newcastle University.

Routledge Studies in Modern British History

Weather, Migration and the Scottish Diaspora
Leaving the Cold Country
Graeme Morton

Science, Utility and British Naval Technology, 1793–1815
Samuel Bentham and the Royal Dockyards
Roger Morriss

Credit and Power
The Paradox at the Heart of the British National Debt
Simon Sherratt

The Casino and Society in Britain
Seamus Murphy

Great Britain, the Dominions and the Transformation of the British Empire, 1907–1931
The Road to the Statute of Westminster
Jaroslav Valkoun

The Discourse of Repatriation in Britain, 1845–2016
A Political and Social History
Daniel Renshaw

The Devil and the Victorians
Supernatural Evil in Nineteenth-Century English Culture
Sarah Bartels

Lord Dufferin, Ireland and the British Empire, c. 1820–1900
Rule by the Best?
Annie Tindley

For more information about this series, please visit: https://www.routledge.com/history/series/RSMBH

Lord Dufferin, Ireland and the British Empire, c. 1820–1900
Rule by the Best?

Annie Tindley

LONDON AND NEW YORK

First published 2021
by Routledge
2 Park Square, Milton Park, Abingdon, Oxon OX14 4RN

and by Routledge
52 Vanderbilt Avenue, New York, NY 10017

Routledge is an imprint of the Taylor & Francis Group, an informa business

© 2021 Annie Tindley

The right of Annie Tindley to be identified as author of this work has been asserted by her in accordance with sections 77 and 78 of the Copyright, Designs and Patents Act 1988.

All rights reserved. No part of this book may be reprinted or reproduced or utilised in any form or by any electronic, mechanical, or other means, now known or hereafter invented, including photocopying and recording, or in any information storage or retrieval system, without permission in writing from the publishers.

Trademark notice: Product or corporate names may be trademarks or registered trademarks, and are used only for identification and explanation without intent to infringe.

British Library Cataloguing-in-Publication Data
A catalogue record for this book is available from the British Library

Library of Congress Cataloging-in-Publication Data
Names: Tindley, Annie, author.
Title: Lord Dufferin, Ireland and the British Empire, c. 1820-1900 : rule by the best? / Annie Tindley.
Description: Abingdon, Oxon ; New York : Routledge Taylor & Francis Group, 2021. | Series: Routledge studies in modern British history | Includes bibliographical references and index.
Subjects: LCSH: Dufferin and Ava, Frederick Temple Blackwood, Marquis of, 1826-1902. | Diplomats--Great Britain--Biography. | Great Britain--Colonies--Administration--History--19th century. | Governors general--Canada--Biography. | Colonial administrators--Biography. | Viceroys--India--Biography. | Imperialism--Social aspects--Great Britain--Colonies--History--19th century. | Ulster (Northern Ireland and Ireland)--Biography.
Classification: LCC DA17.D9 T56 2021 (print) | LCC DA17.D9 (ebook) | DDC 954.03/54092 [B]--dc23
LC record available at https://lccn.loc.gov/2020046643
LC ebook record available at https://lccn.loc.gov/2020046644

ISBN: 978-0-815-36827-4 (hbk)
ISBN: 978-0-367-71278-5 (pbk)
ISBN: 978-1-351-25528-8 (ebk)

Typeset in Sabon
by SPi Global, India

In this history I know that everything anyone could want to find in the most delectable history is to be found; and if anything worthwhile is missing from it, it's my belief that it's the dog of an author who wrote it that's to blame, rather than any defect in the subject.

Miguel de Cervantes, *Don Quixote*, part I, ch. IX.

This book is dedicated to my husband, Colin, and my mother, Linda.

Contents

List of figures viii
Acknowledgments ix

Prologue 1

1. Introducing Dufferin 4

2. Property 27

3. Irish questions: the empire within 53

4. Will to rule 83

5. Remits of power: governing the self-governed 112

6. Man on the spot: Dufferin as imperial problem solver 141

7. Ornamental empire?: Dufferin as viceroy 164

Conclusion: decline and fall 202

General bibliography and sources 209
Index 231

Figures

1.1 *Lord Dufferin Monument* of 1906 by Frederick W. Pomeroy. Marble. This monument is reproduced by the kind permission of Belfast City Council. The original can be viewed at City Hall, Belfast.   5
1.2 Stipple engraving of Frederick Temple Hamilton-Temple-Blackwood, 1st Marquess of Dufferin and Ava as a young man, 1869 or thereafter. Charles Holl, after Henry Tanworth Wells/Public domain via Wikimedia Commons.   8
1.3 *Frederick Hamilton-Temple-Blackwood, 1st Marquess of Dufferin and Ava* by Henrietta Rae. Oil on canvas. This portrait is reproduced by the kind permission of Belfast City Council. The original can be viewed at City Hall, Belfast.   14
5.1 Lord Dufferin, taken in Ottawa, 1873, aged 47. The Notman studio, Ottawa, William J. Topley, proprietor/public domain via Wikimedia Commons.   114
7.1 Official portrait of Lord Dufferin as viceroy of India, c. 1885. Photo by Bourne and Shepherd of Calcutta. Nineteenth-century albumen print. The original uploader was Fawcett5 at English Wikipedia/Public domain.   165

Acknowledgments

This book has been nearly ten years in the researching and writing, has been through three academic posts, many more house moves, and has jostled for attention among other research and writing projects. The number of debts and influences to be acknowledged and thanked is therefore hilariously considerable.

I was extremely fortunate to benefit from two grants to support the research in the various archives in which Dufferin material is located: first, grateful thanks to the Royal Society of Edinburgh for a research expenses grant made in 2011 and, second, to the British Academy for a small research grant made in 2014.

I am even more fortunate to have worked side-by-side with an assiduous, dedicated and clever researcher: my mother, Linda. She travelled from Chester to London, Oxford and Hatfield on countless visits to read and transcribe hundreds of thousands of words from the archives when I was struggling for time, and is now as much an expert on matters of aristocracy and empire as I am, as I found out when I received back my draft manuscript with numerous suggestions for improvement. Of course, the book has benefitted hugely from those and I want to thank her for everything. I would also like to thank Joe and Janet, my in-laws, for their utmost patience and good humour in the face of their ragged and annoying daughter-in-law turning up for weeks on end to receive dinner, bed and breakfast, and taxi services while working at the Public Record Office of Northern Ireland, an institution that, unfortunately for them, is only 15 minutes from their house.

PRONI is an exemplary repository and it was a pleasure to spend so much time there, benefitting from the kind help and advice of their archivists, especially David Huddleston, Stephen Scarf and Lorraine Bourke. I would also like to thank the British Library, especially the staff in the Asian and African Studies Room; The National Archives, Kew; the Bodleian Library, Oxford; the National Library of Scotland; the Marquis of Salisbury and the archivist at Hatfield House; and the Duke of Argyll and Alison Diamond, archivist for the Argyll Estates at Inveraray Castle. I am also very grateful to Belfast City Hall for their permission to publish two illustrations from their collections: that of the statue to Dufferin still located in their grounds and of the portrait of Dufferin in older age by Henrietta Rae. Lastly, and most importantly, I would like to thank and pay tribute to the late Lady Dufferin, a truly inspirational and defining figure, the heart and soul of Clandeboye in its late twentieth and early twenty-first century iterations. Her vision will continue to shape the future of the estate and the people who live and work on it, which is at least some comfort for those left bereft at her death in October 2020. I would also like to thank most warmly her archivist Lola Armstrong, the (now retired) estate manager and fellow researcher John Witchell, Sir Ian Huddleston, Mark Logan and Karen Kane for their endless help, inspiration and insight.

Some of the initial ideas for this study were knocked around with my first boss, Elaine McFarland, emeritus professor at Glasgow Caledonian University. For her advice and for kindly reading some of this in draft – as well as everything else she has done for me – I would like to thank her. Likewise, my other colleagues at Glasgow Caledonian University, Dr Ben Shepherd, Dr Fraser Duncan, Dr Stewart Davidson and, now my colleague at Newcastle University, Dr Vicky Long. I spent three years in between at the University of Dundee and would like to extend my thanks to my History colleagues there, especially Professor Graeme Morton and Dr Pat Whatley for their friendship, and to my new(er) colleagues at Newcastle, who are a joy and inspiration to work with. I would especially like to thank the School of History, Classics and Archaeology for a semester of research leave in 2019–20, and my friends and colleagues Dr Scott Ashley, Professor Helen Berry, Dr Sarah Campbell, Dr Ruth Connelly, Dr Stacy Gillis, Professor Nigel Harkness, Professor Vee Pollock, Professor Mike Rossington, Dr Claire Stocks and all my fabulous colleagues in the Northern Bridge Consortium – but, most especially, Carole Palmer and Sarah Rylance. I owe a special debt to Dr Karly Kehoe, now of St Mary's University, Nova Scotia, who gave me my first research leave – in the form an Atlantic Canada fellowship – where I was able to complete the two main tranches of the writing up of this book. Her friendship and encouragement over the past fifteen years is one of the great privileges of my working life, as are those of Professor Laura Stewart (University of York), Professor Dauvit Broun (University of Glasgow), Professor David Worthington and his colleagues at University of the Highlands and Islands, Professor Terry Dooley (Maynooth University), Dr John MacAskill (University of Edinburgh), Mr Finlay McKichan and my long-suffering PhD supervisor, Professor Ewen Cameron (University of Edinburgh). Each offered insight and support at critical periods, and some read and commented on drafts: all errors are my own, of course.

General admiration and thanks are also due to my father Roger, my sister Jen, her husband Greg and my two nieces, Isobel and Elsie. I am looking forward to threatening them with reading this (BORING) book in due course. My last debt is the most important: to my husband Colin, who grew up just ten minutes away from Clandeboye and is and has been a constant source of encouragement and support. Sitting here, I find I cannot quite put what I feel into words and so he will need to trust me on this one.

Annie Tindley

Prologue

Skibbereen, Ireland, 1847

In early 1847, two young and earnest Oxford undergraduates left their comfortable lodgings and convivial society life at Christ Church and travelled to the epicentre of Europe's worst nineteenth-century peacetime disaster: Skibbereen, the town at the heart of the Great Irish Famine. Frederick Temple Hamilton-Temple-Blackwood, Baron Clandeboye, later 1st Marquis of Dufferin and Ava, and the Hon. George F. Boyle – fast friends at Oxford and full partakers of the religious spirit then infusing university society – had heard of the horrors unfolding since the previous year and had decided to investigate conditions for themselves.[1] Dufferin had inherited his own Irish estate in County Down in 1841 as a minor and, although the day-to-day management of his property was in the hands of his guardians, he wanted to get to grips with the stark realities of the Irish 'problem'.[2] Together, Dufferin and Boyle sailed to Dublin and travelled by stagecoach to Cork. 'At the end of every stage,' Dufferin wrote later, 'the coach was surrounded by crowds of wretched creatures begging for something to eat. Wan little faces thrust themselves in at the window.'[3] Worse was to come when they arrived at Skibbereen: 'Dead bodies had lain putrefying in the midst of the sick remnants of their families, none strong enough to remove them, until the rats and decay made it difficult to recognise that they had once been human beings.'[4] Lord Dufferin was only twenty-one and about to take up the reins of his own landed estate: witnessing the horrors of the Famine made a fundamental impact on the ways in which he framed his experience of being an Irish landlord and what he regarded as his duties for the rest of his life.[5] His immediate response was to write a pamphlet with Boyle describing what they had seen, in order to publicise the extent of the suffering and drum up charitable donations from his fellow Oxford undergraduates.[6] He personally donated £1000, a large enough sum to draw concerned comments from his mother, Lady Helen, and his uncle, Sir James Graham.[7]

Dufferin's plunge into the misery and despair of the Irish Famine puts into stark relief many of the tensions and contradictions he would face over the coming decades as an Irish landlord. First, was the seemingly inescapable limitations of Ireland's agricultural economy.[8] Although his own estate was situated in the relatively prosperous and diversified economy of Ulster and escaped the worst effects of the Famine, grinding poverty and the steady flow of emigration framed a deeply pessimistic view of the future of the country.[9] There were difficult questions to address about the failure of landowners to provide any effective mitigation of the crisis; indeed, accusations that some had actively sought to profit from it grew amongst Ireland's starving, fleeing peoples.[10] Dufferin was acutely aware from a formative period of the turbulence not only at the heart of Britain's relationship with Ireland, but also between Irish landlords and its peasantry.[11] As he reflected in his pamphlet, 'as we rattled along on a hard dry road, for the wind had changed, and the sun shone brightly, we wondered whether we would ever return to the village of Skibbereen, and what legislation and what influences could soonest make Ireland happy and cheerful, and its poor people industrious and independent.'[12] This was the question that would occupy Dufferin from the late 1840s to the late 1860s; it would dominate his political career as a Whig Liberal in the House of Lords and the management of his Clandeboye estates, where he emphasised improvement, leases, schools, housing and agricultural activity and, later, questions of land reform. He wished to do good for his own tenants and for Ireland, and became a leading voice in all Irish questions in parliament and in print.[13] He sunk large sums of money he did not have into improving his own estate, following the lead of his Whig aristocratic friends, the Sutherlands and Argylls. He wished to demonstrate that a new Ireland was possible, if only its natural leaders – the landed aristocracy and gentry – would show the way.[14] For Dufferin, Ireland was both his life-long anchor and millstone: it defined his identity, his sense of purpose, and framed his later engagement with imperial administration and the diplomatic world. It also instilled an association with Ireland of pessimism, debt and crisis, and a sense of hopelessness in the face of economic stagnation and collapse, and bitterly divided politics. Dufferin was destined to spend much of his life and career outwith Ireland, but he carried its demands and complexities with him. He would move into a prestigious diplomatic and colonial career that added significant variety to his experience of peoples, places and cultures. But there were also many constants, chief of which was his aristocratic inheritance. Whether on tiger hunt in the Raj, receiving the loyal addresses of his tenants at Clandeboye, or hosting skating parties in Quebec, Dufferin was ably performing the role of the aristocrat, setting an example of fine manners, good breeding and quick-thinking. Critical to this was the implicit understanding that his qualities were part of a wider landed and aristocratic inheritance, which had then been refined by a particular kind of education and by personal experience of governing the extensive landed estates that were his birth right.[15] This book examines the enduring power of aristocratic thinking about land, governance and empire in the nineteenth century through the career of one of the most successful diplomats and colonial governors of his age, framing his experience through the prism of his management and ownership of a significant Irish estate.[16]

Notes

1. A. Gailey, *The Lost Imperialist: Lord Dufferin, Memory and Mythmaking in an Age of Celebrity* (London, 2015), pp. 24–5, 30.
2. A. C. Lyall, *The Life of the Marquis of Dufferin and Ava* (London, 1905), pp. 55–8; Gailey, *Lost Imperialist*, pp. 37–40.
3. H. Nicolson, *Helen's Tower* (London, 1937), p. 71.
4. Nicolson, *Helen's Tower*, p. 71.
5. For example, Dufferin, *The case of the Irish tenant, as stated sixteen years ago by the Rt. Hon. Lord Dufferin, in a speech delivered to the House of Lords, February 28, 1854* (London, 1870).
6. Lord Dufferin and the Hon. G. F. Boyle, *Narrative of a Journey from Oxford to Skibbereen during the Year of the Irish Famine* (Oxford, 1847).
7. Christ Church, Oxford, MR iii.c.i 1/6/3, Dufferin to Lady Dufferin (his mother), n.d. [March 1847?]; Public Record Office of Northern Ireland [hereafter PRONI], D1071, H/H/B/G/316, ff. 2, Sir James Graham to Dufferin, 24 Aug. 1847.
8. W. E. Vaughan, An assessment of the economic performance of Irish landlords, 1851–81, in F. S. L. Lyons and R. A. J. Hawkins (eds), *Ireland under the Union: Varieties of Tension* (Oxford, 1980), pp. 177–88.
9. Dufferin, *Irish Emigration and the Tenure of Land in Ireland* (Dublin, 1870); L.P. Curtis, *The Depiction of Eviction in Ireland, 1845–1910* (Dublin, 2011), pp. 1–8.
10. P. Gray, The making of mid-Victorian Ireland? Political economy and the memory of the Great Famine, in P. Gray (ed.), *Victoria's Ireland? Irishness and Britishness, 1837–1901* (Dublin, 2004), pp. 152–66; R. Romani, British views on Irish national character, 1800–1846: an intellectual history, *History of European Ideas*, 23:5–6 (1997), pp. 193–4.
11. T. Dooley, Landlords and the land question, 1879–1909, in C. King (ed.), *Famine, Land and Culture in Ireland* (Dublin, 2001), pp. 116–28.
12. Dufferin and Boyle, *Narrative of a Journey from Oxford to Skibbereen*, p. 23.
13. Dufferin, *Mr Mill's Plan for the Pacification of Ireland Examined* (London, 1868); Gailey, *Lost Imperialist*, pp. 40–5.
14. T. Dooley, *The Decline of the Big House in Ireland: A Study of Irish Landed Families, 1860–1960* (Dublin, 2001), pp. 79–96.
15. P. J. Cain, Character and imperialism: the British financial administration of Egypt, 1878–1914, *Journal of Imperial and Commonwealth History*, 34:2 (2006), pp. 177–8; J. A. Mangan, *Making Imperial Mentalities: Socialisation and British Imperialism* (Manchester, 1990), pp. 1–3.
16. L. P. Curtis, The Anglo-Irish predicament, *Twentieth Century Studies*, 4 (1970), pp. 37–44.

1   Introducing Dufferin

> I do think that the England which we know could not be the England that she is but for the maintenance of a high-minded, proud and self-denying nobility.[1]

In the green and damp fields of north Down, Ireland, is the Clandeboye – once the Ballyleidy-estate, seat of the Blackwoods, barons and, later, marquises of Dufferin and Ava. A grey-stoned, substantial and rambling house sits in the beautiful landscaped demesne, noted for its lakes and the extent and exotic variety of its tree plantations. The house is just a few miles from the edge of Belfast Lough, the Bangor train line running in parallel, only ten miles from the industrial – now post-industrial – imperial city of Belfast. In the grounds of its imposing Victorian white-stoned City Hall is a remarkable example of the kind of flamboyant statue of a Great Man that the late Victorian and Edwardian public excelled in producing and with which the urban landscape of Britain is littered. Even by the usual standards, this particular monument, raised to the memory of Frederick Temple Hamilton-Temple-Blackwood, 1st Marquis of Dufferin and Ava, is almost comically ornate. Dufferin stands proud in court dress under a stone umbrella, his honours, including the Star of India and the Order of St Patrick, displayed proudly on his chest.[2] At his feet are two exotic figures, one a turbaned and moustachioed Indian, the other a Canadian *voyageur* complete with fur cap and snow shoes.

This extraordinary piece of public commemoration, injecting a visual reminder of Belfast's place in and contribution to the British imperial project, is generally ignored by the city's inhabitants and visitors. The world it evokes has receded from public view, having once been a source of immense local pride and global emphasis: a local landowner turned colonial governor and diplomat, at the heart of imperial affairs and European courts.

This book is about that landlord, diplomat, traveller, writer and governor: it examines his career and identity as an Irish landowner, an urbane diplomat, literary sensation, courtier, politician, colonial governor, collector, son, husband and father. It is not a biography in the traditional sense; it does not seek to describe Dufferin's life and experiences but, instead, selects episodes from it in order to illuminate a number of interrelated themes

Figure 1.1 Lord Dufferin Monument of 1906 by Frederick W. Pomeroy. Marble. This monument is reproduced by the kind permission of Belfast City Council. The original can be viewed at City Hall, Belfast.

that require to be disentangled, but are not always conveniently treated in isolation from one another.[3] It seeks to link the landowning and aristocratic culture of Dufferin (and his peers) to his colonial experiences, and to understand the connections and correlations between them. Generally, these two elements have been kept separate by historians: this book slots them back together again, rebuilding the holistic perspective in which aristocratic men and women operated in the nineteenth century. This book is not a hagiographical study of an Eminent Victorian, although Dufferin certainly was one.[4] Instead, it uses Dufferin to argue that there was a defined, if fluid, conception of aristocratic governance and purpose that infused the political and imperial world, and was constructed from two parts: the inheritance and management of a landed estate and Big House, and a well-defined sense of 'rule by the best'.[5] Interesting and creative tensions developed out of the challenges posed to both these elements of aristocratic leadership in the period and this provides one aspect of the value of this study. Political, economic and cultural changes forced the landed classes in Britain and, especially, Ireland, onto the back foot, and obliged them to define their contribution and purpose in increasingly explicit ways. While not taking their analysis of their evolving position at face value, it does provide the historian with an opportunity to understand the ways in which the management of landed estates overlapped with the ideologies of colonial rule, complicating how Britain and Ireland saw themselves and the empire. It identifies a particular kind of atmosphere of empire and aristocracy, one that was riven with tensions and angst, as those who saw themselves as Britain and Ireland's hereditary leaders were challenged by a rising meritocracy and, in Ireland, by a powerful new definition of what Irishness was.

As the face of British power in Ireland, the group labelled the Anglo-Irish Ascendancy found their identities rejected and turned against them in the face of a new Irish nationalism.[6] Dufferin's experience captures these themes; his personal, political and imperial networks illuminate the nature and workings of governing power in Ireland, and the wider imperial and British world.[7] Depending on his context – from Ulster to Prince Edward Island, from Simla to Syria – his beliefs and ideals adjusted, hardened or connected. The political context within Britain and Ireland also had a profound impact on Dufferin; a life-long Liberal and supporter of moderate land reform in Ireland, he became increasingly alienated, like many of his class, by Gladstone's more radical land legislation from 1870 and, more especially, by Irish Home Rule.[8] Indeed, Dufferin would become embittered by the course of land reform and by what he regarded as Gladstone's wrong-headedness on the issue, and would later claim that Irish landlordism had been betrayed by the British government by the 1890s.[9]

The sheer range of political, social and economic issues that Dufferin was affected by or involved in on a global scale means that a fully exhaustive discussion is not possible. This means that, for the most part, Dufferin's prestigious career as a diplomat in the European courts is not touched on directly, with the exception of his term as ambassador to the Ottoman empire in the early 1880s. There are other, more fleeting, but still important areas not discussed: Burmese ruby mine concessions; the management of opium prices in India; tensions with the French over Siam; the detailed history of the Great Game; tariff negotiations between Canada and the USA – the list continues.[10] Instead, the book focuses on wider questions of identity, land and aristocracy.

The first aspect of this investigation is to unravel the complex relationships relative to Dufferin's sense of his Irishness, empire and his status as a landed aristocratic peer, all of which were subject to intense challenge in his lifetime.[11] Although securely a member of the Anglo-Irish Ascendancy, for Dufferin and many of his Irish peers, 'Anglo' never really featured in their identity: they were simply the Irish aristocracy.[12] Dufferin's sixteenth-century forebears were Scottish: the Blackwoods had left Scotland in the wake of the Marian Wars and established themselves in County Down in the 1590s. Dufferin took a great interest in his Scottish antecedents, fuelled by a passion for the work of Sir Walter Scott and his friendships within the Whig aristocratic circle of the Sutherlands and Argylls. Dufferin was not simply a lover of the works of Scott for its literary merit, but believed that the values expressed in them were those closest to his own heart: 'I love Sir Walter Scott', he wrote, 'with all my heart; and, my mother excepted, I think he has done more to form my character than any other influence; for he is the soul of purity, chivalry, respect for women and healthy religious feeling'.[13] But his primary identity was Irish and, although he acknowledged aspects of Ulster's unique history and make-up, he considered himself an Irishman first and an Ulsterman second. This meant that he occupied a liminal space as both an insider (aristocratic, landed, male, elite) and an outsider (Irish, indebted, Ulster, Anglo) in both the British context of Eton, Oxford and Westminster, and the Irish context of Dublin, Orangeism, and political nationalism.[14] He never fitted quite comfortably anywhere and while this subtly destabilised him, it also necessitated a fluidity and ability to fit in, a critical skill in his constantly changing world of royal courts and imperial administrations.[15]

Dufferin's constant anchor was his inheritance of the Clandeboye estates and landed identity. The second aspect of this study therefore explores the relationship between his estates and his illustrious career as an imperial administrator. It considers how Dufferin defined and managed his landed properties, and exposes the nature of the overlap with his imperial administration. In other words, what aspects of landed governance were translated from rural Ireland to the colonial world? This discussion is complicated by Ireland's ambiguous colonial status, as Dufferin was well aware, and echoes the insider–outsider dynamic that he personified. Land was a global issue in the nineteenth century; Dufferin made himself the spokesperson for landed interests in the acrimonious debates over land tenure reform and improvement in the 1850s and 1860s, having witnessed the catastrophe of the Great Irish Famine at first hand.[16] He then transplanted this issue into the global imperial context, where land questions were among the dominant challenges and opportunities for Britain's empire project, from the Canadian prairies to the Nile Delta. Tensions between the rights and responsibilities of property, historicist versus contractual definitions, and the relationship between the good governance and management of land and people anchors land as perhaps the most important imperial and domestic issue of the age.[17] Dufferin found himself working vigorously to challenge the direction of land reform in Ireland and then, watching with mounting alarm, the same principles of reform spread to the imperial world.

Lastly, the book (re)constructs what aristocratic 'rule by the best' looked like and how it actually operated. The challenges facing the landed and aristocratic classes in the nineteenth century were legion; the extension of the franchise and the conduct of national and local politics, the rise of a middle and professional class and a push for reward based on merit, an influx of new industrial and financial wealth, all presented existential challenges to the traditional social, military and political leadership enjoyed by the peerage.[18] This did not mean that landed aristocrats gave up their position without a whimper: the rise of anti-aristocratic feeling generated a stout defence from individuals such as Dufferin, useful to the historian in understanding what they regarded as their will to rule and particular aristocratic style. This book unpacks what Dufferin and his peers meant by this, focusing on the nature of their governance, imperial security and land reform. Every aspect of this rule could be applied equally to their landed estates, to Westminster, or to the imperial territories. British 'character' included gentlemanly codes and behaviours, hierarchy and form, pomp and ceremony, which were not just ornamental froth: they had their hands firmly on the levers of power, were embedded in that power and part of its operation.[19] This had major implications for the nature of British rule in Ireland and across the empire, particularly in understandings of hierarchies of peoples and races, where coercion could justifiably be applied, and how the challenges of nationalism and revolt should be dealt with.[20] It also informed a prescribed definition of 'good' governance: that, in exchange for British dominion, subject peoples could expect internal and external security, liberal and progressive reforms of land tenure, social customs and economic investment in infrastructure.[21] This mirrored expectations on landed estates: deference in exchange for improvement, support when the rural economy atrophied in exchange for rents promptly paid in the good times. This book illuminates the ways in which the aristocratic sinews of power defined the nature of landed rule in Britain, Ireland and across the empire in the nineteenth century. Traditionally seen as a period of ominous existential threat to landed and aristocratic elites, this book suggests a more nuanced view of their responses, and the extent and nature of how aristocratic philosophies remained central to British and imperial political cultures.

Lord Dufferin – an introduction

Figure 1.2 Stipple engraving of Frederick Temple Hamilton-Temple-Blackwood, 1st Marquess of Dufferin and Ava as a young man, 1869 or thereafter. Charles Holl, after Henry Tanworth Wells/Public domain via Wikimedia Commons.

So here's your empire. No more wine then?[22]

Frederick Temple Hamilton-Temple-Blackwood, 1st Marquis of Dufferin and Ava, was born in Florence in 1826, first and only son of a respectable Ulster landowner, Price Blackwood and Lady Helen Selina, a beautiful and artistic society figure and the granddaughter of the playwright Richard Brinsley Sheridan. Dufferin, and his friends, would attribute the wilder and more creative aspects of his character to his 'Sheridanish' inheritance, including his literary merits and, perhaps less glamorously, his troubling ineptitude with finances.[23] Dufferin's personal qualities were linked to those popularly associated with 'Irishness': he was generous – sometimes recklessly so – artistic, exercised a quick temper and was famously charming, witty and adept at putting people at ease: 'in my uncle's own veins the Sheridan blood seethed and tingled like champagne', wrote his nephew Harold Nicolson in later years.[24] The glamorous Sheridan link, through to his mother and two aunts (the Duchess of Somerset and the controversial Caroline Norton), fed Dufferin's refined aesthetic and literary tastes, and he would become a celebrated author in his own right in the 1850s. Dufferin's primary identity was as a member of the Irish landed and aristocratic classes; the Clandeboye estates were a substantial property, with a fine house and demesne, and the family were part of elite local circles including the Hamiltons, Downshires, Abercorns and Londonderrys.[25] The Blackwoods had been in Ulster from the late sixteenth century and, although not in the top rank, they were a long-standing and respectable well-placed family, with over £20,000 per year coming in from the estates Like many such families, they also had a distinguished history of service to Crown and State, principally in the British Navy: Price Blackwood was a naval officer, Captain Robert Blackwood died at Waterloo and Sir Henry Blackwood had fought with Nelson at Trafalgar.[26]

In line with contemporary elite practice, Dufferin was educated mainly in England, firstly at a school in Hampton, and then from May 1839 at Eton, the traditional hothouse for the ambitious aristocrat.[27] Indeed, it would be the lasting friendships he made here (for example, with the future Lord Kimberley and Lord Salisbury), rather than his education, which he remembered as being, 'dominated by idleness', that would set Lord Dufferin on the path of his distinguished imperial career.[28] This was further confirmed when he went up to Christ Church, Oxford, in January 1845. Despite being rather homesick initially, Dufferin soon threw himself into university life, making friends, reading extensively and setting up his own debating club, the Pythic.[29] He occupied a prominent position as a young undergraduate, having inherited the Clandeboye estates in 1841 due to the unexpected death of his father of an opium overdose on the Liverpool to Belfast steam packet service.[30] This was due to the error of a chemist in Liverpool, rather than anything more sinister, but it meant that Dufferin became a landowner in his own right at the young age of fifteen. That he did not quickly run into any trouble – financial or other – was largely due to his close relationship with his mother, Lady Helen.[31] A devoted son, Lord Dufferin wrote to her frequently, often to berate her for not replying frequently or quickly enough. He asked her advice on every matter; from how to shake off a would-be friend he was not keen on, to how to furnish his rooms. Of more concern to Lady Helen than her son's rooms or dislike of morning lectures was the growing pressure on his finances. Despite the close management of Clandeboye by his guardians, including his uncle Sir James Graham, the prominent Whig politician and Home Secretary, the estates were burdened by a concerning level of debt by late 1845. In the same year, a worrying blight was beginning to effect Ireland's potato crop, the implications of which were beginning to seep into the British public consciousness.[32] Oxford life was not cheap, but Lord Dufferin had little choice but to take part in the festivities and cultures that cemented private and public relationships in the university town. As he told his mother: 'The summer clubs are being formed: I belong to two. I thought it was a good way of being civil to some of those men. They are very expensive; what with the dress and dinners amounting to 50£ but it will show them that I will always help to contribute to public amusement when it is necessary'.[33] Despite the financial pressures of Oxford life, Dufferin's investment in it would be repaid handsomely in his later life, as friendships made and social skills honed led to his appointment to prestigious diplomatic and administrative roles across the globe from the 1860s.[34] The establishment of his own club, the Pythic, which seemed to consist largely of, 'immense wine parties' and violent debating, which Dufferin was only able to control by, 'screaming and knocking his head against the table', is another example of this enterprising attitude, although he was also elected to the Oxford Union, becoming its president in 1847.[35] He travelled in these years, as would be expected of a young landed aristocrat; indeed, travel was seen as a central element of elite education, emphasising the development of taste and manners, an appreciation of art and architecture, and developing fluency in the European languages.[36] Dufferin spent his time principally in France, to visit his mother who was living in Paris, and during which lively scenes took place, as in 1847, when he, 'went to the Embassy ball, danced till five in uniform: shoved through a glass door'.[37] Despite this seemingly rakish behaviour, Dufferin was in fact wrestling with larger issues, practical and spiritual, in the mid-1840s. In Oxford, he was involved in the great religious debates of the 1840s or, as he put it in later years, he got into, 'an emotional state of mind, in regard to religion'.[38] In many ways he was a serious and sensitive young man, and successfully took his degree in November 1846, being noted at the time as being interested in, 'political discussion, not only in regards to points of past history, but also to questions of practical administration'.[39] Oxford gave Lord Dufferin the classical education of the time, as it did so many other imperial administrators and politicians, and this would inform his view of governance, both on his Ulster estates and British rule in the Empire.[40] At this time, Dufferin was young, talented and eligible: he was the subject to the high expectations of his mother, frequent advice from his uncles the Duke of Somerset and Sir James Graham, and full of a somewhat directionless potential.[41]

In 1847, Dufferin was celebrating his majority at Clandeboye. He did not stay in Ireland for long, however, and set up in London, where in 1850 he took his seat as Baron Clandeboye in the House of Lords, as a Liberal.[42] He also became a Lord-in-Waiting at Queen Victoria's court, and spent more time travelling on the Continent. In the early 1850s, Dufferin also made one of the most important friendships of his life, one perhaps surprisingly not generated within the confines of Eton or Oxford. This was with George Douglas Campbell, the 8th Duke of Argyll, whom he met through their mutual connections with the ducal family of Sutherland and their young heirs, the Staffords (the 8th Duke of Argyll's first wife was Elizabeth, sister to Lord Stafford, later 3rd Duke of Sutherland).[43] Argyll had been schooled privately – something he felt was to his lasting social and political disadvantage – and was a serious and ambitious intellectual and politician.[44] The strong bond between Dufferin and Argyll was in many ways surprising given their differing temperaments but, nevertheless, would be definitive for them both, anchoring Dufferin's serious side and enabling a more relaxed tone for Argyll. 'I look back and say within myself, "The barbarous people treated us with no little kindness on yon wild island". What droll people you Paddies are! ... Clandeboye dwells on our memories as a green spot across a blue sea', Argyll wrote after his first visit to Clandeboye.[45] A consistent part of their written friendship was this kind of mutual stereotyping of Dufferin's Irishness and Argyll's Scottishness, and it highlights the pervasive and increasingly racialised views of the Irish – particularly the Irish peasantry – in establishment opinion. The friendship between Dufferin and Argyll would ebb and flow until their deaths in 1902, ranging from a serious political correspondence on issues of land reform and Irish Home Rule, to a deeply personal bond that withstood and supported each other through the deaths of wives, children and mothers.[46]

Before all this, Dufferin was to make a name for himself in another field entirely; travel, exploration and the publication of a book spinning tales of aristocratic *sangfroid* on the dangerous seas of northern Europe. In 1856, Dufferin set off on his yacht the *Foam* to undertake a journey around Iceland, the Faeroes and the northern islands of Svalbard.[47] His humorous retelling of these travels in *Letters from High Latitudes* became a best-seller and seemed to set Dufferin on the path of a literary career, but his political and administrative ambitions outpaced those for writing. In 1860, Dufferin was selected by Lord John Russell to represent Britain on a joint commission to Syria, instituted to deal with the aftermath of sectarian massacres in that country, a posting requiring a good deal of sensitivity and diplomacy in dealing with the Ottoman authorities and his European colleagues.[48] It was a test that Dufferin passed, introducing what would be a long and distinguished career in imperial and diplomatic service. In 1862, he married Hariot Rowan Hamilton, who came from a neighbouring Ulster landowning family of distinction but not significant wealth.[49]

12 Introducing Dufferin

Despite the fact she did not bring riches or connections, the marriage would be a great success; she was a shrewd and hard-working diplomatic wife and a significant prop for Dufferin, who – perhaps as a result of his domineering mother, somewhat scandalous relations and energetic personality – was rather sensitive to criticism and lacked the thick skin required by diplomats and administrators.[50] Hariot supported him in this, travelled everywhere with him, operated their exhausting social life, raised their seven children all over the globe, set up a hugely significant medical foundation for women in India and wrote detailed diaries of her experiences, which were published by John Murray, becoming almost as successful an author as her husband.[51] The Dufferins would become a truly imperial family, taking a rounded, holistic view of their colonial duties and opportunities. A number of his children would go onto serve in the imperial and diplomatic world themselves, and in many critical ways his 'incorporated' wife and children were an essential part of Dufferin's success.

Every aspect of Dufferin's birth, education, and social and political milieu spoke to his immense potential and talent, but a suitable arena for it was a long time coming. He threw himself into Westminster politics, quickly becoming a leading Liberal spokesman in the Lords, trusted by Gladstone and other senior party members, speaking with growing conviction on Irish matters and positioning himself as a progressive Liberal on Church, coercion and land questions.[52] To his growing frustration, he was never regarded as serious cabinet material and began, instead, to be offered imperial and diplomatic posts, which seemed to suit his talents for managing tricky situations, his urbane charm and his projection of the aristocratic ideal. Dufferin turned down the presidency of Bombay in 1862, but wrote to Argyll – who was a rising government and cabinet man – to express his frustrated ambitions:

> What I feel is this – that life is slipping by very fast, and that I have very little to show for the years that are gone … whatever there was to be done in this part of the world I have either done, or am in the way of doing, and once a proper system is organised, even an Irish estate does not give sufficient occupation. Of course I should prefer what would keep me at home, but I do not see much chance of any opening occurring there: consequently, I am forced to look abroad … But one thing is certain, I cannot endure to be idle any longer, and though literary occupation is open to me, it will be with great dissatisfaction that I shall subside into that lower form of existence.[53]

Dufferin filled a number of minor government positions, although these would prove important for his later career (Undersecretary of State for India, 1864–66, Undersecretary of State in the War Office, 1866–68, Chancellor of the Duchy of Lancaster, 1868–72), until his appointment to the Canadian viceroyalty in 1872.[54] It was this first senior posting that cemented Dufferin's ambitions for himself, provided a context for his wife and family to operate and shine, and promoted the ideal of aristocratic rule overseas. Canada was a challenging posting in the 1870s, with complex issues surrounding the expansion and consolidation of the Confederation, political corruption and the building of the trans-continental railway dominating Dufferin's agenda. In addition, the role and constitutional powers of the Governor-General remained fluid and open to debate between the Canadian and British establishments.[55] Sir Alfred Lyall, Dufferin's first biographer and an eminent colonial administrator himself, claimed that, 'it was in Canada that British statesmen gradually worked out experimentally the science of colonial administration, and felt their way towards consummating the right relations between a colony and its metropolis by the gradual devolution of internal self-government'.[56] Chapter 5 of this book will discuss the issues in more detail, but Dufferin's actions during the Pacific Scandal affair in 1872–73 led to the establishment on his departure of new agreed constitutional terms for future Governors-General, a signal that he had possibly misread the boundaries of his power.[57] The appointment came with a generous salary, but Dufferin's finances were perhaps too precarious to benefit from this fully; rumours of his monetary difficulties reached Britain, provoking Argyll to write in consternation: 'I hear terrible things about your expenditure. People say that you will be entirely ruined. Do not be too Irish, or too Sheridanish; it is an awful combination'.[58] Alas, Dufferin would be obliged to sell the bulk of his Irish estates in the 1870s, to redeem his debts and restructure his assets onto a more even keel.

In 1878, Dufferin returned from Canada and, the next year, took up the post of ambassador to Russia, where he witnessed the assassination of Tsar Nicolas II. He left relatively swiftly to move to the Sublime Porte, where he took a leading role in Egyptian affairs in the wake of the 'Urabi Revolt, writing a report that would form the blueprint for British dominion in Egypt for decades to come. These experiences gave him valuable experience of dealing with acute challenges to British imperial interests and hammered home the strategic importance of the Suez Canal to Britain. These perspectives would be of demonstrable use when he achieved the crowning glory of his career: Viceroy of India in 1884. This, the most prestigious of all the imperial posts, would be no sinecure for Dufferin.[59] Aside from having to deal with the volatile border arrangements with Afghanistan and the Russian threat, internally he oversaw controversial land reform bills, the establishment of the Indian National Congress, and the occupation and annexation of Burma in 1886.[60] Dufferin was nearly sixty when he took the viceroyalty and found the work exhausting, despite being amenable to the climate.[61] He stood down in 1888 and returned to Europe with his wife and family, first as ambassador in Italy and, lastly, in France.

After a relatively late start and two decades of imperial 'exile', Dufferin's career ended with prestigious diplomatic postings in the heart of Europe, and the new title of Ava granted by the Queen to reward his efforts in Burma. But then, near the end, it all went wrong for Dufferin. At the turn of the new century he was hit by a double blow; first, the death of his eldest

14 *Introducing Dufferin*

son, Archie, Lord Ava, in South Africa where he was fighting the Boers.[62] The second disaster was financial and reputational: he had been persuaded to back a rising company, the London and Globe Finance Corporation, headed by the financial wizard of the day, Whittaker Wright. Wright had generated an immense personal fortune through his financing of mining ventures in Australia among other operations and was seeking some aristocratic gloss for his company. Dufferin agreed to become its chairman and also invested trustingly and heavily. When it went spectacularly bust in November 1900, Dufferin lost all of his investments, as did every other shareholder, a burden of guilt he felt deeply.[63] Wright escaped to America but was successfully extradited and tried in London, before committing suicide in the courtroom on his conviction.[64] It was too late for Dufferin, who seems not to have fully recovered from these twin disasters. Honours continued to shower upon him – Lord Warden of the Cinque Ports; degrees, dinners and speeches in his honour; and election to rector at both St Andrews and Edinburgh universities – but his final years were clouded and after a short illness he died in February 1902 at Clandeboye where he was buried.[65]

Figure 1.3 Frederick Hamilton-Temple-Blackwood, 1st Marquess of Dufferin and Ava by Henrietta Rae. Oil on canvas. This portrait is reproduced by the kind permission of Belfast City Council. The original can be viewed at City Hall, Belfast.

Assessing Dufferin's life and career is a task that presents many contradictions: there are many glittering successes: literary, political, diplomatic and imperial. He was an attractive man who spread happiness, not least to his wife and family, but also to his friends and colleagues. He was quick and clever, but not overly industrious, a quality criticised after his death but which was arguably the best *modus operandi* for a man at the top and on the spot such as he.[66] He was a fully formed self-declared and proud Irishman, and a global and aristocratic citizen, who found his identity under attack and out of kilter with the rising age of Irish nationalism. Although in sum his career was a great success, it was compressed into twenty years. His posthumous reputation has also been somewhat problematic: as mouthpiece for Irish landlordism from the Great Famine to the Land Wars, as viceroy who was highly critical of the Indian National Congress, as Canadian governor general who was seen to have over-stepped the boundaries of his powers, Dufferin has come in for criticism.[67] Mostly, though, he is one of the forgotten of his generation. Alongside men such as Mayo, Lansdowne, Kimberley, Salisbury, even Argyll, he has faded into the background.[68] This is emblematic of his relatively insecure position as an Irish Ulster landlord in the elite worlds of Westminster, the European courts and the empire. Contemporaries would remember how sensitive he was to any criticism and how much emphasis he would put on form and ceremony, both rooted in his insecurity of social position and worth. As this book will show, it is this liminal quality that makes Dufferin such an illuminating historical study; as someone obliged constantly to define and reinforce his position as an Irish landlord, in Ireland and across the world, he gives us a window into how aristocratic and landed elites defined themselves and their duties and privileges at exactly the same time as they were coming under existential attack. Those aristocrats and statesmen more confident of their position are less useful to the historian in this regard. Instead, Dufferin's insider–outsider status, insecurities, and public and private battles with his identity and purpose, whether in Ireland, Westminster or in the empire, can tell us about the nature of aristocratic definitions and purpose in a changing and challenging world.

Historiography

> My work immerses me in documents of all kinds, and compels me to wander in a labyrinth of old letters, memoranda, and blue-books. It is a business for which I have little capacity, so I am easily fatigued by it.[69]

As an 'Eminent Victorian', Dufferin was the subject of autobiographical publications and some early biographical studies, although not to the same extent as many of his contemporaries. Dufferin did not publish an autobiography, but did publish a volume of poems by and for his mother, which includes his own memories of her and their relationship, as well as Dufferin's literary and linguistic interests.[70] His wife, Lady Hariot, kept extensive journals and

16   *Introducing Dufferin*

published three of these: one volume on their time in Canada and two volumes of their time in India.[71] Although in the main a detailed account of their daily activities with little really personal, something of the tone of the household comes across in her lively accounts. On his death in 1902, she commissioned Sir Alfred Lyall, a colleague in India and an extensively published writer of poetry and prose, to write an official biography. This Lyall did, producing a comprehensive, sympathetic and thoughtful account, with a heavy emphasis on Dufferin's official life.[72] In 1903, Charles Drummond Black published a rushed and somewhat superficial account of the life and career of Dufferin, which was not supported by the full access Lyall had to Dufferin's papers and, as such, it does not add much to the standard account.[73] Much more interesting is the 1937 biography by Dufferin's nephew Harold Nicolson, *Helen's Tower*, which still stands up to modern sensibilities as an inventive, amusing but serious and sympathetic account of both Dufferin and his age from the perspective of the clouded and difficult 1930s, from someone who knew Dufferin in his later years and was a fellow diplomat. His most recent biographer is Andrew Gailey, who in 2015 published a major study of Dufferin, covering every aspect of his life and career, with a particular emphasis on his relationship with his mother and earlier years to middle age. Gailey positions Dufferin as a forgotten imperialist, who was driven by insecurities about his position and respectability, who worked hard during his lifetime to manage his reputation effectively and – broadly – speaking successfully, only to be largely forgotten by historians and the wider public alike after his death.[74] This book draws on Gailey's analysis, although the intention is not to (re)produce a biographical angle: it is to draw on Dufferin's life and career to think about how Irish elite identities were constructed in relation to Westminster and empire in a period of turbulent challenge and change. Given the wide geographical range of Dufferin's life and career, this study contextualises numerous sets of historical literature, debates and fields. It does not claim to make any definitive interventions into these distinct fields but, rather, draws on aspects and links them together in new ways to pose new questions and suggest different interpretations. This is the value of taking Dufferin as the focal point for this study: it supports a transnational analysis, drawing out the differences and similarities across national and imperial boundaries.[75] It utilises the historical literature from three main areas, each full of overlapping themes and discussion: nineteenth-century Ireland, empire, and imperialism and aristocracy.

   Nineteenth-century Ireland is well-served by historians, particularly its rural and political history, enabling the historian to anchor Dufferin in his Irish and landowning context. Dufferin inherited the Clandeboye estates in 1841 and took over their management directly once he achieved his majority in 1847; as such, the voluminous historical research available from the Great Famine to the Land Wars to the Wyndham Act is relevant to this study. Dufferin plays a bit part in existing studies of landlord responses to the political, economic and social conditions of the decades from the 1840s: as a vocal champion for liberal landlordism, actively involved in and publishing about land reform, emigration, property and improvement with a fine turn of phrase, his views are often taken as being emblematic of his peers and their decline and fall across the period.[76] By rooting this better-known aspect of Dufferin's activities into his own estate management experiences and practices, this book will offer a more holistic view of his practical and intellectual contribution. This incorporates landed responses to the strictures of political economy, definitions and practice of 'Improvement', emigration and the rights and responsibilities of property. Much of the literature deals in detail with these questions, but does not root it in estate management and the day-to-day decision-making taking place on landed estates. This adds a new perspective to debates around the Ulster Tenant Right in the 1850s, the 1870 Irish Land Act and the 1881 Irish Land Act, grounding debates about the sanctity of property into the reality of estate management.[77] Dufferin spent much of the 1860s fighting not just legislative 'attacks' on the rights of property, but also the – in his view mistaken – assumptions underpinning them. He was concerned about the practical and financial implications of land tenure reform legislation, but equally rejected the implied assumption that Westminster was required to restrain or correct the behaviour of Irish landlords as a particular group that had failed to carry out their fundamental duties, or meet basic expectations of behaviour, during the most significant crisis of the nineteenth century, the Great Famine.[78] These themes link into the historiography of the acrimonious debates about what both Irishness and Britishness was in this period. Dufferin identified as Irish throughout his life, but recognised that others saw him as Anglo, and alien, an interloper and usurper, which he took very much to heart. This was about traditional expectations of social and political leadership and the ways in which he saw his role being increasingly denied to him domestically. Dufferin's struggles nuance a historiographical picture that tends to a traditional narrative of the rise of Irish nationalism and the decline of landed power in the last quarter of the nineteenth century.

A fundamental area of debate within Irish historiography is Ireland's status under the Union and within the empire, which provides this study with a link into the historiographies of the British empire and imperialism.[79] The utility of examining the nature of imperial governance through one individual is that it exposes the practical workings of that governance. The range of places Dufferin was posted to draws in the historiographies of colonial possessions and their strategic architecture. Dufferin's brief service in Syria in the 1860s highlights transnational intellectual exchange around managing sectarian conflict, as well as juggling the demands of European powers and empires through gentlemanly diplomacy, bringing an aristocratic character to the work.[80] Both of these elements were also at the fore in 1882 when Dufferin travelled to Egypt in the wake of the 'Urabi Revolt, tasked with managing the various and competing interests of British and French imperial ambitions. Egypt also exposes how Dufferin defined imperial 'character', and how that related to good governance and financial discipline, a view shared with his elite and landed peers.[81] Some of this thinking had evolved during his tenure as Canada's governor general in the 1870s, particularly that around which colonial peoples were worthy and capable of some measure of self-government and those that were not. This had interesting applications – and, for Dufferin, contradictions – with the Irish context, and, in Canadian constitutional terms, so did its federal model, established in 1867. Irish campaigners would periodically point to Canada, arguing that they were only asking for what already existed in the British imperial world, but to no avail. Dufferin exemplifies this contradiction well: at no point during his tenure in Canada did he argue that the Canadians were not fit to rule themselves (although under imperial supervision), but he would never support Irish home rule. What he did adhere to was the ideal of 'good' governance; that the British had to bring demonstrable benefits to colonial peoples in order to justify their dominion, in exactly the same way that landlords in Ireland and Britain had to support improve their tenantry to justify their privileges and right to rule.[82]

Although the focus of imperial rule was very different in India, many of the underlying issues were shared. Most important was the justification of British imperial power, expressed far more autocratically in India; as in Canada, aristocratic character infused the government of India, with an emphasis on rational governance, improvement and gentlemanly character.[83] The three key issues faced by Dufferin during his tenure as Indian viceroy were also applicable across the other imperial territories he had served in: land reform, the rise of nationalism and imperial security.[84] Each has generated a major literature, some of which makes explicit the connection between Ireland and India in particular, including legislative approaches and philosophies as well as personnel, although almost exclusively focused on the middle, professional and military classes rather than the aristocratic elite.[85] This book draws on these debates, while making other connections – with Canada, Egypt, Syria and others – to illuminate the ways in which aristocratic understandings of empire's purpose and structures infused the entire project.[86] This included the increasing racialised nature and expression of British rule across the empire, something Dufferin shared while rejecting the harsher stereotypes of the Irish. It also informed debates about the style, methods and structures of British imperial governance, justifications of the imperial project, particularly around its periodic expansion, such as the annexation of Burma in 1886. This conflicted with Dufferin's liberal instincts, but his aristocratic outlook was always more important than political loyalties, which had been bitterly tested by Gladstone's Irish and imperial programmes.[87]

This brings us to the third body of literature addressed by this book, and probably the most important to the arguments made: the aristocracy, the challenges it faced, and the extent of the decline and fall of their class, particularly in the Irish and imperial contexts.[88] In the British and Irish contexts, the narrative of decline and fall remains central to much of the historiography, particularly for the period after 1880. For Ireland, this analysis is even more pronounced. Historians have identified earlier roots of this decline, with the constitutional blow of the Union and its removal of a critical seat of power in Dublin, and the failure of Irish landlordism to take advantage of economic opportunities that might have cushioned their financial decline and corrected their dependence on credit. Additionally, the rise of Irish nationalism in the nineteenth century was increasingly defined in ways that excluded elite or aristocratic participation in the construction of a new nation.[89] Much of this rings true for Dufferin although, as he often pointed out, there were nuances for Ulster and it is impossible to dogmatise. While Dufferin was obliged to sell off the majority of his estates in the 1870s, and felt acutely the pressures of the changing political view of Irish landlords, he did so without recourse to any legislation and the Dufferin family still own and occupy Clandeboye, now successfully regenerated and diversified. This book addresses the question of Irish aristocratic exceptionalism in a British and European context: were they as unusual as the majority of historians seem to suggest?[90] The critical arena of the empire offers another angle to this question: David Cannadine has made the influential argument that, as opportunities narrowed and criticisms increased in the domestic context, aristocrats and the landed sought and received imperial posts, where the pomp and deference they were educated for and expected to receive was still a possibility.[91] This book accepts that argument and extends it, suggesting that there was a coherent imperial aristocracy that took its traditional domestic expectation of comprising the governing classes and extended it to the imperial context, underpinned by traditional values of good governance and rule by the best.

The book is structured around these themes, taking episodes in Dufferin's life and career to illustrate them. Chapters 2 and 3 focus on that anchor and millstone of Dufferin's life, Ireland. Chapter 2 examines Dufferin's landed inheritance and its management, including the ways in which his philosophy of improvement and duty was undercut by financial constraints and, eventually, land sales. Chapter 3 looks at the intellectual and political context of Dufferin's engagement with various and often contradictory 'Irish Questions', including land reform and home rule, questions also being asked in the wider imperial context. Chapter 4 asks why aristocratic elites such as Dufferin sought imperial service and how it was utilised to express their own will to rule. It does this by addressing the ways in which concepts of loyalty, unity, power and progress were made real through a variety of approaches including political autocracy, economic dominion, and state violence and terror. Chapter 5 takes what would appear to be a much more settled and peaceful example: the dominion of Canada and Dufferin's tenure as its governor-general in the 1870s. How did Dufferin's aristocratic outlook and understandings around subject peoples and British imperial power operate in a self-governing context? Chapter 6 addresses that context and the idea of the aristocratic 'man on the spot' by putting side-by-side two critical episodes in Dufferin's diplomatic career: Syria in

1860 and Egypt in 1882–83. It asks what elements of the 'man on the spot' were fundamentally aristocratic in nature and what effect this had on volatile and controversial engagements by Britain. Chapter 7 draws all the foregoing themes together in a discussion of Dufferin's tenure as viceroy of India, the ceremonial and autocratic peak of imperial service. In many ways, India provided the most obvious context for the display and exercise of aristocratic rule: this chapter examines that in detail and also asks whether this strengthened British dominion or weakened it.

Dufferin and his peers believed in the benefits of their social and political dominion; thus, what follows is a story with a moral: that historians should not overlook intentions over outcomes, that those individuals who awkwardly rub up against majority identities illuminate for us the nuances and variety of experience, and confound reductionist tendencies. Lastly, it emphasises the value of the personal and lived experience, with all of its inconsistencies, selfishness, tensions, sadness and failures, but equally its joys, good intentions and the happiness spread to others.

Notes

1 A. Trollope, *Phineas Redux*, vol. 2 (London, 1873), p. 157.
2 D. Gilmour, *The Ruling Caste: Imperial lives in the Victorian Raj* (London, 2005), p. 18.
3 Dufferin's biographies to date are: C. D. Black, *The Marquess of Dufferin and Ava* (London, 1903); A. C. Lyall, *The Life of the Marquis of Dufferin and Ava* (London, 1905); H. Nicolson, *Helen's Tower* (London, 1937); A. Gailey, *The Lost Imperialist: Lord Dufferin, memory and mythmaking in an age of celebrity* (London, 2015). The thematic biographical approach taken here has been influenced by, among others: J. Bew, *Castlereagh: enlightenment, war and tyranny* (London, 2011), pp. xxvii–xxx; C. Hall, *Macaulay and Son: architects of Imperial Britain* (New Haven, 2012), pp. xii–xxvi; R. Bourke, *Empire and Revolution: the political life of Edmund Burke* (Princeton, 2015); M. Bentley, *Lord Salisbury's World: Conservative environments in late-Victorian Britain* (Cambridge, 2001), pp. 1–7; A. Jackson, *Colonel Edward Saunderson: land and loyalty in Victorian Ireland* (Clarendon Press, 1995). It has also drawn on aspects of process philosophy to think about transitions on different scales – personal, national and transnational: J. Helin, T. Hernes, D. Hjorth, R. Holt (eds), *The Oxford Handbook of Process Philosophy and Organisation Studies* (Oxford, 2016), pp. 1–4, 10–14.
4 Nicolson, *Helen's Tower*, pp. 246–58, for a flavour of this; F. Campbell, *The Irish Establishment 1879–1914* (Oxford, 2009), pp. 2, 19–25, 307–9.
5 P. Cosgrove, T. Dooley and K. Mullaney-Dignam (eds), *Aspects of Irish Aristocratic life* (Dublin, 2014), pp. 169–75; K. T. Hoppen, *Governing Hibernia: British politicians and Ireland 1800–1921* (Oxford, 2016), pp. 179–99; A. Thompson, The language of imperialism and the meanings of empire, in S. Howe (ed.), *The New Imperial Histories Reader* (London, 2010), pp. 306–10.
6 J. C. Beckett, *The Anglo-Irish Tradition* (Belfast, 1976), pp. 85–96; Gailey, *Lost Imperialist*, pp. 37–41, 105–6; R. Romani, British views on Irish national character, 1800–1846: an intellectual history, *History of European Ideas*, 23:5–6 (1997), pp. 193–4, 207; D. G. Boyce, *Nationalism in Ireland* (Abingdon, 2005), pp. 154, 170–1, 228.

7 There is a strong literature on imperial networks and mobility on which this study draws, including: Z. Laidlaw, Richard Bourke: Irish liberalism tempered by empire, in D. Lambert and A. Lester (eds), *Colonial Lives Across the British Empire* (Cambridge, 2006), pp. 113–22, 144; S. Checkland, *The Elgins, 1766–1917: a tale of aristocrats, proconsuls and their wives* (Aberdeen, 1988), pp. 215–16, 227; Z. Laidlaw, *Colonial Connections 1815–45: patronage, the information revolution and colonial government* (Manchester, 2005), pp. 13–17, 19–21, 35; Z. Laidlaw and A. Lester (eds), *Indigenous Communities and Settler Colonialism: land holding, loss and survival in an interconnected world* (Basingstoke, 2015), pp. 1–12.

8 A. Jackson, *Home Rule: An Irish History, 1800–2000* (London, 2004), pp. 39–49, 66; Gailey, *Lost Imperialist*, pp. 161–3.

9 M. Cragoe and P. Readman (eds), *The Land Question in Britain, 1750–1950* (Basingstoke, 2010); S. Den Otter, 'Thinking in communities': late nineteenth century Liberals, idealists and the retrieval of community, in E. H. H. Green, *An Age of Transition: British politics, 1880–1914* (Edinburgh, 1997), pp. 67–78.

10 Many of these themes are covered by Dufferin's two principal biographers, Alfred Lyall and Andrew Gailey.

11 S. Howe, *Ireland and Empire: colonial legacies in Irish history and culture* (Oxford, 2002), pp. 134–65; J. Lennon, *Irish Orientalism: a literary and intellectual history* (Syracuse, 2004), pp. 167–72, 193–5.

12 J. Ridden, Britishness as an imperial and diasporic identity: Irish elite perspectives, c. 1820–70s, in P. Gray, *Victoria's Ireland? Irishness and Britishness, 1837–1901* (Dublin, 2004), pp. 88–104; D. M. McHugh, Family, leisure and the arts: aspects of the culture of the aristocracy of Ulster, 1870–1925, unpublished PhD thesis (University of Edinburgh, 2011), pp. 1–9, 37–8, 40.

13 Quoted in Nicolson, *Helen's Tower*, p. 41; Gailey, *Lost Imperialist*, pp. 5–6, 51. For a detailed exploration of this 'character', see D. Castronovo, *The English Gentleman: images and ideals in literature and society* (London, 1987), pp. 75–9, 81, 86.

14 D. Fitzpatrick, Ireland and the empire, in A. Porter, *Oxford History of the British Empire: vol. III, The nineteenth century* (Oxford, 1999), pp. 494, 497, 517.

15 Gailey, *Lost Imperialist*, pp. 2, 157, 199–200; J. M. Mackenzie, Irish, Scottish, Welsh and English Worlds? A four-nation approach to the history of the British empire, *History Compass*, 6:5 (2008), pp. 1245–6, 1255–6.

16 W. A. Maguire, *The Downshire Estates in Ireland, 1801–1845* (Oxford, 1972), p. 77; M. Moss, The high price of Heaven: the 6th Earl of Glasgow and the College of the Holy Spirit on the Isle of Cumbrae, *Architectural Heritage*, 22 (2011), pp. 77–98.

17 O. MacDonagh, *States of Mind: a study of Anglo-Irish conflict 1780–1980* (London, 1983), pp. 34, 36–7, 49.

18 L. P. Curtis, The Anglo-Irish predicament, *Twentieth Century Studies*, 4 (1970), pp. 37–61; K. T. Hoppen, Landownership and power in nineteenth century Ireland: the decline of an elite, in R. Gibson and M. Blinkhorn (eds) *Landownership and Power in Modern Europe* (London, 1991), pp. 164–77.

19 A. Porter, Empires in the mind, in P. J. Marshall (ed.), *The Cambridge Illustrated History of the British Empire* (Cambridge, 1996), pp. 185, 218–19, 223; A. Shanks, *Rural Aristocracy in Northern Ireland* (Aldershot, 1988), pp. 111–14, 121–9; D. Cannadine, *Aspects of Aristocracy: grandeur and decline in modern Britain* (New Haven, 1994), pp. 77, 81, 90.

20 Fitzpatrick, Ireland and the empire, pp. 501–20; L. P. Curtis, *Anglo-Saxons and Celts: a study of anti-Irish prejudice in Victorian England* (Bridgeport, 1968), pp. 74–86.

21 J. A. Mangan, *Making Imperial Mentalities: socialisation and British Imperialism* (Manchester, 1990), pp. 1–3; P. J. Durrans, A two-edged sword: the Liberal attack on Disraelian imperialism, *Journal of Imperial and Commonwealth History*, 10:3 (1982), p. 273.

Introducing Dufferin

22 R. Kipling, *One Viceroy Resigns* (1888). This is the opening line of Kipling's poem, written in the imagined voice of Lord Dufferin when he was Indian viceroy (1884–88), to his successor and fellow Irish landowner, Lord Lansdowne.
23 Lyall, *Life of Lord Dufferin*, p. 25; Gailey, *Lost Imperialist*, pp. 315–325.
24 Nicolson, *Helen's Tower*, p. 42; for more analysis on the Sheridan link, see Black, *Dufferin and Ava*, pp. 4–7. Dufferin's financial generosity caused some early concerns for his guardians; Public Record Office of Northern Ireland [hereafter PRONI], D1071, H/B/G/316, ff. 2, Sir James Graham to Dufferin, 24 Aug. 1847.
25 Maguire, *The Downshire Estates*, pp. 1, 7–8, 83–4; L. Proudfoot, The management of a great estate: patronage, income and expenditure on the Duke of Devonshire's Irish property, c. 1816–1891, *Irish Social and Economic History*, 13 (1986), pp. 32–3, 54.
26 Gailey, *Lost Imperialist*, pp. 18–22.
27 J. Gathorne-Hardy, *The Public School Phenomenon* (London, 1977), pp. 68, 137–43.
28 Lyall, *Life of Dufferin*, p. 38. The study of classics was the bedrock of elite education: M. Bradley, Tacitus' *Agricola* and the conquest of Britain: representations of empire in Victorian and Edwardian Britain, in M. Bradley (ed.), *Classics and Imperialism in the British Empire* (Oxford, 2010), pp. 124, 126–7, 157; R. Alston, Dialogues in imperialism: Rome, Britain and India, in E. Hall and P. Vasunia (eds), *India, Greece and Rome, 1757–2007* (London, 2010), pp. 51–7, 75.
29 Lyall, *Life of Dufferin*, pp. 45–6.
30 Lyall, *Life of Dufferin*, p. 40: Lord Price had requested a prescription of opiates to ease an old injury but the chemist made an error in the dosage and he was found dead on arrival in Belfast: Gailey, *Lost Imperialist*, pp. 21–2.
31 Christ Church, Oxford, MR iii.c.i 1/6/3, Dufferin to Lady Helen, 24 Jan. 1845. Gailey tracks this relationship in great detail: see, for instance, Gailey, *Lost Imperialist*, pp. 1, 3, 25–7, 318–19, 345, 350.
32 PRONI, D1071, A/B/6/1: Summary account book for the minority of Lord Dufferin (1841–7); L. P. Curtis, Incumbered Wealth: landed indebtedness in post-famine Ireland, *American History Review*, 85:2 (1980), p. 343.
33 Christ Church, Oxford, MR, iii.c.i 1/6/3, Dufferin to Lady Helen, n.d. [1846?].
34 Nicolson, *Helen's Tower*, p. 68.
35 Lyall, *Life of Dufferin*, p. 46; Sir William Fraser, later historian of the aristocracy, was another founding member of the Pythic. Gailey, *Lost Imperialist*, pp. 27–8, 31–4.
36 R. Ansell, Educational travel in Protestant families from post-Restoration Ireland, *Historical Journal*, 58:4 (2015), pp. 932–40.
37 Lyall, *Life of Dufferin*, p. 49.
38 Lyall, *Life of Dufferin*, p. 49; Nicolson, *Helen's Tower*, p. 69; K. Tidrick, *Empire and the English Character* (London, 1990), pp. 1–4.
39 Lyall, *Life of Dufferin*, p. 50.
40 Bradley (ed.), *Classics and Imperialism in the British Empire*; Alston, Dialogues in imperialism; R. Jenkyns, *The Victorians and Ancient Greece* (Oxford, 1980).
41 Nicolson, *Helen's Tower*, p. 85; Gailey, *Lost Imperialist*, pp. 46–9.
42 Lyall, *Life of Dufferin*, pp. 61–5.
43 I. E. Campbell (ed.), *George Douglas, 8th Duke of Argyll, 1823–1900: autobiography and memoirs*, 2 vols (London, 1906); Gailey, *Lost Imperialist*, pp. 49, 53.
44 H. C. G. Matthew, Campbell, George Douglas, eighth duke of Argyll in the peerage of Scotland, and first duke of Argyll in the peerage of the United Kingdom, *Oxford Dictionary of National Biography* (Oxford, 2004), https://doi-org.libproxy.ncl.ac.uk/10.1093/ref:odnb/4500 (accessed 20 Nov. 2019).
45 Cited in Lyall, *Life of Dufferin*, p. 81; PRONI, D1071, H/H/B/C/95, ff. 1–159, correspondence with the 8th Duke of Argyll.

46 See, for example, PRONI, D1071, H/B/C/95, ff. 146, Dufferin to Argyll, 7 Nov. 1896; N. M. Dawson, Letters from Inveraray: the eight duke of Argyll's correspondence with the first marquis of Dufferin and Ava, with particular reference to Gladstone's Irish Land Acts, in H. MacQueen (ed.), *Miscellany Seven* (Stair Society: Edinburgh, 2015), pp. 367; Argyll, 8th duke of, A Model Land Law: a reply to Arthur Williams MP, *Fortnightly Review*, 41 (1887), pp. 764, 784.
47 Dufferin, *Letters from High Latitudes* (London, 1856); H. Hansson, The gentleman's north: Lord Dufferin and the beginnings of Arctic tourism, *Studies in Travel Writing*, 13:1 (2009), pp. 61–71; Gailey, *Lost Imperialist*, pp. 64–9.
48 F. Zachs, 'Novice' or 'heaven-born' diplomat? Lord Dufferin and his plan for a 'Province of Syria': Beirut, 1860–61, *Middle Eastern Studies*, 36:3 (2000), pp. 160–1, 172.
49 Lyall, *Life of Dufferin*, p. 134.
50 A. T. Q. Stewart, *The Pagoda War* (Newton Abbot, 1974), pp. 21, 25.
51 Dufferin, Lady Hariot, *Our Viceregal Life in India; selections from my journal, 1884–1888* (London, 1889); Dufferin, Lady Hariot, *My Canadian Journal, 1872–8* (London, 1891); R. Davenport-Hines, Blackwood, Hariot Georgina Hamilton-Temple-, marchioness of Dufferin and Ava, *Oxford Dictionary of National Biography* (London, 2004), https://doi-org.libproxy.ncl.ac.uk/10.1093/ref:odnb/56107 (accessed 20 Nov. 2019); Gailey, *Lost Imperialist*, pp. 101–2, 137–41, 273; P. Beaumont and R. Beaumont, *Imperial Divas: the vicereines of India* (London, 2010), pp. 6, 93–4, 148; S. Sehrawat, Feminising Empire: the Association of Medical Women in India and the campaign to found a women's medical service, *Social Scientist*, 41:5–6 (2013), pp. 74–5; D. A. Roberts, Merely birds of passage: Lady Hariot Dufferin's travel writings and medical work in India, 1884–88, *Women's History Review*, 15:3 (2006), pp. 444, 447–9, 453.
52 Gailey, *Lost Imperialist*, pp. 506–7, 72, 92; H. C. G. Matthew, *Gladstone, 1809–1898* (Oxford, 1999), pp. 196–8, 451.
53 PRONI, D1071, H/B/C/95, ff. 11, Dufferin to Argyll, 20 Dec. 1863; Lyall, *Life of Dufferin*, pp. 137–8; Gailey, *Lost Imperialist*, pp. 105–6.
54 R. Davenport-Hines, Blackwood, Frederick Temple Hamilton-Temple-, first marquess of Dufferin and Ava, *Oxford Dictionary of National Biography* (Oxford, 2004), https://doi-org.libproxy.ncl.ac.uk/10.1093/ref:odnb/31914 (accessed 20 Nov. 2019).
55 R. Bitterman, *Rural Protest on Prince Edward Island: from British colonization to the Escheat Movement* (Toronto, 2006), pp. 3–6, 272; D. M. L. Farr, *The Colonial Office and Canada, 1867–1887* (Toronto, 1955), pp. 3–12; B. Messamore, The line over which he must not pass: defining the office of Governor General, 1878, *Canadian Historical Review*, 86:3 (2005), pp. 435–83.
56 Lyall, *Life of Dufferin*, p. 194.
57 B. Messamore, *Canada's Governors General, 1847–1878: biography and constitutional evolution* (Toronto, 2006), pp. 148–75.
58 Lyall, *Life of Dufferin*, p. 203–4; Gailey, *Lost Imperialist*, pp. 115–16.
59 M. Bence-Jones, *The Viceroys of India* (New York, 1982), pp. 130–49.
60 M. P. Callahan, *Making Enemies: war and state-building in Burma* (Ithaca, 2005), pp. 21–32; A. Tripathi and A. Tripathi, *Indian National Congress and the Struggle for Freedom, 1885–1947* (Oxford, 2014), pp. 1–28.
61 B. Martin, The viceroyalty of Lord Dufferin, *History Today*, 10 (1960), pp. 821–30.
62 Nicolson, *Helen's Tower*, p. 264; Gailey, *Lost Imperialist*, p. 335.
63 D. Kynaston, *The City of London, vol. II: the golden years, 1890–1914* (London, 1995), pp. 137–140, 173–4.
64 Kynaston, *City of London*, pp. 180, 216–19; Gailey, *Lost Imperialist*, pp. 335–9, 340.
65 Nicolson, *Helen's Tower*, p. 276; Lyall, *Life of Dufferin*, pp. 548–60.

66 See later criticism from Lord Curzon, for example: G. Curzon, *British Government in India: the story of the viceroys and government houses*, 2 vols (London, 1925), p. 246; J. W. Cell, *Hailey: a study in British Imperialism* (Cambridge, 1992), pp. xi–xii, 1–5; M. Francis, *Governors and Settlers: images of authority in the British colonies, 1820–60* (Basingstoke, 1992), pp. 1–10; Gailey, *Lost Imperialist*, pp. 350–4.
67 L. P. Curtis, Landlord responses to the Irish Land War, 1879–1987, *Eire/Ireland*, Fall–Winter (2003), pp. 137–44; B. Martin, Lord Dufferin and the Indian National Congress, 1885–88, *Journal of British Studies* 7:1 (1967), pp. 68–96; B. Messamore, The line over which he must not pass: defining the office of Governor General, 1878, *Canadian Historical Review*, 86:3 (2005).
68 Gailey, *Lost Imperialist*, pp. 345–53; A. Hawkins and J. Powell (eds) *The Journal of John Wodehouse, First Earl of Kimberley for 1862–1902* (London, 1997), pp. 18, 345; J. W. Mason, The Duke of Argyll and the Land Question in late nineteenth century Britain, *Victorian Studies*, 21 (1978), pp. 149–70.
69 Sir Alfred Lyall on writing his biography of Lord Dufferin, cited in H. M. Durand, *Life of Sir Alfred Lyall* (London, 1913), p. 430.
70 For a full discussion of the archival sources underpinning this study, please see the General Bibliography and Sources: Dufferin, *Songs, Poems and Verses by Helen, Lady Dufferin (Countess of Gifford)* (London, 1894).
71 Dufferin, Lady Hariot, *Our Vicaregal Life in India; selections from my journal, 1884–1888* (London, 1889); Dufferin, Lady Hariot, *My Canadian Journal, 1872–8* (London, 1891).
72 Lyall, *Life of Dufferin*.
73 Black, *Dufferin and Ava*.
74 See, in particular, Gailey, *Lost Imperialist*, pp. 345–53.
75 The growing body of transnational literature has been critical to this study: A. G. Hopkins, Back to the Future: from national history to imperial history, *Past and Present*, 164 (1999), pp. 199, 209–13; E. Delaney, Our Island Story? Towards a transnational history of late modern Ireland, *Irish Historical Studies*, 37 (2011), pp. 599, 605, 615–16; C. A. Bayly, S. Beckhert, M. Connolly, I. Hoffmeyr, W. Kozol, P. Seed, AHR Conversation: on transnational history, *American Historical Review*, 111:5 (2006), pp. 1441–6, 1458–61; A. Jones and B. Jones, The Welsh World and the British Empire, c. 1851–1939: an exploration, *Journal of Imperial and Commonwealth History*, 31:2 (2003), pp. 57, 59, 66; E. Delaney and C. O'Neill (eds), Beyond the Nation: transnational Ireland, *Eire-Ireland*, 51:1–2 (2016), pp. 9–10; N. Whelehan (ed.), *Transnational Perspectives on Modern Irish History* (London, 2015), pp. 1–2, 7–23; R. McMahon and A. Newby, Introduction – Ireland and Finland, 1860–1930: comparative and transnational histories, *Irish Historical Studies*, 41:160 (2017), pp. 166–8, 174; N. Ethrington, *Theories of Imperialism: war, conquest and capital* (London, 1984), pp. 267, 270; D. R. Khoury and D. K. Kennedy, Comparing empires: the Ottoman domains and the British Raj, *Comparative Studies of South Asia, Africa and the Middle East*, 27:2 (2007), pp. 234, 236–7.
76 For example, T. Dooley, *The Decline of the Big House in Ireland: a study of Irish landed families, 1860–1960* (Dublin, 2001), pp. 79–108; O. Purdue, *The Big House in the North of Ireland: land, power and social elites, 1878–1960* (Dublin, 2009), pp. 1–10, 14.
77 T. W. Guinnane and R. I. Miller, Bonds without Bondsmen: Tenant-Right in nineteenth century Ireland, *Journal of Economic History*, 56:1 (1996), pp. 113–16, 121.
78 P. Marshall, The imperial factor in the liberal decline, 1880–1885, in J. Flint and G. Williams (eds), *Perspectives of Empire: presented to Gerald S. Graham* (Harlow, 1973), p. 144.

79 This consists of a vast literature: some illustrative touchpoints for this study include: C. A. Bayly, *The Birth of the Modern World, 1780–1914: global connections and comparisons* (Oxford, 2004), pp. 290–9; L. Colley, What is imperial history now?, in D. Cannadine, *What is History Now?* (Basingstoke, 2002), pp. 133–8, 141; D. Kennedy, Imperial history and post-colonial theory, *Journal of Imperial and Commonwealth History*, 24 (1996), pp. 345–7, 350–1; P. J. Cain and A. G. Hopkins, *British Imperialism, I: Innovation and Expansion; II, Crisis and Deconstruction* (London, 1993), pp. 1–19; C. Kinealy, At home with the empire: the example of Ireland, in S. Rose and C. Hall (eds), *At Home with the Empire: metropolitan culture and the imperial world* (Cambridge, 2006), pp. 78–80.
80 G. Bolton, The idea of a colonial gentry, *Historical Studies*, 13 (1968), pp. 308–9, 315–16.
81 P. J. Cain, Character and Imperialism: the British financial administration of Egypt, 1878–1914, *Journal of Imperial and Commonwealth History*, 34:2 (2006), pp. 177–200; A. Scholch, The 'men on the spot' and the English occupation of Egypt in 1882, *Historical Journal*, 19:3 (1976); R. L. Tignor, *Modernisation and British colonial rule in Egypt, 1882–1914* (New Jersey, 1966), pp. 48–66.
82 B. Porter, *The Absent-Minded Imperialists: empire, society and culture in Britain* (Oxford, 2004), pp. 227–8; A. Kirk-Greene, *Britain's Imperial Administrators, 1858–1966* (London, 2000), pp. 1–2, 202–14, 222–4; T. Koditschek, *Liberalism, Imperialism, and the Historical Imagination: nineteenth-century visions of a Greater Britain* (Cambridge, 2011), pp. 314–31.
83 C. Boylan, Victorian ideologies of improvement: Sir Charles Trevelyan in India and Ireland, in T. A. Boylan and T. P. Foley, *Political Economy and Colonial Ireland: the propaganda and ideological function of economic discourse in the nineteenth century* (London, 1992), pp. 1–4.
84 T. R. Metcalfe, *Land, Landlords, and the British Raj: Northern India in the nineteenth century* (Berkley, 1979); F. Thompson, *The End of Liberal Ulster: land agitation and land reform 1868–1866* (Belfast, 2001), pp. 1–7.
85 T. R. Metcalfe, *Forging the Raj: essay on British India in the heyday of empire* (Oxford, 2005), pp. 41–9; M. Holmes, The Irish and India: imperialism, nationalism and internationalism, in A. Bielenberg (ed.), *The Irish Diaspora* (Harlow, 2000), pp. 235–43; B. Crosbie, *Irish Imperial Networks: migration, social communication and exchange in nineteenth-century India* (Cambridge, 2012), pp. 1–23; S. B. Cook, *Imperial Affinities: nineteenth century analogies and exchanges between India and Ireland* (New Delhi, 1993), pp. 9–37; H. Brasted, Indian nationalist development and the influence of Irish Home Rule, 1870–1886, *Modern Asian Studies*, 14:1 (1980), pp. 37–46.
86 C. A. Bayly, *Empire and Information: intelligence gathering and social communication in India, 1780–1870* (Cambridge, 1996), pp. 1–9, 338–51.
87 M. E. Daly and K. T. Hoppen, *Gladstone, Ireland and Beyond* (Dublin, 2011), pp. 169–78, 179–99; B. Knox, Conservative imperialism 1858–1874: Bulwer Lytton, Lord Carnarvon and Canadian confederation, *International History Review*, 4 (1984), pp. 333–5, 357; D. Cannadine, Lord Strickland: imperial aristocrat and aristocratic imperialist, in D. Cannadine, *Aspects of Aristocracy: grandeur and decline in modern Britain* (New Haven, 1994), pp. 109–10, 128; E. F. Biagini, *Liberty, Retrenchment and Reform: popular liberalism in the age of Gladstone, 1860–1880* (Cambridge, 1992), pp. 50–8.
88 A. Taylor, *Lords of Misrule: hostility to aristocracy in late nineteenth and early twentieth century Britain* (Basingstoke, 2004), pp. 1–15.
89 Dooley, *The Decline of the Big House in Ireland*, pp. 79–108; Purdue, *The Big House in the North of Ireland*, pp. 1–10, 14.

90 E. Frie and J. Neuheiser, Introduction: noble ways and democratic means, *Journal of Modern European History*, 11:4 (2013), pp. 434–48; M. Rendle, Conservatism and Revolution: the all-Russian Union of landowners, 1916–18, *Slavonic and East European Review*, 84:3 (2006), pp. 481–6, 505–6.
91 D. Cannadine, *Ornamentalism: how the British saw their empire* (London, 2001), pp. 3–23, 95, 137–49.

2 Property

> Here you have the whole theory. A man may come of a stock rooted for 600 years in the soil of Ireland – unless he be a Catholic and his name begins with an O' he is to be denounced as an alien, declared incapable of holding landed property, [and] his title ... is to be considered a usurpation.[1]

The Irish landed experience: titles and entitlement

First and foremost, Dufferin was an Irish landowner. But what did this mean, both for his class and for him personally? The answer is not straightforward. The plethora of names given to the Irish landed elite indicates this: Anglo, Anglo-Irish, the Ascendancy – each offers a nuanced, politicised, misused and misunderstood indication of the complexity of identities inhabited or rejected by landlords in nineteenth-century Ireland. This chapter explores Dufferin's Irish landed inheritance and the political, intellectual and imperial paradoxes resulting from his propertied, elite position. By tracking Dufferin's experience of land management, investment, consumption and debt – from improving, Whig-Liberal idealist to demoralised seller of the bulk of his estates – the domestic context of his imperial career can be exposed.[2] This prompts another question: how did Dufferin understand and mobilise his identity and with what consequences?[3] He certainly identified himself as one of a class of increasingly embattled Irish landowners – a man whose forebears had established a strategically and economically valuable foothold in County Down in the late sixteenth century that, from the 1840s onwards, turned from a privileged entitlement into a problematic symbol and source of existential tension.[4] One of the ways in which he was able, at least to some degree, to escape the pressures of Irish landlordism was to move into the world of imperial administration and diplomacy, as later chapters will show.[5] His estates tied him permanently to Ireland; however, he – along with his peers – was to witness a transformation of Protestant Ireland in his lifetime. From the confident enthusiasm of the early part of the century, by the 1880s and 1890s Protestant Ireland reflected an altogether less secure and disillusioned outlook – economically, politically and culturally. Dufferin was happy to display and celebrate particular elements of his Irishness, principally his Sheridan inheritance, partly for reasons of literary pedigree, but partly to consolidate and emphasise his genuine Irish heritage in the face of external denials of it.[6] Politically and intellectually, his position as an 'Irish landlord' was his chief identity, defined by his responses to the shifts in the economic and political currents of Irish life that he found himself a witness to and player in: the Great Irish Famine; tenant agitation; the agricultural depression of the 1860s; the Land War; and Irish Home Rule, which raged up to and beyond his death. Dufferin's position as a leading spokesperson for the Anglo-Irish Ascendancy was both a challenge and opportunity as he mobilised his identity for specific purposes throughout his life and career, both at home and overseas. In an Irish context, this identity was being increasingly challenged both politically and intellectually, as a Celtic, Gaelic Irish identity came to the fore in the later nineteenth century, riding the growing tide of nationalism. Dufferin's Anglo-Irish identity became, in the Irish context, increasingly disadvantageous, seen as symbolic of spoliation and conquest, as well as religious distance and tyranny.[7] In the context of Westminster – and more importantly, the empire – his identity was diluted into a more general elite Irishness, with contemporaries commenting on his, 'quick temper', charm and 'blarney', as well as a perceived resistance to hard work, all classic expressions of prejudices held about the Irish, even elite Irish.[8] The performance of identity was not an abstract exercise, but affected how and why Dufferin made decisions about land, financial management, relations with his tenants and, later, imperial governance.[9] His nephew Harold Nicolson argued that, in his landownership, Dufferin was in a conflicted and ultimately false position whereby, 'although [he was] a powerful Irish landlord, his heart was tormented with shame and pity at the plight of the Irish tenants'.[10] There were to be no easy answers. Like many Irish landlords, Dufferin found life at times a financial uphill struggle, seasoned with conflicting and uncomfortable loyalties. Fundamentally, the rural economy in Ireland was increasingly politicised, and so was estate management.[11]

Although Dufferin rose to prominence as a traveller, literary star and courtier, and then as an imperial administrator and diplomat, his Irish inheritance always remained central to his thinking and identity. We can only understand Dufferin's actions in the British diplomatic and imperial context in terms of the complexities of Ireland's socio-economic and political conditions. From the 1860s, he found himself increasingly on the defensive as Irish landlordism came under attack from all sides of the political spectrum, as well as his own tenantry.[12] This raises all kinds of interesting questions: in what ways did Dufferin, as a committed Liberal, think about the rights of property and contract, and their relationship with the evident poverty and destitution of much of the Irish population? What were his views on 'bad' landlordism in Ireland, defined as a rejection of the paternalistic responsibility to improve estates and to resist eviction and rack-renting?[13] In other words, was (Irish) landlordism inherently immoral? Whether some landlords were just bad apples, or whether the whole cart of Irish landlordism was rotten was a question that exercised many political and intellectual contemporaries. Unsurprisingly, Dufferin saw landlordism as a force for good, although not without its historical – and even contemporary – sinners.[14] Lastly, as these Irish question(s) became increasingly bound up in demands for national determination and self-rule, how did Dufferin balance a willingness to countenance reform to promote 'good' governance, while keeping the nationalist wolf from the door?[15] One of Dufferin's central beliefs was that it was both the right and, more importantly, the duty of the landed and aristocratic classes to govern well at home and in the imperial context. He was dismayed by the declining influence of the Irish landed classes over the late nineteenth century, as they were denigrated, not just by Irish nationalists and radicals, but also by their landed and titled brethren in Britain, whose disapproval hardened and sympathy evaporated by the late 1880s.[16]

As well as these universal questions, Dufferin had more immediate and personal difficulties to face as an Irish landowner. Although his Clandeboye estate weathered the Great Irish Famine relatively well, inherited debt and a seemingly immovable weight of rent arrears rested on the books when Dufferin came into his majority in 1847.[17] Aside from financial challenges, Dufferin faced a general and significant increase in the complexity of estate management from the 1830s, as the population continued to increase, economic opportunities became less certain, and the structures of credit and debt became more complicated and expensive. He was dependent throughout his life on the men who managed his estates on the ground, the land agents and estate managers. Much of his correspondence with these men consisted of increasingly frantic requests to think of ways to stabilise and increase the estate's income, clear rent arrears and manage his lines of credit.[18] This came to a head in the early 1870s, when he made the decision to sell the bulk of his estates, leaving himself only Clandeboye house and its demesne, totalling a few thousand acres.[19] This was more than a financial or dynastic decision: without the acres of Irish soil, who was Dufferin?[20]

David Cannadine has delineated the declining spheres of influence of the British aristocracy in the later nineteenth century, identifying the Irish aristocracy as the group that came under the fiercest attack and saw the steepest decline.[21] This has been nuanced by studies by Terence Dooley and Olwen Purdue, who both identify the different pace and nature of change across Ireland's regions, particularly Ulster, and warn against taking the vocal complaints and paranoia of the landed aristocracy too much at face value.[22] The landed classes across Britain faced the same critiques of their authority, but the position in Ireland was made more acute by the ways in which it was bound up in questions of governance and religion.[23] This has led to a remarkable concentration of academic effort on untangling the sinews of landed power and its decline in Ireland, and this chapter will place Dufferin's experience into this context, while addressing three main themes.[24] The first theme is the debate around the extent of landlord improvement in pre- and post-Famine Ireland, including improvement and investment in agriculture, alternative employments and industrialisation. Second, Dufferin's response to the tragedy of the Great Famine will be put into the wider context of landed responses across the island of Ireland, including landed interactions with the British state around expectations of the burden of responsibility, both moral and economic. The third theme is the increasingly acrimonious debate as to whether Irish landlordism was a fundamentally immoral institution. Dufferin violently objected to the view that it underpinned the economic, social and political misery of Ireland in the nineteenth century but, despite his efforts, he was never able to convince public opinion either in Ireland or Britain.[25] For Dufferin, property rights were universal and any detrimental precedents set in Ireland (or India or Canada, for that matter) would inevitably rebound on landed elites in Britain, a fate he railed against, Cassandra-like, for his entire career.

This was one element of Dufferin's decision to look overseas, towards a diplomatic and imperial career, escaping the political and financial turmoil of Ireland. In many ways, his response aligns with that of the British aristocracy more generally, with the empire becoming a far-flung system of outdoor relief for cash-strapped aristocrats looking for a way to bolster fragile incomes with government salaries and cheap living.[26] But this decision was based on much more than financial common sense, it was also a statement about the duty of the landed – and, by definition, governing – classes, and a key part of elite formation.[27] Dufferin was part of a generation of landowners who held genuine convictions as to their responsibilities to British global leadership, whether that was in Ireland or overseas, summarised as 'an aristocracy redeemed by service'.[28] Alongside peers such as the Lords Ripon, Kimberley, Lansdowne and Mayo, Dufferin – inspired, like them, by the political and philosophical zeitgeist and the expansive direction the British empire was taking in the 1870s – felt a duty to govern as part of a service aristocracy.[29] This moves us beyond 'ornamentalism' – the view that the landed classes became increasingly symbolic and ornamental, both in the domestic context and then, later, in the empire, too.[30] Although, overall, this was the dominant pattern, peers such as Dufferin still maintained a belief in both their ability and right to govern for the benefit not only of the empire project, but also for the populations and territories they oversaw. As aristocratic leadership became increasingly impossible in an Irish context, Dufferin withdrew from the vitriolic political world of Westminster and observed it from afar, mobilising his Irish credentials when necessary and bewailing his exile from the metropolis.[31]

'An individual who does not get any rent': the Clandeboye estates – finances and improvement

> The allusion which has been made … to that devastating famine by which Ireland was depopulated in 1846 and 1847 has recalled to my mind very bitter and affecting memories. It so happened that it was in that year I first was called upon to undertake the responsibilities

attaching to the ownership of land in Ireland, and my first invitation to my duties as an Irish landlord consisted in an endeavour to confront the exigencies of that terrible disaster.[32]

Dufferin, raised and educated predominantly in England, did not fully make his mark on his estates until he reached his majority in 1847. On that pre-eminent occasion, he held a dinner for five hundred of his tenants and made a speech on the outlook for an Irish landlord. These were: 'an individual who does not get any rent; a well-dressed gentleman who may be shot with impunity, the legitimate target of the immediate neighbourhood, a superficial index by which to mark the geographical direction of the under currents of assassinations'.[33] Dufferin was being facetious when making this speech to his (presumably not too sympathetic) tenants, but there was truth in the humour. His social circle at Eton and Oxford had shown him what real wealth looked like, and even a cursory glance at his own estate finances would have shown him that – given his own personal ambitions with regard to political, elite and literary society – they were never going fully to support his expectations.[34] What had Dufferin inherited? The total acreage of the estate in 1847 was 18,343; this was not contiguous but, spread across three areas: Clandeboye, Ards and Killyleagh, all in County Down.[35] During Dufferin's minority, the estates were under the primary supervision of one of his guardians, the Hon. and Rev. W. J. Blackwood, supported by Arthur Read and John Howe, who were the resident land agents.[36] Naturally, a cautious approach to estate management was followed during these years, and no major improvements were undertaken. One worrying trend, however, was the growing proportion of arrears of rent: these stood at £2431.13.7 in 1841, and this figure continued to increase by a rate of nearly 5%.[37] In a summary of the minority finances commissioned by Sir James Graham in order to impress upon his young nephew the limitations of his particular inheritance, the auditor noted that average yearly arrears totalled £2098.7.6. These were significant and suggest problematic structural issues relating to rentals on the Clandeboye estate, leaving aside for the moment the impact of the Great Famine from the middle of the decade.[38] To put them into context, the average annual expected rental of the estate totalled £18,770.14.9, although this was topped up from liquid sources, such as investments, to a total income of £21,695.6.10.[39] An income of over £21,0000 was very respectable for a young landowner, although lower than that enjoyed by some of his peers at Eton and Oxford, and certainly lower (catastrophically so), than the incomes of his future social circle.[40] A very small proportion of this income was actually free for Dufferin to use, however; annual expenditure on the estate – which included the upkeep of the house, rates and taxes, as well as family burdens and jointures – swallowed up £21,009.8.4, leaving Dufferin only £680 free for disposable income as he came into his majority.[41] Unsurprisingly perhaps, at about this time Dufferin described inheriting an Irish estate as a, 'more melancholy, saddening employment can scarcely be conceived'.[42]

By 1848, this rather pessimistic view had further deepened through experience and, at a tenant's dinner, he again expounded on his situation:

> I consider a newly constituted Irish landlord is a sublime spectacle. There is something heroic in his situation; his difficulties are so insurmountable, and the destiny against which he hopelessly strives is so ruthless and inexorable, that he becomes extremely affecting … There is nothing that he has not to do, or be, or try to be. Without the slightest warning, he suddenly finds himself wildly ranging through a whole circle of difficulties. In ethics, politics and economics he stands helplessly confronting an entire conglomeration of problems which the ingenious management of his predecessors have invented for his solution … something of this has been, psychologically speaking, my condition during the past year.[43]

Dufferin was expressing the disjuncture between his imagined construction of Irish landlordism with the situation he had found on the ground in the twelve months he had had primary responsibility for his property. Already, he had diagnosed the economic and social structures hemming Irish landlordism in as implacable, indeed, 'insurmountable'.[44] This does not appear to have prevented him from making an effort to reform and restructure his estates.[45] Indeed, this emphasis on improvement was part of his personal and political identity, and was directly influenced by his social circle, which was dominated by other improving Whig-Liberal landlords, mainly Scottish-based.[46] For Dufferin, a key part of the duty and identity of a landlord was improvement – economic and moral – and he was disappointed by the lack of zeal demonstrated by Irish landlords in general, compared to their English and Scottish counterparts.[47] Dufferin was also motivated in his desire to improve by his conception of landlordism as a mechanism for social and economic leadership.[48] In his view, Ireland's economic plight could not be addressed solely through agricultural improvement or land reform but, rather, with, 'the development of commercial enterprise, of our mineral resources, of our manufacturing industry', opportunities perhaps more apparent in the north of Ireland than the south or west.[49] This view was later reflected in the extensive (and expensive) public works programmes he oversaw as Indian viceroy, and the genesis of the Canadian Pacific Railway project while Governor-General. For Dufferin, the provision and financing of economic infrastructure was a central mechanism for putting the theory of landed service into practice, both defining and defending landed privilege.

As an idealistic young graduate, his head stuffed with a classical education and peppered with the latest thought on political economy, Dufferin was burning to begin the management of the Clandeboye estates anew.[50] With this in mind, between 1847 and 1848, he visited, or attempted to visit, every tenant on his land ('I have passed whole days among the bogs') to gain a first-hand view of conditions on his estate under the shadow of the Famine, and formulate a comprehensive plan of improvements.[51] His estates offered significant potential, with good soil and other investment opportunities, such as house building, to cater for a future middle-class exodus from Belfast at Helen's Bay.[52] Dufferin would attempt to develop these opportunities, but both his timing and his financial limitations precluded them from becoming immediate economic successes. Of course, he was undertaking this review under a cloud of perilous economic catastrophe as the potato blight devastated rural Ireland.[53] At Clandeboye, conditions were relatively stable, in part due to the availability of alternative employment, but also because reliance on the potato was not so absolute. This did not mean that distressing poverty and increasing rent arrears were not in evidence, but compared to what Dufferin had seen during a visit to Skibbereen in 1847, the Clandeboye tenantry were relatively well-supported.[54] He was privately critical of the lack of effort of other Irish landlords, particularly those who resorted to large-scale eviction programmes during and in the immediate wake of the Famine. In a letter to Lady Russell after the Queen's visit to Ireland in 1849, he noted his shock at the condition of the people in the south and west, and that, 'great has been the guilt of them who have brought them to this pass ... generation after generation have grown up in ignorance and misery, while those who lived upon the product of their labours have laughed and rioted through life ... and have now left them to die off the face of the earth'.[55] His fear was that this abdication of responsibility and the suffering which ensued would lead to, 'a repetition of the horrors of the [1798] rebellion', demonstrating the way in which he linked in his own mind good landlordism with good governance, but also his fear of the rebellious nature of the Irish, a fear shared by his peers and the British government.[56] Dufferin was never under any illusion about the precarious nature of the Irish rural economy, even in County Down, close to the booming textile industries of Belfast.[57] As well as rent remissions, Dufferin established a number of employment projects to keep his tenants afloat. The most unusual of these was the construction of a folly, Helen's Tower, in tribute to his mother, complete with a five-mile road linking it to Helen's Bay, the small seaside town he was redeveloping.[58] He also improved the demesne, viewing these projects as relief measures, but also as adding long-term value to his estate and capturing his legacy, presumably hoping that their combined cost of just over £78,000 would be reflected in future land values.[59]

Dufferin did not need to look at his tenant's struggles to identify looming economic catastrophe: he just had to look at his own account books. Perhaps unsurprisingly, given the expensive circles in which Dufferin was moving, as he came into his majority he grew increasingly dependent on credit, both to meet general expenditure and to support his improvement projects. He was, in these early years, almost recklessly generous to his tenantry; one of his first acts when he reached his majority was to give a rent remission amounting to just over £2000 per annum.[60] In addition, he was consistently unwilling to engage in acrimonious debate with outgoing tenants as to the value of their improvements, as was the custom in Ulster, leading to astonishing payouts to some individual tenants, as much as £18,000 in one case.[61] This was despite the fact, as he told the 1865 select committee on tenure and improvement of land (Ireland), 'there can be no doubt that agriculture in Ireland is in a backward condition ... even in the most advanced parts of Ireland'.[62]

Rent arrears had long been a problem on the Clandeboye estates, and his guardians had been unable to address the issue before he came into his majority in 1847. As Thomson, his land agent, later explained to him from the vantage point of 1870:

> When your Lordship came of age in 1847 I may say that the entire estate ... was even then suffering through the potato blight [and] your agent received instructions to re-value the entire estate with a view of affording temporary relief ... the abatement under this process amounted to £2000 a year. The distress continuing for some years longer your Lordship decided a further abatement of 10 per cent be allowed and this was continued for a period of 5 and a half or 6 years ... the tenants – not withstanding their leases – were allowed to hold on at the abated rent till 1862 – a period of 15 years – when the rents were finally settled at some £700 below the figure at which your Lordship coming of age found them leased.[63]

Why did Dufferin manage his estate in this financially unsustainable and potentially ruinous way? It was a question his own land agents, friends and family asked with increasing urgency. The answer lies in two parts: first, as revisionist histories of rural and agricultural Ireland have suggested, Irish land was chronically under-rented in the post-Famine period as a general rule. Vaughan has demonstrated that rents lagged behind the value of agricultural outputs and farming profits from the 1850s, although this was matched by low landlord investment in permanent improvements, which were usually left to tenants. There are a number of reasons for this, but it clear that Dufferin was by no means alone in tolerating low rents, although this was perhaps a little more unusual in Ulster, as was his significant investment in improving his estate.[64] The second part of the answer lies in Dufferin's construction of Irish landed identity, combined with his life-long aversion to public criticism ('worrying about "what people thought"').[65] He aspired to an imagined ideal of the 'good' Irish landlord; investing in and resident on his estates, fair to his tenantry, and deserving of their loyalty and his elevated position. He wanted, in fact, to engage in the practical articulation of his qualities as a Whig-Liberal politician and landowner, and to set an example of good governance, just as the cloud of hostility hanging over Irish landlords darkened in the wake of the Great Famine, never again to clear.[66] This makes for an interesting comparison to the estate policies that came in the wake of the potato famine and had been introduced by his friend and fellow Whig-Liberal landowner, the 8th Duke of Argyll who, in the same period, undertook a full rationalisation of his estates, with a specific view to removing the poorest 'surplus' of his estate population, and increased rents. In other words, he sought to modernise and fully commercialise his landed operations in Scotland. Argyll wrote extensively on both the theory behind and the practical management of land, his own estates and those in Ireland included. He argued that, despite popular prejudice, Irish landlords had a history of improvement but that it had been unacknowledged in favour of 'mere sentiment'.[67] This is supported by Curtis, who reminds us that, despite the 'revisionist rush' to acquit Irish landlords, the power of 'myth, memory and emotion' cannot be set aside, a contradiction Dufferin grappled with his whole life.[68] The results of Dufferin's financially risky decision-making can in part be explained with reference to the hostile economic climate of mid-century rural Ireland, but he was also unwilling or unable to curb his personal expenditure, with travel, club life and society, and his passion for yachting all adding up.[69] While these social and cultural activities relate to a long tradition of elite formation and family strategy, their cost outstripped the stagnating financial resources of the estate.[70] To these pressures were added the family jointures and portions which, in the year after Dufferin came into his majority, totalled £4740, the bulk of which was annually distributed to his mother (£1661.8.8) and his grandmother (£923.1.6).[71] Luckily, Dufferin was an only child, and so he did not have to concern himself with portions for brothers and sisters, although providing financially for his own children in later decades would be a constant worry.[72]

The scale of Dufferin's accumulated indebtedness makes frightening reading: between 1848 and 1862 he borrowed a total of £131,364.2.–.[73] Two years later, in 1864, his accountant reported that his total debt then consisted of, 'English loans: £100,500; Irish loans, £75,571.1.11; Interest per annum, £7,958.1.6'. This meant that the interest payments on the debt alone swallowed nearly 40 per cent of Dufferin's annual income.[74] He was unable to slow his spiral into debt and, from 1862 to 1871, he borrowed a further £192,476, although he claimed that at least £150,000 of this was spent directly on estate improvements.[75] By the late 1860s, thanks to repeated warnings from his managers, Dufferin had come to recognise the gravity of his financial situation and began a decade-long process of retrenchment, principally by selling off assets to keep his head above water. This included the sale of smaller properties such as Dufferin House on the Clandeboye estate for £16,200 in 1866–67; No. 8 Grosvenor Square, London, for £9000; the sale in 1871 of Dufferin Lodge, Clandeboye, for £12,000; and most importantly, due to their useful liquidity, the continual sale of shares worth £114,111 between 1847 and 1872.

Dufferin was not alone among the landed classes – British or Irish – in facing financial instability and decline.[76] Even the wealthiest families used their landed assets to leverage credit, and whole generations could find themselves obliged to retrench to clear debt.[77] The problem can be defined in two ways; first, a stagnant or falling income and, second, increased expenditure. Dufferin faced both. Take income first: when Dufferin inherited his estate, the annual income was £21,695.6.10 but the bulk of that was quickly swallowed by essential expenditure.[78] Unlike many a canny and impoverished landlord before him, Dufferin did not marry money either; his wife, Hariot Hamilton, was a happy choice and an essential prop to his career, but she came from a County Down family of proud heritage but modest means and did not represent a financial benefit to his personal or estate finances.[79] What about expenditure? The figure of the profligate and extravagant Irish landlord was well-established in satire long before the 1840s and Dufferin did match some aspects of the stereotype; improving a Big House, having an ornamental demesne designed by a fashionable landscape artist, keeping carriages, subscribing to numerous clubs in Belfast, Dublin and London.[80] The costs of maintaining an establishment in County Down, alongside a London operation with some expensive hobbies thrown in quickly outstripped a stagnant rental roll.

Why did Dufferin feel compelled to spend in this way? The largest proportion of his expenditure was made with a pragmatic and calculating eye to future profit, through the development of his landed and other assets. This included a comprehensive investment in the estate's tenancies, including the refurbishment of the four principal houses on the estate, all rented (and later sold) to affluent Belfast businessmen.[81] It also included the classic landed investment tactic of railway building and land sales to accommodate it. Dufferin was initially wary of a railway running across his estate on aesthetic grounds, but was converted by the long-term economic prospect of being connected into the heart of Belfast.[82] Partly as a result, from the early 1860s he began to develop a small seaside town on his estate, renaming it Helen's Bay for his mother.[83] As well as negotiating an expansion of railway operations at Helen's Bay station (which he designed and built himself, creating one of the most remarkable train stations in Ireland), he began investing heavily in his vision of new 'homes for gentlemen'.[84] He began by constructing a sea wall and esplanade for the town, and then commenced on suitable residential properties, until the financial pressures became too great to continue.[85] Overall, Dufferin calculated that he had spent, 'something like £150,000', on permanent improvements on his estate, expenditure that he was never able to recoup.[86] When Dufferin asked in the same year – with some urgency – whether an increase of the rental on the estate could be implemented, his agent rejected the plan, pointing out that it was, 'unfortunate that the state of money matters prevents the outlay necessary to fully develop the property'.[87] That was a polite way of expressing the seriousness of Dufferin's financial position. Generally, the 1850s and 1860s were decades of high capital investment in both agriculture and communications such as railways in Britain; Dufferin's developments were not out of the ordinary in that context, although they were perhaps more so in an Irish one.[88] The extent to which Irish landlords as a class did, or did not, implement improvements on their estates has been much debated in the historiography.[89] Although significantly revised and nuanced in recent years, particularly for the pre-Famine period, the standard view of the Irish landlord as essentially un-improving, forcing the tenantry to make improvements at their own expense, has retained some traction.[90] Dufferin was relatively unusual, therefore, in sinking large sums of capital in his estates after the Famine, although the nature of this improvement always had one eye on increasing the capital value of his land.[91] But Dufferin's investments never reached a point where they began to pay back and, instead, he was left with their cost, all funded by ballooning and increasingly expensive credit.

Expenditure on items unrelated to permanent improvements and more focused on pleasurable or social activities was, arguably, also made with one eye to advancement. Dufferin, with his minor Irish peerage and relatively small income, had to rely on cultivating influential friends within the circles in which he desired to move.[92] He was helped, of course, by his mother, a prominent society figure along with her two sisters.[93] But he propelled himself up the path of acceptance and promotion with his famously affable manners, humour and charm.[94] He did have to spend more than he had to keep up, but it was a successful tactic, given his glittering diplomatic and administrative career, supported in the early days by influential patrons such as Lord John Russell, Palmerston and Disraeli. Dufferin's decision-making was underpinned by a recognition that a close and politicised handling of estate management was also a pragmatic expression of his theoretical conception of the rights and responsibilities of landlords, a display intended to have an impact locally, but also nationally in Westminster and, later, to exemplify his expectations of landowners in the imperial territories.[95]

Due to the relatively small income Dufferin received from his estate and his mounting financial problems, wherever he happened to be in the world, he kept a close eye on the smallest details of estate management. He was able to do this through a succession of land agents, the most important of whom were John Howe (1846–52) and Mortimer Thomson (1852–82).[96] These were men of significant education and local authority who had jurisdiction over the 18,000 acres of Dufferin's estates, and the upkeep of the house and demesne, kept ready for whenever Dufferin and his family returned.[97] They had charge over the collection of rents and rates, financial management and accounting, repairs, maintenance, relations with tenants large and small, and, of course, reporting to Dufferin on all aspects of their management.[98] For Dufferin, his relationship with Thomson was especially pivotal, although not without its ups and downs. Although grateful for both his agrarian and legal knowledge and the Catholic man's ability to command respect and affection from a largely Presbyterian tenantry, he often found himself scolding him from across the seas for the slow pace of his correspondence.[99] Dufferin was in an immensely frustrating position: he wanted to be kept entirely up to date with activities at Clandeboye and the political temperature on the ground. Thomson attempted to oblige but did not write nearly enough for Dufferin's needs. In 1867, Dufferin was writing furiously that, 'Nobody can write a better letter than you can when you once set about it but it is extraordinarily difficult to get you to put pen

38 *Property*

to paper'.[100] Despite this drawback, Thomson was assiduous in pursuing Dufferin's interests, re-structuring his debt as advantageously as possible and handling the general estate management with all feasible efficiency.

The perilous economic circumstances of mid-nineteenth-century Ireland conspired against effective financial discipline on the Clandeboye estates. His desire to be a popular, improving landlord overwhelmed the financial constraints of his inheritance, and both were in turn overwhelmed by a hostile economic context. He attempted to spend his way to economic security through the development of his land and other assets, but this goal was never achieved. Although the trend for diversification of landed assets into industry and finance was a common and often successful method of managing a landed fortune, Dufferin was precluded from this by a combination of unlucky timing of his investments – the impact of the Great Famine and the agricultural depression of the 1860s being the most important – as well as a failure to recognise the essential restrictions the relative smallness of his estate created.[101] Economies of scale were not possible on Clandeboye, and Dufferin lacked the liquidity required to soak up major investments or losses.[102] The consequences would come home to roost in the early 1870s.

Debt, land sales and retrenchment

> We must make Clandeboye keep itself by hook or by crook.[103]

Dufferin's most pressing financial problem was the management of his ever-increasing burden of debt, which might have remained manageable if not for the impact of economic and political downturns for Irish landed interests from the 1860s. His papers are littered with correspondence tracking the negotiation and re-negotiation of loans, both capital and interest, throughout the 1860s and 1870s. He was facing an uphill battle in this regard: the smaller and poorer the landowner, the more expensive – and less likely – obtaining credit became.[104] Curtis has expressed the position of Irish landowners as, 'a financial limbo, caught somewhere between luxury and austerity'.[105] By the late 1860s, this was certainly proving the case for Dufferin, who was already a long-standing debtor.[106] Dufferin had borrowed heavily by 1868, mortgaging his properties to a total of forty-three creditors. By far the largest was John Mulholland (later Lord Dunleath), the outrageously successful Belfast textiles magnate.[107] These mortgages were regularly renewed and extended by Dufferin until the early 1870s, when Mulholland began to tighten the screws, refusing to maintain an interest rate below 5 per cent.[108] Dufferin became increasingly desperate, and gradually moved towards the sale of his estates as the only possible solution, a decision supported by Thomson:

> I wish to increase the amount I borrow, from £160,000 to £180,000 ... Even as it is I fear that the annual rental we offer is hardly sufficient to cover the £160,000 ... I have already explained that on no account

whatsoever are any fresh arrears are to be permitted to accrue ... I must also request you to keep in mind that although *I do not wish it to be known in the county* I have quite made up my mind to sell Clandeboye and the whole estate if I can obtain an advantageous offer.[109]

The early 1870s represented financial Armageddon for Dufferin. The auditor's report for 1871–72 laid out the difficulties in stark terms: the total rental for that year was £19,809.2.1, but Dufferin's debts towered over that and he was struggling to pay even the interest on his loans.[110] When Thomson totted up the total debt in 1873, it came to the heart-stopping total of £299,171.1.11, with £120,346 of that owed to Mulholland, which had fallen due.[111] In early 1874, Thomson wrote to Dufferin, then in Ottawa, estimating that year's income to be £21,635, but that interest payments would immediately claim £14,421 of that.[112] With the rest of the essential expenditure taken into account, Dufferin would have only £153 of free income. Like many indebted landowners, Dufferin was struggling between renegotiating his debts when they fell due, or facing steep and rising interest rates to do so.[113] Thomson spelt it out in 1874: 'Mr Mulholland tho' willing to facilitate us by not insisting on his rights, was not inclined to reduce his interest to 4 and a half per cent'.[114] The costs of borrowing were high for small and struggling landowners in Dufferin's position, and this, alongside the difficulty in finding new creditors and the scale of the debt, meant that there was no other option but land sales.[115] In a joint memorandum written in November 1875, Dufferin's advisors spelt out plainly that, in order to clear his debts and be left with a suitable income, major land sales and financial reconstruction would be required, and, even then, the resulting income would likely only be enough to support a moderate domestic operation at Clandeboye, with nothing left over for a permanent London establishment.[116]

The sale of Irish land in a difficult market at a time of economic depression was no simple task, as Dufferin knew very well, despite the operation of the Encumbered Estates Act.[117] He was also keenly aware of the pressure on him as the man who was proposing to sell his family's patrimony; it was difficult to offer another interpretation aside from failure.[118] He recognised the symbolic as well as the practical step he was taking, and emphasised the high stakes to Thomson: 'I need not remind you that we are now embarking upon a most momentous operation upon the successful issue of which will depend the future prospects and position not merely of myself, but of my children'.[119] As well as this, he was keenly aware of the reputational damage public land sales might have, 'as it would be very disagreeable if a report got abroad that I was getting rid of the whole of the property because I was "ruined"'.[120] This concern highlights contradictory pressures on Dufferin, relating to the actual state of his finances on one hand, and questions of reputation and identity on the other. Was Dufferin truly 'ruined'? Arguably, although he faced serious financial challenges – inherited debt, Ulster tenant right costs and problems of rent arrears – that probably could have been predicted, those of recurrent agricultural depression and famine could not have been. These were issues faced by nearly all Irish landowners, but Dufferin's financial insecurity and ultimate sale of the majority of his ancestral estate were in large part caused by his determination to be a 'good' landlord; namely, by investing in ambitious and ultimately unprofitable development projects, rent abatements and generous payments to outgoing tenants for improvements, all of which were ultimately beyond his means. Despite the major land sales required, Dufferin was not ruined by the end of the 1870s: his and his family's long-term capital underpinning was severely weakened but Clandeboye was still a significant Ulster property, and his imperial and diplomatic career secured his reputation and position.[121]

As with most Irish land sales in this period, the actual process was slow and fraught with difficulty.[122] One advantage Dufferin possessed was the fact that his estates were not contiguous, and so could be carved up into lots and separately marketed with relative ease. This meant – in theory – that portions of the estates could be sold over a longer period, allowing time for the best offers to come forward.[123] The difficulty lay in getting the right price: Dufferin had to achieve sales of at least 25 years purchase (his preference was 28 years) in order to clear his debts and have something left over.[124] Dufferin calculated in 1877 that, if they could achieve 28 years purchase on the estate, he could realise £540,000 from the sale of 17,400 acres (out of a total estimated estate value of £700,500, by leaving the Clandeboye demesne out of the sale).[125] Thomson took a more realistic view, noting that 25 years purchase was more likely, and that from a verified rental of £12,663 per annum they could expect to make £316,550 from a sale.[126]

Dufferin hired a land agency based in Manchester, Carrick, Brockbank and Wilson, to manage the piecemeal sale of his estates, which took place between 1875 and 1880.[127] They were instructed to find buyers for the various lots, or, failing that, a long-term lease on the properties. To help them, in 1877 Dufferin wrote a memorandum of the history and value, as he understood it, of his landed patrimony.[128] He stressed the attractive qualities of the estate, knowing that his agents would be using the memorandum as the basis from which to attract purchasers. As such, he was quick to point out that the estate was, 'almost exclusively occupied by Scotch-Irish Protestants, and no landlord has ever been connected with a more orderly, industrious or friendly tenantry'.[129] Dufferin was aware that increasing agitation and hardening racialised attitudes about Ireland could negatively affect his chances of getting a good price, or even achieving a sale. As such, he stressed the particular location of Clandeboye, in 'the most flourishing part of the county, the neighbourhood of Belfast enhancing of course the value of all landed property around it'.[130] Dufferin's ideal scenario was to find a private purchaser for the whole of the property, and for this he would be happy to drop his overall projected price of £700,500.[131] It was not to be; piece by piece, land sales were made between 1875 and 1878 and, although Dufferin's crushing debts were cleared, it was at the future cost of a much-reduced base of landed capital and financial leverage.[132]

Although direct and unsentimental in his letters to his agent, Dufferin was clearly very disappointed and anxious about these sales; that he had to make them at all, and the further worry that he would not achieve the best possible price for them and therefore cheat himself and his descendants out of their patrimony.[133] He indulged in these more bitter reflections when writing to Argyll:

> The sense of bitter injustice involved in these transactions is so painful, as to render one's position intolerable nor am I required by any conceivable call of duty to undergo this species of annoyance. God knows I have done my duty by my tenantry only too liberally for my own advantage and now that they are well protected against any possible exaction at the hands of strangers, I shall make my escape. I shall have to leave something like £150,000 behind me in the shape of improvements, from which I have had no time to reap no other advantage than the ameliorated condition of the farmers themselves, but an Irish estate is like a sponge, and an Irish landlord never so rich as when he is rid of his property ... In many ways it will be a great pain to part with a possession that has been for nearly 300 years in my family and which I had done so much to embellish, but there are many counteracting considerations and the interests of those who come after me, I am inclined to think that Great Britain will afford a firmer foothold than poor dear Old Ireland.[134]

This private assessment constituted a common cry from Irish landlords, from the 1840s to the 1920s.[135] There is little in his assessment addressing any personal responsibility for the parlous state of his finances. Perhaps as early as 1847 he was aware his income would never be able to keep pace with his social and political ambitions, and the Great Famine and depression of the early 1860s encouraged a fatalistic approach to financial matters.[136] In his mind, circumstances had conspired against him and it is not surprising that he would come to this conclusion.[137] He was not alone in his troubles among his class in Ireland, or indeed Britain. The early 1860s and late 1870s were periods of acute agricultural depression in both and, although Dufferin had been in receipt of some salaried government posts in the 1860s, it was not until his appointment to Canada in 1872 that these began to represent an effective income.[138] In his case, a 'firmer foothold' would materialise in the empire, rather than Ireland.

What his letter to Argyll really demonstrates is the impact the sale of his estates had on Dufferin's sense of identity and purpose. This was fundamentally that of an Irish landowner but, after the 1870s, he could no longer claim to have maintained the land he had inherited to support that primary identity. As well as this, although the sale of his lands freed Dufferin to serve across the empire, this did not represent any psychological freedom from the burden of estate ownership; rather, he felt this change as a loss. His first biographer speculated as to whether these sales had the opposite intended effect, by removing a curb on Dufferin's already somewhat reckless approach to finances – his 'incautious magnificence' – with no property to conserve for his children.[139] Certainly, later affairs – including Dufferin's ill-fated support of the London Globe and Finance Company – could be seen as evidence for this.[140] Due to the shifting ground beneath his feet, Dufferin was obliged to re-think the expression of his Irish identity and, instead, mobilised it in lobbying on Irish issues throughout his colonial and diplomatic career. From the early 1880s, the focus of his correspondence with his land agent shifts from finance and land sales to reputational difficulties, as the 1879 agricultural downturn and Irish Land League began to bite. Now Dufferin faced public complaints to newspapers and petitions from his tenants as to rent reductions and unfair estate policies, which further unsettled Dufferin's view of himself as a good landlord who had made financial sacrifices for his tenantry.[141] He was outraged and anxious when, in early 1881, he received a petition from his Clandeboye tenants requesting a 30 per cent rent reduction, particularly when he had, 'shown [them] the greatest kindness and indulgence … and made them the men they are'.[142] Eventually Dufferin agreed to a 15 per cent abatement, principally to get the rents paid to some extent and to avoid coming, 'publicly into collision with any of my tenants'.[143] After the passage of the 1881 Irish Land Act – of which Dufferin was highly critical, if despondingly resigned – the tone of the correspondence shifts subtly once again towards a less emotive discussion of how best to manage the legislation in relation to the interests of his finances and family.[144] The long-term shifts in Dufferin's priorities – from concern with political economy and improvement in the 1840s and 1850s, through to the financial pressures of credit and debt in the 1860s and 1870s, to resignation and reputational concerns from the 1880s – mirror his changing relationship with the ideals of Irish landlordism and the wider fortunes of Irish landlords in this period. Dufferin was tireless in mobilising his private political connections to paint a picture of the good undertaken by many Irish landlords in terms of low rents, improvements and charitable works in the face of the highly critical narrative that emerged by the 1870s in both Ireland and Westminster. In his view, 'The Irish Landlords have become the victims of a revolution … our rents have never been raised for such a long period, in spite of the enormous sums of money I have spent upon the property … I should be glad if our cases come into Court that the fact of my great expenditure on my estate, as set forth in my evidence, should be duly recorded'.[145] As time passed, he began to frame his land sales as a prudent manoeuvre, given the direction of Irish policy from the 1880s onwards, particularly that around land purchase; that he, 'got a good lot out of the fire in time'.[146]

'This will be an economy in Paddy Land'[147]

> I hear terrible things about your expenditure. People say that you will be entirely ruinated. Do not be too Irish, or Sheridanish; it is an awful combination.[148]

Over the course of the nineteenth century, the deteriorating reputation of Irish landlords became an increasing source of weakness, undermining their power and influence both in Ireland and in Britain. Even before the catastrophe of the Great Irish Famine, some commentators saw them as already discredited as a class, and their responses to the crisis years further established negative perceptions, both in public opinion generally but also – critically for the coming decades – at Westminster.[149] But the law was not keeping up with fluctuating reputations: it still gave landlords great power over their properties and tenants, as well as in politics and parliament. Their power rested on what was, in the mid-nineteenth century, still a relatively deferential and paternalistic rural society, but that advantage was undercut both financially and culturally by the responsibilities landed paternalism imposed back onto landlords: the unspoken contract that demanded a return of economic support in the form of rent reductions, charitable and employment projects, and other measures when times were hard, which they frequently were, even in industrialising Ulster.[150] Dufferin took both sides of the reputational coin extremely seriously, but was constrained by tough financial realities, the widespread shift away from traditional social deference of tenants, and by a hostile intellectual and political environment.

Dufferin constructed a particular kind of Irishness, utilising definitions of property ownership and the heritable principle. It is perhaps unsurprising that a landowner and peer should be so influenced by the idea of inheritance – of family 'traits', as well as the translation of property and assets – but Dufferin perhaps took this to extremes, a result of the insecurity of his religious, social and political position.[151] How far Dufferin's construct matched the realities of his experiences as a landowner, and where the disjuncture appeared between expectation, construction and experience is clear. Dufferin was continually disappointed by the widening gap between his experiences and his ideals as a landlord. He held – perhaps unsurprisingly – a positive image of Irish landlordism close to his heart, far distant from the stereotypes of Castle Rackrent.[152] Instead, he emphasised a Romantic persona, partially inspired by Sir Walter Scott, where the spirit of generosity, paternalism and deference were as central to landlordism as a sound head for figures. These qualities of Romanticism and derring-do made up the construction of Irish identity that Dufferin held most closely to his heart; but they were very far removed from the realities of mid- to late-nineteenth-century rural Ireland or despotic imperial governance.[153] Dufferin's most important influences were popular literature and European Romanticism, and the religious fervour that gripped Oxford in the 1840s.[154] It is unsurprising that when, in 1847, he reached his majority and threw himself into the role of Irish landlord, he was shocked and disappointed. The very select social circles he moved in – the royal court, the great Whig landed families – shaped his expectations as to his lifestyle, but the income generated by Clandeboye fell far short in meeting the cost of these. It was also perhaps unwise to act with reckless generosity instead of cool-headed commercialism when it came to the management of any estate, not least a small, indebted Irish one reeling

44 *Property*

from the impact of the Great Famine. Dufferin was also taken aback and later became very cynical about the realities of sectarian division in Ireland. Although not something that ever became a serious issue on the Clandeboye estate – Dufferin's Anglican beliefs did not generate much comment or dissatisfaction among his predominantly Presbyterian tenantry – he was keenly aware of the growing nationalist discourse from the 1870s, which related Catholicism with 'true' Irishness and Protestantism with the oppression of the Anglo-Irish Ascendancy and Castle Government by the British state.[155] As Olwen Purdue has rightly stressed, the Anglo-Irish landowning classes struggled with their conflicted identity: 'their home was in Ireland but their culture was English. They felt Irish but their loyalty was to the British Empire'.[156] Dufferin became embittered over what he saw as his exclusion from an Irish future on the basis of his religion and class status; in his own mind, he was one of the natural governing elite – educated, connected. But he never had the chance to govern in Ireland: instead, he was obliged to govern elsewhere in the empire.[157]

At the heart of these questions of identity and governance was Dufferin's relationship to Clandeboye. After 1880, Dufferin was an Irish landlord without a great deal of land, in a period just before the great land purchase acts put many other Irish landowners into the same position.[158] The loss of his landed estates did not translate into a loss of Dufferin's identity, or adherence to his landed patrimony or self-constructed role of Irish landlord; instead, he translated these into other avenues. Some of these will be explored in Chapter 3, which will examine Dufferin's contributions to the great debates on Irish land management and reform, emigration and home rule. But his principal efforts were saved for diplomacy, governance and administration overseas, where he was able to channel his governing passion in a way no longer possible in Ireland or Westminster. Dufferin had been educated and brought up to expect his role in life to consist of the governance and improvement both of his landed estates, and imperial polities and territories – a role that encompassed economic imperatives, but also deeply felt social privileges and responsibilities.[159] When these were removed from his control, Dufferin translated his ideal construction of Irish landownership to his methods and philosophies of imperial governance.

Notes

1 Public Record Office of Northern Ireland [hereafter PRONI], Dufferin & Ava Papers, D1071, H/B/C/95, ff. 30, Dufferin to 8th Duke of Argyll, 11 Jan. 1869.
2 C. O'Grada, Irish Agricultural History: recent research, *Agricultural History Review*, 38:2 (1990), p. 169; E. Heggs, Whig politics and the 3rd duke of Leinster (1791–1874), in P. Cosgrove, T. Dooley and K. Mullaney-Dignam (eds), *Aspects of Irish Aristocratic Life* (Dublin, 2014); A. Gailey, *The Lost Imperialist: Lord Dufferin, memory and mythmaking in an age of celebrity* (London, 2015), pp. 109–114.
3 J. Ridden, Britishness as an imperial and diasporic identity: Irish elite perspectives, c. 1820–70, in P. Gray, *Victoria's Ireland? Irishness and Britishness,*

1837–1901 (Dublin, 2004), pp. 88–90; R. Romani, British views on Irish national character, 1800–1846: an intellectual history, *History of European Ideas*, 23:5–6 (1997), pp. 193–4.

4 W. H. Crawford, Landlord-Tenant relations in Ulster, 1609–1820, *Irish Economic and Social History*, 2 (1975), pp. 5–11, 20–1.

5 See the discussion in C. A. Bayly, Ireland, India and the Empire, 1780–1914, *Transactions of the Royal Historical Society*, 6th ser., 10 (2000), pp. 381, 389, 391.

6 See, for instance, Dufferin, *Helen's Tower* (private print: London, 1884); Dufferin (ed.), *Songs, Poems and Verses by Helen, Lady Dufferin (Countess of Gifford)* (London, 1894), pp. 7, 32–3; H. Nicolson, *Helen's Tower* (London, 1937), pp. 41–2.

7 A. T. Q. Stewart, *The Ulster Crisis* (London, 1967), pp. 43–4.

8 L. P. Curtis, *Anglo-Saxons and Celts: a study of anti-Irish prejudice in Victorian England* (Bridgeport, 1968), pp. 87–8; T. A. Boylan and T. P. Foley, *Political Economy and Colonial Ireland: the propaganda and ideological function of economic discourse in the nineteenth century* (London, 1992), p. 118; G. Bolton, The idea of a colonial gentry, *Historical Studies*, 13 (1968, pp. 308–9, 315–16; R. Romani, British views on Irish national character, 1800–1846: an intellectual history, *History of European Ideas*, 23:5–6 (1997), pp. 193–4.

9 Bayly, Ireland, India and the empire, pp. 390–2.

10 Nicolson, *Helen's Tower*, pp. 78–83.

11 L. Kennedy and P. Ollerenshaw (eds), *An Economic History of Ulster 1820–1940* (Manchester, 1985), pp. 10, 16, 25–7; A. Jackson, *Home Rule: an Irish history, 1800–2000* (London, 2004), p. 40; K. T. Hoppen, Landownership and power in nineteenth century Ireland: the decline of an elite, in R. Gibson and M. Blinkhorn (eds), *Landownership and Power in Modern Europe* (London, 1991), pp. 166, 168, 176.

12 O. Purdue, *The Big House in the North of Ireland: land, power and social elites, 1878–1960* (Dublin, 2009), pp. 10, 23–9.

13 W. E. Vaughan, An assessment of the economic performance of Irish landlords, 1851–81, in F. S. L. Lyons and R. A. J. Hawkins (eds), *Ireland under the Union: varieties of tension* (Oxford, 1980), p. 174.

14 Dufferin frequently compared Irish estate management and agriculture unfavourably to that in Britain, particularly Scotland. See, for instance, PP 1881 [Cd. 2779, I–III] *Evidence and Report of Her Majesty's Commissioners of Inquiry into the working of the Landlord and Tenant (Ireland) Act 1870*, evidence from Lord Dufferin, p. 1020, Q. 33118; House of Lords Debates, 23 Mar. 1866, vol. 182, cc. 831–7; R. Perren, The landlord and agricultural transformation, 1870–1900, *Agricultural History Review*, 18 (1970), pp, 42, 46, 50; see also, on 'bad' landlords, P. Bull, *Land, Politics and Nationalism: a study of the Irish land question* (Dublin, 1996), pp. 13–19; J. C. Beckett, *The Anglo-Irish Tradition* (Belfast, 1976), pp. 91–2.

15 A. Warren, Gladstone, land and social reconstruction in Ireland, 1881–1887, *Parliamentary History*, 2 (1983), pp. 155–6.

16 A. Taylor, *Lords of Misrule: hostility to aristocracy in late nineteenth and early twentieth century Britain* (Basingstoke, 2004), pp. 2, 12, 15; F. Campbell, *The Irish Establishment, 1879–1914* (Oxford, 2009), pp. 36–40; E. F. Biagini, *Liberty, Retrenchment and Reform: popular liberalism in the age of Gladstone, 1860–1880* (Cambridge, 1992), pp. 50–8.

17 PRONI, D1071, A/B/6/1, Summary account book for the minority of Lord Dufferin, 1841–1847; W. A. Maguire, *The Downshire Estates in Ireland, 1801–1845* (Oxford, 1972), p. 21.

18 M. W. Dowling, *Tenant Right and agrarian society in Ulster, 1600–1870* (Dublin, 1999), pp. 241–6.

46 *Property*

19 PRONI, D1071, A/R: Landed Estates Court, Sales.
20 D. Large, The wealth of the greater Irish landowners, 1750–1815, *Irish Historical Studies*, 15 (1966), p. 27.
21 D. Cannadine, *The Decline and Fall of the British Aristocracy* (London, 1990), pp. 36, 57, 63–6.
22 T. Dooley, *The Decline of the Big House in Ireland: a study of Irish landed families, 1860–1960* (Dublin, 2001), pp. 79–108; O. Purdue, *The Big House in the North of Ireland: land, power and social elites, 1878–1960* (Dublin, 2009), pp. 1–12.
23 Cannadine, *Decline and Fall*, pp. 103–6; T. Dooley, *The Big Houses and Landed Estates of Ireland: a research guide* (Dublin, 2007), p. 47; L. P. Curtis, Landlord responses to the Irish Land War, 1879–1987, *Eire–Ireland*, Fall–Winter (2003).
24 A quick overview of this literature would contain: Purdue, *Big House*; Dooley, *The Big Houses and Landed Estates of Ireland*; J. S. Donnelly, *The Land and the People of Nineteenth Century Cork* (London, 1975); R. D. C. Black, *Economic Thought and the Irish Question, 1817–1870* (Cambridge, 1960); L. P. Curtis, Incumbered wealth: landed indebtedness in post-famine Ireland, *American History Review*, 85:2 (1980); T. Dooley, *Decline of the Big House in Ireland*; Curtis, Landlord responses, pp. 179–180.
25 Curtis, Landlord responses, p. 134.
26 F. M. L. Thompson, English landed society in the twentieth century III: self-help and outdoor relief, *Transactions of the Royal Historical Society*, series 6, vol. 2 (1992), pp. 1–23.
27 This was an established pattern for Irish gentry families, as discussed by R. Ansell, Educational travel in Protestant families from post-restoration Ireland, *Historical Journal*, 58:4 (2015), pp. 932, 949, 958.
28 C. Dewey, Celtic agrarian legislation and the Celtic revival: historicist implications of Gladstone's Irish and Scottish Land Acts, 1870–1886, *Past and Present*, 64:1 (1974), pp. 59–60; Catherine Hall has raised the question about the implications for the 'British' that their national identity became associated with ruling others in the nineteenth century: see C. Hall, *Macaulay and Son: architects of imperial Britain* (New Haven, 2012), p. xiii; M. Bentley, *Lord Salisbury's World: conservative environments in late-Victorian Britain* (Cambridge, 2001), p. 72.
29 See, for instance, Bayly, Ireland, India and the Empire, pp. 377–8; P. J. Cain, Capitalism, aristocracy and empire: some 'classical' theories of imperialism revisited, *Journal of Imperial and Commonwealth History*, 35:1 (2007), pp. 25, 27, 41; B. Knox, The Earl of Carnarvon, empire and imperialism, 1855–90, *Journal of Imperial and Commonwealth History*, 26:2 (1998), pp. 48, 57, 63; P. J. Cain, Character and imperialism: the British financial administration of Egypt, 1878–1914, *Journal of Imperial and Commonwealth History*, 34:2 (2006), pp. 177–8.
30 D. Cannadine, *Ornamentalism: how the British saw their empire* (Oxford, 2002), pp. 4–5, 85–6.
31 See, for instance; British Library [hereafter BL], Gladstone Papers, Add MS 44151, Vol. LXVI, correspondence with Lord Dufferin, ff. 143, Dufferin to Gladstone, 13 Dec. 1879, when Dufferin talks about his 'Arctic banishment' to the embassy in St Petersburg.
32 H. Milton (ed.), *Speeches of the Earl of Dufferin* (Toronto, 1878). See also A. Lyall, *The Life of the Marquis of Dufferin and Ava* (London, 1905), pp. 55–7.
33 Quoted in Lyall, *Life of Dufferin*, p. 58; Dufferin did receive some criticism on this speech from his uncle and mentor, Sir James Graham, who warned him off making any promises to his tenants. Graham was clearly concerned that Dufferin's generous temper would be the ruin of an estate with an already limited financial capacity; see PRONI, D1071, H/B/G/316, ff. 2, Graham to Dufferin, 24 Aug. 1847; J. Parry, Graham, Sir James Robert George, second baronet (1792–1861), *Oxford Dictionary of National Biography* (Oxford, 2004):

https://www.oxforddnb.com/view/10.1093/ref:odnb/9780198614128.001.0001/odnb-9780198614128-e-11204 (last accessed 12 Aug. 2019); T. MacKnight, *Ulster as it is, or Thirty Years' experience as an Irish Editor* (London, 1896), pp. 88, 90.
34 Dufferin appears to have partially recognised this while at Oxford; see Christ Church Archives, MR iii.c.i 1/6/3, Dufferin to Lady Helen Dufferin, 24 Jan. 1845; 27 Feb. 1846. This did not stop him from spending £26,000 on yachts between 1852 and 1872, however; Campbell, *Irish Establishment*, p. 45; Nicolson, *Helen's Tower*, p. 68–9.
35 PRONI, D1071, A/F rentals; A/F/24 estate survey (1870); Gailey, *Lost Imperialist*, p. 36.
36 PRONI, D1071, A/B/6/1: Summary account book for the minority of Lord Dufferin (1841–7).
37 PRONI, D1071, A/B/6/1: Summary account book for the minority of Lord Dufferin (1841–7); L. P. Curtis, Incumbered Wealth: landed indebtedness in post-famine Ireland, *American History Review*, vol. 85:2 (1980), p. 343.
38 PRONI, D1071, A/B/6/1: Summary account book for the minority of Lord Dufferin (1841–7).
39 That is, the theoretical maximum income: PRONI, D1071, A/B/6/1: Summary account book for the minority of Lord Dufferin (1841–7); Gailey, *Lost Imperialist*, pp. 115–16.
40 The duke of Sutherland, for example, at this time relished an annual income of over £120,000 per annum, and Dufferin's great friend the 8th Duke of Argyll also enjoyed a much higher income than Dufferin from his extensive Scottish estates encompassing 160,000 acres; A. Tindley, *The Sutherland Estate: aristocratic decline, estate management and land reform* (Edinburgh, 2010), p. 3–4; K. Mulhern, The Intellectual Duke: George Douglas Campbell, 8th Duke of Argyll, 1823–1900, unpublished PhD thesis (University of Edinburgh, 2006).
41 PRONI, D1071, A/B/6/1: Summary account book for the minority of Lord Dufferin (1841–7); A/C/3/31, explanation of encumbrances affecting the estate of the Rt. Hon Lord Dufferin and Clandeboye, 1 Sept. 1848.
42 Quoted in Lyall, *Life of Dufferin*, p. 60.
43 Quoted in Lyall, *Life of Dufferin*, pp. 61–2; Gailey, *Lost Imperialist*, pp. 34, 56.
44 For pre-1840s context, see Large, The wealth of the greater Irish landowners, p. 21–44; O'Grada notes that historians have revised this bleak post-famine outlook: O'Grada, Irish Agricultural History, p. 169.
45 F. Thompson, *The End of Liberal Ulster: land agitation and land reform, 1868–1886* (Belfast, 2001), pp. 12–13.
46 A. Tindley, The Iron Duke: land reclamation and public relations in Sutherland, 1868–95, *Historical Research*, vol. 82, no. 216 (2009), pp. 303–19; E. A. Cameron, *Land for the People? The British government and the Scottish Highlands, c. 1880–c. 1925* (East Linton, 1996), pp. 25–6.
47 Dufferin often stressed the importance of landlord investments and improvements in the House of Lords; see, for instance, HL Debates, 23 Mar. 1866, vol. 182 cc.831–7. Bentley, *Lord Salisbury's World*, pp. 95; C. O'Grada, The investment behaviour of Irish landlords 1850–75: some preliminary findings, *Agricultural History Review*, 23 (1975), pp. 146, 151, 153; Maguire, *Downshire Estates*, pp. 72–3, 77–8.
48 W. E. Vaughan, An assessment of the economic performance of Irish landlords, 1851–81, in F. S. L. Lyons and R. A. J. Hawkins (eds), *Ireland under the Union: varieties of tension: essays in honour of T. W. Moody* (Oxford, 1980), p. 174.
49 Dufferin, *Irish Emigration and the Tenure of Land in Ireland* (Dublin, 1870), p. 7; Lyall, *Life of Dufferin*, pp. 152, 156; W. E. Vaughan, Landlord and tenant relations in Ireland between the famine and the land war, 1850–1878, in L. M. Cullen and T. C. Smout (eds), *Comparative Aspects of Scottish and Irish Economic and Social History, 1600–1900* (Edinburgh, 1977), pp. 222–3.

48 *Property*

50 Gailey, *Lost Imperialist*, pp. 37, 40–1; P. Bull, Irish Land and British politics, in M. Cragoe and P. Readman, (eds), *The Land Question in Britain, 1750–1950* (Basingstoke, 2010), p. 128. For an indication of Dufferin's university reading, see: Christ Church, MR, iii.c.i. 1/6/3, Dufferin to Lady Helen Dufferin, no date [late 1845?]; PRONI, D1071, H/B/G/316, ff. 1, Sir James Graham to Dufferin, 9 Nov. 1846. This included the works of David Hume, Adam Smith and Edmund Burke.
51 Lyall, *Life of Dufferin*, p. 62.
52 PRONI, D1071, A/R/12, Lord Dufferin's descriptive memorandum of the Clandeboye demesne and estate (1877).
53 K. T. Hoppen, Landownership and power in nineteenth century Ireland: the decline of an elite, in R. Gibson and M. Blinkhorn (eds), *Landownership and Power in Modern Europe* (London, 1991), p. 164.
54 Dufferin and G. F. Boyle, *Narrative of a journey from Oxford to Skibereen during the year of the Irish Famine* (Oxford, 1847), pp. 5, 11, 23; Lyall, *Life of Dufferin*, pp. 55–6; Dufferin later referred to this visit when lobbying Gladstone for an Irish peerage: BL, Add MSS 44151, ff. 102, Dufferin to Gladstone, 13 Sept. 1871; P. Gray, *Famine, Land and Politics: British government and Irish society, 1843–50* (Dublin, 1999), pp. 326–7.
55 The National Archives [hereafter TNA] PRO 30/22.8a, Dufferin to Lady Russell, 10 Sept. 1848; Gailey, *Lost Imperialist*, pp. 34–5, 36–9.
56 Christ Church, Oxford, MR iii.c.i 1/6/3, Dufferin to Lady Dufferin [nd. 1846?]; Curtis, *Anglo-Saxons and Celts*.
57 Thompson, *End of Liberal Ulster*, p. 22; PRONI, D1071, H/B/C/95/32, Dufferin to Argyll, 14 Jan. 1869: 'a new world has come into being since 1846'. Also, Hall, *Macaulay and Son*, pp. 185–6, 310, 316–18.
58 C. D. Black, *The Marquess of Dufferin and Ava: diplomatist, viceroy, statesman* (London, 1903), p. 18.
59 Nicolson, *Helen's Tower*, p. 84.
60 PRONI, D1071, A/K/1/B/20/1, Thomson to Dufferin, 10 Mar. 1870; Nicolson, *Helen's Tower*, p. 84.
61 The issue of Ulster Tenant Right will be discussed in Chapter 3. Dufferin raised this case in the Lords; HL Deb, 14 Mar. 1870, vol. 199, cc. 1857–60; Nicolson, *Helen's Tower*, p. 84. See Dufferin's own retrospective account of his estate management policies in his evidence to the 1865 Select Committee: PP 1865, *Evidence and Report of the Select Committee on the Tenure and Improvement of Land (Ireland) Act* [hereafter PP 1865 *Select Committee Evidence*], Dufferin, p. 46, Q. 990; and his evidence in 1881 to the Bessborough Commission: *Bessborough Commission Evidence*, Dufferin, p. 1015, Q. 33044.
62 PP 1865 *Select Committee Evidence*, p. 44, Q. 960; J. S. Donnelly, *The Land and the People of Nineteenth Century Cork* (London, 1975), pp. 187–9, 199.
63 PRONI, D1071, A/K/1/B/20/1, Thomson to Dufferin, 10 Mar. 1870.
64 Vaughan, An assessment, pp. 176–86.
65 Nicolson, *Helen's Tower*, p. 120.
66 See, for example, Dufferin's justifications to Gladstone: BL, Add MS 44151, ff. 64, Dufferin to Gladstone, 12 Nov. 1869; and to the 1865 Select Committee: PP 1865 *Select Committee Evidence*, Dufferin, p. 56, Q. 1103; B. Mac Suibhne, *The End of Outrage: post-famine adjustment in rural Ireland* (Oxford, 2017), pp. 1–19.
67 Argyll, 8th Duke of, New Irish Land Bill, *Nineteenth Century*, 9 (1881), pp. 882, 887, 895; Argyll, 8th Duke of, *Crofts and Farms in the Hebrides: being an account of the management of an island estate for 130 years* (Edinburgh, 1883). See, in comparison, G. F. Trench, *The Land Question: Are the landlords worth preserving? Or, forty years' management of an Irish estate* (London and Dublin, 1881), pp. 22–3.

68 L. P. Curtis, *The Depiction of Eviction in Ireland, 1845–1910* (Dublin, 2011), pp. 1–2.
69 Lyall, *Life of Dufferin*, pp. 74, 86–9, 94; Curtis, Landlord responses, p. 138; I. d'Alton, Aquatic gentlemen …: the sport and status of sailing in the gentry's world from the 1830s to the 1920s, in T. Dooley and C. Ridgway (eds), *Sport and Leisure in the Irish Country House* (Dublin, 2019), pp. 86, 92; Gailey, *Lost Imperialist*, pp. 58–60, 302–3.
70 Ansell, Educational travel, pp. 932–6.
71 PRONI, D1071, A/C/3/31: Explanation of encumbrances affecting the estate of the Rt. Hon. Lord Dufferin and Clandeboye, 1 Sept. 1848.
72 PRONI, D1071, A/N/4/5, Correspondence connected with the Trusteeship (1902); for a discussion of the impact of providing family portions and jointures, see Curtis, Incumbered wealth, pp. 338–9; Purdue, *Big House*, p. 27.
73 PRONI, D1071, A/B/6/3, Index schedule of accounts, 1847–1868; Curtis, Incumbered wealth, pp. 340, 348, 359.
74 PRONI, D1071, A/C/3/9, Report of William Hartley, public auditor and accountant', Jan. 1864.
75 PRONI, D1071, A/B/6/3, Index schedule of accounts, 1847–1868; C. O'Grada, The investment behaviour of Irish landlords, 1850–1875, pp. 140–1; PP 1865 *Select Committee Evidence*, Dufferin, p. 62, Q. 1216 and HL Deb, 14 Jun. 1870, vol. 202, cc. 4–98. His estate investments did assist him in gaining a promotion in the peerage in 1871: BL, Add MS 44151, Gladstone Papers, ff. 102, Dufferin to Gladstone, 13 Sept. 1871.
76 For the general trends, see Purdue, *Big House*, pp. 26, 29, 37; Curtis, Incumbered wealth, pp. 335–6, 347, 367; Large, The wealth of the greater Irish landowners, pp. 32–3, 44; Campbell, *Irish Establishment*, p. 45; Dooley, *The Big Houses and Landed Estates of Ireland*, pp. 47–8.
77 D. Cannadine, The landowner as millionaire: the finances of the dukes of Devonshire, c. 1800–c. 1926, *Agricultural History Review*, 25:2 (1977), pp. 77–91.
78 PRONI, D1071, A/B/6/1 Summary account book for the minority of Lord Dufferin (1841–47).
79 PRONI, D1071, A/N/4/3, Lord Dufferin's marriage settlement, 1877. Historians have argued that Irish landowners often found it harder to identify and marry heiresses than English ones: Large, Wealth of the greater Irish landowners, p. 41.
80 For a list of the fourteen clubs to which Dufferin subscribed, plus twenty further pages detailing his expenses, see PRONI, D1071, A/L/21/4, Particulars of monthly payments, 1868.
81 PRONI, D1071, A/K/1/B/26/1, Dufferin to Thomson, 25 Mar. 1876.
82 This was the Belfast and Bangor line, see R. Masefield, *Be Careful, Don't Rush: celebrating 150 years of train travel between Bangor and Holywood* (Newtownards, 2015), pp. 36–9. Railway investment and expansion was a subject Dufferin spoke on in general terms in the House of Lords: HL, DEB, 23 Mar. 1866, vol. 182, cc. 831–7. See also similar investments made by landowners in the Scottish Highlands to facilitate sporting tourism: J. MacGregor, *The West Highland Railway: 120 Years* (Stroud, 2014).
83 Thompson, *End of Liberal Ulster*, pp. 2–3.
84 PRONI, D1071, A/R/12, Lord Dufferin's descriptive memorandum of the Clandeboye demesne and estate, 1877.
85 PRONI, D1071, A/R/12, Lord Dufferin's descriptive memorandum of the Clandeboye demesne and estate, 1877.
86 Although there is no conclusive evidence that this expenditure led directly to his financial difficulties; PRONI, D1071/H/B/C/95, ff. 70, Dufferin to Argyll, 7 May 1874.
87 PRONI, D10771/A/K/1/B/24/1, Thomson to Dufferin, 27 Feb. 1874.

88 For detail on the railway building and urban investments made by landowners in Britain, see D. Cannadine, *Aspects of Aristocracy: grandeur and decline in modern Britain* (London, 1994), pp. 56–61.
89 W. L. Burn, Free trade in land: an aspect of the Irish Question, *Transactions of the Royal Historical Society*, 31 (1949), pp. 62–3.
90 See, for instance, O'Grada, The investment behavior of Irish landlords; Curtis, Incumbered wealth, pp. 359–61; Dooley, *The Big Houses and Landed Estates of Ireland*, pp. 37, 40; O'Grada, Irish agricultural history: recent research, pp. 166, 169.
91 Bentley, *Lord Salisbury's World*, pp. 106–7.
92 Black, *Dufferin and Ava*, p. 23. He was given an English peerage, the first of a number of advancements, in 1850.
93 The Duchess of Somerset and the rather more infamous Caroline Norton: Gailey, *The Lost Imperialist*, pp. 12, 118.
94 Nicolson, *Helen's Tower*, p. 17.
95 Thompson, *End of Liberal Ulster*, pp. 11–13.
96 Dufferin expressed the importance of these men publicly in 1881: *Bessborough Commission Evidence*, p. 1018, Q. 33083, 33089.
97 For more on the relationship between the big house in Ireland and the empire, see S. Barczewski, Country houses and the distinctiveness of the Irish imperial experience, in T. G. McMahon (ed.), *Ireland in an Imperial World* (Cambridge, 2017), pp. 25–38.
98 A. Tindley, They sow the wind, they reap the whirlwind: estate management in the post-Clearance Highlands, c. 1815–c. 1900, *Northern Scotland*, 3 (2012), p. 66–85; Thompson, *End of Liberal Ulster*, pp. 11–13.
99 See PP 1865 *Select Committee Evidence*, Dufferin, p. 77, Q. 1499.
100 PRONI, D1071, A/K/1/B/22/1, Dufferin to Thomson, 4 Sept. 1872.
101 For a detailed examination of this economic downturn, see J. S. Donnelly, The Irish Agricultural Depression of 1859–64, *Irish Economic and Social History* (1976), pp. 33–4, 45–6, 52; O'Grada, Investment behavior, p. 150–4; W. E. Vaughan, An assessment of the economic performance of Irish landlords, 1851–81, in F. S. L. Lyons, and R. A. J. Hawkins (eds), *Ireland under the Union: varieties of tension: essays in honour of T. W. Moody* (Oxford, 1980), pp. 186–7; T. W. Guinnane and R. I. Miller, Bonds without Bondsmen: Tenant-Right in c19th Ireland, *Journal of Economic History*, 56:1 (1996), pp. 113–16, 121; B. Solow, *The Land Question and the Irish Economy 1870–1903* (Massachusetts, 1971), pp. 11–12.
102 Vaughan, An assessment of the economic performance of Irish landlords, pp. 188, 192–8; R. W. Kirkpatrick, Origins and development of the land war in mid-Ulster, 1879–85, in F. S. L. Lyons and R. A. J. Hawkins (eds), *Ireland under the Union: varieties of tension: essays in honour of T. W. Moody* (Oxford, 1980), pp. 213–15. See, in comparison, A. Jackson, *Colonel Edward Saunderson: land and loyalty in Victorian Ireland* (Oxford, 1995), pp. 174–81.
103 PRONI, D1071, A/K/1/C/2/1, Dufferin to Howe, 24 Aug. 1880.
104 Curtis, Incumbered wealth, pp. 335, 339; Thompson, *End of Liberal Ulster*, pp. 170–4.
105 Curtis, Incumbered wealth, p. 336.
106 PRONI, D1071, A/L/21, Schedule of liabilities chargeable on the Dufferin and Clandeboye estates, 1847, 1868.
107 L. A. Clarkson, Mulholland, John, first Baron Dunleath (1819–1895), *Oxford Dictionary of National Biography*, Oxford University Press, 2004: http://www.oxforddnb.com/view/article/48077 [accessed 13 January 2020]; Purdue, *Big House*, pp. 15, 29; Curtis, Incumbered wealth, p. 349; D. M. McHugh, Family, leisure and the arts: aspects of the culture of the aristocracy of Ulster, 1870–1925, unpublished PhD thesis (University of Edinburgh, 2011), pp. 53–4.

Property 51

108 Curtis, Incumbered wealth, pp. 345, 347; Gailey, *Lost Imperialist*, p. 116; Maguire, *Downshire Estates*, pp. 95, 97.
109 PRONI, D1071, A/K/1/B/22/1, Dufferin to Thomson, 27 Nov. 1872 and D1071, A/K/1/B/24/1, Thomson to Dufferin, 27 Feb. 1874.
110 PRONI, D1071, A/F/24, Summarised schedule of the acreage and rental of the Clandeboye, Ards and Killyleagh estates, for the year ending 1 Nov. 1870.
111 PRONI, D1071, A/L/41, Schedule showing claimants on Dufferin's estate. The next single largest lender was Coutts Bank, to which Dufferin owed £40,000.
112 PRONI, D1071, A/K/1/B/24/1, Thomson to Dufferin, 27 Feb. 1874; Curtis, Landlord responses, p. 141.
113 Curtis, Incumbered wealth, p. 339; L. Proudfoot, The management of a great estate: patronage, income and expenditure on the Duke of Devonshire's Irish property, c. 1816–1891, *Irish Social and Economic History*, 13 (1986), pp. 43, 53–4.
114 PRONI, D1071, A/K/1/B/24/1, Thomson to Dufferin, 27 Feb. 1874.
115 For instance, an attempt was made to arrange a mortgage with the Royal Exchange Assurance Company, in early 1874, but negotiations collapsed: PRONI, D1071, A/K/1/B/24/1, Thomson to Dufferin, 27 Feb. 1874.
116 D1071, A/K/2/B/7/2, Thomson, Filgate and Pattisson to Dufferin, 4 Nov. 1874.
117 Bentley, *Lord Salisbury's World*, pp. 99–100.
118 T. M. Dooley, Landlords and the Land Question, 1879–1909, in C. King (ed.), *Famine, Land and Culture in Ireland* (Dublin, 2001), pp. 124–6; and a comparative study of the dukes of Leinster in T. Dooley, *The Decline and Fall of the Dukes of Leinster, 1872–1948* (Dublin, 2014), pp. 55–6.
119 PRONI, D1071/A/K/1/B/21/1, Dufferin to Thomson, 24 Dec. 1874; M. W. Dowling, *Tenant Right and Agrarian Society in Ulster, 1600–1870* (Dublin, 1999), pp. 241–52, 312–4.
120 D1071, A/K/2B/6/1, Dufferin to Pattisson, 30 Apr. 1874.
121 Dooley, Landlords and the land question, 1879–1909, p. 124.
122 Purdue, *Big House*, p. 66.
123 PRONI, D1071, A/R/1, Earl of Dufferin's estate: report as to Landed Estates Court proceedings, Apr. 1874.
124 PRONI, D1071 A/L/41, Schedule showing the individual claimants, the amount due to each and the period at which – with due notice – the several amounts ought to be paid, 1873; twenty-five years seemed to be the expected standard in county Down in the 1870s: see Maguire, *Downshire Estates*, p. 19.
125 PRONI, D1071, A/R/12, Lord Dufferin's descriptive memorandum of the Clandeboye demesne and estate, 1877; Campbell, *Irish Establishment*, p. 38.
126 PRONI, D1071, A/K/1/B/25/1, Thomson to Dufferin, 15 Jan. 1875.
127 PRONI, D1071, A/R/3: Land Agent's Papers. Carrick, Brockbank and Wilson changed their name to Brockbank, Wilson and Mulliner in late 1875.
128 He wrote this from memory while resident in Canada: PRONI, D1071, A/R/3, Brockbank, Wilson and Mulliner to Pattison, 7 Dec. 1876; PRONI, D1071, A/R/12, Lord Dufferin's descriptive memorandum, 1877.
129 PRONI, D1071, A/R/12, Lord Dufferin's descriptive memorandum, 1877.
130 PRONI, D1071, A/R/12, Lord Dufferin's descriptive memorandum, 1877.
131 PRONI, D1071, A/K/2B/6/1, Dufferin to Pattison, 19 Mar. 1874.
132 PRONI, D1071, A/K/1/B/26/1, Dufferin to Thomson, 27 Nov. 1876 and 4 Dec. 1876; A/K/1/C/2/1, Dufferin to Howe, 17 Jul. 1880; A/K/1/C/3/2, Dufferin to Howe, 2 Aug. 1881.
133 Dewey, Celtic agrarian legislation and the Celtic revival, pp. 30–1.
134 PRONI, D1071, H/B/C/95/70, Dufferin to Argyll, 7 May 1874; J. W. Mason, The Duke of Argyll and the land question in late nineteenth century Britain, *Victorian Studies*, 21:2 (1978), pp. 168.

52 Property

135 Bentley has characterised Irish landlords in this period as, 'a class marked by wailing and gnashing of teeth', *Lord Salisbury's World*, pp. 100, 109; Purdue, *Big House*, pp. 25–6; Dooley, *The Big Houses and Landed Estates of Ireland*, pp. 47–8.
136 Black, *Dufferin and Ava*, p. 383.
137 Bentley, *Lord Salisbury's World*, pp. 113–14.
138 Dufferin earned £10,000 per annum as Governor-General, but still asked for a pay rise. For problematic economic conditions in the 1860s and 1870s, see O'Grada, The investment behaviour of Irish landlords, 1850–1875, pp. 154–5; Donnelly, Irish agricultural depression, p. 33; F. H. A. Aalen, Constructive Unionism and the shaping of rural Ireland, c. 1880–1921, *Rural History*, 4:2 (1993), p. 138; Campbell, *Irish Establishment*, pp. 39–40, 48.
139 Lyall, *Life of Dufferin*, p. 190.
140 Lyall, *Life of Dufferin*, p. 556.
141 PRONI, D1071, A/K/1/8/20/1, 10 Mar. 1870; A/K/1/B/30/1, 3 Dec. 1880; A/K/1/B/31/1, 18 Feb. 1881, 20 Feb. 1881, 22 Feb. 1881.
142 PRONI, D1071, A/K/1/C/3/1, Dufferin to Howe, 7 Jan. 1881; Dooley, Landlords and the land question, 1879–1909, pp. 120–2.
143 'The language they use is very scurrilous and the lies they tell enough to make one's hair stand on end', as he described it to Lady Dartrey: PRONI, D1071, H/B/D/78, ff. 95, 24 Feb. 1881; A/K/1/C/3/1, Dufferin to Howe, 7 Jan. 1881; H/B/C/95, ff. 83, Dufferin to Argyll, 6 Jan. 1880.
144 D1071, A/K/1/C/3/2, Dufferin to Howe, 10 Aug. 1881.
145 PRONI, D1071, A/K/1/C/4/1, Dufferin to Howe, 13 Feb. 1882.
146 PRONI, D1071, H/B/S/251B, ff. 5, Dufferin to Brinsley Sheridan, 25 Feb. 1881.
147 PRONI, D1071, H/B/S/204, ff. 9, Duke of Somerset to Dufferin, 27 Aug. 1869.
148 Quoted in Lyall, *Life of Dufferin*, pp. 203–4, Argyll to Dufferin, 1872.
149 Purdue, *Big House*, p. 25.
150 Jackson, *Colonel Edward Saunderson*, pp. 181–3.
151 Gailey, *Lost Imperialist*, pp. 2, 98–100.
152 Curtis, Landlord responses, p. 139.
153 D. Castronovo, *The English Gentleman: images and ideals in literature and society* (New York, 1987), pp. 75–8.
154 Lyall, *The Life of Dufferin*, p. 49; J. Parry, *Democracy and Religion: Gladstone and the Liberal Party, 1867–1875* (Cambridge, 1986), pp. 66–7.
155 PRONI, D1071, H/B/C/95, ff. 30, Dufferin to Argyll, 11 Jan. 1869.
156 Purdue, *Big House*, p. 233.
157 In 1868, for instance, there had been some discussion about Dufferin being appointed viceroy of Ireland, but this never came to fruition: BL, Add MS 44151, ff. 26, Gladstone to Dufferin, 9 Dec. 1868; ff. 27, Dufferin to Gladstone, 11 Dec. 1868; Gailey, *Lost Imperialist*, pp. 105–6.
158 Curtis, Incumbered wealth, p. 359.
159 J. W. Mason, Political economy and the response to socialism in Britain, 1870–1914, *Historical Journal*, 23:3 (1980), pp. 565, 568, 578.

3 Irish questions
The empire within

> I am rather inclined to think that whatever ability I possess would be more usefully employed in literary than Parliamentary labours and that five or six years spent writing a really good impartial history of Ireland would be as useful an employment as any other and might help soothe and compose the angry reminiscences which so embitter the relations with Catholics and Protestants and of their country with England.[1]

Ireland in the abstract

Dufferin left Oxford in 1847 with a thorough grounding in classical political economy and, for the next twenty years, attempted to solve the Irish Question with it. Only just taking up the reins of estate management, Dufferin was in these early days, 'confounded, but never despairing', on Irish political and economic questions.[2] Indeed, his strenuous efforts demonstrate his ambitions for Clandeboye and Ireland, echoing contemporaries such as Palmerston in his political approach to his estate and its management – in contrast to his later reputation as a somewhat lazy man, his engagement with his estates and Irish questions demonstrates this was far from the case. Until 1860, Dufferin held no formal government post but was nonetheless in the thick of parliamentary activity, writing pamphlets and letters, lobbying and debating within the Liberal party and with his chief, William Gladstone. His motivation was his belief, alongside many of his class and generation, in his duty to govern, and that Britain, Ireland and the empire deserved government by 'the best' through a service aristocracy.[3] Much, if not all, of this activity revolved around a succession of highly contested Irish questions: disestablishment, land tenure reform, the electoral franchise, emigration, education, coercion and, latterly, Home Rule.[4] He identified himself first and foremost as an Irish landlord: whether resident in Ottawa, Cairo, or Paris, he remained involved in the great debates circling Ireland from the mid-nineteenth century.[5] He was at the forefront of a group of Irish elites who, in the wake of the Great Irish Famine, attempted to develop a liberal model of empire, whereby they could find a place as colonisers while still retaining a sense of their Irishness.[6] Dufferin argued that the union had not been an unqualified benefit to Ireland and he saw it as an incomplete project; at the same time, it had opened access to imperial opportunities for Irishmen at all social levels, as well as himself and his family. His support for emigration as one of the solutions for Ireland's economic malady was one expression of this, as were his liberal views on religion.[7]

This chapter will examine Dufferin's relationship with the Ireland beyond his own estate, considering contemporary questions around morality and governance: what was British rule in Ireland *for*, and how could it be justified?[8] For Dufferin, the decades of the 1840s through to the 1870s saw Irish questions increasingly framed by imperial concerns and perspectives. His other key intellectual framework was history, particularly that of Anglo-Irish relations and their mediation through the landowning Ascendancy. For Dufferin, Ireland's history was clouded by sectarianism and religious strife, rebellion, spoilation and revolution, and he believed that this history fundamentally defined and constrained the present, including Ireland's ability (or lack of) to rule itself without dissolving into civil as well as religious conflict.[9] There is a natural chronological division in Dufferin's approach to Irish issues, between the late 1840s, when he began actively to apply himself to his estate, political life, cabinet ambitions and writing, and the late 1870s, with the beginning of the Irish Land War and passage of Gladstone's 1881 Irish Land Act. Although never publicly separating himself from the Liberal Party, after 1881 Dufferin's heart was no longer with it. A few years later, he was appalled by Gladstone's conversion to Irish Home Rule; he was passionately opposed to self-government for Ireland and feared the consequences for the integrity of Britain's overseas empire.[10]

The first section of this chapter deals with Dufferin's early engagement with the questions thrown up in the wake of the Great Irish Famine, including diagnoses of 'surplus' population and what should be done about it, and the responsibilities of the state and of landlords, both in the heat of the crisis itself but also in creating the conditions for and shaping the outcome of the tragedy. This was against a background for Dufferin of embarking on the management of his own property, the financial limitations of which meant it was never really able to live up to his ambitions for it, beyond acting as an effective calling card for his political career. The second section addresses the period of the Irish Land War from 1879 and the rise of Irish nationalism into the 1890s, both of which dismayed and embittered Dufferin. As he had already sold significant portions of his estates before the Land War began to bite, Dufferin was able to claim that there was no personal gain or loss to concern him. Instead, he framed his interventions in this period as disinterested and increasingly drew on his imperial experience to make direct comparisons with Ireland to stoke fears around imperial security and decline. Irish Home Rule split the Liberal Party and the nation and, finally, divided Dufferin from his old chief, Gladstone.[11] Dufferin's thinking on key Irish issues – land agitation and reform, including Ulster Tenant Right, emigration, economics and governance – draw out the tensions in his position as he struggled to balance his liberal instincts with the constitutional, social and economic realities of British power in Ireland.[12]

The political economy of Ireland, 1847–1879

> At present the relationship between landlord and tenant in that country [Ireland] is almost of a barbarous character.[13]

Dufferin's early views on Ireland were influenced by his experiences as an Oxford undergraduate, which were dominated by the orthodoxies of political economy, classical studies – especially Rome and its empire – and contemporary religious controversies.[14] Even as a student, Dufferin was active in attempting to apply his book learning to the brutal realities of Irish rural life, as he came face to face with the Great Irish Famine on two visits, one to Skibbereen in 1847 and another in 1849 as part of Queen Victoria's entourage (he had been made a lord-in-waiting in January 1849).[15] Dufferin, watching with alarm the 1848 revolutions in Europe, connected chronic economic mismanagement, the near destitution of the majority of the population and a landlord class failing to carry out fundamental aspects of their duties with the realisation that revolution and disaster could await for Ireland.[16] In later years, Dufferin would extend this point more explicitly to a recognition that, in order to maintain imperial security, the British state could not afford to allow such crises to pass as a judgement on their fitness to rule.[17] For his own part, he noted that as far as Irish landownership was concerned, 'a more melancholy, saddening employment can scarcely be conceived'.[18]

Dufferin contributed £1000 to his relief effort, a large sum of money that he could ill afford, but that he felt to be, 'the duty of an Irish landlord and legislator'.[19] By this, he meant as much a moral as an economic duty, part of the implicit social contract between landlord and tenant and one that he felt had been broken by at least some members of the Irish landed elite.[20] He attempted to lead by example at Clandeboye, as we have seen, visiting the tenantry, and introducing rent rebates and employment projects. Dufferin, following a problem-oriented trend in Irish political economy, diagnosed two central causes of Irish destitution and suffering: an ever-increasing population and agricultural mismanagement.[21] The first he blamed on potato dependency; the second on a combination of peasant and landlord inertia, and on implacable market forces beyond his, or any landlord's control.[22] 'The majority of Ireland's misfortunes may be traced to this fact', he argued, 'viz., that a prolific people have been confined within an island ... in a country without manufactures, without commerce, without emigration and without a poor law.'[23] His views were influenced by his observations of the management of the Scottish estates of his friends the 8th Duke of Argyll and the 3rd Duke of Sutherland. Western and northern Scottish Highland estates faced many of the same challenges that Dufferin identified in Ireland but, as Scotland was in the vanguard of the Industrial Revolution, there were escape routes for the peasantry out of rural poverty. As this was not the case in Ireland, he regarded population decrease through emigration as key to preventing a recurrence of the Famine. In August 1849, he travelled to Dublin to attend the Queen's visit, dismayed still to find, 'great destitution and disease', and became further convinced that emigration, not relief, was the only permanent solution to the Gordian knot of that particular Irish Question.[24] In the late 1840s and 1850s, Dufferin would see his wish coming true as hundreds of thousands of destitute Irish people escaped as best they could to Britain and the New World.[25] Dufferin's views on emigration were practically orthodox at this time; even radicals on the Irish question regarded the reduction of Ireland's population as essential to its future economic and political development.[26] This did not equate to forgiveness for evictions made during the Famine years, however; one of the chief accusations made against Irish landlords was the part – direct and indirect – they played in the vast emigration from the country through mass evictions. As Curtis points out, numbers alone will never tell the full story: the political and cultural legacies of eviction were equally important. The images of dispossession that sprang from the Famine years and snowballed in the decades following exposed the harsh face of landlordism, despite all that liberal landlords such as Dufferin and political economists would claim.[27]

And he did so claim. Dufferin argued that emigration – rather than being a symptom of disfunction – was the most urgent solution to Ireland's problems, calling it a 'curative process'.[28] Along with many other commentators in the late 1840s, he saw the end of the Famine and the Queen's visit as the start of Ireland's regeneration, the start of a new era of possibility and prosperity for Ireland: the Famine had broken dependence on the potato and encouraged a large proportion of the population to leave.[29] The alternative, he explained, was further sub-division, poverty and destitution – fates that even the, 'Highland ghillie and Kentish yokel' had rejected.[30] For Dufferin, emigration was not simply an Irish issue, but an imperial one and his views on it were framed by his colonial perspective, something Irish tenants could not possibly share.[31] He regarded the Irish diaspora as potentially the empire's greatest asset and emigration as an essentially entrepreneurial act, even when, in some cases, it threatened British power and reputation overseas. 'To lament the exhibition of so much enterprise, vital energy and colonising power, in the race to which we belong, seems to me more perverse than to stigmatise as a curse the blessing originally pronounced on those who were first bidden "to go forth and multiply and replenish the earth."'[32] Dufferin would be less enthusiastic about the Irish diaspora while Canada's governor-general in the 1870s, facing both civic disorder around Orange Order activities in Montreal and the bitter aftermath of Fenian raids from across the United States border.[33]

Emigration was not the only question facing the future of Ireland's rural population; for those who stayed, reform of the agricultural system and tenancy structure was their foremost priority, including the mysteries of Ulster Tenant Right.[34] This customary practice – which, until the 1870 Irish Land Act, was primarily but not exclusively found in Ulster – can be defined as the mechanism by which tenants exiting a lease were entitled to demand a payment from the incoming tenant to compensate for any improvements they may have made and to secure their 'good will'.[35] A renegotiation of the rights of tenants and the responsibilities of landlords to promote the improvement of agricultural holdings was initially embraced by Dufferin, although his more experienced advisors urged caution. His uncle, Sir James Graham, wrote to him in August 1847 after reading a newspaper report on a speech Dufferin had given to his tenants at Clandeboye, which Graham felt was rather rash: 'the whole subject of the present state of Ireland must come under the review of the new Parliament: and I strongly advise you to stand aloof and to await the result ... Let your tenants experience your active kindness and considerate indulgence, while you walk among them, but be cautious in promising any extension of their *rights*.'[36] Despite his financial constraints, Dufferin energetically committed himself to the improvement of his estates as the principal duty of an Irish landlord – or, indeed, any landlord. This was despite, in his words, 'the evils being so gigantic and so independent of the landlord's control'.[37] For Dufferin, it was part of his construction of what an Irish landlord should be, tinged with romanticism, a strong moral drive and, at this stage, optimism, 'that improvement once in progress acquires itself the innate power of motion, and if not in this, at all events in the next generation, the whole tone of people's habits might be raised. Such', he continued, 'is the kind of work that Irish landlords have now on their hands.'[38] Dufferin, like most Irish landlords, was prepared to tolerate tenant right in the context of low rents and tenant-led improvements, but rejected the suggestion it should be enshrined in law, as we will see.[39] There was more than just its economic cost at stake: it became a source of acrimonious complexity because of what it symbolised – the fundamental lack of control of landlords over their own properties. Tenant right was, in fact, a form of property owned by tenants. It was tolerated by landlords and estate managers because the burden of improvements then rested on the tenant and it allowed them to manage tenants in other ways, principally in encouraging timely and full rent payments without the threat of eviction.[40] The frustration for Dufferin was that he tried to keep his rents at a moderate level and invested in his estates, and yet the tenant right system effectively took both the increasing rental value and investment for themselves in the form of tenant right.[41] His reputation also suffered as, ironically, it was those landlords who tried to encourage agricultural improvement who came in for the fiercest criticism in Ireland.[42]

In 1850, supported by Sir James Graham, Dufferin had lobbied for and received an English peerage, and on 31 January 1850 he took his seat in the House of Lords as Baron Clandeboye of Clandeboye.[43] It is within the political context of his parliamentary career that we must view Dufferin's ongoing tussle with land tenure reform and landlord–tenant relations, not just in Ireland but elsewhere in Britain and the empire. He played an intriguing role in parliamentary politics, never sampling life in the Commons; this may have been of little regret, as he was then able to avoid the most divisive and unpleasant controversies. By nature, Dufferin preferred a diplomatic rather than dogmatic approach, and his public and political activities

58   Irish questions

up to his first imperial posting in 1872 are tinged with discomfiture, both with the form of political debates over Ireland and with some of its key protagonists. His nephew and biographer Harold Nicolson diagnosed this uneasiness as originating from, 'his loyalty to the caste of Irish landowner; his loyalty to Mr Gladstone, and his loyalty to the Irish peasant whom he pitied but whom he did not really love'.[44] Dufferin did, however, feel that reform was necessary, for both tenant and landlord. As he expressed it: 'it is impossible for anyone who has passed three or four years of his life amid the endless embarrassments attendant upon the management of Irish property, not to perceive that at present the relationship of landlord and tenant in that country is almost of a barbarous character'.[45] Again, he stressed the moral aspects of landownership: for Dufferin, the economic and moral were inextricably linked, and their separation or rejection by Irish landlords was the primary explanation for agitation not just over land issues, but over the question of whether Ireland should be governed from Westminster. The irony for Dufferin was that the economic limitations of his estate meant that he was unable to demonstrate fully the benefits of good governance by landlords, no matter the effort and influence he applied.

One of his first notable appearances in the Lords was to speak to two bills brought forward in February 1853, one for the better regulation of relations between landlord and tenants, and the other on Ulster Tenant Right.[46] Dufferin, still being relatively inexperienced in the ways of both Irish estate management and the House of Lords, regarded the most important issue surrounding any reform of Irish land tenure as being the 'past'.[47] Dufferin was making a general point here, rather than specifically arguing for a historicist interpretation of landownership and management, to which he was opposed. His view was that Ulster Custom had arisen for a range of historical and social reasons, but that did not mean that a fully historicist view of tenant right should be considered a panacea for Ireland's economic and agricultural 'backwardness'. Unfortunately for Dufferin, the relatively flourishing state of Ulster's economy acted as a proof for those who were arguing for the extension of tenant right across the whole island.[48] The 'past' – or a historicist framing of contemporary political difficulties – would become, by the late 1860s, a highly influential Liberal rhetoric and historicist constructions of land reform ('simply retrospective') would bedevil Dufferin and his future thinking on land in Ireland, Canada, Egypt and India.[49] Dufferin's economics were arguably sound, but his political position was, from the mid-1860s, rapidly becoming anachronistic.[50]

Dufferin became increasingly unsatisfied with his parliamentary activities, where he was respected and useful, but not regarded as cabinet material. He wrote to his great friend (and source of Liberal patronage), the 8th Duke of Argyll, 'that life is slipping by very fast, and that I have very little to show for the years that are gone'.[51] He was casting around for an appointment and, although at this stage he most coveted the Irish Lord Lieutenancy, he was already considering the overseas empire, noting Canada or one of the Indian presidencies for preference.[52] 'Whatever there was to be done in this part of the world [Ireland], I have either done, or am in the way of doing and once a proper system organised, even an Irish estate does not give sufficient occupation', he wrote to Argyll, somewhat disingenuously.[53] Perhaps he spoke too soon, as Dufferin's contributions to the debate over Irish land reform in the late 1860s were far from over. In May 1865, he gave voluminous evidence to a select committee established to consider the workings of the 1860 Tenure and Improvement of Land (Ireland) Act, running to more than forty pages of wide-ranging discussion.[54] Dufferin's analysis of Irish rural and agricultural issues was robust. He first identified a number of intellectual and practical problems with the existing state of landlord–tenant relations – the first and most important being the significant variation within Ireland as to quality of land and the complicating factor of local customs such as Ulster Tenant Right.[55] Although he believed Irish agriculture as a whole to be 'less advanced' than that of England or Scotland, Dufferin nonetheless pointed to gradations of quality within Ireland, identifying the west of the country as the least advanced agriculturally and the north as the most.[56] Added to this was the problem of 'minute subdivision', of land by tenants, creating a fundamentally uneconomic structure and one over which the majority of landlords had failed to impose any discipline.[57] He further identified the lack of, 'an independent class, whose interests are so entirely distinct from either those of the landlord or the tenant', that could promote sustainable change in the rural economy of Ireland by spreading both cost and risk, and setting a moral, as well as an economic, example.[58] In his view, there was no utility in a blanket legislative solution, so what did he propose? His thinking can be divided into social and legislative approaches. First, to combat the 'evil effects' of the growing Irish population, Dufferin regarded emigration of large numbers of people combined with the diversification of the Irish economy into manufactures as the key starting points of amelioration and reconstruction.[59] But this had to be supported by other fundamental changes: the increasing gradation of social class in the country, so that rural society was not simply divided between landowners and tenants but, rather, would include an influential middle class, 'whose intervention as arbitrators would inspire the tenants and the landlords with equal confidence'.[60] Dufferin saw a role for government in the appointment of arbitrators to decide on cases of compensation for improvements between landlords and tenants, so as to avoid placing, 'tenants in a position hostile to their landlords'.[61] For Dufferin, this was preferable to the unregulated 'custom' of Ulster Tenant Right, of which he disapproved and would certainly not wish to see extended across the country.[62]

Dufferin's contributions to the debate continued, as internal Liberal discussion on the issue swirled in alarming directions. Dufferin felt strongly enough on the matter to build up a portfolio of speeches, pamphlets and reviews between 1866 and 1870.[63] These constitute some of the best-constructed liberal defences of Irish landlordism of the time, although his actual practical impact was limited. He also made little or no impression upon the more influential economists, campaigners, thinkers and politicians, who identified the origins of Ireland's problems as being its landlords. He was well aware of the political threat to British governance presented by the simmering discontent of Ireland, and this concern would be echoed throughout his imperial postings, particularly in India.[64] Only by providing effective and good governance could British rule in Ireland – or in the imperial territories – be justified.[65] In a speech in March 1866 in the Lords on a new coercion bill, Dufferin acknowledged the barriers to political content in Ireland: 'unhappily there exists among the less educated portion of the community a traditional hostility to the Government of England, a hostility once justified by the evil treatment that country received for centuries at your hands.'[66] This had recently been inflamed by the horrors of the Great Famine – but how to counter it? Dufferin argued that coercive legislation was pointless: if landlords were at the root of Ireland's problems, then the salvation of Ireland also lay in their hands, the natural governing class. But landowning culture in Ireland had to change first: most importantly, chronic absenteeism had to end. Dufferin pleaded, 'It is your presence, your sympathy, that your people want; the sight of your wives and daughters moving through the villages on their errands of charity and mercy, the tangible proof that you regard them as your fellow-citizens, and Ireland as your common country, that your own pride and happiness are interwoven with the welfare of the people.'[67] Of course, what Dufferin was not acknowledging was the history of Irish landlordism, stemming from conquest and plantation. This Ascendancy – of which Dufferin was very much a member – often owned land in Britain, and regarded their Irish estates as a secondary asset at best, with many rarely visiting their properties there.[68] Dufferin was an exception to this, owning only Irish land and being a frequent resident at Clandeboye in these years and, as much as was possible, during his years of overseas postings. The evils of absentee landlordism had to be stamped out in his view and, 'the action of those natural economic laws', diversifying the economic and employment prospects of the people. This, rather than unworkable or ineffectual legislation, was Dufferin's proposed reform programme.[69]

Of course, by putting his head above the parapet in this way Dufferin laid himself open to attack from those who disagreed with both his diagnosis and landlord-focused solutions to the troubles of Ireland, such as Isaac Butt and John Stuart Mill, who both argued that only a radical curb on landlord power could conciliate the Irish to British rule.[70] Public opinion in England was beginning to outpace Irish policy by the late 1860s, in part due to Fenian violence, but also due to the high-profile political debates that raged from 1866 to 1870, posing increasingly fundamental questions about Ireland.[71] This included debate over whether there should be specifically Irish solutions for Irish questions, land reform being the chief expression of that. Historicist and evolutionist frameworks for Irish economic development were gradually accepted by many British Liberals, slowly overtaking the views of political economists who had argued from the early nineteenth century that the market should prevail and the state act consistently, no matter the economic conditions on the ground. This included, by 1869,

Gladstone, despite Dufferin's best efforts to persuade him otherwise.[72] One of the most influential pressures on Gladstone was John Stuart Mill's radically controversial *England and Ireland*, which argued that hundreds of years of English misgovernment and outright oppression in Ireland justified unique palliative measures in the present, or England would lose its moral right to govern Ireland or any other imperial territory.[73] Dufferin, while fully committed to the union, admitted that, 'in past days, Ireland has suffered ill treatment and injustice', but argued that, 'for generations England has strained every nerve to make reparation for those wrongs'.[74] He was therefore in partial agreement with Mill, as he was on Mill's assertion that Ireland required special institutions and treatment.[75] Where they parted was on Mill's damning indictment of Irish landlordism: for Mill, only when 'the superstitions of landlordism' were cast off would Ireland be content.[76] Other writers were less sensational but, arguably, had as great an influence on the direction of British policy in 1869–70, including Sir James Caird, whose *Irish Land Question*, published in 1869, argued for special measures for Ireland, including Ulster Tenant Right, to be recognised in law and the introduction of a moderate scheme for tenant land purchase.[77] Most influential was Sir George Campbell, who mobilised his Scottish background and later experiences in Russia, India and Prussia to address the Irish land question in a truly global context. He supported a more moderate approach that would effectively police the actions of 'bad' landlords and include fixity of tenure for occupiers of land.[78] Dufferin was stung into writing a number of rebuttals to these publications, principally Mill's polemic, denying the charges made against his 'obnoxious class'.[79] He claimed that Mill's proposals amounted to 'confiscation' and pointed out that, if allowed in Ireland, it would only be a matter of time before his English peers faced the same menace. He would defend Irish landlords to the end against Mill's assertion that 'a landlord is an immoral entity'. This cut to the quick for Dufferin, whose identity was predicated on the ideal of a paternalistic, improving and morally upright landlord.[80]

Dufferin's efforts to defend Irish landlordism provide us with a clear insight into his view of its role as a route to the better governance of the country, rather than the source of its discontent.[81] From the outset, Dufferin was in a false position: as a man of progressive views, he acknowledged the history of spoliation that had resulted in his – and many other landlords' – wealth, privileges and patrimonies. He recognised that, historically, the Irish landed classes could be open to the description as being, 'the political garrison of England … backed in their secure possession by all the latent prejudices of anti-Celtic feeling in the English mind', as Michael Davitt would later express it.[82] Closer to home, he was fully aware of the evils of absentee landlordism, sectarian tensions between the landlord and tenant, and the pressures created by an ever-increasing population contained within a relatively undeveloped agrarian economy.[83] He wanted to support his party loyally, but ultimately could not come to terms with the direction Gladstone was taking it. 'I have hardly ever conversed with him [Gladstone] that I have not felt my face burn with irritation when I left his presence', he later admitted, and his bafflement and disappointment would only increase over the years.[84] Dufferin's problem was that he wanted to defend what was fast becoming the indefensible.[85] Gladstone was unfailingly polite in his response to Dufferin's efforts to influence him with letters, statistics and memoranda on Irish matters, but there was to be no meeting of minds.[86] He developed an increasing contempt for Irish landlords, combined with conviction that only good governance – which by definition could not be provided by the landed classes in Ireland – could reconcile Ireland to the rule of Westminster.[87]

Dufferin fumed to the only person who would understand: Argyll, then Secretary of State for India.

> Do any of your 15 deities, sitting in your ministerial Olympus, cast an eye towards these forlorn regions? If you do, you may perhaps learn that a good many people have been shot lately, and it may occur to you, in a languid sort of manner that not an unimportant function of government is the preservation of life and property … People may talk as they choose, but these crimes are but the simple translation with fact of the benevolent theories which have been so complacently professed of late by our transcendental moralists and philosophers.[88]

This *cri de coeur* would become a recurring refrain throughout Dufferin's political and administrative career: standing on the sidelines, attempting to expose the perceived threat to imperial rule and the sacrosanct rights of property to the Westminster powers that be.[89] Dufferin never attained senior cabinet position; he did not regard himself as having the necessary toughness to become a true statesman like his friends Argyll or Kimberley. Instead, he took on a Cassandra-like role, the man on the spot, advising and warning when necessary. And he saw much to warn of in Ireland by 1870.[90] It was Dufferin's misfortune that the tone and direction of Irish debate would turn so far against his views as to increasingly exclude him even from the deliberations of his own party, an exclusion that would be later echoed during his imperial career. Dufferin would remain on the outside, knocking on the windows to gain the attention of the 'deities', but never quite succeeding in doing so.[91]

Despite – or perhaps because of – the years of debate and disagreement, in 1870 Dufferin was asked to introduce to the Lords both the Peace Preservation and Irish Land bills, which he did, but with feelings of, 'repugnance, mortification and disappointment'.[92] The speech he gave on the Irish Land Act did not have quite the effect desired by his party, being met with, 'a considerable amount of cheering by the Opposition and dead silence from his own side'.[93] His obvious distaste for the provisions of the Act effectively to extend Ulster Tenant Right across Ireland he likened to the execution of the murderer of an illegitimate child: 'I do not approve of adultery but the creature being there has a right to the protection of the law.'[94] Two wrongs did not make a right, in other words, and Dufferin's sacrifice on the altar of

Gladstone's land reform was met with Tory amusement and sour faces on the Liberal benches.

There was no parting of the ways for Dufferin and the Liberal party in 1870, however. Gladstone wrote to thank Dufferin – almost without irony – for supporting the bills in the Lords, and the following year a discussion took place about a promotion in the English peerage for him.[95] This was in September 1871 and Dufferin, perhaps disillusioned by the passage of the 1870 Act and the fact that his Westminster career had stalled, wrote to Gladstone that he believed his service so far entitled him to an elevation in the peerage, 'before quitting a political for a literary career'.[96] There does seem to have been a genuine desire on Dufferin's part to turn to Irish history writing and he began a study of the 1798 Rebellion during these months. Typically, Dufferin was more interested in the characters of the chief protagonists than a stringent historical analysis. 'Indeed', he wrote to Argyll, 'I am ashamed to say that of all the personages of that date Wolf Tone in spite of his folly and his wrong-headedness is by far the most amusing and the most attractive of the Patriot heroes.'[97] He would later have a far less romantic view of self-proclaimed 'Patriot heroes' operating in the imperial context, such as Louis Riel in Canada.[98] For Dufferin, history was to be the healing balm that would calm the fire of Irish political disaffection and sectarian division. As he explained to Gladstone, instead of wasting his time as a bit-part player in the Lords, he could instead write, 'a really good impartial history of Ireland ... and might soothe and compose the angry reminiscences, which so embitter the relations with Catholics and Protestants and of their country with England'.[99] It was neither as a political stalwart in the Lords nor as a historian that Dufferin was to spend his future days, however: in early 1872, he was offered the Canadian governorship-general and he, Lady Dufferin and their children sailed for Quebec in June that year.

There was no escape from the workings of the 1870 Act, however: in March 1870, a critical article appeared in the *Northern Star*, a Belfast newspaper, mocking the issuing of leases on the Clandeboye estate in the wake of the new legislation as 'confiscation'. 'Why should the liberal, generous, enlightened, high-minded Lord Dufferin be anxious to hide his light under a bushel?', it asked ironically.[100] Dufferin's land agent, Thomson, was furious:

> It is very vexatious to find that after all the anxiety and labour expended in the effort to plant the tenant in a position of comparative independence in relation to his landlord that certain parties – outsiders – are endeavouring to interrupt the good feeling that has always existed between the tenant and the proprietor by misrepresenting the tenor of the lease, and by imputing the want of money for its issue at the present time.[101]

At the same time, rumours were beginning to circulate locally about Dufferin's financial difficulties. This pattern of press criticism would only continue and increase as the decade progressed, leaving Thomson with an increased workload in rebuffing these attacks.[102] Removed from the magnetic presence of Gladstone, Dufferin's views on Irish issues and radical Liberal responses to them began to harden.[103] His life-long correspondence with Argyll darkened from the late 1870s as both landowners began to rebel – Argyll openly from 1881, Dufferin only privately – against Gladstone's Irish and land reform policies.[104] This was also the decade when Dufferin sold off the bulk of his estates, which no doubt contributed to his sense of despair over the declining position of the Irish landlord, a fate he was sure would soon be shared by his peers in Britain.[105] It was not only the British and Irish context where Dufferin saw warning smoke rising into the sky; as governor-general he watched in horror as the legislature of Prince Edward Island introduced a Bill in 1874, 'expropriating landowners in the Island under very unfair conditions', linking this to the appearance in Westminster of a 'monstrous Tenant Right Bill' introduced by his old combatant Isaac Butt.[106] The 1870s were a defining period for Dufferin's understanding of Irish landownership and identity. After the failure of his efforts to influence the direction of Liberal Irish policy in 1870, he was suddenly physically removed from the Westminster sphere of action to take up his first imperial appointment in Canada. This represented no escape from the defining issues of the age, however; wherever he looked – back to Ireland, to Prince Edward Island, or to Egypt and India – the hydra-headed land issue haunted him.[107] As a member of the landed, governing elite, constantly in communication with his peers at home, he tried to make his voice heard, to maintain his vision of the ideal of Irish landlordism. This task would become increasingly difficult after 1879.

The Irish Land War and the Home Rule movement, 1879–1902

> The defence of property is as sacred a duty as the defence of liberty, and men are as much bound to sacrifice their lives for the one as for the other.[108]

A sea change took place in debates over land reform and tenant right from 1879, when the Irish Land War took hold of the country in earnest and the stakes – political and ideological – increased exponentially. A potent mix of anger and despair generated by the severe economic downturn of the late 1870s – further proof that the long-expected regeneration of the Irish economy after the Famine was never going to come – as well as land hunger and nationalism were at the root of the Land War.[109] It was the most organised and widespread tenant agitation of the nineteenth century, with radical tactics including violence against persons, animals and property; rent strikes; demands for rent reductions; and utilisation of the press in Ireland and Britain to damage both landlord reputations and purses.[110] Memories of the Famine and of the mass evictions of that period drove tenant anger, which was in turn effectively marshalled by a leadership determined to settle the agricultural crisis at the expense of the landlords.[111] As a class, Irish landowners had not helped their own position: they faced these challenges from a weakened platform of continued indebtedness, exacerbated by the economic downturn of the late 1870s.[112] Dufferin's almost continuous overseas postings in this period meant that involvement in terms of parliamentary attendance and debate tailed off after the early 1880s.[113] Despite this, he maintained a close and increasingly cynical eye on Irish affairs, and made sure his opinions were known by his cabinet and political allies in the Liberal party and friends on the Conservative benches, such as Lord Carnarvon and Lord Salisbury.[114] Like Argyll, he diagnosed Gladstone's policies towards Irish land from the early 1880s as revolutionary and destructive – more than this: a betrayal.[115] As he received reports of Irish agitation, rent strikes and agrarian violence while in Ottawa, and then observed with despair if not surprise the passage of the 1881 Irish Land Act, he became openly critical of his old hero, Gladstone.[116] 'The Irish landlords have become the victims of a revolution and the prospect of obtaining anything like justice … is evidently hopeless', he wrote to Howe, his land agent at Clandeboye.[117] Naturally, he was most unguarded in his condemnations when writing to Argyll, who resigned from the cabinet in 1881 over the Act.[118] Although Dufferin recognised that since he had sold the bulk of his estates he was, as he put it, 'beyond the reach of even a communistic revolution', he did, 'confess my sense of justice would be very much outraged if I thought the political party to which I belong would be tempted … to countenance Mr Parnell's proceedings'.[119] Dufferin was to find that he was not personally immune from the agitations and heart-burnings of the Land War, however; he faced disturbance on his own estate, principally meetings about tenant right from which criticisms emerged over the rent conditions of new leases then being drawn up.[120] As was the case on most Irish estates at this time, proprietors were being forced to re-interrogate past management decisions, particularly around leases and evictions, as the press, agitators and reformers exposed the past to justify their demands. Most historical attention rested on the Great Famine and its aftermath, and Dufferin was obliged to conduct an audit of the Clandeboye estate, investigating the number of evictions carried out in order to combat the hostile press coverage.[121] Dufferin recoiled under criticism of any type and, having had his fingers burnt over estate and land issues, his imperial management and policies would be cautious in tone and sensitive to predicted public reaction.

There was more to come: in late 1880, he received reports from Howe that the Clandeboye tenants had published a petition requesting rent reductions and had sent it to no less a person than Gladstone.[122] This was alongside local newspaper reports critical of Dufferin's record as a landlord and, together, they sent him into a hurricane of anxiety and activity.[123] Dufferin struggled with criticism of any kind, being a sensitive man and also acutely aware of the power of reputation, politically and socially, for Irish landlords. Also, despite the anger he directed at Gladstone and his Irish policy, he still regarded him as Britain's greatest living politician, and was sensitive to the value of his patronage and attention for future appointments.[124] He was also aware of a growing sense of anger against Irish landlords among the political classes in Westminster (and shared to some extent by both party leaders), and this feeling increased in the 1880s. Why should the British state, it was asked, bail out a class of feckless, cruel and failing landlords, who had long ago repudiated the responsibilities of property but were now crying out for assistance?[125] Dufferin was acutely aware of this view and of his immediate need to limit the damage done, to him personally and his class more widely, by these negative reports and the petition.[126]

Dufferin immediately wrote a long letter to Gladstone, having gathered as much evidence as he could from his land agent of his beneficent record as a landlord.[127] Acknowledging the petition to be 'a bitter indictment' against his estate management, Dufferin went on, in several thousand words, to refute every detail of the attack.[128] He was at pains to stress what he saw as evidence of his kindliness as a landlord: that he had dismissed, in 1847, the land agent in place due to his 'unsympathetic manner in dealing with the tenants', and quoted the substantial sums both invested and written off since that date for the benefit of his tenantry.[129] The real force of the document rests in Dufferin's anguished summary of the lot of an Irish landlord and the moment when the optimism Dufferin had expressed on his inheritance finally evaporated:

> I cannot tell you, my dear Mr Gladstone, what a pain and humiliation it has been to me to write this letter … I think I may fairly say that I have endeavoured to do my duty faithfully and honestly in the difficult situation in which I have been placed. Up till now I have certainly succeeded in retaining the affectionate regard of my tenantry … and I can only regard the present diatribe as resulting from the unhealthy state of public feeling which has lately been generated in Ireland.[130]

In his private letters to Argyll he was more forthright, being confident of a sympathetic hearing.[131] 'The Irish mess is more hopeless than ever', he claimed, expressing his pessimistic diagnosis of the future not simply of Irish landlordism (dire), but of Irish civil society and the security of the British imperial state itself.[132] Feeling betrayed by the promise that the 1870 Land Act was to be 'a final settlement', only to find that just ten years later the Liberals were now, 'insisting upon the necessity of radical reform of the land laws of Ireland', Dufferin, aware perhaps of Argyll's impending resignation, noted that it would have been a, 'very bitter mortification to me if I had not been able to support him [Gladstone] on an Irish question'.[133] He warned that these attacks would not be limited to Irish landlordism, but would inevitably spread to Britain and the imperial territories.[134] Rebellion and violence committed by Irish people in Ireland and beyond its shores was viewed by Dufferin, as it was by many contemporaries, as being part of the national character of the Irish politically, culturally and even racially. It was also linked to how the landed aristocracy evolved a governing mentality based on traditional views borne out of social elitism: that they had the good qualities and ability to govern and defend an 'inferior race' of people. The repeated cycle of coercion and extraordinary legislation required to govern Ireland in this period was both recognised and criticised by Dufferin, but he also worried that these policies were an indication not of the strength of British government in Ireland but, rather, of its weakness and experimental nature, trends he would also identify in India in the 1880s.[135] In both contexts, Dufferin struggled to balance his liberal instincts with the brutal realities of British power.

Although by now well-established in his overseas career, Dufferin made a last public appearance on the Irish land issue in 1881 when he gave evidence before the Bessborough Commission, appointed to investigate the workings of the 1870 Irish Land Act.[136] Dufferin's evidence was reflective, ranging back and forth from the optimism of his early days as an Irish landlord, his thoughts on the deep-rooted causes of Irish poverty, criticisms of the 1870 Act, and his condemnation of proposals to grant the Three Fs under what would become the 1881 Irish Land Act.[137] These Fs constituted fair rent, freedom from eviction and free sale, the last of these being of most concern to Dufferin.[138] Much of his evidence focused on the issue of improvements: who made and paid for them, and how they were to be compensated, the waters muddied by differing interpretations of Ulster Tenant Right.[139] He spelt out very clearly to the Commissioners his objections to the Three Fs; identifying the fundamental shift in power such a reform would introduce:

> The effect of the Act of 1870 was to put the tenant into the same bed as his landlord, and the first impulse of the tenant has not unnaturally been to kick the landlord out of bed … The government will now be tempted, with the view of quieting the disturbance, to give the tenant a little more of the bed. The effect of this, however, will be exactly the opposite. The tenant will say to himself, "One good kick more, and the villain is on the floor."[140]

Beyond this, Dufferin believed the Three Fs would finally remove any real interest the landlord may have in his property beyond its rental value. Improvements and management would be ignored, social discipline would crumble. Instead, Dufferin urged, why not look to land purchase by government along the Russian model, observed while ambassador there?[141] 'Let us rather take a leaf out of the Russian book, and convert this rent to a fixed charge or land rate to be collected by local authorities.'[142] Dufferin stressed that he only suggested land purchase to avoid 'proposals of a far more revolutionary character'.[143] 'By adopting the Russian principle of interposing the Commune between the Government and the rent-payers, it would be possible, I think, to obviate the manifest dangers you indicate [of land purchase].'[144] Despite his vigorous defence of property, Dufferin was disappointed (if not surprised) by the eventual Bessborough Report; indeed, he went so far as to draft a letter of dissent to the Commission's secretary, Sir

George Young, although in the end he refrained from sending it.[145] Perhaps he understood that such a defence no longer chimed with the prevailing mood at Westminster, or even at Clandeboye. As he wrote wryly to Howe: 'I expect that I shall be a good deal abused when the evidence I have given … comes out. Please take care that the Land League does not send emissaries to burn Clandeboye House down. I should be very sorry to lose my family papers and pictures.'[146] The threat was far more real for other Irish landowners at this time as, flippancy aside, Dufferin understood all too well. He settled into his usual course of private lobbying, writing to Gladstone to dissuade him from the Three Fs, and to Argyll to stiffen his spine for cabinet conflict.[147] He was also, from St Petersburg and then from Constantinople, in constant correspondence with his land agent at Clandeboye, absorbing the view from the front line.[148]

Having made his objections, Dufferin maintained a close eye on the workings of the 1881 Act, which he regarded as fulfilling all of his negative expectations.[149] For Dufferin, the Three Fs were only the beginning of the 'abducting away of the landlord's rights'.[150] This view seemed to him to be confirmed in the early 1880s when a new tenant agitation burst out in the Scottish Highlands and Islands, eventually resulting in more Liberal land reform: the 1886 Crofters Holdings (Scotland) Act.[151] This act was constructed along the same principles as the 1881 Irish Land Act, granting Highland crofters the Three Fs.[152] For Dufferin, then viceroy in India and overseeing the stormy passage of the Bengal and Oudh Tenancy Acts, the first half of the 1880s marked a sea change in the fortunes of landlords in the British world, when fundamental responsibilities were taken from landlords by the state, which then became an intermediary between landlords and tenants.[153] Like many of his class in Ireland and Britain, faced with the horrors of 'dual ownership' under the Three Fs, Dufferin increasingly, if reluctantly, turned to land purchase as the best of a bad job for Irish landowners.[154] 'Property only entails expense and responsibilities far in excess of the income derived from it', he lamented in 1893.[155] Having spent three decades resisting the symbolic reduction of landownership to mere rent collection, encouraging his fellow landowners to be resident, leaders of their communities for moral as well as political and economic reasons, by the 1890s Dufferin had given up that ideal.[156] Instead, like many an embittered landowner, he saw a future where the burdens of landownership were shifted onto the shoulders of the state.[157] If the people, the political classes and government were so critical of private landownership in Ireland, then they could take responsibility for it.[158] It was a remarkable intellectual turnaround, one resulting from his tumultuous experiences, financial, political and imperial. Although his position was shared by many of his peers, his was one of the longest journeys to this end point, a place where morality was no longer the driver of landowning philosophies.[159] With the benefit of hindsight, he regarded himself as fortunate in having sold his estates before the 1881 Act and in having sidestepped a political career under the shadow of bitterness caused by Irish issues, not least Home Rule.[160] If Dufferin saw hope for Ireland's future, it was in the growing manufacturing power of Belfast, not in its agrarian economy or population, which the 1881 Act had worked on to 'destroy the moral sense of the Irish people'.[161] His view has been borne out to some extent by later historians and economists, who have argued that neither the 1870 nor the 1881 Acts did much in the way of improving Irish agricultural efficiency, because of their minimal impact on reallocating land in a productive way.[162] That was beside the point, however: the Acts were political in intention and result, as Dufferin recognised. His sense of despair was only compounded by the ongoing debate over Irish nationalism and imperial unity from the mid-1880s.[163]

The first Home Rule movement had been launched by Dufferin's old sparring partner on the land question, Isaac Butt, with tacit support for and from the Fenian movement. This was bad enough for Dufferin and others of his class, but at least Butt was essentially a parliamentarian, a social conservative and reformer, not a revolutionary.[164] By the 1880s, the picture was very different: the rural economy had been politicised through the activities of the Land League and two land reform acts – of 1870 and 1881 – had symbolically undermined Irish landed power. With Home Rule, disruption and radicalism infected the heart of empire at Westminster. Despite this, Irish Home Rule and the parliamentary factions and crises it engendered were never directly part of Dufferin's public or political activities.[165] By the time Gladstone converted to the cause in the mid-1880s, Dufferin had been working overseas for nearly fifteen years, and was then occupying the most prestigious of all imperial posts, the viceroyalty of India.[166] Unlike the debates surrounding land reform – in Ireland, Britain and the imperial territories – Dufferin did not publicly comment on Irish Home Rule. It was too radical, too threatening to his by now purely sentimental loyalty to the Liberal party and Gladstone, and he had, since 1881, been wholly fatalistic about the fate of landowners in Ireland.[167] Dufferin was also too thin-skinned to make an effective public contribution in the context of a bitterly acrimonious Westminster. Instead, he acted as a promoter of imperial unionism, privately lobbying his friends and colleagues in Britain and Ireland. These included correspondents from across the political and social spectrum, from the Queen ('The Queen hopes the Viceroy is well. What does he say to all our troubles at home?')[168], to his India Office masters, Lords Kimberley, Churchill and Cross.[169] Friends and colleagues picked up through years of colonial service also corresponded with Dufferin, usually to offer words of encouragement and support for his views on Irish Home Rule and the dangers it represented for other imperial territories.[170] Sir Samuel Baker can stand for all of them when he wrote: 'We already possess a terrible example in Ireland of the ruin that must result from the agitation stirred up by professional disturbers for selfish gains; this would be repeated in India upon a gigantic scale unless supressed by crushing them before the period of incubation.'[171] This was also what Dufferin feared: the 'germ theory' of agitation taking hold across the empire leading to the ruination of imperial security and glory.[172] For these reasons, Dufferin's contributions (always made privately) were framed through imperial concerns and consequences, as the safest way for him to engage with and address Irish Home Rule.

Dufferin's anguish around Irish Home Rule also exposed the fundamental tensions in his position and that of other Irish peers and landowners who took a leading role in imperial governance.[173] Dufferin performed a certain kind of Irish identity – romantic, literary, quick-tempered – and actively played on the differences this generated between himself and his English and Scottish peers. As a result, he was deeply concerned by other constructions of Irish identity that began to take hold and harden from the 1870s – that of the rebellious, violent and credulous paddy.[174] As a member of a transnational ruling elite, he was obliged to engage with legislation for coercion, land and constitutional reform. In India, the question was clearer: Britain's interest was imperial security against any genuine shift to self-government. But as an Irishman and member of the British imperial elite, Dufferin's views on the benefits of empire to Ireland were much more ambivalent.[175] At a time when British domestic wealth and overseas power was at its peak, the economic condition and divided society of Ireland was an embarrassment and a challenge to the 'civilising mission' of England, and Dufferin felt this acutely.[176]

He recognised with dismay the ways in which Irish nationalists had bound up the question of self-rule with that of land reform and attacks on landlordism, but his greatest fear was that this nationalism would seep into vulnerable imperial polities such as India, and this framed his response to Irish Home Rule.[177] As he wrote to Lord Kimberley from Calcutta:

> I cannot help having a strong suspicion that the course of events at home in regard to Ireland has produced a very considerable effect upon the minds of the intelligent and educated sections of our own native community [in India] … I cannot help asking myself how long an autocratic Government like that of India – and a Government which everyone will admit for many a long year to come must in its main feature remain autocratic – will be able to stand the strain implied by the importation *en bloc* from England, or rather from Ireland, of the perfected machinery of modern democratic agitation.[178]

Dufferin's belief in the necessity of despotic government for India was in part based on his belief in the inherent racial inferiority of Indians, an echo of contemporary racialised views about the Irish.[179] This was where the danger lay, in Dufferin's view, as 'evidently India is not a country in which the machinery of European democratic agitation can be applied with impunity'.[180] The contradictions in this position are fascinating: Dufferin's liberal instincts came into direct conflict with the necessity of autocratic rule in India to preserve British power and status. The issues were not dissimilar in Ireland, but Dufferin was unable to support British policy there fully after 1881. This was because much unionist thought in the mid-1880s was influenced by Anglo-Saxon thinking, which argued that the Irish, like the Indians, were not ready for self-rule, partly for reasons of inherent racial and cultural inferiority, and partly because the ancient liberties of the English were specifically designed by and for Anglo-Saxons and were not suitable for Celts.[181] Dufferin shared some of these concerns but was by no means a fully paid-up member of the Anglo-Saxonist crew.[182] His diagnosis of the threat centred on questions of governance and fitness to rule, and he regarded the gravest error of British government in Ireland to be their ritual sacrifice of Irish landed interests at the behest of Irish agitators. He saw this as a mistake, not just because it affected his interests personally, but also because the landed and aristocratic classes were natural allies of British power.[183] He strongly promoted this view in India, deploying pomp and ceremony and his diplomatic skills on the princely states and nobility. To fail to act would be an abdication of responsibility, with serious consequences. And, indeed, the emerging nationalist movement in India in the early 1880s was and would continue to be a threat to the authority of the Raj. As Dufferin wrote to Kimberley: 'The instinctive desire which now possesses them [Indian nationalists] is to ape the tactics and organisation of the Irish Revolutionists. With this object they denounce the whole Indian Administration and its various services as brutally inimical to native interests.'[184] This was dangerous talk indeed: although he never openly broke with the Liberal party, Dufferin's correspondence with Gladstone henceforth avoided political questions, and he wrote privately to Salisbury with his support for Conservative resistance to any measure of Irish Home Rule.[185] Informed by his experiences as an imperial administrator, Dufferin opposed self-rule for Ireland as enthusiastically as he did for India. For him, there was little difference between the two in imperial terms; both must be loyal, but the British must earn that loyalty through good governance – that is, better governance than could be managed by Indians or the Irish themselves. Above all, his Irish experience defined and framed his views on imperial governance throughout his overseas career. His political and personal identity was moulded by Irish questions and, throughout his work in the British imperial world, the empire within continued to shape and influence every action he took.

Irreconcilable difference?

> [Gladstone] spent his declining years trying to guess the answer to the Irish Question; unfortunately, whenever he was getting warm, the Irish secretly changed the Question.[186]

By the late 1880s, Dufferin had become embittered and embattled over the various Irish questions he faced, at home and overseas. His diagnosis was heavily influenced by his early commitment to political economy, his experience of owning a landed estate and, later, by his imperial service. It was a vision that incorporated contemporary thinking on racial hierarchies, Malthusian logic, a belief in inherent British superiority as a liberal parliamentary society, as well as the British state's ability – through its hereditary,

72   *Irish questions*

landed governing class – to rule both with a sense of fair play and without democracy. As such, his own estate at Clandeboye was in many ways a vehicle for social and economic positioning, even if a rather unreliable one. Because landed, Anglo-Irish loyalties were so closely attached to property, religion and caste, Dufferin and his peers were in direct opposition to the great national movements of land reform and demands for self-government.[187] However, his views – informed by a belief that the Irish 'past' was the defining factor in its present and future, and that landownership and governance was as much a moral as an economic exercise – led to some interesting, if ultimately unsuccessful, interventions into the debates over political economy, land reform and self-government. Dufferin took these Irish questions with him on every appointment and they constituted an inherent part of his mental furniture. It was also the case that, due to the autocratic nature of much of British imperial rule, his views gained greater traction outwith the British and Irish Isles.

Dufferin was never able wholly to resolve the question of what British rule in Ireland was for, or how it could be justified, morally or politically. While he rejected the view that Britain's record in Ireland corrupted its self-image as a liberal, moral, parliamentary system and acted as a bastion for non-autocratic systems across the world, he could also not deny that, mediated by Ascendancy landownership, this image belied the realities of Irish life. His riposte was to encourage his fellow landowners to take their responsibilities seriously, but he was whistling into the wind. Both the economic and political structures of Irish landownership made internal change unlikely and so that had to come from Westminster, ultimately resulting in the beginning of a process of the wholesale purchase of Irish land by the state in the early twentieth century. Ultimately, the Irish landowning class were more the victims of impossible circumstances than the creators of their own downfall, in spite of the history, the debt and the Famine. They were too vulnerable to the accusation that – however long their family lineage – they were interlopers and usurpers, and were unable to make common cause with their tenantry and Irish society more broadly. Fatally, they were also unable to convince the British political classes of this either. Dufferin's interest had been the examination of the Irish past for the roots of the dislocation and conflict he grappled with over the course of his life, a conflict that sat in tension with his preferred romantic, Scott-infused reading of history. Dufferin carried with him an internal conception of Ireland – its complexities and tensions – which constituted an empire within for his whole life, framing and locating imperial problems both consciously and unconsciously.

Notes

1 British Library [hereafter BL], Gladstone papers, Add MSS 44151, Vol. LXVI, correspondence with Frederick Temple Hamilton Blackwood, Lord Dufferin, ff. 102, Dufferin to Gladstone, 13 Sept. 1871; C. Kinealy, At home with the empire: the example of Ireland, in S. Rose and C. Hall (eds), *At Home with the Empire: Metropolitan Culture and the Imperial World* (Cambridge, 2006), pp. 88–9, 96–7.

2 A. Lyall, *The Life of the Marquis of Dufferin and Ava* (London, 1905), p. 62; W. H. Crawford, Landlord-tenant relations in Ulster, 1609–1820, *Irish Economic and Social History*, 2 (1975), pp. 20–1.
3 M. Bentley, *Lord Salisbury's World: conservative environments in late-Victorian Britain* (Cambridge, 2001), p. 72. Gladstone also idealised the concept of an 'aristocracy redeemed by service', itself a historicist proposition: C. Dewey, Celtic agrarian legislation and the Celtic revival: historicist implications of Gladstone's Irish and Scottish Land Acts, 1870–1886, *Past and Present*, 64:1 (1974), p. 60; J. R. Vincent, *Disraeli, Derby and the Conservative Party: the political journals of Lord Stanley 1849–69* (Hassocks, 1978), p. 176; J. Epstein, Taking class notes on empire, in S. Rose and C. Hall (eds), *At Home with the Empire: Metropolitan Culture and the Imperial World* (Cambridge, 2006), pp. 251–6, 270.
4 House of Lords Debates, 5 Jul. 1869, vol. 197, cc. 1108–65; HL Deb, 4 Aug. 1870, vol. 203, cc. 1541–5; HL Deb, 5 Mar. 1872, vol. 209, cc. 1384–8; HL Deb, 7 May 1872, vol. 211, cc. 363–8.
5 This is best exemplified by the long-running correspondences between Dufferin and the 8th Duke of Argyll, W. E. Gladstone and Lord Salisbury; Public Record Office of Northern Ireland [hereafter PRONI], Dufferin Papers, D1071/H/B/C; BL, Add MSS 44151; Hatfield House, papers of the 3rd Marquis of Salisbury.
6 P. Bull, Irish Land and British Politics, in M. Cragoe and P. Readman, *The Land Question in Britain, 1750–1950* (Basingstoke, 2010), p. 128; A. Gailey, *The Lost Imperialist: Lord Dufferin, memory and mythmaking in an age of celebrity* (London, 2015), pp. 40–1.
7 J. Ridden, Britishness as an imperial and diasporic identity: Irish elite perspectives, c. 1820s–70s, in P. Gray (ed.), *Victoria's Ireland? Irishness and Britishness, 1837–1901* (Dublin, 2004), pp. 89–93; Gailey, *Lost Imperialist*, pp. 40, 106–12.
8 E. Delaney, Our Island Story? Towards a transnational history of late modern Ireland, *Irish Historical Studies*, 37:148 (2011), pp. 599–601; Bull, Irish Land and British Politics, pp. 126–143.
9 C. A. Bayly, Ireland, India and the Empire, 1780–1914, *Transactions of the Royal Historical Society*, 6th ser., 10 (2000), pp. 390–1.
10 P. Davis, The Liberal Unionist party and the Irish policy of Lord Salisbury's government, 1886–1892, *Historical Journal*, 18 (1975), pp. 88, 103–4; H. Brasted, Indian nationalist development and the influence of Irish home rule, 1870–1886, *Modern Asian Studies*, 14:1 (1980), pp. 37–63.
11 Delaney, Our island story? pp. 616–17; C. Townshend, *Political Violence in Ireland: government and resistance since 1848* (Oxford, 1984), pp. 103–4, 105, 128, 133.
12 C. O'Grada, The investment behaviour of Irish landlords 1850–75: some preliminary findings, *Agricultural History Review*, 23 (1975), p. 139; J. R. Roszman, 'Ireland as a weapon of warfare': Whigs, Tories and the problem of Irish outrages, 1835 to 1839, *Historical Journal*, (2017), pp. 3, 6–7, 24–5.
13 Dufferin, *The case of the Irish tenant, as stated sixteen years ago by the Rt. Hon. Lord Dufferin, in a speech delivered to the House of Lords, February 28, 1854* (London, 1870), p. 7.
14 Gailey, *Lost Imperialist*, pp. 24–8, 31–4.
15 Dufferin and the Hon. G. F. Boyle, *Narrative of a journey from Oxford to Skibbereen during the year of the Irish Famine* (Oxford, 1847); Lyall, *Life of Dufferin*, p. 151.
16 Christ Church, Oxford, MR iii.c.i 1/6/3, Lord Dufferin to Lady Helen Dufferin, no date [late 1847?]. Indian and Irish comparisons have been made here, too: J. Bender, The imperial politics of famine: the 1873–4 Bengal Famine and Irish parliamentary nationalism, *Eire–Ireland*, 42:1 (2007), pp. 132, 135, 151.

74 Irish questions

17 A. Hawkins, Parliamentary government and Victorian political parties, c. 1830–c. 1880, *English Historical Review*, vol. 104, No. 412 (1989), pp. 641, 646–7.
18 Lyall, *Life of Dufferin*, p. 60.
19 C. D. Black, *The Marquess of Dufferin and Ava: diplomatist, viceroy, statesman* (London, 1903), p. 20.
20 G. Bigelow, *Fiction, Famine and the Rise of Economics in Victorian Britain and Ireland* (Cambridge, 2003), pp. 112, 116.
21 Lyall, *Life of Dufferin*, p. 68; P. Gray, The making of mid-Victorian Ireland? Political economy and the memory of the Great Famine, in P. Gray (ed.), *Victoria's Ireland? Irishness and Britishness, 1837–1901* (Dublin, 2004), p. 152.
22 Lyall, *Life of Dufferin*, p. 62.
23 Dufferin, *The case of the Irish tenant*, p. 8; R. D. C. Black, *Economic Thought and the Irish Question, 1817–1870* (Cambridge, 1960), pp. 235–7.
24 Lyall, *Life of Dufferin*, p. 68; Black, *Economic Thought*, p. 235–8.
25 Black, *Economic Thought*, pp. 235–7.
26 P. Gray, *Famine, Land and Politics: British government and Irish society, 1843–50* (Dublin, 1999), pp. 326–7.
27 L. P. Curtis, *The Depiction of Eviction in Ireland, 1845–1910* (Dublin, 2011), pp. 1–8.
28 Dufferin, *Irish Emigration*, p. 9; Lyall, *Life of Dufferin*, pp. 159–62. See also his run-in with John Bright, MP: HL Deb, 25 Mar. 1867, vol. 186, cc. 454–7.
29 Gray, Making of mid-Victorian Ireland, pp. 155–6.
30 Dufferin, *Irish Emigration*, p. 11.
31 B. Mac Suibhne, *The End of Outrage: post-famine adjustment in rural Ireland* (Oxford, 2017).
32 Dufferin, *Irish Emigration*, p. 13; Gailey, *Lost Imperialist*, p. 40.
33 Delaney, Our island story? p. 613; D. A. Wilson, *The Orange Order in Canada* (Dublin, 2007), pp. 12–16; H. Senior, *The Fenians and Canada* (Toronto, 1978), pp. 136, 142, 146–7; P. Toner, The green ghost: Canada's Fenians and the raids, *Eire–Ireland*, 16:4 (1981), pp. 27–9, 45–6.
34 F. Thompson, *The End of Liberal Ulster: land agitation and land reform 1868–1866* (Belfast, 2001), pp. 35–41; Bull, Irish land and British politics, pp. 131–2; Bentley, *Lord Salisbury's World*, pp. 99, 115.
35 W. L. Burn, Free trade in land: an aspect of the Irish Question, *Transactions of the Royal Historical Society*, 31 (1949), pp. 65–7.
36 PRONI, D1071, H/B/G/316, ff. 2, Sir James Graham to Dufferin, 24 Aug. 1847.
37 Lyall, *Life of Dufferin*, p. 62.
38 Lyall, *Life of Dufferin*, p. 62. See also, F. Campbell, *The Irish Establishment, 1879–1914* (Oxford, 2009), pp. 25–8, 30; P. Bew and F. Wright, The agrarian opposition in Ulster politics, 1848–87, in S. Clark and J. S. Donnelly (eds), *Irish Peasants: violence and political unrest, 1780–1914* (Manchester, 1983), p. 193; W. E. Vaughan, *Landlords and Tenants in Mid-Victorian Ireland* (Oxford, 1994), pp. 67–8.
39 E. D. Steele, *Irish Land and British Politics: tenant-right and nationality, 1865–1870* (Cambridge, 1974), pp. 9, 21–2.
40 M. W. Dowling, *Tenant Right and agrarian society in Ulster, 1600–1870* (Dublin, 1999), pp. 241, 253–5.
41 W. E. Vaughan, *Landlords and Tenants in Mid-Victorian Ireland* (Oxford, 1994), p. 72.
42 K. T. Hoppen, Landownership and power in nineteenth century Ireland: the decline of an elite, in R. Gibson and M. Blinkhorn (eds), *Landownership and Power in Modern Europe* (London, 1991), p. 171.
43 Lyall, *Life of Dufferin*, p. 64–5.
44 H. Nicolson, *Helen's Tower* (London, 1937), p. 79.
45 Dufferin, *The case of the Irish tenant*, p. 7.

46 These were the Landlord and Tenant (Ireland) Bill and the Leasing Powers (Ireland) Bill; Black, *Dufferin and Ava*, p. 24; Dufferin, *The case of the Irish tenant*.
47 J. W. Burrow, *A Liberal Descent: Victorian historians and the English past* (Cambridge, 1981), pp. 1–22; P. Readman, *Land and Nation in England: patriotism, national identity and the politics of land, 1880–1914* (Suffolk, 2008), pp. 137–8, 147.
48 Vaughan, *Landlords and Tenants*, p. 81; C. W. Bouton, John Stuart Mill on Liberty and History, in E. J. Eisenach (ed.), *Mill and the Moral Character of Liberalism* (Pennsylvania, 1999), p. 263.
49 Dufferin, *The case of the Irish tenant*, p. 25; Dewey, Celtic agrarian legislation, p. 44–5; for an imperial parallel that affected Dufferin directly, see R. Bitterman and M. McCallum, Upholding the land legislation of a 'communistic and socialist assembly': the benefits of confederation for Prince Edward Island, *Canadian Historical Review*, 87:1 (2006), pp. 3, 8, 13, and, especially, 16–17.
50 Dowling, *Tenant Right*, pp. 291–2.
51 PRONI, D1071, H/B/C/95, ff. 12, Dufferin to Argyll, 20 Dec. 1863.
52 PRONI, D1071, H/B/C/95, ff. 13, Argyll to Dufferin, 18 Oct. 1864.
53 PRONI, D1071, H/B/C/95, ff. 12, Dufferin to Argyll, 20 Dec. 1863; Nicolson, *Helen's Tower*, p. 137.
54 PP 1865, *Report and Minutes of Evidence from the Select Committee on Tenure and Improvement of Land (Ireland) Act* [hereafter *Select Committee 1865*].
55 O. Purdue, *The Big House in the North of Ireland: land, power and social elites, 1878–1960* (Dublin, 2009), pp. 313–23; Black, *Economic Thought*, pp. 51–7, 65; Thompson, *End of Liberal Ulster*, pp. 36–7.
56 *Select Committee 1865*, Dufferin, pp. 44, Q960; p. 46, Q985–7. As George Campbell would later claim: 'God made Ireland a bog'; G. Campbell, Land legislation for Ireland, *Fortnightly Review*, new ser., xix (1881), p. 26.
57 *Select Committee 1865*, Dufferin, p. 47, Q994.
58 *Select Committee 1865*, Dufferin, p. 48, Q1010.
59 *Select Committee 1865*, Dufferin, p. 78, Q1503; see also Dufferin, *The case of the Irish tenant*, p. 5.
60 *Select Committee 1865*, Dufferin, p. 71, Q1408.
61 *Select Committee 1865*, Dufferin, p. 51, Q1042.
62 T. W. Guinnane and R. I. Miller, The limits to land reform: the land acts in Ireland, 1870–1909, *Economic Development and Cultural Change*, 45:3 (1997), pp. 594, 601.
63 Thompson, *The End of Liberal Ulster*, p. 63.
64 For example, British Library, Mss Eur F130, Papers of the 1st Marquess of Dufferin as Viceroy of India 1884–88, ff. 97, Dufferin to Lord Kimberley, 12 Jun. 1885; ff. 157, Dufferin to Lord Randolph Churchill, 19 Oct. 1885; ff. 45, Dufferin to Kimberley, 26 Apr. 1886.
65 K. T. Hoppen, Landownership and power in nineteenth century Ireland: the decline of an elite, in R. Gibson and M. Blinkhorn (eds), *Landownership and Power in Modern Europe* (London, 1991), pp. 168, 176–7.
66 Dufferin, *Contributions to an Inquiry into the State of Ireland* (London, 1866), p. 43–4. See also HL Deb, 11 May 1866, vol. 183, cc. 745–65.
67 Dufferin, *Contributions to an Inquiry into the State of Ireland*, pp. 47–8.
68 Hoppen, Landownership and power, pp. 168, 171.
69 Dufferin, *Contributions to an Inquiry into the State of Ireland*, p. 48.
70 Lyall, *Life of Dufferin*, pp. 159–60; K. Blake, *Pleasures of Benthamism: Victorian literature, utility, political economy* (Oxford, 2009), pp. 195–9, 215–16; D. Thornley, The Irish conservatives and home rule, 1869–73, *Irish Historical Studies*, xi, 43 (1959), pp. 200–5; Black, *Economic Thought*, pp. 245–6.

76 Irish questions

71 Mill was writing in the context of the Fenian threat when he wrote *England and Ireland*: E. D. Steele, J. S. Mill and the Irish Question: reform and the integrity of Empire, 1865–70, *Historical Journal*, 13:3 (1970), p. 420; Dowling, *Tenant Right*, p. 296. Compare to Butt's views: D. Thornley, *Isaac Butt and Home Rule* (London, 1964), pp. 62, 64, 68–70, 77.
72 Black, *Economic Thought*, pp. 51–7, 65, 246; R. C. D. Black, Economic policy in Ireland and India in the time of J. S. Mill, *Economic History Review*, 21:2 (1968); B. Kinzer, J. S. Mill and Irish land: a reassessment, *Historical Journal*, 27:1 (1984), pp. 111–13, 115, 121; J. Loughlin, *Gladstone, Home Rule and the Ulster Question, 1882–93* (Dublin, 1986), pp. 172, 175, 177, 251–5; B. Solow, *The Land Question and the Irish Economy 1870–1903* (Massachusetts, 1971), pp. 15–23, 32, 43.
73 Mill argued it was possible to govern Ireland effectively, as it had already been achieved in India; J. S. Mill, *England and Ireland* (London, 1868), pp. 22–3. E. D. Steele, J. S. Mill and the Irish Question, pp. 216–17, 235–6; L. Zastoupil, Moral government: J. S. Mill on Ireland, *Historical Journal*, 26:3 (1983), pp. 708–10, 712, 714; E. Sullivan, Liberalism and imperialism: John Stuart Mill's defence of the British Empire, *Journal of the History of Ideas*, 44 (1983), pp. 599–603, 616.
74 Dufferin (ed. Milton), *Speeches of the Earl of Dufferin* (Toronto, 1878), p. 109, from a speech made to the Montreal Brigade, 24 May 1879.
75 J. S. Mill, *England and Ireland* (London, 1868), p. 8; Steele, Reform and integrity of empire, pp. 430–3; J. Pitts, *A Turn to Empire: the rise of imperial liberalism in Britain and France* (New Jersey, 2005), pp. 133, 136–7, 149.
76 Mill, *England*, p. 41; N. Capaldi, *John Stuart Mill: A Biography* (Cambridge, 2004), pp. 320, 324.
77 J. Caird, *The Irish Land Question* (London, 1869), p. 24. See also G. Fitzgibbon, *The Land Difficulty of Ireland with an Effort to Solve it* (London, 1869).
78 G. Campbell, *The Irish Land* (London and Dublin, 1869), pp. 4, 51, 85–7; G. Campbell, Land legislation for Ireland, *Fortnightly Review*, 19 (1881), pp. 18–19, 23–4, 29; E. D. Steele, Ireland and the Empire: imperial precedents for Gladstone's First Irish Land Act, *Historical Journal*, 11:1 (1968), pp. 64, 72–6; D. Omissi, A most arduous but a most noble duty: Gladstone and the British Raj in India, 1868–98, in M. E. Daly and K. T. Hoppen (eds), *Gladstone, Ireland and Beyond* (Dublin, 2011), pp. 181–2, 199.
79 Dufferin, *Irish Emigration and the Tenure of Land in Ireland* (Dublin, 1870), p. 1; Steele, Reform and integrity of empire, pp. 442–3; M. Bentley, *Politics without Democracy, 1815–1914: perception and preoccupation in British government* (Oxford, 1984), pp. 141–2; R. Foster, *Paddy and Mr Punch: connections in Irish and English History* (London, 1995), p. 239. Argyll also wrote rebuttals against land reform proposals for Ireland and Highland Scotland: J. W. Mason, The Duke of Argyll and the Land Question in late nineteenth century Britain, *Victorian Studies*, 21 (1978), pp. 149, 153, 169–70.
80 Dufferin, *Mr Mill's plan for the Pacification of Ireland examined* (London, 1868), p. 15, 35; J. Ridden, Making good citizens: national identity, religion and liberalism among the Irish elite, c. 1800–1850, unpublished PhD thesis (King's College London, 1998), pp. 7–9, 12–13, 18, 21.
81 Dowling, *Tenant Right*, pp. 290–7.
82 M. Davitt, *The Fall of Feudalism in Ireland* (London, 1904), p. xvii; M. Davitt, *Speech delivered by Michael Davitt in defence of the Land League* (London, 1890), pp. 187–212.
83 S. Den Otter, Thinking in Communities: late nineteenth century Liberals, idealists and the retrieval of community, in E. H. H. Green (ed.), *An Age of Transition: British Politics, 1880–1914* (Edinburgh, 1997), pp. 68, 76–8.

84 Nicolson, *Helen's Tower*, p. 85; BL, Gladstone Papers, Add MS 44151, ff. 18, Dufferin to Gladstone, 25 Apr. 1867 and ff. 24, Dufferin to Gladstone, 9 Mar. 1868; Black, *Economic Thought and the Irish Question*, pp. 64–5; Bentley, *Politics without Democracy*, p. 146; D. Thornley, The Irish Conservatives and home rule, 1869–73, *Irish Historical Studies*, xi, no. 43 (Mar. 1959), pp. 202–3.
85 He was by no means the only one: see G. F. Trench, *The Land Question: Are the landlords worth preserving? Or, forty years' management of an Irish estate* (London and Dublin, 1881); W. Bence-Jones, *The Life's Work in Ireland of a Landlord who tried to do his duty* (London, 1880).
86 PRONI, D1071, H/B/G/172, ff. 2, Gladstone to Dufferin, 18 May 1866; ff. 3, Gladstone to Dufferin, 13 Oct. 1869 and ff. 9, Gladstone to Dufferin, 3 Nov. 1869; H. C. G. Matthew, *The Gladstone Diaries: volume VII* (Oxford, 1978), pp. 160, 170; Bentley, *Lord Salisbury's World*, p. 111; Bentley, *Politics without Democracy*, pp. 146–7; H. C. G. Matthew, *Gladstone, 1809–1898* (Oxford, 1999), pp. 196–8, 436.
87 Increasingly, this became a cross-party view: Bentley, *Lord Salisbury's World*, pp. 121–3; Campbell, *Irish Establishment*, p. 48.
88 PRONI, D1071, H/B/C/95, ff. 30, Dufferin to Argyll, 11 Jan. 1869; D. Howell, The Land Question in nineteenth century Wales, Ireland and Scotland: a comparative study, *Agricultural History Review*, 61:1 (2013), pp. 84, 93, 99.
89 Thompson, *End of Liberal Ulster*, pp. 63, 79–80, 102.
90 PRONI, D1071, H/B/C/95, ff. 30, Dufferin to Argyll, 11 Jan. 1869, and A. Hawkins and J. Powell (eds), *The Journal of John Wodehouse, First Earl of Kimberley for 1862–1902* (London, 1997), entries for 16 Dec. 1868, p. 229, and 6 Feb. 1870, p. 265.
91 Thompson, *End of Liberal Ulster*, pp. 73–7.
92 Lyall, *Life of Dufferin*, p. 168; see also BL, Add MS 44151, Gladstone Papers, ff. 62, Dufferin to Gladstone, 16 Oct. 1869; ff. 64, Dufferin to Gladstone, 12 Nov. 1869 and HL Deb, 26 Jul. 1869, vol. 198, cc. 665–70; HL Deb, 29 Mar. 1870, vol. 200, cc. 788–828; HL Deb, 31 Mar. 1870, vol. 200, cc. 970–82; Purdue, *The Big House*, pp. 35–6; Bentley, *Politics without Democracy*, pp. 142–3, 146; Matthew, *Gladstone*, pp. 196–8.
93 Lyall, *Life of Dufferin*, p. 170. See HL Deb, 5 May 1870, vol. 201, cc. 265–8 and HL Deb, 14 Jun. 1870, vol. 202, cc. 4–98; Black, *Economic Thought and the Irish Question*, pp. 65, 67.
94 Lyall, *Life of Dufferin*, p. 170; Black, *Dufferin and Ava*, pp. 71, 75; Bentley, *Lord Salisbury's World*, pp. 99–100, 124.
95 PRONI, D1071, H/B/G/172/16, Gladstone to Dufferin, 16 Feb. 1870; BL, Gladstone Papers, ff. 89, Dufferin to Gladstone, 16 Feb. 1870; D. Cannadine, *Ornamentalism: how the British saw their empire* (London, 2001), p. 21.
96 BL, Gladstone papers, Add MS 44151, ff. 102, Dufferin to Gladstone, 13 Sept. 1871. He was awarded this promotion and became Viscount Clandeboye and Earl of Dufferin.
97 PRONI, D1071, H/B/C/95, ff. 56, Dufferin to Argyll, 21 Dec. 1871.
98 See, for instance, HL Deb, 16 Apr. 1875, vol. 223, cc. 1065–77.
99 BL, Gladstone papers, Add MS 44151, ff. 102, Dufferin to Gladstone, 13 Sept. 1871.
100 PRONI, D1071/A/A/5/1, for a copy of the *Northern Star* article, 8 Mar. 1870.
101 PRONI, D1071, A/K/1/B/20/1, Thomson to Dufferin, 10 Mar. 1870.
102 See, for instance, PRONI, D1071, A/K/1/B/30/1, Dufferin to Thomson, 3 Dec. 1880, describing an attack made in the *Morning News*; see also Curtis, Incumbered wealth, pp. 339–40, 365–6.
103 PRONI, D1071, H/B/C/95, ff. 77, Dufferin to Argyll, 15 May 1871.

78 Irish questions

104 Argyll resigned from Gladstone's cabinet in 1881. Black, *Economic Thought*, pp. 64, 67; F. Thompson, Attitudes to reform: political parties in Ulster and the Irish Land bill of 1881, *Irish Historical Studies*, 24 (1985), pp. 327–8, 336–9; N. M. Dawson, Letters from Inveraray: the eighth duke of Argyll's correspondence with the first marquess of Dufferin and Ava, with particular reference to Gladstone's Irish Land Acts, in H. MacQueen (ed.), *Miscellany Seven* (Edinburgh, 2015), pp. 362, 364, 371–7.
105 PRONI, D1071, H/B/C/95, ff. 70, Dufferin to Argyll, 7 May 1874.
106 PRONI, D1071, H/H/1/2, Dufferin to Lord Carnarvon, 29 May 1874; see also a similar comparison made between civil order in Ireland and Canada, H/H/1/3, Dufferin to Carnarvon, 29 Oct. 1875; Steele, Ireland and the Empire in the 1860s, pp. 64–5; Bitterman and McCallum, Upholding the land legislation, pp. 16–19; J. Moir, K. A. MacKirdy and Y. F. Zoltvany (eds), *Changing Perspectives in Canadian History: selected problems* (Ontario, 1971), p. 246; D. Wilson (ed.), *Irish Nationalism in Canada* (Toronto, 2009), pp. 3–8, 20–1.
107 Dufferin was not alone in this, of course: G. Peatling, Race and empire in nineteenth century British intellectual life: James Fitzjames Stephen, James Anthony Froude, Ireland and India, *Eire–Ireland*, 42:1 (2007), pp. 157, 159, 171; R. Romani, British views on Irish national character, 1800–1846: an intellectual history, *History of European Ideas*, 23:5–6 (1997), pp. 193–4, 201; S. Howe, *Ireland and Empire: colonial legacies in Irish history and culture* (Oxford, 2002), pp. 45, 49, 65–6.
108 PP 1881 [Cd. 2779, I, II, III] *Report and Evidence of Her Majesty's Commissioners of Inquiry into the working of the Landlord and Tenant (Ireland) Act, 1870, and the acts amending the same* [hereafter *Bessborough Evidence*] Dufferin, p. 1022, Q.33162.
109 R. W. Kirkpatrick, Origins and development of the land war in mid-Ulster, 1879–85, in F. S. L. Lyons and R. A. J. Hawkins (eds), *Ireland under the Union: varieties of tension* (Oxford, 1980), pp. 202, 208, 221, 232; Thomson, *End of Liberal Ulster*, pp. 170–7; D. A. Hamer, The Irish question and Liberal politics, 1886–1894, *Historical Journal*, 12:3 (1969), pp. 511, 513, 515, 518, 522; L. M. Geary, *The Plan of Campaign, 1886–1891* (Cork, 1986), pp. 2–3, 7–9, 140–2.
110 T. Dooley, *The Decline of the Big House in Ireland: a study of Irish landed families, 1860–1960* (Dublin, 2001), pp. 91–6; T. Dooley, Landlords and the land question, 1879–1909, in C. King (ed.), *Famine, Land and Culture in Ireland* (Dublin, 2001), pp. 118–20; Purdue, *The Big House*, pp. 31–63.
111 P. Bew, *Enigma: a new life of Charles Stewart Parnell* (London, 2011), p. 54; Dooley, Landlords and the land question, pp. 116–22; Davitt, *Speech Delivered*, pp. 187–212.
112 L. P. Curtis, Landlord responses to the Irish Land War, 1879–1987, *Eire–Ireland*, Fall–Winter (2003), p. 137.
113 Purdue, *The Big House*, pp. 21–3.
114 Bentley, *Lord Salisbury's World*, pp. 109, 111.
115 Dewey, Celtic agrarian legislation, p. 59; J. W. Mason, Political economy and the response to socialism in Britain, 1870–1914, *Historical Journal*, 23:3 (1980), pp. 565–8, 578.
116 Bentley, *Politics without Democracy*, pp. 168–74; Dooley, Landlords and the land question, pp. 122, 127; Gailey, *Lost Imperialist*, pp. 37–8, 106, 109.
117 PRONI, D1071, A/K/1/C/4/1, Dufferin to Howe, 13 Feb. 1882; see also A/K/1/C/4/2, Dufferin to Howe, 22 Aug. 1882; 26 Oct. 1882; Bull, Irish land and British politics, pp. 136–7.
118 K. Mulhern, The Intellectual Duke: George Douglas Campbell, 8th Duke of Argyll, 1823–1900, Unpublished PhD thesis (University of Edinburgh, 2006); 8th Duke of Argyll, New Irish Land Bill, *Nineteenth Century*, 9 (1881); Matthew, *Gladstone*, p. 446.

119 PRONI, D1071, H/B/C/95, ff. 83, Dufferin to Argyll, 6 Jan. 1880; Bigelow, *Fiction, Famine*, p. 115; 8th Duke of Argyll, A model land law: a reply to Arthur Williams MP, *Fortnightly Review*, 41 (1887), pp. 764, 784.
120 PRONI, D1071, A/K/1/B/20/1, Thomson to Dufferin, 10 Mar. 1870; R. V. Comerford, The land war and the politics of distress, in W. E. Vaughan (ed.), *A New History of Ireland, vol. 6: Ireland under Union, 1801–1921, II, 1870–1921* (Oxford, 2010), pp. 28, 42, 46–7.
121 For example, PRONI, D1071, A/K/1/B/31/1, Dufferin to Thomson, 18 Feb. 1881.
122 PRONI, D1071, A/K/1/B/31/1, Dufferin to Thomson, 22 Feb. 1881; BL, Gladstone Papers, Add MS 44151, ff. 153, John Patterson to Gladstone, 11 Feb. 1881; Gailey, *Lost Imperialist*, pp. 160–3.
123 Purdue, *The Big House*, pp. 50, 52.
124 British Library, Gladstone Papers Add MS 44151, Vol. LXVI, ff. 303, Dufferin to Gladstone, 29 Dec. 1897.
125 Bentley, *Lord Salisbury's World*, pp. 118–19; Foster, *Paddy and Mr Punch*, p. 239; O. MacDonagh, *States of Mind: a study of Anglo-Irish conflict 1780–1980* (London, 1983), pp. 34, 36–9, 42, 48–9.
126 PRONI, D1071, A/K/1/B/30/1, Dufferin to Howe, 3 Dec. 1880; A/K/1/B/31/1, Dufferin to Howe, 18 Feb. 1881; 20 Feb. 1881; Lyall, *Life of Dufferin*, pp. 182–4; Nicolson, *Helen's Tower*, p. 82.
127 BL, Gladstone Papers, Add MS. 44151, ff. 154, Dufferin to Gladstone, 22 Feb. 1881. See also ff. 167, Dufferin to Gladstone, 10 Mar. 1881; ff. 169, Dufferin to Gladstone, 10 Mar. 1881. Dufferin was Ambassador to Russia and living in St Petersburg at this time.
128 BL, Gladstone Papers, Add MS. 44151, ff. 154, Dufferin to Gladstone, 22 Feb. 1881.
129 BL, Gladstone Papers, Add MS. 44151, ff. 154, Dufferin to Gladstone, 22 Feb. 1881. Dufferin put this figure, made up of various abatements, improvements and cancellation of arrears, at £102,476; Thompson, *End of Liberal Ulster*, pp. 178–88.
130 BL, Gladstone Papers, Add MS. 44151, ff. 154, Dufferin to Gladstone, 22 Feb. 1881; see Nicolson, *Helen's Tower*, p. 169, for a picture of an increasingly pessimistic Dufferin.
131 Argyll, New Irish Land Bill,; Argyll, Land reformers, *Contemporary Review*, 48 (1885); J. W. Mason, The Duke of Argyll and the land question in late nineteenth century Britain, *Victorian Studies*, 21:2 (1978), pp. 149–50, 152–3.
132 PRONI, D1071, H/B/C/95, ff. 89, Dufferin to Argyll, 2 Sept. 1880.
133 PRONI, D1071, H/B/C/95, ff. 89, Dufferin to Argyll, 2 Sept. 1880.
134 PRONI, D1071, H/B/C/95, ff. 89, Dufferin to Argyll, 2 Sept. 1880; H/B/C/95, ff. 96, Dufferin to Argyll, 5 Jan. 1881; H/B/C/95, ff. 97, Dufferin to Argyll, 9 Jan. 1881. Bayly, Ireland, India and the Empire, pp. 377, 389–92.
135 N. Whelehan, *The Dynamiters: Irish nationalism and political violence in the wider world, 1867–1900* (Cambridge, 2012), pp. 1, 3, 20.
136 *Bessborough Evidence*; Matthew, *Gladstone*, pp. 439, 441; A. Warren, Gladstone, land and social reconstruction in Ireland, 1881–1887, *Parliamentary History*, 2 (1983), p. 155; Thompson, *End of Liberal Ulster*, pp. 238–9.
137 For context, see R. W. Kirkpatrick, Origins and development of the land war in mid-Ulster, 1879–85, in F. S. L. Lyons and R. A. J. Hawkins (eds), *Ireland under the Union: varieties of tension: essays in honour of T. W. Moody* (Oxford, 1980), pp. 201–35.
138 Burn, Free trade in land, p. 65.
139 *Bessborough Evidence*, Dufferin, pp. 1015–17, Q.33039–33066.
140 *Bessborough Evidence*, Dufferin, p. 1020, Q.33127.
141 *Bessborough Evidence*, Dufferin, p. 1021, Q.33139, Q.33142; p. 1022, Q.33145, Q.33149a.

80 Irish questions

142 *Bessborough Evidence*, Dufferin, p. 1023–4, Q.33168; M. Rendle, Conservatism and revolution: the all-Russian Union of landowners, 1916–18, *Slavonic and East European Review*, 84:3 (2006), pp. 481–3, 505.
143 *Bessborough Evidence*, Dufferin, p. 1024, Q.33168.
144 *Bessborough Evidence*, Dufferin, p. 1025, Q.33189.
145 PRONI, D1071, A/K/1/C/3/2, Dufferin to Sir George Young, 16 Jun. 1881.
146 PRONI, D1071, A/K/1/C/3/1, Dufferin to Howe, 3 Jan. 1881.
147 BL, Gladstone Papers, Add MS 44151, ff. 146, Dufferin to Gladstone, 7 Dec. 1880; ff. 148, Dufferin to Gladstone, 24 Dec. 1881; PRONI, D1071, H/B/C/95, ff. 104, Dufferin to Argyll, 4 Mar. 1881; H/B/C/95, ff. 108, Dufferin to Argyll, 6 Aug. 1881; Lyall, *Life of Dufferin*, p. 287; Matthew, *Gladstone*, pp. 442, 446; Warren, Gladstone, land and social reconstruction, pp. 157–9.
148 For instance, PRONI, D1071, A/K/1/C/2/2, Howe to Dufferin, 11 Nov. 1880.
149 See, for instance, PRONI, D1071, A/K/1/C/4/2, Dufferin to Howe, 22 Aug. 1882 and 26 Oct. 1882; Nicolson, *Helen's Tower*, pp. 84–5.
150 PRONI, D1071, H/B/C/95/93, Dufferin to Argyll, 24 Dec. 1880; H/B/C/95, ff. 102, Dufferin to Argyll, 18 Feb. 1881; Curtis, Landlord responses, p. 167; Bentley, *Politics without Democracy*, pp. 167–8; Matthew, *Gladstone*, p. 451.
151 Mason, The Duke of Argyll and the land question, pp. 157–61.
152 See E. A. Cameron, *Land for the People? The British government and the Scottish Highlands, c.1880–c.1925* (East Linton, 1996); for a Welsh perspective, see M. Cragoe, A contemptible mimic of the Irish: the land question in Victorian Wales, in M. Cragoe and P. Readman (eds), *The Land Question in Britain, 1750–1950* (Basingstoke, 2010), pp. 92, 102; Dewey, Celtic agrarian legislation, pp. 61–8.
153 PRONI, D1071, H/B/C/95, ff. 119, Argyll to Dufferin, 31 Jan. 1891; for contemporary context, see A. Mackenzie, Ireland and the Irish Land Act from a Highland point of view, *Celtic Magazine*, X (1884–5), pp. 17–27; G. Campbell, The tenure of land in India, in J. W. Probyn (ed.), *Systems of Land Tenure in Various Countries* (London, 1876), pp. 150, 155, 183; and, later, Davitt, *The Fall of Feudalism in Ireland*, pp. 79–95. Bayly, Ireland, India and the Empire, pp. 391–2.
154 Purdue, *The Big House*, p. 68; Warren, Gladstone, land and social reconstruction, pp. 163–5, 168–9; L. P. Curtis, *Coercion and Conciliation in Ireland, 1880–1892: a study in conservative unionism* (New Jersey, 1963), pp. 138–49; Foster, *Paddy and Mr Punch*, p. 257; Gailey, *Lost Imperialist*, pp. 160–4.
155 PRONI, D1071, A/K/1/C/17/1, Dufferin to Howe, 2 Jun. 1893. See also Sir Randolph Churchill's view on land purchase as a measure to 'greatly conciliate all Irish landlords',: BL, India Office Select Materials, Mss Eur IOR, Reel 4351, ff. 60, Churchill to Dufferin, 24 Jul. 1885; and that of Lord Hartington, PRONI, D1071, H/B/C/243, ff. 14, Hartington to Dufferin, 27 Jan. 1889 and ff. 17, Hartington to Dufferin, 14 Sept. 1890.
156 A. T. Q. Stewart, *The Ulster Crisis* (London, 1967), pp. 34, 37, 43–4.
157 F. H. A. Aalen, Constructive Unionism and the shaping of rural Ireland, c. 1880–1921, *Rural History*, 4:2 (1993), pp. 140–2; N. C. Fleming, The landed elite, power and Ulster Unionism, in D. G. Boyce and A. O'Day, (eds), *The Ulster Crisis 1885–1921* (Basingstoke, 2005), pp. 86, 88–9, 103.
158 Davitt, *Speech Delivered*, pp. 187–212, for a sample of criticism of landlords; M. Bence-Jones, *Twilight of the Ascendancy* (London, 1987), p. 71.
159 A. Jackson, *The Ulster Party: Irish Unionists in the House of Commons, 1884–1911* (Oxford, 1989), pp. 150–4, 167.
160 *Bessborough Evidence*, Dufferin, p. 1024, Q.33177; BL, Gladstone Papers, Add MS 44151, ff. 267, Dufferin to Gladstone, 15 Sept. 1888; Curtis, *Coercion and Conciliation in Ireland*, p. 138.

Irish questions 81

161 PRONI, D1071, H/B/C/95, ff. 135, Dufferin to Argyll, 8 Dec. 1894; see also Hatfield House, Papers of the 3rd Marquess of Salisbury, ff. 41, Dufferin to Salisbury, 31 Aug. 1889; Curtis, Incumbered wealth, p. 355.
162 T. W. Guinnane and R. I. Miller, The limits to land reform: the land acts in Ireland, 1870–1909, *Economic Development and Cultural Change*, 45 (1997), pp. 591, 598.
163 Dufferin believed in the potential for Ireland to reap the benefits of imperial rule: Aalen, Constructive Unionism, pp. 137–8; D. G. Boyce, *Nationalism in Ireland* (Abingdon, 2005), pp. 154–6, 170–1, 228; R. B. McDowell, *The Irish Administration, 1801–1914* (London, 1964), pp. 52–6, 68–9; S. Checkland, *The Elgins, 1766–1917: a tale of aristocrats, proconsuls and their wives* (Aberdeen, 1988), p. 216.
164 A. Jackson, *Home Rule: An Irish History, 1800–2000* (Oxford, 2004), p. 39; Davitt, *Fall of Feudalism*, pp. 79–85; D. Thornley, *Isaac Butt and Home Rule* (London, 1964); D. Thornley, The Irish Conservatives and home rule, 1869–73, *Irish Historical Studies*, 11, 43 (1959), pp. 204–5, 221–2; D. Brundage, *Irish Nationalists in America: the politics of exile, 1798–1998* (Oxford, 2016), pp. 4–6, 88–9; Comerford, Isaac Butt and the home rule party, pp. 1–4; P. Townend, *The Road to Home Rule: anti-imperialism and the Irish national movement* (Madison, 2016), pp. 3–16, 17–37.
165 Jackson, *Home Rule*, pp. 49–52, 62–6; J. Parry, *The Rise and Fall of Liberal Government in Victorian Britain* (New Haven, 1993), pp. 294–5, 300–3.
166 Porter has argued, for example, that Gladstone was attempting to liberate some colonies (Ireland, the Transvaal) in B. Porter, Gladstone and imperialism, in M. E. Daly and K. T. Hopkins (eds), *Gladstone, Ireland and Beyond* (Dublin, 2011), p. 172.
167 Unlike Argyll; see 8th Duke of Argyll, *Irish Nationalism: an appeal to history* (London, 1893), or his future son-in-law Ronald Munro-Ferguson, who supported Irish home rule: Gailey, *Lost Imperialist*, p. 327; A. Jackson, *The Ulster Party: Irish Unionists in the House of Commons, 1884–1911* (Oxford, 1984), p. 134; P. Davis, The liberal unionist party and the Irish policy of Lord Salisbury's government, 1886–1892, *Historical Journal*, 18:1 (1975), pp. 88, 100–4; U. S. Mehta, *Liberalism and Empire: a study in nineteenth century British Liberal thought* (Chicago, 1999), pp. 1–7, 11–15, 24, 30.
168 BL, India Office Select Materials, Mss Eur IOR, Reel 4351, ff. 32, Queen Victoria to Dufferin, 21 May 1886.
169 BL, India Office Select Materials, Mss Eur IOR, Reel 4351, ff. 1, Churchill to Dufferin, 16 Apr. 1886; ff. 19, Kimberley to Dufferin, 16 Apr. 1886; W. T. Russell, *Ireland and the Empire: a review* (London, 1901), p. vi–iii, x.
170 T. Koditschek, *Liberalism, Imperialism, and the Historical Imagination: nineteenth century visions of a greater Britain* (Cambridge, 2011), pp. 314–35; B. Porter, *The Absent-Minded Imperialists: empire, society and culture in Britain* (Oxford, 2004), pp. 227–31, 244.
171 PRONI, D1071, H/B/B/35, ff. 6, Sir Samuel Baker to Dufferin, 14 Dec. 1888; for similar tales of woe, see D1071, H/B/C/95, ff. 115, Argyll to Dufferin, 19 Feb. 1889; D1071, H/B/D/252, ff. 24, Sir Mountstuart Grant Duff to Dufferin, 8 Dec. 1890; Gailey, *Lost Imperialist*, pp. 106, 109.
172 Bayly, Ireland, India and the Empire, pp. 391–2; Brasted, Indian nationalist development, pp. 37, 40, 42–3 and, especially, 44–6; Matthew, *Gladstone*, p. 437.
173 Such as Lord Lansdowne and Lord Mayo: P. A. Townend, *The Road to Home Rule: anti-imperialism and the Irish national movement* (Madison, Wisconsin, 2016); Jackson, *The Ulster Party*, pp. 131–7.

Irish questions

174 L. P. Curtis, *Anglo-Saxons and Celts: a study of anti-Irish prejudice in Victorian England* (Bridgeport, 1968), pp. 74–88; I. Sheehy, The view from Fleet Street: Irish nationalist journalists in London and their attitudes towards empire, 1892–1898, in S. J. Potter (ed.), *Newspapers and Empire in Ireland and Britain* (Dublin, 2004), p. 148.
175 He was, however, a proponent of the 'constructive unionism' of this period, Aalen, Constructive Unionism, pp. 138–9; R. McMahon and A. Newby, Introduction – Ireland and Finland, 1860–1930: comparative and transnational histories, *Irish Historical Studies*, 41:160 (2017), pp. 166–8, 174.
176 Aalen, Constructive unionism, p. 161.
177 Lyall, *Life of Dufferin*, pp. 435, 497–9; Porter, Gladstone and imperialism, p. 172; Gailey, *Lost Imperialist*, pp. 332. He was far from alone in this fear, of course: Bentley, *Lord Salisbury's World*, p. 235; Steele, J. S. Mill and the Irish question, p. 425; P. Davis, The Liberal Unionist Party and the Irish Policy of Lord Salisbury's government, 1886–1892, *Historical Journal*, 18 (1975), pp. 103–4.
178 BL, India Office Select Materials, Mss Eur IOR, Reel 4351, ff. 12, Dufferin to Kimberley, 21 Mar. 1886.
179 Steele, J. S. Mill and the Irish question, p. 431; Cannadine, *Ornamentalism*, pp. 5–6.
180 BL, India Office Select Materials, Mss Eur IOR, Reel 4351, ff. 17, Dufferin to Kimberley, 26 Apr. 1886.
181 Curtis, *Anglo-Saxons and Celts*, pp. 78–80, 98–9; T. Foley and M. O'Connor (eds), *Ireland and India: colonies, culture and empire* (Dublin, 2006), pp. xiii, xviii; T. Ballantyne, The sinews of empire: Ireland, India and the construction of British colonial knowledge, in T. MacDonagh (ed.) *Was Ireland a Colony? Economics, Politics and Culture in Nineteenth Century Ireland* (Dublin, 2005), pp. 146–9, 158.
182 Gailey, *Lost Imperialist*, pp. 262–3; A. Porter, Empires in the mind, in P. J. Marshall (ed.), *The Cambridge Illustrated History of the British Empire* (Cambridge, 1996), pp. 185, 218–19, 223.
183 Curtis, *Anglo-Saxons and Celts*, pp. 98–105; Stewart, *Ulster Crisis*, pp. 34, 37.
184 BL, India Office Select Materials, Mss Eur IOR, Reel 4351, ff. 17, Dufferin to Kimberley, 26 Apr. 1886.
185 BL, Gladstone Papers, Add Ms 44151, ff. 267, Dufferin to Gladstone, 15 Sept. 1888; ff. 302, Dufferin to Gladstone, 4 Jun. 1896; Hatfield House, Papers of the 3rd Marquess of Salisbury, ff. 19, Dufferin to Salisbury, 11 Aug. 1887; ff. 22, Dufferin to Salisbury, 13 Nov. 1887; Omissi, A most arduous but most noble duty, pp. 181, 196–9; A. Gailey, *Ireland and the Death of Kindness: the experience of constructive unionism, 1890–1905* (Cork, 1987), pp. 3, 10; E. D. Steele, *Palmerston and Liberalism 1855–1865* (Cambridge, 1991), pp. 317–9, 329–32; Gailey, *Lost Imperialist*, pp. 290, 329.
186 W. C. Sellar and R. J. Yeatman, *1066 And All That* (London, 1930), p. 108; Gailey, *Lost Imperialist*, pp. 102–3.
187 L. P. Curtis, The Anglo-Irish predicament, *Twentieth Century Studies*, 4 (1970), p. 44.

4 Will to rule

> He [Dufferin] talked – at first to me directly, then sliding into a reverie – of his work in India, Canada, and the world at large. I had seen administrative machinery from beneath, all stripped and overheated. This was the first time I had listened to one who had handled it from above. And unlike the generality of Viceroys, Lord Dufferin *knew*. Of all his revelations and reminiscences, the sentence that stays with me is: 'And so, you see, there can be no room,' (or was it 'allowance'?) for good intentions in one's work.[1]

'His present difficult burden'[2]

This chapter examines Dufferin's relationship to imperial governance and empire as a starting point for a wider discussion of landed, aristocratic engagement in implementing colonial rule globally in the nineteenth century. What were the specific contributions made by the many landed and aristocratic men – such as Dufferin – appointed into the top echelons of colonial administration in the nineteenth century? The question is important because of their numerical and cultural dominance of the highest-ranking imperial posts, which were hardly ever filled by commoners or the non-landed. The contribution of the landed and titled elite was as much cultural and intellectual as it was practical and political, though. Through their monopoly of senior imperial roles, they created a governing culture, a will to rule of which Dufferin was at the heart. This chapter places Dufferin explicitly into his aristocratic context, outwith the constraints and pressures of particular geographies, in order to discuss the aristocratic aspects of British imperial dominion in the nineteenth century.[3] Dufferin was at the heart of the aristocratic monopoly of imperial governance and his imperialism was firmly grounded in the conviction that the British aristocracy could provide 'good' governance to rule the world. He could extoll the benefit of British rule for the colonies, but there were inherent weaknesses in the model that his experiences in Ireland should have taught him.

Within historiographies of the personnel of empire, emphasis has been traditionally laid on upper middle-class and professional colonial officials, civil servants, merchants and officers because, numerically, they constituted the bulk of the governing imperial classes. They were both the intellectual and practical engines of empire: those generations of missionaries, doctors, surveyors, revenue collectors, military officers and others who actually ran the show, with the aristocrats at the top constituting a ceremonial froth, but little more.[4] Dufferin's career demonstrates that they were more than ornament, both practically and also in terms of understandings of British, Irish and imperial society.[5] Aristocrats sought to replicate their class values and system in the empire while attempting to maintain a delicate balancing act between metropolitan power and the power devolved onto the man 'on the spot'.[6] Dufferin described this responsibility as a source of 'great anxiety', and he struggled to, 'work in a spirit of earnest and hearty loyalty towards my employers and to place myself as much as possible in sympathy with them. I have always been able to do this without in any way withholding from them my independent opinions.'[7] He and his peers did more than simply execute instructions, however; they were instrumental in developing the specific character of British imperial rule on the ground.[8] The scale of the task they undertook should not be underestimated, particularly the burden of responsibility for British policy and reputation, which they believed they were born to shoulder. As landowners, legislators and statesmen, they regarded themselves as the natural governing class, with the requisite education and status to take on political and imperial responsibility. This did not mean they never felt pressure, however; 'Indeed when I consider the heavy responsibilities attaching to my office and the enormous areas over which they extend', wrote Dufferin after two years in India, 'I often stand aghast at the spectacle.'[9] This discussion will be divided into two linked sections: the first will consider aristocratic engagement with empire in theory, and the second will examine the translation of those ideals into the application of colonial rule in practical terms. Dufferin provides us with an example through which the wider culture of aristocratic imperial power can be explored, in part because of his Irish origins. An examination of the lists of imperial office holders of the nineteenth century shows that, as well as their predominantly landed or titled antecedents, they were also mainly of Scottish or Irish origin, in either title or estate. By contrast, the cabinet secretaries that held the imperial briefs in Westminster at the Colonial and India Offices were more often English, or, where they owned lands and titles in both England or Scotland and Ireland, regarded their English estates as the basis for their primary identity. This chapter will discuss why that may have been the case and the impact it had, considering the insider/outsider status that Dufferin struggled with, as did many others of his fellow aristocratic peers of the 'Celtic fringe'.[10]

Although the members of the landed aristocracy were regularly satirised by contemporaries for their perceived laziness, anti-intellectualism and frivolous, immoral lives, there was a good deal of coherent thinking around aristocratic purpose, service and duty as it related to Britain's empire project.[11] This goes to the heart of what Britain and Ireland's aristocracy thought they were for, and how their rights and privileges were justified. As a class whose position was inherited, their chief strength as they saw it lay in the continuity they represented: of family, position and service. Governing characteristics were seen as inherited, not something that could be earned or merited. This was then supplemented by a specific type of education in certain institutions that stressed expertise on classical history and culture, particularly that of Rome and its empire.[12] As a dutiful aristocracy, a culture of governance was performed and, as political challenge to their dominance increased domestically, it increasingly shifted to the imperial context. In the past, that service had been expressed chiefly through military means, in support of the Crown through turbulent centuries. By the nineteenth century, as military service was increasingly professionalised, aristocratic duty shifted to political and colonial leadership, representing the Crown overseas and upholding British interests in Europe. Dufferin was recognised by contemporaries as being an early pioneer of this approach.[13] The management of landed estates was seen as a crucial training ground for Westminster and overseas administration. Dufferin's landed inheritance gave him all the experience he needed and, more importantly, he was part of and understood the cultural expressions of aristocratic character and power. A number of other aspects of the intellectual underpinning of aristocratic governance flowed from the central concept of the service aristocracy. One was its impact on understandings of class structures among British communities throughout the empire, and the extent to which they reflected the aristocratic ideal. It is tempting to assume that the dominance of aristocrats in the top roles translated into a replica of domestic class structures, with an upper middle-class layer of colonial professionals and officials, and a working-class layer consisting of the army and navy, migrant settlers and suchlike. It has been argued that many aristocrats were attracted to the empire for this very reason: that the challenges of domestic political and social reform could be escaped, and old certainties preserved.[14] It is arguable how far any of these certainties were in place in the colonial context, however; although wrapped into debates around race and gender, class and hierarchy were as fluid in the empire as they were in the domestic context.[15]

In Dufferin's view, British governance was principally about the art of the possible; pragmatism expressed as a system, supported by precedent, tradition and inherited values, as well as his experiences as a landlord. This was the bedrock of the sense of imperial 'mission' or ideology among colonial aristocrats, which framed a more general intellectual agenda for empire. Over and above all was the concept of duty: empire as a burdensome exile from the beating heart of civilisation: London and all it represented.[16] On his appointment to Paris in 1892, for instance, Dufferin wrote to his Indian colleague and later biographer Sir Alfred Lyall that, 'at last, too, after having lived for sixteen years always upon the outskirts of civilisation, we shall be placed in its very heart'.[17] In the same way that their forebears had to undertake often perilous military service, nineteenth-century aristocratic imperialists resided across the world in dangerous climates and in what they regarded as less civilised societies to ensure the maintenance

86 Will to rule

of British power overseas.[18] This was no easy task, as Dufferin constantly complained: in India he noted the 'exceptional anxieties and difficulties, and the burden and responsibilities of this government are very heavy'.[19] He described it to Granville as, 'very like a man who has been suddenly pitched head foremost into a cauldron of hot water, who has risen to the top, choking and spluttering, and who finds it very difficult to keep his head above the rising inundation of business that pours in on him from every side'.[20] Symbolising British power was aristocratic management of its pomp and ceremony; the honours, the soirees and *durbars*, that endless stream of occasions and the grand tours that took these displays on the road for maximum impact.[21] This was more than ornamentalism: it was display with a purpose, which generated both intended and unintended consequences.[22] Aristocrats understood themselves to be the most suitable figureheads for these ceremonial activities: as representatives of the Crown, as the owners of landed estates and as individuals trained in the ceremonial from public school to Parliament.[23] As such, the presence of members of the British royal family in the empire was also usually welcomed, as Dufferin pointed out in the case of India: 'Speaking from a political point of view I have always considered it a very good thing that one of H. M.s sons should be in India. The presence of the Duchess of Connaught also exercises a very wholesome effect upon Indian society.'[24] The monarchy and aristocracy were one family, and regarded themselves as the most fitting representatives of British power overseas.

This challenges assumptions about aristocratic attitudes to the hard graft of governance and administration. After all, one of the defining features of the landed classes was their leisured status; their incomes secured from rent rolls and investments, they were free to undertake either a life of pure leisure, engaging in literary, architectural and artistic pursuits, or political leadership. As such, many worked hard, especially those in Parliament, government and cabinet. Imperial office also entailed a good deal of work, as well as a requirement to live overseas. Dufferin continually stressed these sacrifices to his friends and colleagues, particularly because he was relatively old (over forty) by the time he embarked on his imperial career, ending it as the oldest Indian viceroy in the history of the office. Perhaps because of this, his colleagues remember him as having a somewhat laid-back approach to his workload, happy to delegate to his officials and unwilling to get bogged down in the detail of questions and decisions unless he had to.[25] Sir Henry Durand wrote after Dufferin's death that he would, in vain, attempt to draw his attention to particular cases: 'My dear fellow', he would say, 'I cannot go into that. Life is too short.'[26] Perhaps they were missing the point: inaction and tact were not necessarily evidence of laziness but perhaps of sound judgement, masterly inactivity. By contrast, there was universal recognition that he undertook with energy and skill the ceremonial aspects of office, particularly in Canada and India. We might draw three conclusions from this. The first is that Dufferin stressed the ceremonial over the administrative in his imperial roles, for reasons that will be explored. Second, he knew when to leave questions to the experts. Dufferin saw his role as essentially managerial in nature, acting as umpire between the different factions of the actual government (whether elected or autocratic) of the colonial territories to which he was appointed, providing a steadying hand where required, ensuring 'good' governance was being employed, without personally carrying it out. Lastly, as both the man at the top and the man on the spot, he had to take ultimate responsibility for any policy, action or programme undertaken by the government, and it was this responsibility that aristocrats were conditioned to carry, not day-to-day governance. In a domestic parallel, we can see this pattern in the management of landed estates, where owners would rarely be involved in the daily workings of their estates, instead relying on land agents to carry out that work, while they shouldered the ultimate responsibility for conditions on their land and, equally, the ultimate reward of income and status derived from it.[27]

Linked to the imperial mission was the concept of progress, which was understood and instrumentalised to justify both British and aristocratic rule. Progress was defined in many ways, often contradictory, and was used by British imperialists to link the history of 'Britain' (more often England) to imperial dominion. It was framed politically, in terms of institutions and cultures, and economically, socially, and religiously. Crucially, it was also framed temporally, as part of the past, present and future of Britain and its imperial territories. As these were all subject to interpretation and debate, progress as a concept was also fluid and subject to geographical and historical pressures. There was also a specific aristocratic definition of progress, developed on British and Irish landed estates, which was then taken overseas to be challenged and adapted according to circumstances that changed over time. This is a transnational study of the movement of ideas, therefore; about the nature of the aristocratic ideal of progress and their role as leaders of that process among 'inferiors', however defined, including by race, gender or class.[28]

This chapter examines the application of aristocratic colonial rule in practice, where loyalty, unity, power and progress were made real through a variety of approaches including political autocracy, economic dominion, and state violence and terror. Imperial administration required autocratic rule in which violence was an integral part and it was this that aristocrats believed they were able to provide. Firm but just rule, as Dufferin would put it, which the landed and aristocratic classes brought from their landed estates, where hierarchy, loyalty and paternalism were enforced and expressed though a range of practical and symbolic means. One of these practical applications of aristocratic will to rule was how borders were managed as 'buffers' between the British empire in India and other empires – those of Russia and China – in the later nineteenth century. By examining British treatment of Afghanistan and Burma in the 1880s when Dufferin was Indian viceroy, we can examine the ways in which aristocratic understandings of power were practically elucidated, thrown into relief by the importance of diplomatic nicety and the symbols of power as translated through territorial borders, issues that also exercised them on their landed estates.

By looking at both the theory and practice of aristocratic will to rule, Dufferin is set into his wider class context, so that his activities in particular geographical and temporal contexts can be better understood. Although it is possible to track a distinctively aristocratic contribution to both the practical administration and intellectual underpinnings of empire in this period, this does not mean that there was a single, static aristocratic concept of governance that was rigidly applied in the same way across the world.[29] Instead, it is by looking at the challenges to and shifts in aristocratic thinking that we can unpick their expectations and understanding of their place in the political, cultural and economic fabric of Britain, Ireland and its empire.

Aristocratic abstractions – the man at the top

Aristocrats have rarely been lauded for their intellectual contributions to British and Irish life. They were widely pilloried for being anti-intellectual and increasingly challenged by the idea that merit, not birth, should be the key to advancement: what John Stuart Mill attacked as the 'superstitions of landlordism', a view that had particular traction in Ireland.[30] Nonetheless, they maintained a tight grip on the political and practical applications of colonial rule, and so it is important to ask what they *thought* about the empire: what it was for, where it had come from and what it should be. There are four themes around which many landed, imperial peers constructed their thinking on empire. First, their understanding of the purpose of the empire and how a specifically aristocratic form of governance was required for the security, expansion and justification of that purpose. Empire has often been perceived as a middle-class venture, not an aristocratic one, but there was an aristocratic conception of imperial mission that both converged and diverged from that of other classes. Second, and closely related, was the existential purpose of aristocracy. The nineteenth century was an anxious time of fast-paced change, and aristocrats were required to adapt to the challenges and opportunities presented by industrialisation, urbanisation and political reform, amongst others.[31] When we view his career through an imperial lens, we can see that Dufferin was a relatively successful example of this adaptation. This section will examine the dichotomous concepts of a service aristocracy in relation to the empire and the intellectual underpinnings of aristocratic dominance in the upper echelons of the colonial service. Next, the concept of progress will be discussed in relation to the aristocratic contribution to thinking about empire. Was there a specifically aristocratic understanding of progress – past, present and future – and how was this constructed and applied to empire? Lastly, the ways in which aristocratic imperialists understood their role as both a duty and a burden – 'exiled' from the heart of civilised, metropolitan life to perform their duty, as members of an aristocracy of service to Crown and country – will be discussed.[32]

The underpinning philosophies espoused by governing aristocrats were often only articulated under circumstances of pressure and challenge. Otherwise, they were simply assumed and implied, part of their mental furniture, expressed through actions not words. These assumptions were developed through a set of institutions and cultures that nearly all aristocrats were part of, as a tightly knit, interrelated, intermarried and numerically small elite.[33] The first of these was the public school and university system, with which nearly all male aristocrats came into contact by the middle of the nineteenth century. Dufferin is an excellent exemplar of this; after a few years of private tuition, then attendance at a small preparatory school, he was sent to Eton, where he came to know many of his future colleagues, Lords Salisbury, Carnarvon and Kimberley among them. Then, on to Christ Church, that most aristocratic of the Oxford colleges, where Dufferin built the foundations for his glittering imperial career.[34] As well as consolidating a sense of privilege and building networks, the education he received fed into colonial governance in sometimes surprising ways.[35] Dufferin reported in 1887 on a recent meeting of the Indian National Congress, reassuring Lord Cross, then Secretary of State for India that, 'the character of the discussions was very childish, and reminded the auditor rather of an Eton or Harrow Debating Society or even of the Oxford or Cambridge union'.[36] The curriculum at these institutions emphasised the Classics, particularly the literature and history of Rome and its empire which, in turn, established certain cultural norms among the future governing classes, which they applied to their landed estates and colonial territories.[37] Lyall notes of Dufferin's Oxford education that, 'his bent was obviously towards political discussion, not only in regards to points of past history, but also to questions of practical administration'.[38] This emphasis on the Classics as a rulebook for governance fed the aristocratic classes lessons in the 'science' of administration, of Westminster as a modern Rome, a beacon of civilisation shining in the darkness of colonial barbarism.[39] In 1884, for instance, Dufferin was turning over in his mind how the border between Afghanistan and Russia might be protected and he suggested as one option, 'to follow the example of the Romans and plant 30,000 English emigrants as a military colony in the valley of the Heri Rud', although he did also admit this would be 'far from practicable.[40] Roman imperial history also served as a warning from the past; that, without a moral core, empire would fail.[41] The Roman empire failed to endure, it was generally agreed, because their empire was immoral and so built on foundations of sand. That because it was based on slavery and pagan belief, its imperial and aristocratic classes descending into debauchery, it was bound to collapse.[42] Anxious British governors tried to console themselves as to the longevity of the British empire by remembering that theirs was the empire that had abolished the slave trade and slavery; that theirs was a Christian, moral empire that was bringing the light to barbarian populations.[43] Lastly came the assurance that landed power automatically translated into political and imperial power, so that it could both support the imperial monarchy, and the right to rule (and its concomitant burdens).[44] The power of these four underpinning strands of aristocratic confidence and self-understanding should not be underestimated; institutions, culture and proximity reinforced them powerfully so that, even when serving in far-flung parts of the imperial world, aristocrats performed these ideals and imposed their practical consequences upon their administrations and colonial peoples. Being imperial was part of being aristocratic: it was not an add-on or escape from an increasingly challenging domestic context.[45] To be aristocratic was to *be* imperial: to govern those who could not govern themselves.[46] It was part of their intellectual make-up, and was expressed practically in their monopoly of the most senior postings in empire.

Dufferin is an excellent example of this mindset in action. He was an outspoken imperialist, as his contemporaries would recall, but why? After all, he might have contented himself, as might all landed peers, with the management of their estates, local politics and a Westminster career. Dufferin was imperial because he was, first, landed and aristocratic, and, second, Irish: both an insider and an outsider in elite, Westminster society. He played with this construct later in life, describing himself during a rectorial address as 'an "outlander", one who in the days of James the Sixth would have been disrespectfully described as "a mere Irishman"'.[47] There is no doubt that his views as to the importance of empire had an impact, despite running against the tide when he first began to make his mark in the early 1870s: 'Lord Dufferin was one of the earliest supporters of what are now called Imperialist aspirations, and, during the best part of his career, was strengthening the foundations of what is now a national policy', claimed one of his early biographers.[48] Was his Irishness part of that? Senior imperial officials were predominantly Irish and Scottish of title and estate (even if not primarily resident in the Celtic fringes). The occasional English title appears but, overall, English landed aristocrats tended to remain at Westminster. Those English peers who did serve overseas are those we might identify as labouring under unusual circumstances, putting them in the same insider/outsider category; men such as Lord Ripon, of venerable English family, but who converted to Roman Catholicism in 1874.[49] Gladstone wished to retain him, but it was difficult to do so domestically, so he was appointed to the Indian viceroyalty in 1880 with a mission to retreat from what Gladstone saw as the Tories' bombastic and aggressive imperialism.[50] Although all were members of Britain's most elite and privileged class, there were gradations and nuances that informed patronage and appointments. Dufferin's Irishness was a key part in his appointment to imperial office, as it was for many other Irish – and Scots – aristocrats. They had the requisite inheritance to govern well, having experience of doing so over peoples regarded as being on the fringes – racially, culturally and economically – of 'British' (English) norms and expectations. Despite being relative outsiders, they constituted a key part of understandings of imperial mission and the purpose of the empire they governed.

One of the founding principles of the purpose of empire was that it would bring progress to colonial societies – the 'benefits' of empire – in the same way that landed peers had brought improvement to their estates over the generations. Additionally, as educated, experienced, well-travelled men of the world, they had the requisite perspective on political and constitutional institutions to make judgements for the 'benefit' of others. Lyall was very clear that this was one of Dufferin's great strengths: 'No Viceroy ever came to India who had seen so much as Lord Dufferin had seen of political institutions in different forms and stages, from the free government of Canada to absolutism at its zenith in St Petersburg, and Oriental autocracy at Constantinople.'[51] He knew better than most, then, the ways in which the rapidly shifting mood at Westminster could subvert the ideology of permanence in the imperial territories.[52]

What were the perceived benefits to Britain of empire and how were these defined aristocratically? First, there was a strong promotion of the idea of British sovereignty for its own sake – the primacy of British interests – rather than a dialogue between rulers and ruled.[53] This was in contrast to what was the norm on many landed estates in Britain, where a dialogue – sometimes effective, sometimes not – was in place. Aristocratic power was subject to a finely tuned spectrum of interests, where the privileges and wealth landownership conferred were in balance with responsibilities to tenants, particularly in times of economic crisis. This generated periods of agitation and tension, forcing a dialogue and often resulting in adaptations to landed behaviour.[54] A critical exception to this was Ireland, where many landowners were perceived to have failed their tenants during the blackest crisis of the nineteenth century, the Great Famine. This was framed as a fundamental failure of duty, chalked up to the 'alien' nature of many Irish landlords, that would have significant political consequences.[55]

Another purpose of empire as defined by aristocrats was to bring 'order' to chaotic societies, part of the wider duty of promoting progress.[56] This element was political; by bringing social order, stability and constitutional example, eventually colonial societies would be in a position to govern themselves. Imposing order and the rule of law on 'inferior' peoples was central to the role of aristocrats in Britain and Ireland, too, although their historic dominance in these areas was being challenged through local government and legal reform.[57] They transplanted this role overseas instead. Dufferin put it somewhat grandly: 'It is both the pride and the desire of the Imperial Government to provide impartially for every class and section of Her Majesty's subjects in India, fair and equal opportunities of improving their material condition, and of multiplying their means of moral advancement.'[58] As an Ulsterman often exercised by the challenge of sectarian fraying of the social fabric, he had an especially strong sense of British duty in overcoming all types of social and political 'chaos' in the colonial context.[59] As he reported to the Queen in 1886, 'Lord Dufferin regrets to say that there has been some religious rioting at Delhi and some other places. These riots do not differ in any characteristic from those in Belfast…Delhi unfortunately is inhabited by a rather unruly population, almost as difficult to manage as that of Belfast.'[60] So-called unruly populations were a feature of the empire, ranging from communal and sectarian disorder to outright rebellion against British rule; aristocrats were seen as having the requisite 'character' to deal with them skilfully. Ireland was the ultimate imperial challenge, particularly for Liberals. Irish violence and agitation were seen as a direct threat, not just domestically but for the wider empire, particularly for India, which many Whigs – including Dufferin – saw as vulnerable to infection by Irish-style violence.[61] This linked directly into contemporary understandings of the purpose of aristocracy. The intellectual foundation provided by their education and the practical training of governance from their estates together created a service aristocracy that was able to provide 'rule by the best', domestically or in the overseas empire.

The third element of aristocratic understanding of empire lay in the concept of progress. Domestically, landed leadership was seen as a historically grounded, traditional duty from the Norman Conquest up to enclosure, 'improvement', and political and economic enlightenment. This further translated to political and administrative leadership in order to enact progress on colonial societies. The empire, with its developing sense of imperial mission and national destiny, was in itself both a vehicle for and expression of progress. The British pointed to history to justify their supremacy: the world's first industrial nation, the first to abolish the slave trade and slavery, a wealthy nation that had undergone no violent revolution in its route to liberal parliamentary government and constitutional monarchy. The empire was seen as a mirror in which Britain's historical greatness and uniqueness was reflected. It stood apart from empires that had come and gone, due to its moral foundations and domestic history of peaceful, constitutional progress. The aristocracy saw themselves as constituting the heart of this process; leading either through military might or political guile, old landed families could always point to some ancestor or another who had played a leading role in one of the great events narrated by contemporary Whig historians such as David Hume or Thomas Macaulay. They saw themselves as the golden threads in the tapestry of Britain's national history.[62] This was why landed peers placed such emphasis on the heritable principle and the 'past' as a justification – both moral and practical – for their contemporary privileges and right to rule.[63]

A second aspect of the nature of progress as defined by the landed aristocracy was that applied to colonised societies. First had to come order, only after which the journey towards self-rule could begin. There was much debate over when colonial societies would be 'ready'. There was concern around making sure this did not happen too early, when those societies were not mature enough to manage the application of liberal parliamentary government or self-rule in any form. This debate was really about the ways in which the temporality of progress was defined: what were the steps by which it would be achieved, how long did they assume it would take, and what was the eventual goal? Self-government or independence for all colonies was the implicit assumption, eventually lifting the 'burden' of empire from Britain's shoulders, but the details were always vague. The glorious future age of independence was always out of reach, certainly after the lifetimes of those pondering the future progress of empire at any particular time. Dufferin confidently declared in India in 1888 that, 'thirty years is a very short time in which to induce a self-governing nation from its primordial elements'.[64] The British often pointed to the thousand years of constitutional development of their islands as a way to beat back political aspirations in the colonies.

These concerns about progress were not limited to Crown colonies under direct British rule, as the Irish case demonstrates. Dufferin also found much to concern him in Canada. The British view was that Canada was unable to defend itself militarily from its aggressive neighbour and could not be trusted to rule completely independently due to the political corruption evident in their elections, and so the British 'connection' was still required.[65] Dufferin thought they were thirty years or more away from real 'independence' in the 1870s, pushing the promised outcome back out of his own lifetime. The issue of who was really in control was always to be resolved at some future time, but never in the present. 'Evidently India is not a country in which the machinery of European democratic agitation can be applied with impunity', wrote Dufferin, not needing to explain why this was the case, because he knew Kimberley would understand.[66] They only had to look to Ireland for the closest geographical example, but there were many others. The answer was firm but fair government, demonstrating British fitness to rule. In India, Dufferin advised that he was prepared to, 'examine carefully and seriously the demands ... to give quickly and with good grace whatever it may be possible or desirable to accord, to announce that these concessions must be accepted as a final settlement of the Indian system for the next ten or fifteen years and to forbid mass meetings and incendiary speechifying'.[67] There are echoes here of his urging of Gladstone to make the 1870 Irish Land Act the 'final settlement' of the Irish land question and perhaps a realisation with personal experience of colonial governance that such 'final' settlements were not likely to materialise in the messy realities of even autocratic rule. He frequently compared Ireland to India in this regard:

> Take the case of Ireland. In spite of an enormous army, and a most efficient and numerous Constabulary, it has been found impossible to suppress either the raids of moonlighters or the dynamite explosions; and if such a state of things is found arduous to cope with in Ireland ... how much more difficult [in India].[68]

Dufferin remained convinced that, 'it is essential to the efficiency of British Rule in India that the real executive control over all the districts should remain in English hands'.[69] A second example, which very clearly articulates this temporal understanding of progress, can be seen in Dufferin's approach to constitutional reform in Egypt in 1883. In the wake of the 'Urabi revolt and British takeover, he wrote an influential report on the future governance and management of Egypt, prefaced by remarks upon Egypt's long and illustrious history, where he compared ancient and contemporary conditions among the peasantry as well as the three-thousand-year history of autocratic government of the country.[70] This had been informed by his visits to Egypt in the 1850s and 1860s as a tourist, cruising the Nile, deciphering hieroglyphics and digging up items to ship home to Clandeboye.[71] A sense of place-in-time, tradition and historicism infused his thinking around empire and progress, influenced by growing contemporary British and European scholarship on 'Oriental' societies.[72] The application of 'good' governance and the latest scholarship would – it was believed – facilitate progress among colonial peoples, justifying British political and economic dominion, as well as frequent resort to military oppression and conquest.

But there was a price to be paid, a price that was part of aristocratic duty and service: the burdens of empire and the 'exile' it imposed. Dufferin's parliamentary career was not a striking success and, by his fortieth birthday, he was actively seeking appointment to an overseas post to allow him to fulfil his class destiny: 'I cannot endure to be idle any longer', he wrote to Argyll, 'and though literary occupation is open to me, it will be with great disappointment that I shall subside into that lower form of existence.'[73] He desired the opportunity to perform recognised aristocratic duties and his elite circle was able to lever their patronage to aid him in an illustrious career. However, when Dufferin later complained bitterly about his 'exile' in Canada, and again in Russia and India, it was more than a personal complaint. It was part of the cultural loneliness and anxiety shared by all British overseas and for men in Dufferin's position, recognised by their 'masters'.[74] Salisbury wrote to Dufferin almost apologetically to ask him to take up the Russian embassy only six weeks after returning from Canada: 'I quite feel the extreme inconvenience to which a move must put you after so long an absence: and I almost am ashamed of any considerations in favour of such a course. But I am in duty bound to speak only in public interests: and I am constrained therefore to appeal to your public spirit to give us as early a day as you can.'[75] The loneliness they referred to was in part that of carrying the ultimate responsibility for the security and good governance of the imperial territories under their command, as well as the pangs of separation felt from friends, family and 'civilised' metropolitan society.[76] Westminster was Rome for nineteenth-century proconsuls, and it exercised great power over their imagination and actions.[77]

The work of imperial administration could indeed be heavy in terms of both volume and the personal responsibility of being the man on the spot, often obliged to act in the dark, without the support of Westminster or Whitehall before doing so.[78] This was especially the case when it came to military action. As a result, Dufferin, like all in his position, was highly sensitive about his personal reputation and public opinion at home.[79] The aftermath of the annexation of Burma in 1886 was a difficult period for Dufferin, for instance, as he struggled to manage the high expectations of British public opinion in the wake of a blisteringly successful initial campaign, followed by a lengthy period of occupation and unrest, peppered with British casualties and a scandal around the treatment of Burmese combatants sensationally exposed by a correspondent for the London *Times*.[80] In the aristocratic worldview, almost nothing was more important than reputation.[81] Dufferin went on the offensive, writing a long memorandum on the conduct of the campaign that he had privately printed and circulated to the leading politicians of the day. In his covering letter to Gladstone, he explained his reasons thus: 'It does not refer to a pleasant subject, for wars and annexations, even when inevitable, are always hateful topics, but I think it will show you that my government has not failed to carry out its anxious task but in as effective, and as humane a manner as possible; nor have I any doubt that the ultimate result of what we are doing will prove of permanent advantage to a country which for years past has evidently been the theatre of chronic anarchy and bloodshed.'[82] This highlights again the temporal understanding of progress and the way in which emphasis was laid on the ends, rather than the means, of imperial action. Although birth and inheritance were basic requirements of belonging to the aristocratic world, the maintenance of social expectations as to gentlemanly conduct was also essential and was expressed as much through imperial governance as it was in London's clubland.[83] All three contexts were tightly interlinked by individuals, families and networks. Dufferin belonged to the exclusive Breakfast Club, for example, and he noted in 1884 as he embarked for India that, 'I left the Breakfast Club in anything but a weak state. They had acquired quite an Imperial Roman milieu from the consciousness of sending forth so many kings to govern the world.'[84] On the other hand, those whose conduct was identified as being ungentlemanly faced a great deal of censure, reinforcing the importance of reputation.[85]

Britain and Ireland's landed aristocracy saw imperial governance as the natural extension of their local and national power.[86] It required no great mental leap to link their traditions of service to Queen and country to that of empire and Empress, described by Dufferin as being, 'responsible for the welfare of those millions of human beings to whom the British Crown and the British flag are the emblems of peace, safety, liberty and justice'.[87] The same characteristics were required: the ability to lead under pressure, to govern with justice, and the confidence to apply violence and coercion when required.[88] All of these characteristics were seen as part of the landed inheritance of the aristocratic classes and a contemporary adaptation to longstanding duties and purpose. By carrying out these duties, they justified their economic, political and social privileges – which, even in a period of sustained domestic attack by land reformers, political radicals and others, was perhaps surprisingly secure, and especially so in the colonial context.

Iron fists in kid gloves – the man on the spot[89]

> Of course I do not mean to say that the Burmese like having their country taken from them; but, as far as I can ascertain, the great mass of the people would cheerfully acquiesce in our rule if only they see that we can give them protection from their tormentors, justice, and decent government.[90]

96 Will to rule

The aristocratic governors of empire were known more for their practical application of the will to rule than their intellectual justifications for it. Given the extent to which the actions of many imperial governors actively contradicted the intellectual underpinnings of their role, this is unsurprising. There is a further issue to consider: the role of the state – political, economic and military – in both constraining and unleashing the desires of Britain's aristocratic imperial elites. Understanding how aristocrats understood the nature and purpose of the state and their role in it is vital to any understanding of the practical application of their governance in the empire. A major part of their conception of the state was framed by the imperial Parliament at Westminster, in which they more often than not held seats in either the Commons or the Lords. If they did not, they certainly interacted with those who did, the succession of men Dufferin called his 'masters' in the Colonial and India offices.[91] But the state also incorporated the monarchy, and loyalty to the Queen – both as the individual personification of the office, as well as the institution – was a key driver of aristocratic service. This was certainly the case for Dufferin; he had been made a lord-in-waiting by Victoria in 1849, and would become a life-long friend and correspondent of hers, selected to give the eulogy on the death of the Prince Consort in the House of Lords in 1861.[92] But the institution was as important as the individual; after all, aristocracy was an extension of monarchy, the existence of one not possible without the other, with hundreds of years of history to evidence their interdependence. Part of protecting the British monarchy was making sure that those who held royal status in the colonial territories were managed carefully to maintain the primacy of hierarchy. This was a particular issue in India, where princely families were central to British control of the subcontinent, particularly after 1858. Dufferin was highly sensitive to these issues and a dedicated follower of protocol.[93] His contemporaries noted his tendency to be a stickler for form; it was not simply a formality for Dufferin, it was the public expression of the hierarchies that underpinned an ordered society. In both Canada and India, Dufferin instituted a great deal more touring by the viceroy to ensure he – as the personification of British rule – was as visible as possible to his subjects, from prince to peasant. Dufferin argued that touring in India, 'enabled me, in fact, to get something like a personal hold upon the most intelligent representative men in the country and the more I see of India, the more I am convinced that everything depends upon personal influence'.[94] For Dufferin, this was a positive revelation and aligned to his landed upbringing and particular set of social and political skills. He regarded it as a proven success in Canada and, despite the manifest differences in the constitutional arrangements between India and that country, the ceremonial visibility of the figurehead was an integral part – in Dufferin's view – of the governing cultures of both. The role of the state as both a driver of and restriction on aristocratic governance is therefore a key question: aristocrats did not see themselves as separate from the state – they symbolised it, domestically and overseas.[95]

The state acted as a driver of aristocratic imperial activity, first and foremost by emphasising the requirement for security of British sovereignty in the colonies. Power was what rested at Westminster: sovereignty was what aristocratic proconsuls exercised and symbolised in the imperial territories. The distinction is an important one and we can see it in Dufferin's unwillingness to exercise power directly. Some contemporaries described this as laziness, but Dufferin – unlike his later successor Lord Curzon, who criticised Dufferin's perceived inactivity – understood the nature of his position in a more nuanced way. He took a monarchical view – especially of the Canadian governorship-general and the Indian viceroyalty – and, utilising his experiences as a courtier, emphasised symbolic sovereignty rather than political power. Contemporaries noted his skill, endurance and good humour throughout the heavy programmes of social events, ceremonies and levees he undertook wherever he was posted.[96] This should not be treated as a frivolous aspect of his activities, to be set aside in order to examine 'real' issues: this was the purest expression of his role as he understood it in the empire. Dufferin's Irish background conditioned him to assert that, if colonial peoples could not be persuaded to be loyal to British power, perhaps they could to British sovereignty.[97] The British demanded loyalty from their colonial subjects in return for the benefits of good governance, which was displayed through ceremony. In the case of Canada, Dufferin argued strongly that Canadians valued the British connection, and the British people and their politicians urgently needed to recognise this:

> Indeed, until lately, they [the British] scarcely realized the yearning desire felt by the British colonial populations for the due recognition of their kinship … The fact has now been brought home to the imagination of Englishmen that beyond the narrow seas which encircle their island, there lie vast regions peopled by powerful communities, owing allegiance, and proud to owe it, to Queen Victoria, animated by the same ideas as themselves.[98]

Confusion and agitation arose when the British demanded political loyalty in autocratic systems, when – as Dufferin demonstrated – loyalty to sovereignty was more feasible. The drive on the part of the state for security overseas then could turn into a restriction, as the examples of India and Ireland both demonstrated.

In Ireland, a key turning point in this narrative of loyalty and sovereignty came with the Great Famine. The responses of Irish landowners were seen to have undermined the accepted social and moral contract underpinning tenant–landlord relations. Rather than coming to the aid of the people at a time of acute and deadly crisis, landlords attempted to dodge their responsibilities and carried out evictions of even the most vulnerable.[99] The popular and political view was that landlords were as much to blame for the death and despair of those years as the British state: indeed, as symbolic representatives of the British state in Ireland, both had failed together.[100]

Similar accusations were made over British handling of recurrent famine in India, and both Irish and Indian nationalists certainly made the connection between British sovereignty and bad governance, as led by the landed classes. But for Dufferin and his peers, loyalty was not to be subject to the vicissitudes of the harvest, or any other short-term political or economic cause. Because he placed loyalty alongside sovereignty, he saw criticism in terms of betrayal and could not understand how or why 'agitators' could deny or reject the sovereignty of Britain.[101] He did accept that, for this loyalty to operate, there needed to be 'good' governance and this was one of the burdens of imperial dominion that his class had to shoulder. The consequences of not doing so could be severe and Dufferin often reverted to the anxious, doom-laden tone of many of his peers: 'It is wonderful to think what may be the ultimate effect upon our social system of the power which has now evidently been acquired by irresponsible individuals and weak minorities to scatter death and destruction at will.'[102] To prevent these attacks they had to, 'promote by every means in our power the best possible relations between the native population of India and their British fellow-subjects; to unite them in the bonds of a common loyalty; and, under the aegis of an impartial executive, to extend to all and each of them the blessings of justice and good government'.[103] This is why he and his peers would often blame resistance or rejection, whether in India, Ireland, Egypt or elsewhere, on 'external' agitators; evil counsellors acting for their own interests and purposes, not the greater good.[104] This was because Dufferin believed it was he who was acting for the greater good, at great cost to himself, his class and Britain as the imperial superpower. It was an essentially optimistic and paternalistic view, based on the premise that people *were* fundamentally capable of improvement.[105] Dufferin, like his peers, saw himself as fashioned for leadership in Irish and British society but, as this was increasingly challenged there, he readily took his paternalism overseas, arguing that firm direction was required to 'improve' backwards societies.[106] The challenges presented to this view both by Ireland and empire forced Dufferin to articulate and defend his ideas publicly and privately.

All this talk of loyalty and sovereignty, and how it had to be earned by good governance, was quite different from the reality. In practice, loyalty was enforced by political autocracy and violence, sanctioned and executed by aristocratic leadership. Dufferin was operating under no illusions about the true nature of British rule, or about the weaknesses to which it exposed British interests:

> I cannot help having a strong suspicion that the course of events at home in regard to Ireland has produced a very considerable effect upon the minds of the intelligent and educated sections of our own native [Indian] community … I cannot help asking myself how long an autocratic Government like that of India – and a Government which everyone will admit for many a long year to come must in its main features remain autocratic – will be able to stand the strain implied by

the importation *en bloc* from England, or rather from Ireland, of the perfected machinery of modern democratic agitation.[107]

Whatever the qualms of a liberal over the methods of rule, Dufferin and his peers were certain that they were the men best placed to carry it out.[108] A good example of this is the Third Anglo-Burmese War of 1885–86.[109] The causes of this conflict have been much debated, but were formed of a combination of factors.[110] One of these was the active efforts by the Burmese monarch Thibaw to develop new and threatening alliances (in British eyes), principally with the French, which stoked the fears of the British mercantile community in Lower Burma and the industrial cities of northern England.[111] Two previous conflicts had led to a hardening of Burmese patriotism under the shadow of British expansion in the face of a political and fiscal crisis in the Burmese state.[112] The other factor drew on British fears as to the security of the borders of the Raj, a fear stoked by identical concerns about Afghanistan and the Russian threat, a far more strategically problematic situation, which influenced the rush to war in Burma.[113] The Conservative Secretary of State, Lord Randolph Churchill, was keen to press forward on the Burmese campaign, because of commercial pressures in Britain, but also to signal the power of British electoral pressure over Indian and – to some extent – Anglo-Indian opinion.[114] The British had therefore been half-heartedly discussing further intervention in Burma from the mid-1870s, but the re-emergence of active Burmese–French relations, fears around border security and a hawkish Secretary of State in Churchill led to outright conflict in late 1885. The immediate pretext was a dispute between the Burmese state and the Bombay Burma Trading Company over alleged illegal logging: an ultimatum was issued that Thibaw was inevitably unable to accept, and Dufferin duly ordered in military forces.[115] This was in the face of Dufferin's oft-stated concerns that British political opinion had mistaken the viability of Burma as a buffer, 'it is quite enough to be worried by a buffer policy on the west without replicating it on the east', arguing further that Burma could never be an effective 'buffer', being too, 'soft and pulpy'.[116] As his later successor, Curzon, pointed out, the annexation of Burma was fundamentally an unplanned episode and pushed Dufferin out of his cautious comfort zone repeatedly from 1886, not least in terms of managing his legacy and reputation.[117]

The initial military invasion was quick and smooth, and the British quickly secured Thibaw and the rest of the royal family as well as his capital, Mandalay.[118] A high-level discussion then took place between Dufferin, his council, Churchill and the India Office over the constitutional fate of Burma. This exposed a number of key points around imperial anxiety, loyalty and sovereignty. Initially, Dufferin was opposed to the idea of a full annexation of Burma, fearing the burden of a territory the size of France, wracked with dacoity and relatively undeveloped economically.[119] Although Dufferin could see the long-term value of Burma for Britain – principally in teak production and ruby mining – he was frightened by the steeply mounting short-term costs, both in military casualties and infrastructure investment, and questioned whether it was worth the candle.[120] He was to be proven correct in this, not least when the escalating costs of the invasion and troubled occupation began to sky-rocket. The cost of the campaign was initially estimated at around £30,000 but, by mid-1886, the Government of India had spent £635,000 and by 1888 that figure had doubled, pushed upwards by the requirement for an extra 40,000 British and Indian troops and military police.[121] Lord Randolph was a pro-annexationist from the start, with one eye on the volatile political situation at home and Conservative electoral requirements for some imperial vim.[122] On the 1 January 1886, the annexation was formally announced and, in February, Dufferin travelled to Mandalay on a viceregal visit. Dufferin by now accepted that only formal annexation would secure Burma; he regarded the indigenous state institutions as an unsuitable foundation upon which to build a protectorate and justified annexation on those grounds.[123]

In early 1886, the Burmese campaign was regarded as having been a remarkably successful operation, but this complacency was not to last. Although the invasion and deposition of Thibaw and his court was quick and (fairly) clean, there followed five years of violent conflict – 'pacification' was the term used by the British – to contain the guerrilla warfare and banditry that erupted across Burma. There had already been what one historian has termed an 'anarchic' situation under Thibaw, but the removal of the monarch, court and the Hluttaw – critical for its engagement with Burmese hereditary landowners and gentry – turned an unstable situation into an organised and violent resistance.[124] Attempting to contain the situation, which was beginning to draw critical attention from Britain, Dufferin approved a significant increase in troop numbers, forces that instituted a harsh crackdown including the burning villages accused of supporting dacoits, forcibly relocating people and carrying out extra-judicial executions.[125] It was this last that was exposed by an Irish journalist for the London *Times*, E. K. Moylan: he wrote a series of long and highly critical articles for the newspaper, generating an international outcry and questions in Parliament, whipping Dufferin up into a defensive frenzy.[126] One of his first actions was to write to the proprietor of the *Times*, John Walter, asking for Moylan to be replaced with a new reporter; he was ill-advised in attempting this rather clumsy interference, as swiftly became clear. Walter did not reply but Dufferin did receive a letter from the *Times*' head of the Foreign Department, who made it clear they were going to stand by their man.[127] Dufferin would have to take matters into his own hands.

An interesting comparative aspect of Dufferin's engagements between Burma and his Irish estate can be seen in the way in which his sensitivity to criticism – as a liberal and improving landlord on his estate, or an efficient and moderate viceroy – generated intense efforts to manage his reputation.[128] In the Burmese case, Dufferin was accused of being parsimonious in funding military and police forces, spurring him to write a long justification in February 1886. This was a public document, but he assiduously sent it with covering letters to his old Westminster colleagues and combatants, including Gladstone and Salisbury, as well as old India hands such as Northbrook and Kilbracken.[129] This memorandum, structured as a discussion of the measures best calculated for the future peace and economic regeneration of Burma, went over the old ground of the reasons for the initial military campaign, stressing that it had been carried out by a 'large and efficient force'.[130] He went on to discuss in detail the constitutional options open to the British government, with an emphasis on 'rescuing' the Burmese from the long-standing state of 'lawlessness and anarchy' under which it laboured, stressing British fitness to rule where the Burmese were perceived to be unable to do so.[131] This he put down to the national characteristics in the people, including their monarchy; qualities such as 'restlessness', 'credulous and childlike', but with 'a strain of savagery and cruelty'. Like other such peoples, Dufferin recommended that only by 'firm and even severe handling', could these tendencies be overcome and the Burmese convinced to shuffle along the long road of progress.[132] A further long minute was published in October 1886 to counteract the public row that had erupted after Moylan's reports of extra-judicial executions in Burma appeared in the *Times*.[133] Dufferin stressed the difficulty the Government of India had in securing Burma after their initial military success due to the fragmented nature of Burmese society. 'Nor, as in most countries, is there in Burmah a territorial aristocracy with estates to lose, upon whose hopes and fears we can act, or through whose instrumentality the masses can be influenced', he complained. Dufferin's description of the missing link in Burma is not a million miles away from a description of the traditional role of the Irish Ascendancy.[134]

The empire, then, was not always an aristocratic playground. Although sovereignty and loyalty were key to the operation of power on the spot, there were restrictions, too – principally, British anxiety around imperial security.[135] Once a commitment had been made, the necessity of maintaining those values arose. Dufferin had this practically built into his DNA as an Irish landowner who had spent the best part of twenty years debating the nature of Ireland's constitutional, economic and social position, and how it might be secured on a more liberal footing without recourse to either attacks on property or coercion. This demonstrates the existential tension between the requirement for 'good' governance in order to justify British dominion, and the equal requirement for coercion to maintain it. The contradiction between the violent, repressive reality and the ideal of liberalism through reform and progress was, in fact, unresolvable. British and Irish aristocratic imperial governors were at the heart of this tension, and their careers in various ways expressed and symbolised it. The reality was that the means always took second place to the ends in the empire.

The British imposed their intensely hierarchical view of the world onto the indigenous societies with which they came into contact, an implicit set of assumptions that ultimately acted as a restriction on the effectiveness of their decision-making.[136] An example of this was Dufferin's conduct of relations between British India and Afghanistan, at a very sensitive juncture of European and imperial politics.[137] This was driven by British Russophobia and a fear of Russian invasion of India through Afghanistan; indeed, there was some expectation that Britain and Russia would come to war over the North-West Frontier while Dufferin was viceroy – the political stakes could not have been higher.[138] The question was also one of imperial reputation: as Dufferin put it, 'it is out of the question that all England and India should be thrown into a flurry of excitement and a deluge of expense every time a wretched Cossack chooses to shake his spear on the top of a sand hill over the Panjdeh'.[139] It was Dufferin's aim to secure the loyalty of the Amir, promoting a stable and friendly Afghanistan as the best way to maintain British interests. He promised the Amir that, if the Russians did step over his borders, the British would come to his aid, while hoping this situation would never arise.[140] The situation came to a head during the Rawalpindi *durbar* hosted by Dufferin in 1885 at which the Amir was present.[141] Negotiations had been proceeding well when news came into the camp that the Russians had attacked Panjdeh in Afghanistan. Happily for the British, Dufferin was able to manage the Amir's response, being there in person to do so, and so war with Russia was averted.[142] The Panjdeh Incident, as it came to be known, was a classic example of the perceived value of the man on the spot and the requirements of such individuals. As per British expectations, the situation turned out well because Dufferin – an aristocratic, landed gentleman – could be trusted to handle it correctly thanks to the characteristics of his class, even when dealing with a 'savage' such as the Amir.[143] Of course, Dufferin also had at his disposal the Indian treasury and, by May 1885, had handed over in the region of £200,000 and significant caches of arms to keep the Amir on side.[144] Dufferin wrote at some length to the India Office about his feeling when meeting the Amir; parlaying with a man who had killed other men, describing a cunning yet child-like personality, easily swayed by the pomp and ceremony laid on by the British.[145] 'I do not anticipate very much pleasure in shaking hands with a gentleman who has cut so many throats', he wrote.[146] But, in reality, how different was British aristocratic rule, or at least the mechanisms by which it was maintained? Both ruled by the sword and both glossed that violent rule with the ceremonial, calculating advantage through the lens of hierarchy. They both invested in the sheen of civilisation, carefully cultivated and expressed on the British side by the aristocratic governors of empire. This was their strength: their relish of ceremony, their knowledge of how to behave in public contexts in a way their middle-class and professional colleagues could not be trusted to achieve. The reality was always messier than the ideal: Dufferin was obliged to spend a good deal of his viceroyalty in India bolstering the buffer policy instituted by his predecessor Ripon as an alternative to outright war. In Burma, this failed to prevent armed conflict and, for Afghanistan, he was made uneasy by the constant demands made on the Indian treasury and army, the obligations of such a relationship being 'very absolute and specific', while Afghanistan's government was 'weak and uncivilised'.[147] Dufferin battled with the tension between his ideal of British governance as firm and moral in tone, and the practical and messy necessity of dealing with 'uncivilised' neighbours to secure India's borders.

'Moderate and statesmanlike'?[148] Ideals and realities

When Dufferin returned to Europe in 1888 as ambassador to Italy, he had ahead of him nearly fifteen years to reflect on his colonial experiences and the ways in which his own will to rule had been manifested. He claimed to Rudyard Kipling that he had no system, nor 'good intentions'; that he was not an aggressive imperialist in the mould of Lord Curzon, Cecil Rhodes or Joseph Chamberlain, with any racial philosophy or ideological drive. He was, however, firmly committed to the view that Britain alone could provide the qualities of good governance that made imperialism a benefit to the world, despite the failures he had witnessed in Ireland. After four years in India, Dufferin was sure on this point: 'for the good government of the country, and for the general content of all classes, and especially of the people at large … England should never abdicate her supreme control of public affairs'.[149] This brings us to the crux: how the reality of empire so often fell short of the ideal. Dufferin reflected at length on this, writing to the Queen and his colleagues and landed peers in cabinet, attempting to summarise the good works achieved by the British in India under his viceroyalty:

> He may have committed some errors, or failed to execute portions of his task as successfully as he could have wished; but he is in hopes that no very grave miscarriages can be laid at his charge. He feels that he is handing over this vast Empire to his successor under sufficiently favourable conditions. There is no cloud on the horizon anywhere along our frontiers; the Princes of India are thoroughly loyal and contented … and the condition of the population at large gives no cause for alarm.[150]

But what were – in theory and in practice – the aristocratic characteristics of British colonial rule? First, the emphasis placed on hierarchy, which could also be seen on landed estates across Britain and Ireland. As the representatives of the British Crown and government overseas, certain images of power were projected by aristocratic officials, hence the inordinate amount of attention paid to colonial honours lists, promotions in the peerage, tours and *durbars*: this was the fundamental architecture of imperial power – how everything *appeared*. This linked to the belief that they were simply performing an old duty in a new context; that of the service aristocracy, earning their wealth and privileges through onerous duty to Crown and country.[151] For Dufferin, this meant service overseas, representing Queen and nation to the growing numbers of colonial peoples, operating under a range of different constitutional structures. This was the aristocratic sense of imperial mission, however loosely defined. Dufferin was essentially a realist about what the eventual effects of British imperialism were, a view informed by his Irish background. However, doubts were never expressed by him in public; instead, in the countless speeches he gave over the course of a long career, he extolled the benefits of British rule for colonised societies. This was not without its own problems, however, as he increasingly recognised during his tenure as viceroy, whether in India or Ireland. He wrote to Sir Henry Verney from Calcutta that:

> Of course I am a Unionist, no Ulster man could be otherwise, and I fully believe now that we shall win, although I quite agree with you in thinking that the present condition of Ireland is our own fault, and the fault of English statesmen, and of that intolerable and vulgar brutality which the strong English race always manifests towards inferior and more sensitive populations. We are irritating the natives out here in exactly the same manner as for hundreds of years we have been irritating the Irish, and now they are beginning to borrow Irish methods of political agitation.[152]

This was closely related to the final characteristic of aristocratic rule, a commitment to progress and their role as the leaders of this progress – political, social or economic. The pride of the British was that they had arrived at their contemporary domestic supremacy through the largely peaceful means of parliamentary reform: no revolutions or terrors for them.[153] It was this model of calm before chaos, of reason, moderation and rationality that Dufferin and his peers were promoting across the empire as one of the benefits of their dominion, an aspect of the progress they would bring to colonial peoples.[154] Of course, the reality was significantly more complicated and oppressively violent than this ideal. So concerned were the British to maintain power that the means by which it was secured broke free from any liberal constraints, in Ireland, India and across the empire.

Notes

1 R. Kipling, *Something of Myself: for my friends known and unknown* (London, 1937), pp. 56–7; A. Gailey, *The Lost Imperialist: Lord Dufferin, memory and mythmaking in an age of celebrity* (London, 2015), pp. 288–9.
2 British Library [hereafter BL], India Office Papers, Papers of Lord Dufferin as viceroy, Mss Eur, F130, IOR Neg 4325–4370, ff. 75, 7 Feb. 1888, Dufferin to Queen.
3 M. Francis, *Governors and Settlers: images of authority in the British colonies, 1820–60* (Basingstoke, 1992), pp. 1–10; P.J. Cain, Character and imperialism: the British financial administration of Egypt, 1878–1914, *Journal of Imperial and Commonwealth History*, 34:2 (2006), pp. 177–80; C. Hall, *Macaulay and Son: architects of imperial Britain* (New Haven, 2012), pp. 207–50.
4 D. Cannadine, *Ornamentalism: how the British saw their empire* (London, 2001), p. 57; P. J. Cain and A. G. Hopkins, *British Imperialism, I: Innovation and Expansion; II, Crisis and Deconstruction* (London, 1993), pp. 13–14; C. Dewey, *Anglo-Indian attitudes: the mind of the Indian Civil Service* (1993), pp. 3–8; M. Holmes, The Irish and India: imperialism, nationalism and internationalism, in A. Bielenberg (ed.), *The Irish Diaspora* (Harlow, 2000), pp. 235–43.

5 T. Koditschek, *Liberalism, Imperialism, and the Historical Imagination: nineteenth-century visions of a Greater Britain* (Cambridge, 2011), p. 320; J. Epstein, Taking class notes on empire, in S. Rose and C. Hall (eds), *At Home with the Empire: metropolitan culture and the imperial world* (Cambridge, 2006), pp. 251–6.
6 A. Taylor, *Lords of Misrule: hostility to aristocracy in late nineteenth and early twentieth century Britain* (Basingstoke, 2004), p. 7.
7 BL, Cross Papers Add MS 51269, Vol. VII, ff. 132, Dufferin to Cross, 27 May 1887.
8 Cain, Character and imperialism, pp. 177–200.
9 BL, India Office Papers, F130/5, ff. 45, Dufferin to Kimberley, 26 Apr. 1886; Gailey, *Lost Imperialist*, pp. 207–11.
10 B. Crosbie, *Irish Imperial Networks: migration, social communication and exchange in nineteenth-century India* (Cambridge, 2012), pp. 4–10; A. Kirk-Greene, *Britain's Imperial Administrators, 1858–1966* (London, 2000), p. 208; Z. Laidlaw, *Colonial Connections 1815–45: patronage, the information revolution and colonial government* (Manchester, 2005), pp. 13–14; J. M. Mackenzie, Irish, Scottish, Welsh and English Worlds? A four-nation approach to the history of the British empire, *History Compass*, 6:5 (2008), pp. 1250, 1254–6; S. B. Cook, *Imperial Affinities: nineteenth century analogies and exchanges between India and Ireland* (New Delhi, 1993), pp. 9–15, 30–7.
11 The novels of both Anthony Trollope and Charles Dickens often satirised the intellectual weakness of the aristocracy: see, for example, the character of Sir Felix Carbury in A. Trollope, *The Way We Live Now* (London, 1875); and the Barnacle family in C. Dickens, *Little Dorrit* (London, 1857).
12 For an overview, see M. Bradley (ed.), *Classics and Imperialism in the British Empire* (Oxford, 2010).
13 C. D. Black, *The Marquess of Dufferin and Ava* (London, 1903), pp. 134–5. This was why he was invited to the AGMs of the British Empire League; PRONI, D1071, H/H/B/C/243, ff. 23, Hartington to Dufferin, 15 Nov. 1896.
14 D. Cannadine, Lord Strickland: imperial aristocrat and aristocratic imperialist, in D. Cannadine, *Aspects of Aristocracy: grandeur and decline in modern Britain* (New Haven, 1994), pp. 109–10, 128.
15 G. Peatling, Race and empire in nineteenth century British intellectual life: James Fitzjames Stephen, James Anthony Froude, Ireland, and India, *Eire–Ireland*, 42 (2007), pp. 157, 159–60; R. Romani, British views on Irish national character, 1800–1846: an intellectual history, *History of European Ideas*, 23:5–6 (1997), p. 201.
16 Lyall, *Life of Dufferin*, p. 286; Laidlaw, *Colonial Connections*, pp. 17–27; Gailey, *Lost Imperialist*, pp. 153–4, 158, 166.
17 BL, India Office Papers, Papers of Sir Alfred C. Lyall, F132/46, ff. 113, Dufferin to Lyall, 8 Jan. 1892.
18 Black, *Dufferin and Ava*, p. 174; see Wallace, D. M. (ed.), *Speeches delivered in India, 1884–1888 by the Marquis of Dufferin and Ava* (London, 1890), p. 269, St Andrews Day speech, 30 Nov. 1888; 'I believe that the moral ascendency exercised by Englishmen in the East is becoming more and more powerful'.
19 BL, India Office papers, Papers of Arthur Godley, Lord Kilbracken, F102/10, ff. 24, Dufferin to Kilbracken, 10 Apr. 1887.
20 Lyall, *Life of Dufferin*, pp. 361, 355–6.
21 Black, *Dufferin and Ava*, p. 312; Gailey, *Lost Imperialist*, pp. 261, 292.
22 Black, *Dufferin and Ava*, p. 113; G. Bolton, The idea of a colonial gentry, *Historical Studies*, 13 (1968), pp. 316, 326; Cannadine, *Ornamentalism*, pp. 41–57.
23 Bodleian Library, Kimberley Papers, MS Eng C4086, ff. 2, Dufferin to Kimberley, 24 Apr. 1872; Cannadine, *Aspects of Aristocracy*, pp. 77, 82–4.

106 Will to rule

24 Hatfield House, Papers of the 3rd Marquis of Salisbury, correspondence with Lord Dufferin, ff. 13, Dufferin to Salisbury, 6 Aug. 1885. See similar debates for Ireland, R. B. McDowell, *The Irish Administration, 1801–1914* (London, 1964), pp. 68–9.
25 Lyall, *Life of Dufferin*, p. 446; Gailey, *Lost Imperialist*, pp. 209, 292.
26 Lyall, *Life of Dufferin*, p. 565.
27 See, for example, C. J. Reilly, *The Irish Land Agent, 1830–60: the case of King's county* (Dublin, 2014); L. A. Rees, C. J. Reilly and A. Tindley (eds), *The Land Agent, 1700–1920* (Edinburgh, 2018).
28 University of Edinburgh, *Address by the Marquess of Dufferin*, p. 42; Public Record Office of Northern Ireland [hereafter PRONI], D1071, H/H/B/B/251B, ff. 11, Dufferin to his uncle Brin, describing the 'child-like' Burmese, 3 Dec. 1885; A. Porter, Empires in the mind, in P. J. Marshall (ed.), *The Cambridge Illustrated History of the British Empire* (Cambridge, 1996), pp. 185, 218–19, 223.
29 E. Frie and J. Neuheiser, Introduction: noble ways and democratic means, *Journal of Modern European History*, 11:4 (2013), pp. 438, 446–8; U. S. Mehta, *Liberalism and Empire: a study in nineteenth century British Liberal thought* (Chicago, 1999), pp. 4, 7, 30.
30 C. A. Bayly, *The birth of the modern world, 1780–1914: global connections and comparisons* (Oxford, 2004), pp. 296–7; K. Blake, *Pleasures of Benthamism: Victorian literature, utility, political economy* (Oxford, 2009), pp. 200–4.
31 C. A. Bayly, Ireland, India and the empire: 1780–1914, *Transactions of the Royal Historical Society*, 6th ser., 10 (2000), pp. 377–8.
32 Another word used for this was 'destiny': Lyall, *Life of Dufferin*, pp. 443, 487; T. Ballantyne, The sinews of empire: Ireland, India and the construction of British colonial knowledge, in T. MacDonagh (ed.), *Was Ireland a colony? Economics, Politics and Culture in Nineteenth Century Ireland* (Dublin, 2005), pp. 147, 157.
33 M. D. McHugh, Family, leisure and the arts: aspects of the culture of the aristocracy of Ulster, 1870–1925, unpublished PhD thesis (University of Edinburgh, 2011), pp. 1–41.
34 Although as an educational experience, Dufferin remembers Eton as being 'dominated by idleness': Lyall, *Life of Dufferin*, p. 38; Gailey, *Lost Imperialist*, pp. 15, 17–18, 21; J. Gathorne-Hardy, *The Public School Phenomenon* (London, 1977), pp. 68–70, 137–8; B. Knox, The Earl of Carnarvon, empire and imperialism, 1855–90, *Journal of Imperial and Commonwealth History*, 26 (1998), pp. 49, 51; M. Bentley, *Lord Salisbury's World: Conservative environments in late-Victorian Britain* (Cambridge, 2001), p. 3.
35 J. A. Mangan, *Making Imperial Mentalities: socialisation and British imperialism* (Manchester, 1990), pp. 1–3.
36 BL, India Office Papers, F130/8, ff. 1, Dufferin to Cross, 4 Jan. 1887; B. Martin, Lord Dufferin and the Indian National Congress, 1885–88, *Journal of British Studies*, 7:1 (1967), pp. 84–96; A. Parel, Hume, Dufferin and the origins of the Indian National Congress, *Journal of Indian History* (Dec. 1964), pp. 707, 715–16.
37 R. Alston, Dialogues in imperialism: Rome, Britain and India, in E. Hall and P. Vasunia (eds), *India, Greece and Rome, 1757–2007* (London, 2010), pp. 51–2, 54, 74–5.
38 Lyall, *Life of Dufferin*, p. 50; see, in comparison, J. W. Cell, *Hailey: a study in British Imperialism* (Cambridge, 1992), pp. 2–4; Gailey, *Lost Imperialist*, pp. 31–4; R. Symonds, *Oxford and Empire: the last lost cause?* (Oxford, 1992), pp. 25, 31, 33–5.
39 M. Bradley, Tacitus' *Agricola* and the conquest of Britain: representations of empire in Victorian and Edwardian Britain, in M. Bradley (ed.), *Classics and Imperialism in the British Empire* (Oxford, 2010), pp. 127, 133–4, 157.

40 BL, India Office Papers, F130/2, ff. 5 Dufferin to Kimberley, 30 Dec. 1884.
41 Dufferin, *Address delivered at St Andrews University April 6, 1891 by the Marquess of Dufferin and Ava, Lord Rector* (Edinburgh, 1891), pp. 22, 33–4.
42 Lyall, *Life of Dufferin*, p. 426.
43 R. S. Mantena, Imperial ideology and the uses of Rome in discourses on Britain's Indian empire, in M. Bradley (ed.), *Classics and Imperialism in the British empire* (Oxford, 2010), pp. 54, 58, 67; Gailey, *Lost Imperialist*, pp. 28–31, 35.
44 For the benefits of a transnational approach to thinking about power, see E. Delaney, Our island story? Towards a transnational history of late modern Ireland, *Irish Historical Studies*, 37 (2011), pp. 616–17; Crosbie, *Irish Imperial Networks*, pp. 14–23.
45 Bentley, *Lord Salisbury*, pp. 72–5.
46 Bentley, *Lord Salisbury*, pp. 72–3; R. Jenkyns, *The Victorians and Ancient Greece* (Oxford, 1980), pp. 331–5.
47 University of Edinburgh, *Address by the Marquess of Dufferin and Ava (Lord Rector)*, (Edinburgh, 1901), p. 2.
48 Black, *Dufferin and Ava*, pp. 362–3; A. Thompson, The language of imperialism and the meanings of empire, in S. Howe (ed.), *The New Imperial Histories Reader* (London, 2010), pp. 306–8, 310.
49 PRONI, D1071, H/H/B/C/95, ff. 88, Argyll to Dufferin, 28 Apr. 1880.
50 A. F. Denholm, Robinson, George Frederick Samuel, first marquess of Ripon (1827–1909), *Oxford Dictionary of National Biography*, Oxford University Press, 2004; online edn, May 2009 [http://www.oxforddnb.com/view/article/35792, accessed 11 Aug 2017]; A. Denholm, *Lord Ripon, 1827–1909: a political biography* (London, 1982), pp. 139–79; S. Gopal, *The Viceroyalty of Lord Ripon, 1880–1884* (Oxford, 1953), pp. 1–5, 214–7; D. Omissi, A most arduous but a most noble duty: Gladstone and the British Raj in India, 1868–98, in M. E. Daly and K. T. Hoppen (eds), *Gladstone, Ireland and Beyond* (Dublin, 2011), pp. 189–92; Martin, Lord Dufferin and the Indian National Congress, pp. 71–5; Koditschek, *Liberalism, Imperialism, and the Historical Imagination*, pp. 314–17.
51 Lyall, *Life of Dufferin*, p. 426.
52 J. Darwin, *The Empire Project: the rise and fall of the British world-system, 1830–1970* (Cambridge, 2009), p. 200.
53 J. Wilson, *India Conquered: Britain's Raj and the chaos of empire* (London, 2016), pp. 278, 296.
54 J. C. Beckett, *The Anglo-Irish Tradition* (Belfast, 1976), pp. 85, 87–9, 92–6; L. P. Curtis, The Anglo-Irish predicament, *Twentieth Century Studies*, 4 (1970), pp. 44, 61.
55 E. F. Biagini, *Liberty, Retrenchment and Reform: popular liberalism in the age of Gladstone, 1860–1880* (Cambridge, 1992), pp. 53–4; Bentley, *Lord Salisbury*, pp. 116–20.
56 See, for instance, University of Edinburgh, *Address by the Marquess of Dufferin*, pp. 5–6; J. W. Cell, *British Colonial Administration in the Mid-Nineteenth Century: the policy-making process* (London, 1970), pp. vii–xi; A. G. Hopkins, Back to the future: from national history to imperial history, *Past and Present*, 164 (1999), pp. 209–10, 211.
57 This, of course, included Ireland: PRONI, D1071/H/H/B/F/175, ff. 8, Dufferin to Lansdowne, 3 Nov. 1880; ff. 15, Dufferin to Lansdowne, 17 Dec. 1886.
58 Dufferin, *Speeches given in India*, Address from the Anjumani Islam: Dufferin's response, 8 Dec. 1884, p. 24; Gailey, *Lost Imperialist*, pp. 262–4.
59 Dufferin, *Speeches given in India*, Farewell speech in Calcutta, 22 Mar. 1888, pp. 199–201; Queen's Jubilee speech, 17 Feb. 1887, p. 156.
60 BL, India Office Papers, F130, reel 4351, ff. 51, Dufferin to Queen, 16 Oct. 1886.

108 *Will to rule*

61 P. Marshall, The imperial factor in the Liberal decline, 1880–1885, in J. Flint and G. Williams (eds), *Perspectives of Empire: presented to Gerald S. Graham* (Harlow, 1973), pp. 134–6.
62 C. Hall, *Macaulay and Son: architects of imperial Britain* (New Haven, 2012), p. 175; B. Porter, *The Absent-Minded Imperialists: empire, society and culture in Britain* (Oxford, 2004), pp. 228–31; C. C. Eldridge, *England's Mission: the imperial idea in the age of Gladstone and Disraeli* (London, 1973), p. 86.
63 Dufferin noted with pleasure that his successor to the Indian viceroyalty, Lord Lansdowne, was 'high bred': BL, Kilbracken Papers, F102/10, ff. 80, Dufferin to Kilbracken, 13 Mar. 1888.
64 Dufferin, *Speeches given in India*, St Andrews Day speech, 30 Nov. 1888, p. 229; Gailey, *Lost Imperialist*, pp. 262–3; Hopkins, Back to the future, pp. 211, 213, 222.
65 University of Edinburgh, *Address by the Marquess of Dufferin*, pp. 13–14; Gailey, *Lost Imperialist*, pp. 143–6; W.P. Morrell, *British Colonial Policy in the Mid-Victorian Age* (Oxford, 1969), pp. 10, 24.
66 BL, India Office Papers, F130/5, ff. 17, Dufferin to Kimberley, 26 Apr. 1886.
67 BL, India Office Papers, F130/5, ff. 45, Dufferin to Kimberley, 26 Apr. 1884.
68 BL, India Office Papers, F130/5, ff. 85, Dufferin to Cross, 6 Aug. 1886.
69 BL, India Office Papers, F130/5, ff. 111, Dufferin to Cross, 3 Sept. 1886, and F130/26b, ff. 61, Dufferin to Meredith Townsend, 5 Jul. 1887.
70 Lyall, *Life of Dufferin*, pp. 99, 309–10, 331.
71 H. G. Nicolson, *Helen's Tower* (London, 1937), p. 186; M. Jasanoff, Collectors of empire: objects, conquests and imperial self-fashioning, *Past and Present*, 184 (2004), pp. 110–11, 114–16.
72 J. Lennon, *Irish Orientalism: a literary and intellectual history* (Syracuse, 2004).
73 PRONI, D1071/H/H/B/C/95, ff. 11, Dufferin to Argyll, 20 Dec. 1863; Lyall, *Life of Dufferin*, p. 138; Gailey, *Lost Imperialist*, pp. 185–93.
74 O. Gust, The perilous territory of not belonging: exile and empire in Sir James Mackintosh's letters from early nineteenth century Bombay, *History Workshop Journal*, 86 (2018), pp. 2, 9–10, 17.
75 PRONI/D1071/H/H/B/S/250, ff. 3, Salisbury to Dufferin, 5 Feb. 1879.
76 See, for instance, PRONI/D1071/H/H/B/D/78, ff. 58, Dufferin to Lady Dartrey, 2 Oct. 1877, and ff. 82, Dufferin to Lady Dartrey, 4 Jun. 1880; Lyall, *Life of Dufferin*, p. 123.
77 Lyall, *Life of Dufferin*, p. 487.
78 PRONI, D1071/H/H/B/C/95, ff. 79, Dufferin to Argyll, 16 Mar. 1879, on how he 'hates being idle'.
79 Lyall, *Life of Dufferin*, pp. 405, 407, 462.
80 Lyall, *Life of Dufferin*, pp. 397–8; Gailey, *Lost Imperialist*, pp. 238–9, 241.
81 Dufferin, *Speeches made in India*, p. 98, speech to Lord Roberts and armed forces in Mandalay, Burma, 17 Feb. 1886; D. Castronovo, *The English Gentleman: images and ideals in literature and society* (1987), pp. 75–8.
82 BL, Gladstone Papers, Add MS 44151, Vol. LXVI, ff. 248, Dufferin to Gladstone, 20 Oct. 1886.
83 Dufferin belonged to the Travellers Club and the Breakfast Club, which limited itself to just 12 members and in 1885–86 could boast that four of its members were administering Canada, India, and the Madras and Bombay presidencies; Black, *Dufferin and Ava*, p. 373.
84 BL, India Office Papers, Papers of Sir Mountstuart Elphinstone Grant Duff, Mss Eur F234, ff. 3, Dufferin to Grant Duff, 21 Dec. 1884; Lyall, *Life of Dufferin*, p. 507.
85 Dufferin noted that one of his senior officials in India, Sir Lepel Griffin, had very little judgement, 'Nor is he a gentleman, I fear'. BL, Kilbracken Papers, F102/10, ff. 30, Dufferin to Kilbracken, 16 Apr. 1887. Sir Lepel never received the Lieutenant Governorship of the Punjab, which he felt he deserved, as a result of the general censure on his behaviour.

86 A. Ramm (ed.), *The Political Correspondence of Mr Gladstone and Lord Granville, 1876–1886, vol. II, 1883–1886* (Oxford, 1962), 1032. Gladstone to Granville, p. 51.
87 University of Edinburgh, *Address by the Marquess of Dufferin*, p. 4.
88 Hopkins, Back to the future, p. 223; A. Seal, Imperialism and nationalism in India, in J. Gallagher, G. Johnson and A. Seal, *Locality, Province and Nation: essays on Indian politics, 1870–1940* (Cambridge, 1973), pp. 6–9.
89 *Country Life*, 22 February 1902, obituary of Lord Dufferin.
90 BL, Gladstone papers, Add MS 44151, Vol. LXVI, ff. 263, Dufferin to Gladstone, 28 Dec. 1886.
91 BL, Kilbracken Papers, F102/10, ff. 107, Dufferin to Kilbracken, 4 Dec. 1888.
92 Nicolson, *Helen's Tower*, p. 131; Gailey, *Lost Imperialist*, pp. 92, 94.
93 See, for example, BL, India Office Papers, Papers of Sir Henry Durand, Mss Eur D727, ff. 159, Durand to Sir Lepel Griffin, 1 Sept. 1886.
94 BL, India Office Papers, F130/8A, ff. 10, Dufferin to Cross, 8 Mar. 1887.
95 Dufferin, *Speeches given in India*, Speech given to Calcutta Trades Association, 8 Dec. 1884, pp. 24, 29.
96 Lyall, *Life of Dufferin*, pp. 65, 200; Nicolson, *Helen's Tower*, pp. 153–4.
97 See his comments on, 'the occasional eccentricities of my lively countrymen, whose avowed object is to disorganise the deliberations of Parliament and to render its proceedings futile', University of Edinburgh, *Address by the Marquess of Dufferin*, p. 12.
98 Dufferin, *Speeches Delivered in India*, speech made at the Empire Club, London, 1883, pp. 2–3; Gailey, *Lost Imperialist*, pp. 143–6.
99 L. P. Curtis, *The depiction of eviction in Ireland, 1845–1910* (Dublin, 2011), pp. 1–8.
100 P. Gray, *Famine, Land and Politics: British government and Irish society, 1843–50* (Dublin, 1999).
101 PRONI, D1071/H/H/B/F/175, ff. 7, Dufferin to Lansdowne, 4 Jul. 1880.
102 PRONI, D1071/H/H/B/D/78, ff. 97, Dufferin to Lady Dartrey, 17 Mar. 1881.
103 Dufferin, *Speeches given in India*, Speech to the Northbrook Club, London, 1 Nov. 1884.
104 PRONI, D1071/H/H/B/B/35, ff. 6, Sir Samuel Baker to Dufferin, 14 Dec. 1888; C. Townshend, *Political Violence in Ireland: government and resistance since 1848* (Oxford, 1984), pp. 94–5, 127.
105 Castronovo, *The English Gentleman*, pp. 76–7.
106 K. Tidrick, *Empire and the English Character* (London, 1990), pp. 1–4; P. J. Cain and A. G. Hopkins, *British Imperialism, I: Innovation and Expansion* (London, 1993), pp. 319–20; A. M. Burton, *At the Heart of the Empire: Indians and the colonial encounter in late-Victorian Britain* (Berkeley, 1998), pp. 12, 14, 19; Z. Laidlaw, Richard Bourke: Irish liberalism tempered by empire, in D. Lambert and A. Lester (eds), *Colonial Lives Across the British Empire* (Cambridge, 2006), pp. 119, 143.
107 BL, India Office Papers, F130/5, ff. 25, Dufferin to Kimberley, 21 Mar. 1886; Gailey, *Lost Imperialist*, pp. 276–86; R. J. Moore, *Liberalism and Indian Politics, 1872–1922* (London, 1966), pp. 53–4.
108 D. M. Wallace, India under the Marquis of Dufferin, *Edinburgh Review*, 169 (1889), pp. 2–5.
109 Maung Htin Aung, *Lord Randolph Churchill and the Dancing Peacock: the British conquest of Burma 1885* (New Delhi, 1990).
110 A. T. Q. Stewart, *The Pagoda War* (Newton Abbot, 1974), pp. 61–74; M. Yasin, *India's Foreign Policy: the Dufferin years* (New Delhi, 1994), pp. 118–52.
111 D. P. Singhal, *British Diplomacy and the Annexation of Upper Burma* (New Delhi, 1981), pp. 72, 80–1, 92–3; E. Chew, The Fall of the Burmese Kingdom in 1885: review and reconsideration, *Journal of Southeast Asian Studies*, 10:2 (1979),

110   *Will to rule*

p. 372; M. P. Callahan, *Making Enemies: war and state-building in Burma* (Ithaca, 2005), pp. 22–3; Thant Myint-U, *The Making of Modern Burma* (Cambridge, 2001), pp. 188–9.
112   Myint-U, *Making of Modern Burma*, p. 186.
113   Chew, The fall of the Burmese Kingdom, pp. 378–9.
114   PRONI, D1071/H/H/M/17/1, Viceroy's notebook, ff. 25, G. Bernard's views on annexation, 31 Oct. 1884; R. Foster, *Lord Randolph Churchill: a political life* (Oxford, 1981), pp. 206–8; Gailey, *Lost Imperialist*, pp. 223–5.
115   M. Durand, *The Life of Field-Marshall Sir George White, V.C., vol. I* (Edinburgh, 1915), pp. 308–9; Black, *Dufferin and Ava*, pp. 246–50. See also C. E. Crothswaite, *The Pacification of Burma* (London 1912), pp. 1–16, 102; A. C. Lyall, The conquest of Burma, *Edinburgh Review*, 165 (1887), pp. 489–91; Myint-U, *Making of Modern Burma*, pp. 189–90.
116   BL, India Office Papers, F130/2, ff. 157, Dufferin to Churchill, 19 Oct. 1885 and PRONI, D1071/H/H/M/17/1, Minute, 1886; Maung Htin Aung, *Lord Randolph Churchill and the Dancing Peacock*, pp. 87–8, 165, 198–9.
117   Marquis of Curzon, *British Government in India: the story of the viceroys and government houses, vol. II* (London, 1925), p. 246; Moore, *Liberalism and Indian Politics*, pp. 44, 49.
118   Black, *Dufferin and Ava*, pp. 251–2; BL, India Office Papers, F130/2, ff. 159, Dufferin to Churchill, 26 Oct. 1885; ff. 169, Dufferin to Churchill, 30 Nov. 1885; Stewart, *Pagoda War*, p. 108.
119   Maung Htin Aung, *Lord Randolph Churchill and the Dancing Peacock*, pp. 198–9, 213–14.
120   Foster, *Lord Randolph Churchill*, p. 209; Gailey, *Lost Imperialist*, pp. 227–30.
121   PRONI, D1071/H/H/M/17/1, Viceroy's notebook, ff. 371, estimated expenditure on the Burmese expedition, 12 Feb. 1886; Myint-U, *Making of Modern Burma*, p. 191; Callahan, *Making Enemies*, p. 25.
122   Omissi, A most arduous, p. 192; Bentley, *Lord Salisbury*, pp. 236–8; A. B. Cooke and J. B. Vincent, *The Governing Passion: cabinet government and party politics in Britain, 1885–6* (Brighton, 1974), p. 8.
123   Myint-U, *Making of Modern Burma*, pp. 191, 196; Stewart, *Pagoda War*, pp. 115–16, 134–9.
124   Myint-U, *Making of Modern Burma*, pp. 197–9.
125   PRONI, D1071/H/H/M/13/2/5, Report by Major General Sir George White on the principal military incidents in Burma, 6 Jul. 1889; Myint-U, *Making of Modern Burma*, pp. 201–2.
126   PRONI, D1071/H/H/M/17/1, Viceroy's notebook, ff. 573, Mr E. K. Moylan, 8 Mar. 1886; C. Kaul, *Reporting the Raj: the British press and India, c. 1880–1922* (Manchester, 2003), pp. 99–116; Stewart, *Pagoda War*, pp. 120–30; Gailey, *Lost Imperialist*, p. 241.
127   Stewart, *Pagoda War*, pp. 165–6.
128   Stewart, *Pagoda War*, pp. 21, 171–5.
129   A. P. Kaminsky, The India Office in the late nineteenth century, in R. I. Crane and N. G. Barrier (eds), *British Imperial Policy in India and Sri Lanka, 1858–1912 – a reassessment* (New Delhi, 1981), pp. 28–9.
130   PRONI, D1071/H/H/M/17/1, Viceroy's notebook, ff. 69, Minute by his excellency the viceroy and governor general of India, Feb. 1886; Bentley, *Lord Salisbury*, p. 234.
131   Minute, p. 20.
132   Minute, p. 21.
133   PRONI, D1071/H/H/M/17/1, Viceroy's notebook, ff. 86, Minute by his excellency the viceroy and governor general of India, Oct. 1886; Foster, *Lord Randolph Churchill*, p. 210.

134 Minute, p. 29; S. Keck, Involuntary sightseeing: soldiers as travel writers and the construction of colonial Burma, *Victorian Literature and Culture*, 43:2 (2015), pp. 389, 402.
135 A. Kirk-Greene, *Britain's Imperial Administrators, 1858–1966* (London, 2000), pp. 1–7, 9, 16, 206–8.
136 Yasin, *India's Foreign policy*, pp. 8–39; P. J. Durrans, A two-edged sword: the Liberal attack on Disraelian imperialism, *Journal of Imperial and Commonwealth History*, 10:3 (1982), pp. 275–8.
137 Almost as soon as Dufferin took up his post, Afghan difficulties dominated his correspondence: BL, India Office Papers, F130/2, ff.3, Dufferin to Kimberley, 23 Dec. 1884; Gailey, *Lost Imperialist*, pp. 218–22.
138 P. Hopkirk, *The Great Game: on secret service in High Asia* (London, 1990), pp. 6, 423–4, 435–7.
139 BL, India Office Papers, F130/2, ff. 70, Dufferin to Kimberley, 13 Apr. 1885.
140 A. Preston, Sir Charles MacGregor and the defence of India, 1857–1887, *Historical Journal*, 12:1 (1969), pp. 76–7.
141 Black, *Dufferin and Ava*, pp. 223, 227–8, 244–5.
142 Lyall, *Life of Dufferin*, pp. 371–8.
143 PRONI, D1071/H/H/B/J/1/1, ff. 1, Duke of Somerset to Dufferin, 21 Jan. 1879, reporting that Disraeli had called him 'a first-rate man', on the spot; Lyall, *Life of Dufferin*, p. 264; B. Martin, The viceroyalty of Lord Dufferin, *History Today*, 10 (1960), pp. 827–8.
144 BL, India Office Papers, F130/2, ff. 89, Dufferin to Kimberley, 29 May 1885.
145 See, for instance, PRONI, D1071/H/H/M/17/1, Viceroy's notebook, ff. 309, Character and views of the Amir, 31 Mar. 1885; BL, Grant Duff Papers, F234/194, ff. 5, Dufferin to Grant Duff, 23 Apr. 1885; BL, Kilbracken Papers, F102/10, ff. 17, Dufferin to Kilbracken, 26 Jan. 1885; BL, Add MSS 951/10, ff. 111, Dufferin to Lyall, 4 Mar. 1885.
146 BL, Grant Duff Papers, F234/194, ff. 4, Dufferin to Grant Duff, 26 Feb. 1885; Hatfield House, Papers of the 3rd Marquis of Salisbury, ff. 19, Dufferin to Salisbury, 11 Aug. 1887; PRONI, D1071/M/17/1, ff. 309, Dufferin's notes on 'Character and views of the Amir', 31 Mar. 1885.
147 BL, India Office Papers, F130/2, ff. 119, Dufferin to Churchill, 30 Jul. 1885.
148 Black, *Dufferin and Ava*, p. 232; Gailey, *Lost Imperialist*, pp. 281, 290–1.
149 Dufferin, *Speeches made in India*, St Andrews Day speech, 30 Nov. 1888, p. 243; Speech to the Municipality of Lucknow, 30 Jan. 1885, p. 62; N. Ethrington, *Theories of Imperialism: war, conquest and capital* (London, 1984), pp. 263–4, 270; J. Ridden, Making good citizens: national identity, religion and liberalism among the Irish elite, c. 1800–1850, unpublished PhD thesis (King's College London, 1998), pp. 12–13, 21.
150 BL, India Office papers, F130, Neg 4351, ff. 84, Dufferin to the Queen, 3 Dec. 1888: see also a more detailed letter to Kilbracken, BL, Kilbracken Papers, F130/43c, ff. 76, Dufferin to Godley, 10 Apr. 1887 and the official printed material prepared on his departure in PRONI, D1071/M/13/7.
151 See Dufferin's expressions of this feeling: BL, Kilbracken Papers, F102.10, ff. 20, Dufferin to Kilbracken, 12 Aug. 1885; McDowell, *The Irish Administration*, pp. 54–6.
152 BL, India Office Papers, F130/29a, ff. 28, Dufferin to Sir Henry Verney, 6 Jan. 1888; Gailey, *Lost Imperialist*, pp. 276–86.
153 Hatfield House, Papers of the 3rd Marquess of Salisbury, Dufferin correspondence, ff. 11, Dufferin to Salisbury, 3 Jul. 1885; a view maintained by Lord Elgin: S. Checkland, *The Elgins, 1766–1917: a tale of aristocrats, proconsuls and their wives* (Aberdeen, 1988), pp. 216, 227.
154 Lyall, *Life of Dufferin*, p. 194.

5 Remits of power
Governing the self-governed

> There is no doubt the world is best administered by Irishmen! … But still we must be generous, and it is right Scotchmen should have a turn. Nay, I will go a step further – I would even let the poor Englishman take an occasional try at the helm – if for no other reason than to make him aware how much better we manage the business.[1]

'Keeping us all in hot water'[2]

The Canadian governorship-general was Dufferin's first major imperial appointment, in terms of both prestige and length of tenure.[3] Canada was an interesting starting point for imperial service, for two reasons; first, because it was a self-governing dominion and, second, because it had confederated only five years previously, a process that was still in flux when Dufferin arrived in Quebec in 1872.[4] He was inexperienced in colonial governance, although he would not have seen it that way.[5] As a peer and landowner, Dufferin by definition had the requisite qualities and experience to lead and, as an Irish peer and landowner, he knew something about the nature of colonial power.[6] His real problem was failing to recognise that his role, 'was not to save Canadians from themselves'.[7] It was worth the trouble, at least financially: as for many landed administrators, one of the key attractions of the post was the salary and cheap living that could be found overseas.[8] The Canadian governorship-general offered an annual salary of £10,000 plus expenses, two properties and other perks.[9] Despite this, and perhaps not surprisingly considering Dufferin's personal and estate financial management, this failed to cover his costs and, in 1877, he was writing home to request an extension to his term, 'to have an opportunity of bringing my Canadian accounts a little straight. At the present moment the balance is a good deal on the wrong side.'[10] His expenditure in Canada was sometimes extraordinary; for instance, when he built a tobogganing rink and bowling alley at Rideau Hall.[11] Although the financial opportunities were not Dufferin's primary reason for taking up the post – it was prestigious and aligned to his status – it is worth highlighting in order to demonstrate the mix of pressures and objectives in the appointment of aristocratic governors.[12] As Dufferin argued when his Colonial Office superior and old friend Lord Kimberley warned him about his escalating living costs:

> By dint of a great deal of bodily exertion and I admit by a considerable amount of expenditure at the chief cities of the Dominion I have succeeded in making the GG a personage who fills the public eye, and whose social influence is recognised and regarded ... but in order to effect anything of this kind the Governor General must be something more than a *nominis umbra* registering Minutes of Council in Rideau Hall and so straightened in his circumstances as to incur obloquy for his parsimonious mode of living.[13]

This was a very aristocratic framing of the nature and purpose of the role.[14] As he pointed out to Lord Lorne, his successor, 'When I first drove up to the door of "Rideau Hall", as it used to be called, I was very nearly driving straight back to the steamer ... for at that time it was nothing more than a very small villa, such as would suit the needs of some country banker.'[15] Clearly, standards were not what was expected for a man and family of his status, and he worked hard to build up the glamour and visibility of the role. In this, he was ably assisted by his wife, Lady Hariot, who was critical to achieving his aim of increasing the profile of the post. She accompanied him everywhere on his travels and would often be found sitting in the parliamentary gallery to report back to him the latest debates. Canada cemented her role in his imperial life and reputation, supporting him through his speeches and appearances, and constructing with him the general social whirl. When they left in 1878, much of the press comment reflecting on his tenure stressed this aspect of his work in appreciative terms and highlighted the work of Lady Dufferin in arranging and supporting it. Canada (alongside India) was where the Dufferins' holistic, family-centric view of empire came most to the fore and, as a result, they became a truly imperial family.[16]

The three themes discussed in this chapter are land, loyalty and unity, which together examine the practical impact on empire of Dufferin's aristocratic and landed cultural inheritance. First, imperial unity, both within and outwith Canada. Ottawa's struggles to keep British Columbia in the confederation and Dufferin's (not always helpful) interventions will be discussed, as will the wider cultural project of building imperial unity across the north American continent and the Atlantic.[17] Dufferin's deeply held convictions about the qualities and value of a service aristocracy ('I am conscious that the desire to serve my country has never ceased to be the great passion of my life', as he said in a speech in Belfast before he left for Canada), were challenged in Canada, where there was resistance to the idea of aristocratic rule; indeed, for many, this was something they or their forebears had emigrated to escape.[18] Unsurprisingly, then, both the means and the ends of imperial unity were subject to the *sturm und drang* of private and public conflict between Dufferin and the Canadian political classes he was there to 'advise'. The issues were wide-ranging: the Irish diaspora in both

Figure 5.1 Lord Dufferin, taken in Ottawa, 1873, aged 47. The Notman studio, Ottawa, William J. Topley, proprietor/public domain via Wikimedia Commons.

Canada and the United States, the threat of annexation by the latter and Dufferin's approach to indigenous rights.[19] The second theme deals with loyalty and a consideration of the nature of nation-building within imperial structures. How did British expectations and colonial understandings of loyalty shape that evolution? Dufferin saw part of his role as building the national self-confidence of the Canadians, celebrating their achievements, balancing that against the requirement for loyalty to Britain.[20] The third theme examines land and property. The principles of property and contract were the bedrock of British politics, particularly aristocratic political engagement. They were coming under increasing pressure in this period and those tensions were translated into the imperial territories. Many of the issues stemmed from unusual land tenure systems, or land allocation models that had been put in place in the seventeenth or eighteenth centuries. These types of legacies were nothing new to Dufferin, whose inheritance was framed by the Ulster Plantation.[21] For him, property rights were universal, and any changes in one part of British territory must necessarily have an impact everywhere.[22]

Dufferin was an assiduous promoter of Canada and the imperial connection, both to Canadians and the British.[23] He was making a deliberate effort to counteract the negative impact in Canada of political debates in Britain in the late 1850s and the 1860s, which had questioned the economic value of the self-governing territories, which should, at the least, pay for their own defence and ideally be supported to full independence.[24] These debates had had a damaging effect in Canada, and so Dufferin set out to promote the idea of a secure British world to counteract it, something that mainstream Canadian political and public opinion recognised and welcomed.[25] He did this primarily by being a highly visible governor, working with his wife to run an ambitious programme of public events, parties, balls and soirees. He and Lady Hariot also travelled extensively across the dominion, with Dufferin giving speeches pressing home a number of consistent points; first, Canada's glowing future, blessed with space and natural resources; second, Canada's loyalty to Queen and empire, and how this loyalty was supported, not undermined, by its political autonomy.[26] Lastly, he encouraged the flow of European migration into Canada as the best support for the bright future he predicted for the dominion.[27] Of course, just because Dufferin claimed in speeches that Canadians were, 'satisfied to be subjects of the Queen – satisfied to be subjects of the Empire', did not mean that there was no criticism of the British connection.[28]

Dufferin defined the governorship-general both morally and hierarchically. and in terms of a benevolent paternalism, informed by his landed background.[29] This is why the visibility of his wife was so important: it reflected the paternalistic model of the landed estate at home, of a Lady Bountiful. He also took very seriously his symbolic position as the representative of the Crown in Canada, arguing that the governorship-general should be promoted to a viceroyalty, and for more honours to be given to Canadians to reward their loyalty and demonstrate the benefit of the British connection.[30] He was driven in part by his desire to ensure Canadian institutions and norms differed as far as possible from those of the United States: 'it has been my object to lose no opportunity of stamping upon all our [that is, Canadian] institutions, whether social or political, such a character as would most tend to remove them from the American and approximate them to the English type.'[31] Having criticized the absentee landlords of Ireland and watched with concern Queen Victoria's retreat into private life after the death of the Prince Consort in 1861, he understood the importance of visibility.[32] He was also quick to point out to the Canadian administration that the cost of his establishment (which he calculated to be £13,200 in his first six months of arriving in Canada) would be, 'what in England would be considered a modest establishment for a Peer or an ordinary country gentleman'.[33] Dufferin led a pattern of aristocratic activity in Canada that was evident across the other dominions and which offered the greatest scope for the replication of Britain's social hierarchy. This was the 'aristocratic thread' that ran through the settler colonies, stratifying those societies, underpinned by the appointment of aristocratic governors such as Dufferin, who headed up social regimes of unprecedented activity, cost and magnificence.[34]

Dufferin's vision did not meet with universal approval in Canada and, on occasion, openly conflicted with that of the Canadian administrations, especially that of the Liberals under Alexander Mackenzie and his colleague Edward Blake, who regarded Dufferin as interfering well beyond the constitutional boundaries of his office.[35] Dufferin was realistic about the possibility of an eventual constitutional break between Britain and Canada – and was much more sanguine about this than for Ireland – although he remained a passionate advocate of the benefits of the British connection, for both Britain and Canada. His analysis was that French Canada spearheaded discontent, with Montreal acting as the 'head quarters of the Anti-British School'. His relatively relaxed attitude may have been due to the fact he regarded the leading figures as not very 'able men or having definite ideas'.[36] But his principal view was that Britain's imperial dominance had to be justified by 'good' governance, particularly in the settlement and self-governing dominions.[37] In order to implement this good governance, an understanding of Canada's priorities – which Dufferin on a number of occasions thought he was able to identify more accurately than Canada's political classes – was required.[38]

Dufferin took a hands-on approach to his role and quite quickly bumped up against its limits, noting to Kimberley that, 'in administering a Constitutional Government one has but little opportunity of much action in positive usefulness'.[39] This did not prevent him trying, however, bringing strain and tension into his relations with Canadian ministers and public opinion, at times. Their feathers were no doubt also ruffled by his patrician, paternalistic manner; he believed that, as a man of cosmopolitan education and experience, with a landed inheritance and being part of an aristocratic elite, it was his role to improve the conduct and quality of Canadian politics.[40] In Dufferin's view, Canada's politicians were parochial and limited, a result of their humble or middle-class backgrounds: he never tired of pointing out that Alexander Mackenzie had been a stonemason, and had actually 'worked with his hands'.[41] There were some exceptions: he regarded Edward Blake as the most able politician in Canada, despite his advanced views on Canada's position in relation to Britain, 'as might have been expected, [as he] is an Irishman'.[42] This improving instinct was an integral part of Dufferin's cultural identity and, as might easily be imagined, Canada's politicians (and its electors) were resistant to it.

Wider external and domestic pressures help explain these tensions. Internally, Canada's new confederation was only five years-old when Dufferin arrived in 1872 and, although its creation had been a political triumph, disagreements had emerged between the provincial and federal governments, as new challenges and new modes of response developed.[43] The geographies of tension during Dufferin's term of office centred on Prince Edward Island's negotiation with, and eventual entry into, the confederation and British Columbia's turbulent relationship with the federal government due to delays to the Canadian Pacific Railway.[44] The severe economic depression that afflicted Canada from 1873 constrained possibilities for the federal government and dented national confidence. Second, there was the aftermath of the Red River Rising to deal with, including the fate of Louis

Riel, Ambroise-Dydime Lepine and their compatriots.[45] The dream of Canadian confederation was a nightmare for some, as Riel's Metis and Canada's indigenous nations knew.[46] In addition, there was ongoing religious tension, principally between Protestant Orange and Roman Catholic (often Francophile) communities. Dufferin was no stranger to sectarianism and, comparing his responses in Ulster and Canada (and later in India), highlights the transnational nature of Dufferin's elite thinking.[47] Lastly, there were many external pressures on Canada, mainly focused around the United States.[48] Some American politicians had called on Britain to hand over Canada to the United States as reparation for breaking promises of neutrality during the civil war; some British MPs agreed, arguing this was a good opportunity to rid Britain of one imperial burden.[49] In the short term, the thorny negotiation of a new Reciprocity Treaty between the two nations had to be faced – which, in a time of economic depression, became a critical point of national interest.

His first major overseas appointment, Dufferin's experiences in Canada challenged nearly all aspects of his landed, aristocratic identity and, far from being an easy sinecure, was a period that Lord Carnarvon rightly diagnosed as, 'keep[ing] us all in hot water'.[50] Dufferin resisted the challenges robustly but, in almost every case, the eventual outcome would constitute a victory for the Canadian interpretation of Anglo-Canadian relations and constitutional powers. The distinction between British interests and his aristocratic views was often blurred, with his Colonial Office masters on more than one occasion moved to rein him in to preserve accepted constitutional boundaries and good working relations.[51] Unsurprisingly, both the Liberal and Conservative secretaries of state for the colonies during Dufferin's tenure, Lord Kimberley and Lord Carnarvon, shared Dufferin's landed, aristocratic background – indeed, they were his old school and university friends.[52] They shared Dufferin's general outlook, but both regarded Canada as the least of their imperial worries, not sharing the pressures Dufferin was under as the man on the spot.[53] It was for this very reason that men of Dufferin's class and background were selected to serve; as landed, educated men of the world, they could be trusted to maintain British interests without day-to-day supervision.[54] But the tension created by his insider/outsider position never dissipated, with Dufferin exercising extreme caution before taking any action, sensitive to any action that might damage his reputation (the most precious commodity of his class), and at the same time champing at the bit to exercise real power in a way not possible in Britain.[55]

Unity – 'Canada is more British than Britain'[56]

> I shall be glad when my term is over. The Governorship of a colony with Constitutional advisers does not admit much real control over its affairs and I miss the stimulus of responsibility.[57]

Dufferin was complaining to Lord Carnarvon, his Colonial Office master, that, as the Crown's representative in a self-governing colony, he found himself with not enough real power.[58] This would not be for want of trying. One of the aspects of transnational imperial governance faced by Dufferin was that of territorial and constitutional unity.[59] This issue expressed itself during his tenure through one of the greatest political challenges of the decade: the Pacific Scandal. This was a constitutional corruption affair that broke in 1873, bringing down Sir John A. Macdonald's Conservative government, but the consequences of which rumbled on into 1876, bringing Dufferin into sharp conflict with both the Liberal administration over the position of British Columbia in the confederation and wider Canadian public opinion. The episode throws into sharp relief Dufferin's conception of his role as governor-general, not only with regard to constitutional terms, but also his wider governing priorities.[60] Both came into direct conflict with Canadian political and public opinion, and generated a debate about the ideal limits of British power, particularly in domestic political crises. Dufferin had very defined ideas about how the Canadian federal administration should act: his view was that it was falling short in enacting 'good' governance, and that it was his duty to get them on the straight and narrow.[61] Dufferin's landed and aristocratic background meant he placed great emphasis on the moral, personal aspects of governance; of fair play and political purity. He wished to uphold British standards of political life in Canada, regarding its political culture as inferior, fuelled by electoral corruption and a bitterly factional newspaper press. He held a particularly dim view of the Liberal administration under Alexander Mackenzie, and there is little doubt that Dufferin showed a good deal of personal and political favouritism towards Sir John A. Macdonald and his Conservative colleagues.[62] 'Sir John is by far the ablest public man in Canada, experienced, and as far as I can see really anxious for the good of his country', he wrote to Kimberley, although the extent and consequences of Sir John's problematic drinking were also regularly reported back to the Colonial Office.[63] 'The liability of one's Prime Minister to remain drunk for several days in succession at uncertain periods, a good deal complicates one's power of prognosticating the future', he ruefully noted.[64] He regarded most Canadian politicians as being too inexperienced to govern effectively: 'their greatest lack is official experience. In this they are frightfully deficient. Mackenzie whom personally I like very much, is cautious, but small and narrow.'[65]

With this as his starting point, it is perhaps not surprising that, when intense political or constitutional pressures were applied to Dufferin's relationship with leading politicians, acrimonious outbursts were the result, necessitating the personal intervention (twice) of the colonial secretary and generating meetings between Dufferin, Mackenzie and Blake that descended into shouting and tears of rage on both sides.[66] Despite his robust stance, Dufferin effectively lost every one of these arguments.[67] The government argued passionately against British interference in both the Pacific Scandal and the later British Columbia negotiations, seeing them both as purely domestic issues over which neither the Colonial Office nor the governor-general had any jurisdiction and they eventually established this point.[68]

In order to avoid similar confrontations in the future, after Dufferin's departure in 1878 they also agreed with the Colonial Office new Letters Patent, spelling out explicitly the limitations of the office of governor-general.[69]

Dufferin was faced with his first crisis early on in his tenure when the Pacific Scandal broke, shaking Canadian politics and forcing him to take a clear line in a confused context.[70] The crisis was born of the efforts of Sir John and his Conservative administration to get the great Canadian Pacific Railway project off the ground. It had been promised in 1871 as part of the agreement bringing British Columbia into the confederation, and was one of the most ambitious and expensive railway schemes in the world. The Canadian government was struggling to attract contractors to take on the project but, eventually, an agreement was reached with a consortium headed up by Sir Hugh Allan, a Saltcoats-born Canadian capitalist. He – and Sir John – declared that the majority of the consortium's investment was from Canadian, not American, sources, in line with the stipulations of the legislation passed to approve the building of the railway.[71] Behind this was a fear on the part of Canadians that their national railway project would be hijacked by the United States, furthering the annexationist agendas of some Americans.[72] The railway was more than a major infrastructural project; it would open up central and western Canada to agricultural emigrants, and secure the vast territories of the west away from encroachments by the United States.[73] The resulting crisis consisted of two elements; first, accusations were made that Sir Hugh Allan had lied and that, in fact, many of his backers *were* American, and, second, that Sir John had corruptly requested and received a large sum of money ($247,000) from Sir Hugh for election expenses in exchange for commissioning his consortium.[74] Uproar ensued and Sir John was forced to appoint a parliamentary committee in August 1873 to investigate the scandal, resulting in an immediate question as to whether Parliament should be prorogued, a decision that Dufferin as governor-general had to make. A prorogation would delay the inquiry, and so was vehemently opposed by the Opposition and the press. The political classes split down party lines, raging and accusing each other of corruption.[75] Dufferin agonised over the decision, recognising that if he did prorogue Parliament, he would be accused of favouritism towards Sir John and his Conservatives, even if constitutionally it was right to do so. 'We are in a devil of a mess here and my position is not to be envied. The whole country is in a violent state of excitement from one end to the other and the language of the newspaper press is becoming perfectly rabid', he wrote to Kimberley.[76] On the advice of the Colonial Office, he did prorogue Parliament, on condition it met again within two months, generating outrage in Parliament and the press. His public profile, so jealously guarded and a point of great sensitivity for Dufferin, was attacked and no doubt weakened permanently in the eyes of many Canadians.

The other issue this crisis highlighted was the constitutional extent of British involvement when difficulties – constitutional, economic or political – emerged. Dufferin was aware of the sensitivities and was – as can be seen throughout his career – inherently cautious, preferring to execute the explicit instructions of the Colonial Office on contentious issues, rather than develop his own policy, a balance that was not always appreciated in Whitehall.[77] As he admitted to Kimberley: 'I know that I am not sent here in order that the Colonial Office may have the trouble and responsibility of governing Canada from Downing Street and I hope to be able to pull through all right.'[78] The Pacific Scandal was precisely the kind of situation Dufferin abhorred; he was protective of his reputation and above all desired popularity.[79] However, when looking back after the immediate scandal had passed, he saw he had come through the fire unscathed: 'I have been very much bored and worried, and it is vexatious being dragged into such a dirty quarrel and I regret coming into collision with any section of my Canadians, but … I am not sorry to have an opportunity of shewing them that however anxious I may be to be gracious and civil I don't care a damn for anyone when a matter of duty is involved.'[80] Kimberley, though, wrote with a cautionary note in the aftermath, to urge Dufferin to be absolutely sure that he did not grow overconfident and overstep the boundaries of his role: 'It is no doubt very tempting to act in one's own opinion, but if once the Gov.r General comes forward beyond the limits of his constitutional prerogative, the whole machine would get out of gear.'[81]

The consequences of the Pacific Scandal lasted much longer for the Canadian government and, in 1876, Dufferin reported that work had still not begun on the railway. Worse was the Liberal administration's outspoken condemnation of the Conservative government for having ever agreed to build the railway as far as Victoria, and rising protest in British Columbia that it was not being treated fairly and would secede from the confederation unless the railway was built.[82] This would have been the ultimate disaster in Dufferin's view; that during his tenure the confederation would be broken and reduced. As a result, he spent most of 1876 joining battle with Alexander Mackenzie and Edward Blake – who were highly critical of the original deal made with British Columbia – over the issue.[83] Dufferin thought that the Liberals were failing to offer good governance by reneging on a promise made, however inconvenient that now was, and saw himself as a stern but fond schoolmaster enforcing discipline on the child-like Canadians.[84] 'My own opinion so far as I am prepared to express one at present, is, that British Columbia has infinitely more cause to complain of what my ministers have said, than of what they have done, or failed to do', he wrote to Carnarvon, then the colonial secretary.[85] As he put it somewhat patronisingly: 'If only I can get my ministers to use a little good temper and liberality our difficulties with the province would be readily got over, but the pettiness of Colonial politics is inconceivable until you come to be mixed up with them.'[86] He had Mackenzie in particular in his sights: 'Mackenzie is a small man without creative genius or any real initiative, or power of forecast. When the elements of a problem are laid before him he has good sense and judgement sufficient to reach a right conclusion, but that is all and his whole Pacific Railway policy has been full of mistakes and miscalculations.'[87] Despite this disapproval, Dufferin by no means got his own way during the crisis. Mackenzie and Blake put up a robust defence of Canadian privileges against the limits of imperial interference in domestic matters during a series of highly charged and emotional meetings.[88] The stinging after-effects of these echo in the ensuing correspondence and it is clear that very strong words were exchanged, not just on the details of British Columbia's position, but also on the purpose and limits of the Anglo-Canadian connection.[89] Dufferin pushed very hard for the Canadian government to accept arbitration over the British Columbian question by the colonial secretary Lord Carnarvon, which was eventually agreed, although the resulting 'Carnarvon Terms' only generated more discontent.[90] During a furious meeting, Mackenzie put forward his objections to the tone and content of the Terms, the content of which can be gleaned from Dufferin's letter to him afterwards:

> You asked me the other day – after all who is Lord Carnarvon? It is true Lord Carnarvon is nobody ... but though Lord Carnarvon is personally nothing beyond what his abilities have made him, he is the official representative and spokesman of the Power upon whom Canada is dependent for her nationality, her autonomy, and her protection both by sea and by land, and for whose sake, though this view of the case seems seldom to be considered on this side of the Atlantic, England is content to run perpetual risks, and to submit to what many consider humiliating, and all admit to be mortifying sacrifices.[91]

Mackenzie was forced to placate Dufferin's offended dignity, although his irritation over the nature of the dispute – which Dufferin was quick to personalise as an insult to Carnarvon and himself – is evident: 'I certainly had no desire or disposition to entertain or show anything but a conciliatory disposition in this prolonged dispute. I certainly never for a moment doubted Lord Carnarvon's earnest desire to aid us, or Your Excellency's disposition to aid the govt [sic] in reaching firm ground of some sort.'[92] Rather than withdraw, Dufferin again overstepped the bounds of his role by offering to travel to British Columbia as an independent agent and negotiator to try and settle the question, when he had no constitutional powers to do so.[93] He did undertake the visit, but only in his ordinary capacity of a governor-general and during the last two years of his tenure avoided further controversy.[94]

For a man concerned with the principles of imperial unity, Dufferin ran into a good deal of trouble attempting to maintain good relations across the confederation and with the administrations.[95] At root, this was because he believed he was qualified to promote good governance in Canada, perhaps to a greater extent than the Canadian political classes, but he was resisted because he tried to act as a head of government, rather than a head of state. This was due to a combination of two factors: first, even if Canadian politicians agreed in principle that there were problems with their political system, it was not for Britain, represented by Dufferin, to tell them how to reform it.[96] As a self-governing dominion, Canadian governments were as free to make mistakes in their policies as any other country. Second, Dufferin's handling of both crises was too patrician in tone to encourage compromise. Although he understood in theory the limits of his powers as governor, he did not always adhere to them in practice due to his aristocratic inheritance.[97] He was one of a cadre of men born to rule and his attempts to do so in Canada led to conflict and eventual defeat. Dufferin's conceptions of governance evolved over time in response to the reception his actions received, principally from Liberals such as Mackenzie and Blake. He became more cautious and, when preparing to leave, he wrote to his successor that, 'with regard to the degree the G.G. shd [sic] interfere with the administration of the country. My plan has been to fidget as little as possible with the details and minor matters of govt, and to reserve all my strength for great occasions, so that when I did intervene it shd [sic] be in an effectual manner.'[98] Whether or not Dufferin was entirely effectual on minor or major matters of government can be questioned.

Loyalty – 'a certain amount of Celtic effervescence'[99]

> We find that we can manage the Irish that come straight out to us very well. If not subjected to improper influences they become good and loyal members of society, but if they undergo a preliminary Yankification they scarcely ever become reconciled to our Government.[100]

Dufferin identified other challenges and opportunities for British dominion in Canada that, again, were related to his landed and Irish patrimony. Assumptions about various national and racial attributes were embedded in contemporary thinking and were applied both to Dufferin as an Irishman and to emigrant Canadian society. As one British editorial commented on Dufferin: 'Irish blood and breeding will stand him in good stead among a people variously composed of Celt and Teuton, yet strongly attached to the old country.'[101] This racial stereotyping was very much present in Ireland and British opinion on Ireland and was something Dufferin had a mixed relationship with, sometimes playing on his Irish 'traits', but also rejecting some of the negative extremities applied to his countrymen.[102] This section will examine what Dufferin regarded as the most serious challenges to the fabric of Canadian loyalty to Britain, as well as how he tried to avert them.

The first was the most important external pressure on Canada: the United States. 'What a set these Yankees are!' Dufferin exclaimed in 1876, reflecting commonly held attitudes towards the republic and its people among British elites.[103] This was largely based on the poor relations between Britain and the United States since the American Civil War, but Dufferin had his class and nation's typical elitist view of American politics, society and manners. His main concern as governor-general was that it would be Canadian-American relations, 'that we shall eventually find the relations of the

Dominion with the Mother Country work with the greatest amount of friction'.[104] Disagreement between Canada and Britain on all aspects of relations with the United States – after all, Canada's neighbour and a growing global power – was bound to create tension, particularly as Britain had ultimate jurisdiction over Canada's foreign and diplomatic activities. 'The fact is the diplomatic relations of Canada with the Yankees is one of the tender spots in the relations with the Dominion with the mother country, and some of these days the question will have to be seriously considered', as Dufferin gloomily noted.[105] In the 1870s, there were many potential areas of friction, including Britain's conduct during the American Civil War and the arguments of some American politicians that Canada should be handed over by the British as reparation for their failure to adhere to neutrality. Perhaps more concerning for Dufferin was the small minority of internal pro-annexation Canadian voices.[106] Dufferin regarded his primary duty on arriving in Canada as combating these calls: 'You may depend upon my doing my best both to weld this Dominion into an Imperium solid enough to defy all attraction from its powerful neighbour across the line, and to perpetuate its innate loyalty to the Mother Country', he wrote to Carnarvon.[107] As for the annexationists, Dufferin was confident they were no serious threat internally, but he was less confident as to the longer-term constitutional future of Canada, and he regarded independence as their ultimate destiny:

> There may indeed be a few individuals at Montreal, Bankers, Capitalists and others, whose material interests are so implicated with various commercial undertakings in the States, as to make them wish for a change, but the whole current of popular sympathy runs in an opposite direction. But ... I cannot help suspecting that there is a growing desire amongst the younger generation to regard 'Independence' as their ultimate destiny. Nor do I think that this novel mode of thought will be devoid of benefit, provided it remains for the next twenty or thirty years a vague aspiration and is not prematurely converted into a practical project.[108]

This highlights again Dufferin's conception of Canadians as somewhat child-like and immature in their development, requiring British guidance as well military protection.[109] He therefore regarded the looming presence of the United States as beneficial for the connection between Britain and Canada, noting to his friend and regular correspondent Lady Dartrey that, 'their [Canadian's] loyalty is fanatical, bred of their hatred to the Yankee, and their fear of being absorbed by the States'.[110] Ideally, Canadian loyalty would be grounded on a more positive basis than this. Dufferin had his doubts, however; as well as labouring under differences of race and religion to an extent of even 'greater embarrassment even than they do in our beloved Ireland', the very newness of the Canadian confederation generated an inherent instability through constant questioning of the future, 'namely, as to whether the country is to be Imperial, Independent or American'.[111] This uncertainty was successfully manipulated for the benefit of maintaining loyalty to Britain. He used the spectre of the United States during the British Columbia crisis, for instance, in order to press upon the Liberal ministry how high the stakes were in terms of Canada's security along the western border.[112]

The second challenge facing Dufferin consisted of tensions within the Irish community in Canada, divided along Protestant Orange and Roman Catholic lines.[113] Initially, Dufferin was pleasantly surprised by the attitudes he found among the Irish communities in Canada: 'even my Brother Paddies are without a grievance', as he expressed it to Argyll.[114] He was being facetious, but his racialised language set him apart from the mass of Irish migrants of a lower social status than himself and, anyway, this sanguine view was not to last. Dufferin was acutely sensitive towards Irish nationalism, wherever he found it – in Ireland, Canada, the United States or India – and he subscribed to what he called the 'germ theory': that nationalist agitation was contagious and was spreading across the empire. In Canada, this threat had been manifested through the Fenian movement, principally based across the border in the United States, from which various ill-starred raids had taken place.[115] Although Dufferin was somewhat dismissive of these raids, at the time they had generated a good deal of concern in Canada over Britain's ambivalent response, a result of trying to balance public and political opinion in the Dominion with relations with the United States that were still tricky.[116] Dufferin saw Fenians in Canada more as bandits than dangerous political radicals and he put the movement down to 'a certain amount of Celtic effervescence'.[117] In contrast, Dufferin was pleased to see that, in some cases, his long-standing contention that the solution to Ireland's problems rested on emigration seemed to be borne out by what he saw in Canada.[118] As he wrote to Lord Lansdowne:

> Now I have seen in Canada what is the result of the Irish peasant having been compelled by circumstances to quit his potato ground, and put his shoulder to the wheel in a *bona fide* manner, and nothing can be more satisfactory … he becomes prosperous, industrious and contented, and no one can see the Canadian or Yankee descendants of the Irish cottiers of 19 or 20 years ago without being made to feel what is the real remedy for the miserable condition of Irish agriculture, and the perennial wretchedness of the Irish population of the West.[119]

While Dufferin was secure in his position as a Protestant (Anglican) and regarded Roman Catholicism as problematic on its own terms, and especially in relation to social relations in Ireland, he rarely expressed these views publicly or politically; of far greater concern in his eyes was how sectarianism presented a civil problem, not only in Ulster, but in Canada. Almost as soon as he arrived, he had to deal with conflict in Quebec city between Protestant Irish and French Canadian ship-loaders, the former threatening to prevent the latter from working. As Dufferin pointed out, 'this business has made me feel as if I was back again in the old country amid the ship-carpenters of Belfast'.[120] He disapproved of expressions of both Irish nationalism and Protestant loyalty, mainly in the form of the Orange Order.[121] It was this that meant Dufferin uncoupled the typical racial stereotypes of the Irish from sectarian prejudices. Dufferin disapproved of the Orange Order on class grounds – for example, regarding them as unrespectable working class rabble – but also because their 'bounce and bluster' created a destabilising social effect.[122] 'The conduct of the Orangemen and the language of the Orange Press has been equally offensive and exasperating', he noted in 1878, as yet another spell of civic disorder brewed in Montreal.[123] Dufferin was quick to draw on his Irish experiences when in Canada, and to press the government to do so, too.[124] He argued that the rule of law had to be supported by military force as was the case in that other city of empire, Belfast: 'There is absolutely no force whatever behind the Law', he complained, 'What we want is a body like the Irish Constabulary living in Barracks secluded from all contact with the population and disciplined and controlled by the Central and not the subordinate authority.'[125] Dufferin was, in general, more restrained in his approach to sectarian disorder than some of his cabinet superiors. Kimberley, for instance, wrote, 'Your Quebec election riot is also an improvement on English riots tho' it hardly comes up to the Belfast standard. You will see the Belfast people have greatly distinguished themselves. For the life of me I can't understand why the authorities did not order the police and if necessary the soldiers to fire at the mob point blank on the first shot being fired by the mob.'[126] Dufferin knew better than that: yes, some degree of 'firmness' was helpful, but if it stepped over any constitutional lines, it would constitute the opposite of the good governance he promoted for Canada (and Ireland).[127] His concern was to prevent religious denominations from linking themselves to political parties, something he abhorred in Ireland and regarded as a retrograde step for Canada, so early on in the confederation's history.[128]

Dufferin saw a source of weakness in the treatment of Canada's indigenous nations, both in terms of the violence perpetrated on them and the destruction of their land and other rights through the treaties signed before and during his tenure that either pushed them onto reservations or into new western and northern territories.[129] Where does Dufferin's ideal of good governance sit when we consider Canada's indigenous population? His view was informed by a romantic conception of indigenous peoples as 'noble savages', a common stereotype and one that was consolidated when he undertook his expedition to the Artic in the 1850s. His account of that journey, the best-selling *Letters from High Latitudes*, is replete with descriptions and drawings of the noble savages of those regions. For Dufferin, although perhaps noble, Canada's indigenous peoples would always remain primarily savages: 'I should hardly have thought these savages capable of so extended a diplomacy', he noted when informed of ongoing negotiations with a band of Sioux in the west.[130] He believed in British racial superiority and, although he felt sympathy for their plight, he saw them as on the wrong side of history, destined to be swept away on the tide of inevitable progress. In this way, they were less to blame for their actions than Irish or Indian nationalists, whom he regarded as pointlessly refusing to accept the realities of British power despite having the capacity to do so.[131] As such, he attempted to enforce the rule of law for Canada's indigenous peoples, however exploitative and violent that was in practice. In 1877, he lambasted the British Columbian provincial government for not following the standard practice elsewhere of signing treaties for lands. As he complained to Carnarvon: 'instead of following the example of Canada and buying up the Indian title the whites in British Columbia have simply claimed the land as their own, and though they have made certain Indian reservations in various places a great deal of injustice has been perpetrated both in regard to their allotment and the subsequent resumption of portions of them'.[132] He was concerned that Britain's reputation for good governance would be damaged by such actions and did his part by giving speeches encouraging indigenous peoples to give up their traditional ways of life to learn agriculture, to submit to treaties and reservations, to become good Canadians and enjoy the benefits of British rule.[133] His efforts towards making Canadian administrations and settlers desist from the worst outrages and injustices, while at the same time cajoling native communities to submit to the loss of their lands and way of life, was little different to those of his predecessors and successors in Canada and was as ineffectual.[134]

What constituted Canadian loyalty to Britain? First, Britain had to show an interest, a willingness to consider Canadian issues and demonstrate Canadian problems were understood. Dufferin faced an uphill battle rebuilding trust after years of British neglect and a political debate that had questioned the value of the Canadian connection entirely. This was why he was keen to introduce a 'native' aristocracy and honours system, and argued for the elevation of the governorship-general to a viceroyalty. In his worldview, establishing hierarchies and honours based on inheritance alongside a constitutional monarchy was the hallmark of British governance. As the representative in Canada of that monarchy, Dufferin made himself a visible figurehead, giving speeches, holding events, handing out prizes and meeting hundreds of ordinary Canadians in the process.[135] Although on the surface this seems like a superficial approach, it was in fact how Dufferin conceptualised good governance. In the same way as he criticised Irish landowners for being absentee and neglecting their responsibilities, he worked in Canada to be as visible as possible to remind the population there of the importance of the British connection and the demonstration of imperial loyalty.

Land – 'so troublesome a species of property'[136]

As with any discussion about land issues – economic, political or cultural – in any geographical context, in Canada multiple layers of meaning and consequence were intertwined, creating the combustible conditions for disagreement that we can see globally during Dufferin's career.[137] He was no stranger to controversies over land reform; indeed, his entire perspective on land in the dominions and colonies was framed and conditioned by his personal ownership of land in Ireland and the challenges to it. While in Canada, he was horrified to see the same issues emerge and he was quick to identify international links between land reform movements.[138] Witness his outrage when first made aware of a potential land act for Prince Edward Island (PEI): his language was certainly not that of compromise and spoke of a growing paranoia about an international threat to landed power: 'There has also come up from the Local Legislature of Prince Edward Island a Bill expropriating land owners in the Island under very unfair conditions. I have told my Government that I could not consent to it becoming law.'[139] He carried on in the same private letter to criticise Irish land reform measures being debated at Westminster, explicitly linking the two land questions.[140] He was also acutely aware of land reform tussles ongoing in India and in Australia and, in his later appointment in India, would reinforce the global and transnational view of the threat of land reform that he brought to Canada.[141] The concept of good governance also linked these controversies, but not in ways with which Dufferin agreed. For PEI's reformers, maintaining landlord rights at the point of the bayonet was not feasible; failing to act would fatally undermine the state's (provincial, federal and, by extension, imperial) authority and jeopardise negotiations over confederation.[142] Canada was a settlement colony, and part of its attraction to European emigrants was the opportunity to own land outright, escaping the whims of Old World landlordism.[143]

There were really a number of different issues at stake in the island province; first, was the legacy of the land lottery held in eighteenth-century London that left large portions of the island's excellent arable land in the ownership of a small number of mainly absentee private individuals and families.[144] A royal commission appointed in 1860 had condemned the original settlement of the lots and recommended a Land Purchase Act to unravel the great absentee holdings. The commissioners suggested that the British government guarantee a loan of £100,000 to underwrite this legislation, but this was refused by the Colonial Office, which suggested that if PEI joined the confederation it might reconsider.[145] A long period of tenant agitation ensued, including rent strikes, as no action was taken at all.[146] There were also constitutional issues to consider: in 1873, PEI came into the confederation, an occasion Dufferin marked by visiting the island to celebrate.[147] 'Nothing could have been more joyous or exuberant than our reception', he wrote to Kimberley, 'the whole population are unanimous in their delight at Confederation, but regard it as the annexation of the Dominion to the Island.'[148] It was not all happy celebration, however; the high cost of confederation linked the two issues of land and constitutional politics. Economic support was demanded by PEI to compensate for a failed railway-building project on the island, as well as support (legislative and financial) for the long-awaited Land Purchase Act, by which the island government proposed to buy out the large absentee landlords on its own account. Land reform would be as expensive in Canada to central exchequers as it was in Ireland or India.

The controversy is interesting on a number of different levels. It reminds us that even in Canada, regarded by most prospective European emigrants as a free, land-rich utopia, land issues were not entirely clear-cut, with competing definitions of the rights and responsibilities of property.[149] Even Dufferin, in his many speeches encouraging migrants to Canada, would often stress as one of its advantages that of, 'the prospect of independence, of a roof over his head for which he shall pay no rent, and of ripening cornfields around his homestead which own no master but himself'.[150] Eventually, he admitted that expectations of land rights were necessarily different in Canada to those in Britain, eventually acknowledging that they would need to be reformed in PEI: 'Proprietorial rights, in the sense in which they exist in England, are very unsuitable to the atmosphere of this country, and I imagine a perpetual agitation will prevail in the island until its land tenures are assimilated to those of neighbouring provinces.'[151] It was clear that the majority of PEI's inhabitants did not recognise large-scale absentee landlordism as conducive to their interests, or part of their identity, and this posed a direct challenge to Dufferin – to *his* interests and identity.[152] This was the first occasion where Dufferin was able to think in practical terms about land issues transnationally, particularly the impact reform in PEI might have in Ireland, Britain, or elsewhere.[153] It is also useful to remember that, in these years, Dufferin was pressing forward with the sale of the bulk of his estates and was highly sensitive to issues around land prices, conditions of sale and the darkening political context for landed privilege.[154] Land was not like other assets in Dufferin's view; it endowed financial income, but also social, cultural and political status and leadership. As such, its removal by compulsion he regarded as immoral confiscation, and also as a policy that should be outwith the powers of any liberal parliamentary property-owning democracy. In his view, 'the [PEI] Act is one of simple confiscation under the pretence of arbitration, as it compels owners to sell and no one can believe that they will get the full value of their lands thus forced onto the market'.[155] His efforts to sell his estate coloured his views about the PEI controversy and was why he felt so strongly about the position of the PEI landlords and the conditions by which they were being forced to sell. They put pressure on Dufferin, arguing that land purchase legislation was at odds with the fundamental principles of British society, that it would be used by Irish agitators, and that landlordism would not be safe anywhere.[156] The two aspects of the bill he really objected to were the fact that the PEI government wanted to push through this purchase at very low values, perhaps less than sixteen years' purchase price (he achieved twenty-five years' on his own property in Ireland, albeit he had substantially improved it).[157] Second, due to the tenant agitation, the PEI landlords had not received regular rents and Dufferin fought hard to ensure they were eventually paid the value of these lost rents, plus interest, as part of their compensation package.[158] Dufferin leant on the federal government, and an initial arbitration committee sat in 1875, resulting in the settlement of the first ten cases, totalling, '187,000 acres (out of about 310,000 intended to be purchased by the government) ... and the total of the awards is $306,550'. Although Dufferin had initially been entirely opposed to the land reform programme proposed for PEI, by the end he was able to report that, 'generally I think the proprietors have got all they could expect'.[159] By the early 1880s, when faced with the Irish Land Act of 1881, Dufferin had changed his mind and suggested to the Bessborough Commission that land purchase, rather than the 'dual ownership' model being proposed by the Liberal government, would be a more equitable solution for Irish landowners.[160] This view was informed by his experiences in Canada and how the 1874 Act for PEI operated in principle and practice. From a position to total hostility in the early 1870s, land purchase was a principle Dufferin would come to support by 1880, promoting it as a more landlord-friendly alternative to the 1881 Irish Land Act. This *volte face* came about because he saw in action the policy in the colonial context, recognised the political and economic realities, and sought a favourable compromise for the interests of private property.

The other transnational aspect to this question was that of economic development and who was to pay for it. There was fairly universal support on PEI – among its residents, provincial politicians and rural tenantry – for the view that ownership of land equalled the power to implement economic and infrastructure development plans. Among the most important of these was a railway, to better facilitate the movement of agricultural and fishing produce, as well as eventually to link up (via a ferry) with the Canadian Pacific Railway. The development of the local economy was tied to suitable infrastructure being put in place, and to the opportunities and restrictions of the particular type of landownership on the island. It was also linked to the development of a Canadian national identity. Although historians have rightly argued that PEI joined the confederation in 1873 principally for short-term reasons, in the long-term they would be part of and contribute to the identity of confederated Canada, an identity that itself was still under construction. Dufferin gave considerable thought to this question and saw it as one of his most important duties as governor to promote the idea of a strong, united Canada. By contrast, Kimberley, then the secretary of state for the colonies, was his usual cynical self: 'The mess they have got into with their railways makes them feel the necessity for Confederation.'[161] The Lieutenant Governor of PEI made no bones about these pressures either: 'Our railway debt ... will not fall short of £660,000 sterling ... Looking the question fairly in the face, my ministers see that there are only two courses open to them; either they must impose heavy additional taxes on the people ... or seek admission into the Union, provided that Canada would thereupon make our railway debt her own.'[162] For Dufferin, it did not really matter, so long as the federal government grasped the opportunity created by the financial travails of the island government to bring it into the confederation and further strengthen the dominion.

130 *Remits of power*

False rumours and extraneous hallucinations

When Dufferin was preparing to leave his Canadian post in 1878, he was forwarded the thanks of the Queen for delivering a successful tenure. In particular:

> Her Majesty's Government have not failed to notice the high estimation and regard in which your Lordship has been held by all classes in Canada and they feel confident that the admirable manner in which you have fulfilled the duties of the Queen's Representative has done much to strengthen and deepen in the hearts of the Canadian people that spirit of loyalty and devotion to the British Crown and Empire of which there have been gratifying evidences.[163]

In this, Dufferin had been successful.[164] He and Lady Hariot had put a great deal of personal energy into travelling around the dominion, actively working with the press and meeting a large number of Canadians of all classes, who recognised and appreciated their efforts. He constantly reinforced the message that Britain appreciated the connection with Canada, that it was different (and superior) to the republic over the border, and that it had a bright future ahead of it, particularly once its population had increased and all the provinces were confederated. He stressed the centrality of this activity to his successor, Lord Lorne, as: 'consolidating the various elements of which the Canadian Community is composed as well as towards creating a more intimate union between the colony and the Mother Country'.[165] Perhaps another indication of his relative success lies in the fact that Sir John A. Macdonald wrote privately to the British government to request that his tenure be extended, arguing that his experience would make it possible to bring Newfoundland into the confederation and press forward with the completion of the Canadian Pacific Railway.[166] The troubles of 1873 and 1876 had evidently faded and Dufferin was trusted to stay in line, and had recovered some of the reputational damage of those episodes. Dufferin's position as both an insider and outsider in the metropolitan context led to some insecurity for him, but also made him adaptable to imperial postings and responsibilities. We can certainly see the benefits of that adaptability when he was in Canada; although he complained of 'exile', he did take to many aspects of Canadian life, something that won over many Canadians.[167]

Dufferin's experience in Canada was not an unqualified success, of course. His self-confident pursuit of 'good' governance, and his belief that only he was qualified to identify and embody it, led him at times across the constitutional boundaries of his office.[168] But what it also demonstrated was the growing self-confidence of Canada's politicians, who, up against Dufferin's clever, quick-tempered patrician manner and the weight of the Colonial Office, successfully maintained their interpretation of the constitutional position.[169] Dufferin's tenure in Canada came at a point of growing Canadian confidence, which manifested itself in a rejection of Dufferin's somewhat high-handed and aristocratic conception of governance, informed by his landed inheritance. But he was too clever to ignore the lessons given, from 1876 sitting back to 'suck his paws in peace' to a much greater degree than before.[170]

Notes

1. Speech by Lord Dufferin to mark the arrival of Lord Lorne (son of his friend the 8th Duke of Argyll and later the 9th Duke), in Canada as his successor to the governorship-general: H. Milton (ed.), *Speeches of the Earl of Dufferin* (Toronto, 1878), p. 116; *Toronto Globe*, 17 Oct. 1878; *Montreal Herald*, 22 Oct. 1878, for comment on this speech; A. Gailey, *The Lost Imperialist: Lord Dufferin, memory and mythmaking in an age of celebrity* (London, 2015), pp. 113–14, 121–2, 126–8; R. Romani, British views on Irish national character, 1800–1846: an intellectual history, *History of European Ideas*, 23:5–6 (1997), pp. 193–4.
2. Public Record Office of Northern Ireland [hereafter PRONI], Dufferin and Ava Papers, D1071, H/H/2/2b, ff. 13, Carnarvon to Dufferin, 19 Mar. 1876.
3. Nearly six years, from 1872 to 1878; A. Hawkins and J. Powell (eds), *The Journal of John Wodehouse, First Earl of Kimberley for 1862–1902* (London, 1997), p. 281; PRONI, D1071, H/B/K/106, ff. 2, Address of Congratulation to the Right Honorable the Earl of Dufferin on his appointment as Governor General of Canada from his Lordship's Friends and Tenants in the town and neighbourhood of Killyleagh, n.d., [1872]. For a contemporary and very uncritical overview of his tenure, see G. Stewart, *Canada under the Administration of the Earl of Dufferin* (Toronto, 1878) and, for a more personal insight, H. Blackwood, Marchioness of Dufferin and Ava, *My Canadian Journal, 1872–1878* (London, 1891).
4. A. C. Lyall, *The Life of the Marquis of Dufferin and Ava* (London, 1905), pp. 214–16; M. Francis, *Governors and Settlers: images of authority in the British Colonies, 1820–60* (Basingstoke, 1992), pp. 1–2.
5. A. Kirk-Greene, The governors-general of Canada, 1867–1952: a collective profile, *Journal of Canadian Studies* 12 (1977), p. 48; B. Messamore, *Canada's Governors General, 1847–1878: biography and constitutional evolution* (Toronto, 2006), pp. 148–9. Examples of Dufferin's surprise at the 'jealousy' of Canadian politicians over Britain's assertion of dominion can be seen in PRONI, D1071, H/H/1/4, Dufferin to Carnarvon, 1 Jun. 1876; H/H/1/5, Dufferin to Carnarvon, 4 Nov. 1876; 23 Nov. 1876.
6. Lyall commented that it was in Canada that 'British statesmen gradually worked out the science of colonial administration', Lyall, *Life of Dufferin*, p. 195; G. Bolton, The idea of a colonial gentry, *Historical Studies*, 13 (1968), pp. 307–9, 316.
7. 'Their [Canadians'] appalling touchiness', his nephew Nicolson would sniffily call it: H. Nicolson, *Helen's Tower* (London, 1937), p. 153; J. W. Cell, *British Colonial Administration in the Mid-Nineteenth Century: the policy-making process* (London, 1970), pp. viii–ix; Blackwood, *Canadian Journal*, pp. 18–19; Messamore, *Canada's Governors General*, p. 9.
8. F. M. L. Thompson, English landed society in the twentieth century, 3: self help and outdoor relief, *Transactions of the Royal Historical Society*, 6th series, 2 (1992).
9. Lyall, *Life of Dufferin*, pp. 203–4.
10. British Library [hereafter BL], Carnarvon Papers, Add MS 60797, Vol. XLI (ff.1–141, 142–246), Dufferin to Carnarvon, ff. 27, 5 Apr. 1877. He may also have looked with an envious eye at the £20,000 per annum salary of the Irish Lord Lieutenancy; R. B. McDowell, *The Irish Administration, 1801–1914* (London, 1964), p. 54; Gailey, *Lost Imperialist*, pp. 115–16.

11 PRONI, D1071, H/H/3/2, ff. 26, Dufferin to Alexander Mackenzie, Canadian PM, 31 Jan. 1874; ff. 140, 7 Jun. 1874; H/H/4/2a, ff. 7, Dufferin to Mackenzie, 7 Jan. 1874; H/H/3/3, ff. 14 and ff. 15, Dufferin to Mackenzie, 14 and 15 Dec. 1874; Messamore, *Canada's Governors General*, pp. 13–14; R. H. Hubbard, *Rideau Hall: an illustrated history* (Montreal, 1977), pp. 20, 34, 38.

12 BL, Gladstone Papers Add MS 44151, Vol. LXVI, ff. 130, Dufferin to Gladstone, 23 Mar. 1872; PRONI, D1071, H/H/1/2, Dufferin to Carnarvon, 13 Nov. 1874; H/H/1/4, Dufferin to Carnarvon, 9 Mar. 1876; H/H/1/5, Dufferin to Carnarvon, 1 Nov. 1877; B. Messamore, The line over which he must not pass: defining the office of Governor General, 1878, *Canadian Historical Review*, 86:3 (2005), p. 461; Francis, *Governors and Settlers*, p. 3.

13 PRONI, D1071, H/H/2/1a, ff. 9, Dufferin to Carnarvon, 21 Feb. 1873; H/H/6/4, ff. 89, Dufferin to Herbert, 11 Sept. 1878; Kirk-Greene, The Governors-General, pp. 39–40; Messamore, *Canada's Governors General*, p. 19; Lyall, *Life of Dufferin*, p. 200; R. Gwyn, *Nation Maker: Sir John A. Macdonald: his life, our times, vol. 2: 1867–1891* (Toronto, 2011), pp. 218–19.

14 Francis, *Governors and Settlers*, p. 8; Kirk-Greene, The Governors-General, pp. 46–7; J. A. Mangan, *Making Imperial Mentalities: socialisation and British imperialism* (Manchester 1990), pp. 1–3; D. Cannadine, *Aspects of Aristocracy: grandeur and decline in modern Britain* (New Haven, 1994), pp. 77–8.

15 PRONI, D1071, H/H/6/4, ff. 27, Dufferin to Lord Lorne, 12 Aug. 1878; Lyall, *Life of Lord Dufferin*, p. 213; Kirk-Greene, The Governors-General, p. 41.

16 D. Cannadine, *Ornamentalism: how the British saw their empire* (London, 2001), pp. 5–8, 27–38. This was imperial governance conceptualised as a personal and moral task: Francis, *Governors and Settlers*, pp. 4–5; J. Wilson, *India Conquered: Britain's Raj and the chaos of empire* (London, 2016), pp. 128, 296, 481.

17 Principally via the Canadian Pacific Railway project: PRONI, D1071, H/H/1/5, Dufferin to Carnarvon, 4 Nov. 1876.

18 Dufferin (ed. Milton), *Speeches of the Earl of Dufferin* (Toronto, 1878), p. 7; PRONI, D1071, H/H/1/2, Dufferin to Carnarvon, 25 Apr. 1874; E. Frie and J. Neuheiser, Introduction: noble ways and democratic means, *Journal of Modern European History*, 11:4 (2013), pp. 442–5.

19 For instance, PRONI, D1071, H/H/1/5, Dufferin to Carnarvon, 27 Jul. 1876; Z. Laidlaw and A. Lester (eds), *Indigenous Communities and Settler Colonialism: land holding, loss and survival in an interconnected world* (Basingstoke, 2015), pp. 1–12.

20 PRONI, D1071, H/H/14, Dufferin to Carnarvon, 1 Jun. 1876; Lyall, *Life of Dufferin*, pp. 199–200.

21 R. Bitterman (with M. McCallum), Upholding the land legislation of a 'communistic and socialist assembly': the benefits of confederation for Prince Edward Island, *Canadian Historical Review*, 87:1 (2006), pp. 1–2.

22 PRONI, D1071, H/B/B/756, ff. 1, Dufferin to Brodick, 25 Sept. 1872.

23 Lyall, *Life of Dufferin*, p. 192; Francis, *Governors and Settlers*, pp. 1–3.

24 These attitudes were also present in the Colonial Office permanent staff until the 1870s: B. Knox, Conservative imperialism 1858–1874: Bulwer Lytton, Lord Carnarvon and Canadian confederation, *International History Review*, 4 (1984), pp. 341, 354; B. Blakely, *The Colonial Office, 1868–1892* (Durham, USA, 1972), p. xi; D. Creighton, The Victorians and empire, *Canadian Historical Review*, 19 (1938), pp. 139–41; P. J. Durrans, A two-edged sword: the Liberal attack on Disraelian imperialism, *Journal of Imperial and Commonwealth History*, 10:3 (1982), p. 263.

25 C. E. D. Black, *The Marquess of Dufferin and Ava* (London, 1903), pp. 76–7, 161; J. W. Cell, *British Colonial Administration in the Mid-Nineteenth Century: the policy-making process* (London, 1970), p. vii; B. Knox, The Earl of

Carnarvon, Empire and Imperialism, 1855–90, *Journal of Imperial and Commonwealth History*, 26 (1998), pp. 48–9, 52, 54; W. P. Morrell, *British Colonial Policy in the Mid-Victorian Age* (Oxford, 1969), pp. 1–2, 9, 24; G. Martin, Anti-imperialism in the mid-nineteenth century and the nature of the British empire, 1820–70, in R. Hyam and G. Martin (eds), *Reappraisals in British Imperial History* (London, 1975), pp. 94–6, 114–15.

26 They were dutifully recorded by local and national newspapers; see, for example, PRONI, D1071/H/H/9/15; Gailey, *Lost Imperialist*, pp. 142–3, 182, 190.

27 See, for example, PRONI, D1071, H/H9/10, speech by Lord Dufferin to members of the Toronto Club, 2 Sept. 1874.

28 PRONI, D1071, H/H9/10, speech by Lord Dufferin to members of the Toronto Club, 2 Sept. 1874; PRONI, D1071, H/H/2/1b, ff. 46, Carnarvon to Dufferin, 20 Dec. 1875; C. W. De Kiewiet and F. H. Underhill (eds), *Dufferin-Carnarvon Correspondence, 1874–1878* (Toronto, 1955), pp. xii; Gailey, *Lost Imperialist*, pp. 129–30.

29 Behind this, as for many imperial governors, lurked a sense of moral superiority: P. J. Cain, Character and imperialism: the British financial administration of Egypt, 1878–1914, *Journal of Imperial and Commonwealth History*, 34:2 (2006), p. 193; Cannadine, *Ornamentalism*, pp. 4–5; Francis, *Governors and Settlers*, p. 4–5; B. Porter, *The Absent-Minded Imperialists: empire, society and culture in Britain* (Oxford, 2004), pp. 229–31.

30 PRONI, D1071, H/H/1/3, Dufferin to Carnarvon, 3 Nov. 1873 and 11 Nov. 1875; H/H/1/6, Dufferin to Sir Michael Hicks Beach, 6 Aug. 1878. This was appreciated by some Canadians, particularly in the pioneer provinces: Anonymous, *Lord Dufferin in Manitoba. Testimony of the Settlers. Shipment of Manitoban Wheat to Europe* (Liverpool, 1878), pp. 1–2; Cannadine, *Ornamentalism*, pp. 21–2; Messamore, The line, p. 472; Francis, *Governors and Settlers*, p. 3–4; J. Pope, *Memoirs of the Rt Hon Sir John Alexander Macdonald*, vol. 2 (Ottawa, 1894), pp. 236–7; BL, Gladstone papers, Add MS 44151, Vol. LXVI, ff. 126, Dufferin to Gladstone, 9 Feb. 1872; PRONI, D1071, H/B/C/88, ff. 7, Dufferin to Duchess of Argyll, 17 Feb. 1873; Kirk-Greene, Canada's Governors-General, p. 40; Gailey, *Lost Imperialist*, pp. 138–41; J. Cowan, *Canada's Governors General, Lord Monck to General Vanier* (Toronto, 1965), pp. 15–17.

31 PRONI, D1071, H/H/1/3, Dufferin to Carnarvon, 11 Nov. 1875; Cannadine, *Ornamentalism*, pp. 27–33; Cell, *British Colonial Administration*, p. viii.

32 Messamore, *Canada's Governors General*, p. 23.

33 As Sir John A. Macdonald, and particularly Alexander Mackenzie (Liberal party leader and later PM), both came from humble origins, this breezy assumption may have come as something of a surprise: PRONI, D1071, H/H/4/1a, ff. 27, Dufferin to Macdonald, 26 Dec. 1872.

34 Cannadine, *Ornamentalism*, pp. 31, 34, 38.

35 See, for example, PRONI, D1071, H/H/4/2a, ff. 101, Mackenzie to Dufferin, 28 May 1877; J. Schull, *Edward Blake: the man of the other way 1833–1882* (Toronto, 1985), pp. 139, 141, 155–6.

36 Bodleian Library, Kimberley papers, MS.Eng.C.4088, ff. 52, Dufferin to Kimberley, 12 Feb. 1873.

37 D. M. L. Farr, *The Colonial Office and Canada, 1867–1887* (Toronto, 1955), p. 6.

38 E. Delaney, Our island story? Towards a transnational history of late modern Ireland, *Irish Historical Studies*, 37 (2011), p. 619.

39 Bodleian Library, Kimberley papers, MS.Eng.C.4088, ff. 72, Dufferin to Kimberley, 19 Feb. 1873.

40 Cain, Character and imperialism, p. 193; Cannadine, *Ornamentalism*, pp. 94–5.

134   *Remits of power*

41 Mackenzie was Liberal Prime Minister: PRONI, D1071, H/H/1/1, Dufferin to Kimberley, 9 Oct. 1873; 13 Nov. 1873; H/H/1/2, Dufferin to Carnarvon, 18 Mar. 1874; H/H/2/1b, ff. 20, Dufferin to Kimberley, 4 Apr. 1873; Inveraray Castle, Argyll estate papers, NRAS1206, 9th Duke's Canadian papers, outbook: 1878–83, ff. 14, Dufferin to Lorne, 22 Aug. 1878.
42 PRONI, D1071, H/B/C/95, ff. 68, Dufferin to Argyll, 27 Nov. 1873; Farr, *Colonial Office and Canada*, pp. 17, 22.
43 Dufferin provided a summary for Lord Carnarvon in 1874: PRONI, D1071, H/H/1/2, Dufferin to Carnarvon, 18 Mar. 1874; Farr, *Colonial Office and Canada*, p. 3; Knox, Conservative imperialism, pp. 333–4.
44 Black, *Dufferin and Ava*, pp. 90–9, 107–9; PRONI, D0171/H/H/1/5, Dufferin to Carnarvon, 4 Nov. 1876.
45 Black, *Dufferin and Ava*, pp. 109–11; Lyall, *Life of Dufferin*, pp. 197–8; S. K. Gibson and A. Milnes (eds), *Canada Transformed: the speeches of Sir John A. Macdonald* (Toronto, 2014), pp. 282–4; Gailey, *Lost Imperialist*, p. 133; A. Todd, *Parliamentary Government in the British Colonies* (London, 1894), p. 362.
46 PRONI, D1071, H/H/1/2, Dufferin to Carnarvon, 12 Oct. 1874; S. K. Gibson and A. Milnes (eds), *Canada Transformed: the speeches of Sir John A. Macdonald – a bicentennial celebration* (Toronto, 2014), pp. 282–4; Gwyn, *Sir John*, pp. 267–8; A. Hardinge, *The Life of Henry Howard Molyneux Herbert, Fourth Earl of Carnarvon, 1831–1890*, vol. 2 (Oxford, 1925), pp. 117–23.
47 PRONI, D1071, H/H/1/2, Dufferin to Carnarvon, 12 Oct. 1874; H/H/I/3, Dufferin to Carnarvon, 29 Oct. 1875; H/H/I/5, Dufferin to Carnarvon, 29 May 1878; 6 Jun. 1878.
48 Farr, *Colonial Office and Canada*, pp. 13–14.
49 PRONI, D1071, H/H/I/5, Dufferin to Carnarvon, 7 Oct. 1877.
50 PRONI, D1071, H/H/2/2b, ff. 13, Carnarvon to Dufferin, 19 Mar. 1876.
51 Messamore, The line, pp. 463–5.
52 Knox, Carnarvon, p. 49; B. Blakely, *The Colonial Office, 1868–1892* (Durham, USA, 1972), pp. vii–x; A. G. Hopkins, Back to the future: from national history to imperial history, *Past and Present*, 164 (1999), pp. 209–11.
53 Cain, Character and imperialism, pp. 177–8; Messamore, *Canada's Governors General*, p. 23.
54 Z. Laidlaw, *Colonial Connections 1815–45: patronage, the information revolution and colonial government* (Manchester, 2005), pp. 13–14.
55 Bodleian Library, Kimberley papers, MS.Eng.C.4092, ff. 73, Dufferin to Kimberley, 13 Oct. 1873; B. Crosbie, *Irish Imperial Networks: migration, social communication and exchange in nineteenth-century India* (Cambridge, 2012), pp. 2–3, 19.
56 PRONI, D1071, H/H/4/2a, ff. 67, Mackenzie to Dufferin, 25 Jun. 1875.
57 PRONI, D1071, H/H/1/2, Dufferin to Carnarvon, 18 Mar. 1874.
58 Hardinge, *Life of Henry Howard Molyneux Herbert, Fourth Earl of Carnarvon*, pp. 114–17.
59 Creighton, Victorians and empire, pp. 151–2.
60 Messamore, *Canada's Governors General*, p. 148.
61 Lyall, *Life of Dufferin*, pp. 246–9.
62 See, for example, his disappointment when Macdonald was ousted in 1873: PRONI, D1071, H/H/1/1, Dufferin to Carnarvon, 9 Oct. 1873; 26 Oct. 1873; 13 Nov. 1873.
63 PRONI, D1071, H/H/2/1b, ff. 22, Dufferin to Kimberley, 23 Apr. 1873; H/H/3/1, ff. 18, Dufferin to Macdonald, 19 Oct. 1873; H/H/4/1b, ff. 21, Dufferin to Macdonald, 31 Jul. 1873; Gwyn, *Sir John*, pp. 219–20, 290; Gailey, *Lost Imperialist*, pp. 129–30.

Remits of power   135

64 Bodleian Library, Kimberley papers, MS Eng.C.4087, ff. 18, Dufferin to Kimberley, 27 Nov. 1872; MS Eng.C.4089, ff. 102, Dufferin to Kimberley, 29 May 1873.
65 PRONI, D1071, H/H/1/1, Dufferin to Kimberley, 26 Oct. 1873; Gwyn, *Sir John*, p. 273.
66 Dufferin was well-known for his hot temper, a personality trait usually ascribed by contemporaries to his Irishness: British Library, Carnarvon Papers, Add MS 60797, Vol. XLI (ff.1–141, 142–246), ff. 1, Carnarvon to Lord John Russell, 18 Sept. 1874; PRONI, D1071, H/H/1, Dufferin to Carnarvon, 13 Nov. 1873; H/H/1/5, Dufferin to Carnarvon, 23 Nov. 1876; Messamore, The line, p. 458.
67 M. Ormsby, Prime Minister Mackenzie, the Liberal Party and the bargain with British Columbia, *Canadian Historical Review*, 26 (1945), pp. 171–2.
68 PRONI, D1071, H/H/1/4, Dufferin to Carnarvon, 1 Jun. 1876.
69 Messamore, *Canada's Governors General*, p. 9; G. Stevenson, *Ex Uno Plures: federal-provincial relations in Canada, 1867–1896* (Montreal, 1993), pp. 259, 264–5, 269.
70 Lyall, *Life of Dufferin*, pp. 207–13; Messamore, *Canada's Governors General*, pp. 156–66; Gailey, *Lost Imperialist*, pp. 129, 131–4.
71 Lyall, *Life of Lord Dufferin*, pp. 204–12; Bodleian Library, Kimberley papers, MS C 4086, ff. 94, Dufferin to Kimberley, 15 Oct. 1872 and ff. 102–119, memorandum by Sir John A. Macdonald, 16 Oct. 1872.
72 Dufferin thought Canadian politics in general was less 'pure' than that in Britain, although better than in the USA: PRONI, D1071, H/H/1/1/, Dufferin to Kimberley, 9 Oct. 1873; H/H/1/2, Dufferin to Carnarvon, 18 Mar. 1874.
73 PRONI, D1071, H/H/2/1b, ff. 7, Dufferin to Kimberley, 12 Feb. 1873.
74 Creighton, *John A. Macdonald*, pp. 141, 157.
75 Bodleian Library, Kimberley papers, MS Eng.C.4089, ff. 41, Dufferin to Kimberley, 25 Apr. 1873.
76 PRONI, D1071, H/H/2/1b, ff. 55, Dufferin to Kimberley, 5 Aug. 1873; Gailey, *Lost Imperialist*, p. 129.
77 Messamore, *Canada's Governors General*, pp. 174–5; PRONI, D1071, H/H/11/1, Confidential minute on the Pacific Scandal by Dufferin, n.d. [1873].
78 PRONI, D1071, H/H/2/1b, ff. 55, Dufferin to Kimberley, 5 Aug. 1873.
79 Gwyn, *Sir John*, pp. 247–9; Messamore, *Canada's Governors General*, pp. 160, 166; Messamore, The line, p. 465.
80 PRONI, D1071, H/2/1/b, ff. 61, Dufferin to Kimberley, 21 Aug. 1873; H/H/61, ff. 86, Dufferin to Thornton, 19 Nov. 1873.
81 PRONI, D1071, H/H/2/1b, ff. 74, Kimberley to Dufferin, 6 Oct. 1873.
82 Ormsby, Prime Minister Mackenzie, p. 150; Creighton, *John A. Macdonald*, pp. 170–2; Gailey, *Lost Imperialist*, pp. 133–5.
83 J. A. Maxwell, Lord Dufferin and the difficulties with British Columbia, 1874–7, *Canadian Historical Review*, 12 (1931), pp. 365–6, 384; A. Perry, *On the Edge of Empire: gender, race and the making of British Columbia* (Toronto, 2001), pp. 124–38.
84 PRONI, D1071, H/H/1/4, Dufferin to Carnarvon, 9 Feb. 1876; 31 Mar. 1876; 6 Apr. 1876; and especially 1 Jun. 1876; H/H/1/5, Dufferin to Carnarvon, 4 Nov. 1876, 23 Nov. 1876; Ormsby, Prime Minister Mackenzie, p. 161.
85 PRONI, D1071, H/H/1/4, Dufferin to Carnarvon, 6 Apr. 1876; H/H/3/4, ff. 10, Dufferin to Mackenzie, 9 Oct. 1876.
86 BL, Gladstone Papers Add MS 44151, Vol. LXVI, ff. 140, Dufferin to Gladstone, 31 Oct. 1876.
87 PRONI, D1071, H/H/1/4, Dufferin to Carnarvon, 1 Jun. 1876; Maxwell, Lord Dufferin and the difficulties with British Columbia, pp. 370, 374.
88 For instance, PRONI, D1071, H/H/3/3, ff. 88, Mackenzie to Dufferin, 19 May 1876; H/H/4/2a, ff. 45, Mackenzie to Dufferin, 17 Dec. 1874; ff. 142, Mackenzie to Dufferin, 20 May 1876. Also see Blake's summary, H/H/4/2a, ff. 51, Blake to

136 *Remits of power*

     Mackenzie, 1 Jul. 1876; Maxwell, Lord Dufferin and the difficulties with British Columbia, pp. 364–5, 387–9; Messamore, The line, p. 478.
89 Messamore, *Canada's Governors General*, p. 206.
90 Messamore, *Canada's Governors Generals* pp. 182–6; Messamore, The line, p. 468.
91 PRONI, D1071, H/H/3/3, ff. 106, Dufferin to Mackenzie, 22 May 1876; see also H/H/3/4, ff. 32, Dufferin to Mackenzie, 19 Nov. 1876; 'You said last night you are not a Crown Colony, which is true, but neither are you a republic'. D. B. Swinfen, *Imperial Control of Colonial Legislation, 1813–1865* (Oxford, 1970), pp. 95, 103–5, 119.
92 PRONI, D1071, H/H/4/2a, ff. 62, Mackenzie to Dufferin, 17 Nov. 1876; Ormsby, Prime Minister Mackenzie, pp. 159, 164.
93 PRONI, D1071, H/H/1/4, Dufferin to Carnarvon, 31 Mar. 1876; 6 Apr. 1876; Black, *Dufferin and Ava*, pp. 122–4; Maxwell, Lord Dufferin and the difficulties with British Columbia, pp. 382–3; Messamore, *Canada's Governors Generals*, pp. 198–202.
94 R. W. Sandwell, Dreaming of the princess: love, subversion and the rituals of empire in British Columbia, 1882, in C. M. Coates (ed.), *Majesty in Canada: essays on the role of royalty* (Toronto, 2006), pp. 45–6, 56, for a comparison with Lord Lorne's tour of British Columbia; Ormsby, Prime Minister Mackenzie, p. 167; Stevenson, *Ex Uno Plures*, p. 256; F. E. M. St John, *The Sea of Mountains: an account of Lord Dufferin's tour through British Columbia in 1876*, 2 vols (London, 1877), p. 322.
95 Black, *Dufferin and Ava*, pp. 127–8.
96 Maxwell, Lord Dufferin and the difficulties with British Columbia, p. 382; Messamore, The line, pp. 479–83.
97 Messamore, *Canada's Governors General*, pp. 177–80; Maxwell, Lord Dufferin and the difficulties with British Columbia, p. 385.
98 PRONI, D1071, H/H/6/4, ff. 80, Dufferin to Lorne, 24 Aug. 1878; and H/H/6/2, ff. 138, Dufferin to General Haly, 24 Apr. 1875; H/H/4/1a, ff. 41, Dufferin to Macdonald, 11 Feb. 1873; Messamore, The line, p. 471.
99 PRONI, D1071, H/H/6/3, ff. 8, Dufferin to Thornton, 22 May 1878; see also H/H/4/2a, ff. 60, Macdonald to Dufferin, 9 Nov. 1876; ff. 146, Mackenzie to Dufferin, 2 Jul. 1878.
100 PRONI, D1071/H/H/1/1, 7 Oct. 1873, Dufferin to Kimberley.
101 Cited in Black, *Dufferin and Ava*, p. 78; L. P. Curtis, *Anglo-Saxons and Celts: a study of anti-Irish prejudice in Victorian England* (Bridgeport, 1968), pp. 75, 83.
102 Knox, Carnarvon, pp. 53–4; Delaney, Our island history? pp. 599–601.
103 PRONI, D1071, H/H/1/4, Dufferin to Carnarvon, 20 Mar. 1876.
104 PRONI, D1071, H/H/1/5, Dufferin to Carnarvon, 7 Oct. 1877; E. D. Steele, *Palmerston and Liberalism, 1855–1865* (Cambridge, 1991), pp. 350–4.
105 PRONI, D1071, H/H/3/4, ff. 78, Dufferin to Mackenzie, 17 Sept. 1877; P. J. Cain and A. G. Hopkins, *British Imperialism, I: Innovation and Expansion* (London, 1993), pp. 229–73.
106 S. Lynn, Before the Fenians: 1848 and the Irish plot to invade Canada, *Eire–Ireland*, 51:1–2 (2016), pp. 62, 67, 86–7; P. Toner, The green ghost: Canada's Fenians and the raids, *Eire–Ireland*, 16:4 (1981), pp. 27, 29, 45–6.
107 PRONI, D1071, H/H/1/2, Dufferin to Carnarvon, 25 Apr. 1874; Durrans, A two-edged sword, pp. 277–8; C. C. Eldridge, *England's Mission: the imperial idea in the age of Gladstone and Disraeli* (London, 1973), pp. 65–9.
108 PRONI, D1071, H/H/1/2, Dufferin to Carnarvon, 25 Apr. 1874.
109 Gwyn, *Sir John*, p. 224.
110 PRONI, D1071, H/B/D/78, ff. 15, Dufferin to Lady Dartrey, 24 Jul. 1872; see also Milton, *Speeches*, p. 99–100.

111 PRONI, D1071, H/B/D/78, ff. 41, Dufferin to Lady Dartrey, 16 Apr. 1874.
112 PRONI, D1071, H/H/3/3, ff. 17, Dufferin to Mackenzie, 4 Jan. 1876.
113 For a discussion on the Roman Catholic hierarchy in Canada and the wider empire, see C. Barr, Imperium in imperio: Irish episcopal imperialism in the nineteenth century, *English Historical Review*, 502 (2008), pp. 611, 620–23, 647; R. Perin, *Rome in Canada: The Vatican and Canadian affairs in the late Victorian Age* (Toronto, 1990), pp. 100–1; D. A. Wilson, *The Orange Order in Canada* (Dublin, 2007), pp. 12–16.
114 PRONI, D1071, H/B/C/95, ff. 62, Dufferin to Argyll, 27 Nov. 1872; D. Brundage, *Irish Nationalists in America: the politics of exile, 1798–1998* (Oxford, 2016), pp. 4–6, 88, 108.
115 PRONI, D1071, H/H/1/2, Dufferin to Carnarvon, 12 Oct. 1874; H/H/1/5, Dufferin to Hicks Beach, 27 May 1878; Lynn, Before the Fenians, pp. 62–4, 66–9, 88–9; D. Wilson (ed.), *Irish Nationalism in Canada* (Toronto, 2009), pp. 3–8, 11, 20–1; G. Stortz, Improvident emigrants: John Joseph Lynch and Irish immigration to British North America, 1860–88, in T. Murphy and G. Stortz (eds), *Creed and Culture: the place of English-speaking catholics in Canadian society, 1750–1930* (Montreal, 1993), pp. 171–4, 177.
116 Bodleian Library, Kimberley papers, MS. Eng.B, 2049, ff. 26–49, papers on Fenian raids on Canada, 1870: ff. 42, memorandum [n.d.].
117 PRONI, D1071, H/H/6/3, ff. 8, Dufferin to Thornton, 22 May 1878; see also H/H/4/2a, ff. 60, Macdonald to Dufferin, 9 Nov. 1876; ff. 146, Mackenzie to Dufferin, 2 Jul. 1878; H. Senior, *The Last Invasion of Canada: the Fenian raids, 1866–1870* (Toronto, 1991), pp. 189, 191; J. Ridden, Making good citizens: national identity, religion and liberalism among the Irish elite, c.1800–1850, unpublished PhD thesis (King's College London, 1998), p. 18.
118 And with other national and religious groups, too, as in the case of the Mennonites of Manitoba, Anonymous, *Lord Dufferin in Manitoba*, p. 14; N. Macdonald, *Canada: immigration and colonisation, 1841–1903*, (Toronto, 1966), pp. 123, 211–12 and men of his own class: P. Dunae, *Gentlemen Emigrants: from the British public schools to the Canadian frontier* (Toronto, 1981), pp. 1–10.
119 PRONI, D1071, H/B/F/175, ff. 7, Dufferin to Lansdowne, 4 Jul. 1880; Lyall, *Life of Dufferin*, p. 245; Dufferin, *Irish emigration and the tenure of land in Ireland* (Dublin, 1870).
120 Bodleian Library, Kimberley papers, MS C.4086, ff. 31, Dufferin to Kimberley, 16 Aug. 1872.
121 Delaney, Our island story? pp. 613, 615; D. A. Wilson, *The Orange Order in Canada* (Dublin, 2007), p. 89, 107; W. J. Smyth, *Toronto, the Belfast of Canada: the Orange Order and the shaping of municipal culture* (Toronto, 2015), p. 11.
122 PRONI, D1071, H/H/1/2, Dufferin to Carnarvon, 12 Oct. 1874; Cannadine, *Ornamentalism*, p. 20.
123 PRONI, D1071, H/H/1/6, Dufferin to Hicks Beach, 11 Jul. 1878; 13 Jul. 1878.
124 PRONI, D1071, H/H/1/5, Dufferin to Carnarvon, 29 May 1878.
125 PRONI, D1071, H/H/1/3, Dufferin to Carnarvon, 29 Oct. 1875.
126 PRONI, D1071, H/H/2/1a, ff. 6, Kimberley to Dufferin, 28 Aug. 1872.
127 PRONI, D1071, H/H/4/1a, ff. 55, Dufferin to Macdonald, 27 Feb. 1873; S.K. Kehoe, Catholic identity in the diaspora: nineteenth century Ontario, in T. Bueltmann, A. Hinson and G. Morton (eds), *Ties of Bluid, Kin and Countrie: Scottish associational culture in the diaspora* (Guelph, 2009), pp. 85, 87, 89.
128 PRONI, D1071, H/H/6/2, ff. 239, Dufferin to the Bishop of Armagh, 27 Mar. 1878.
129 Black, *Dufferin and Ava*, p. 139; Laidlaw and Lester, *Indigenous communities and settler colonialism*, pp. 12–15; see, for Australian comparisons, P. Dwyer and L. Ryan, Reflections on genocide and settler-colonial violence, *History Australia*, 13:3 (2016), pp. 335–6, 339–42; A. Nettlebeck, Colonial protection

138   *Remits of power*

and the intimacies of Indigenous governance, *History Australia*, 14:1 (2017), pp. 32–7.
130 PRONI, D1071, H/H/2/1b, ff. 29, Dufferin to Kimberley, 2 May 1873. Macdonald had a dismissive view of their 'diplomacy': H/H/4/1a, ff. 16, Macdonald to Dufferin, 14 Oct. 1872.
131 Lyall, *Life of Dufferin*, p. 257.
132 PRONI, D1071, H/H/1/5, Dufferin to Carnarvon, 27 Jul. 1877; see also H/H/1/1, Dufferin to Kimberley, 24 Dec. 1873. See also H/H/3/2, ff. 130, Dufferin to Mackenzie, 23 May 1874.
133 See, for example, his speech to the Six Nations Indians at the Mohawk reservation: PRONI, D1071, H/H/12/3, *Narrative of the Visit of the Governor General and the Countess of Dufferin to the Six Nations Indians, 25th August 1874* (1875); Cannadine, *Ornamentalism*, p. 5; A. Porter, Empires in the mind, in P. J. Marshall (ed.), *The Cambridge Illustrated History of the British Empire* (Cambridge, 1996), pp. 218–19, 223.
134 Weaver, *Great Land Rush*, pp. 133–77.
135 Many of those speeches were about Queen Victoria: for example, Milton, *Speeches*, p. 61, 116; E. Forsey, The role of the Crown in Canada since confederation, *Parliamentarian*, 60 (1979), pp. 15–16; J. Moir, K. A. MacKirdy and Y. F. Zoltvany (eds), *Changing Perspectives in Canadian History: selected problems* (Ontario, 1971), pp. 246, 252; C. M. Coates (ed.), *Majesty in Canada: essays on the role of royalty* (Toronto, 2006).
136 PRONI, D1071, H/H/1/4, 2 Mar. 1876, Dufferin to Herbert. Dufferin sold much of his estate while in Canada: H/B/S/251b, ff. 4, Dufferin to Brinsley Sheridan [his uncle], 6 Feb. 1881.
137 J. C. Weaver, *The great land rush and the making of the modern world, 1650–1900* (Montreal, 2003), pp. 3–10, 133–77; Messamore, *Canada's Governors General*, p. 151.
138 E. S. E. Childers, *The Life and Correspondence of the Right Hon. Hugh C. E. Childers, 1827–1872* (London, 1901), p. 231; Bitterman, Upholding, p. 5; R. Bitterman, *Rural Protest on Prince Edward Island: from British colonization to the Escheat Movement* (Toronto, 2006), pp. 3–4.
139 PRONI, D1071, H/H/1/2, Dufferin to Carnarvon, 29 May 1874; see also H/H/6/2, ff. 21, Dufferin to Herbert, 7 May 1874; Bitterman, Upholding, pp. 3, 11–12; R. Bitterman and M. McCallum, *Lady Landlords of Prince Edward Island: imperial dreams and the defense of property* (Montreal, 2008), pp. 3–14.
140 Both the PEI government and Colonial Office recognized similar pressures ongoing in Ireland; Bitterman, Upholding, p. 9.
141 A. Behm, Settler historicism and anticolonial rebuttal in the British World, 1880–1920, *Journal of World History*, 26:4 (2015); Cook, *Imperial Affinities*; Z. Laidlaw, Richard Bourke: Irish liberalism tempered by empire, in D. Lambert and A. Lester (eds), *Colonial Lives Across the British Empire* (Cambridge, 2006).
142 Bitterman, *Rural Protest*, p. 272; I. R. Robertson, Political alignment in pre-confederation Prince Edward Island, 1863–1870, *Acadiensis*, 15:1 (Autumn 1985), pp. 35, 58.
143 PEI is a rare example of the use of state power to compel redistribution of resources for the benefit of ordinary citizens in Canada: Bitterman, Upholding, p. 2; PRONI, D0171/H/H/1/4, Dufferin to Carnarvon, 18 Feb. 1876; 2 Mar. 1876; J. McLaren, A. R. Buck, and N. E. Wright, Introduction, in J. McLaren, A. R. Buck, and N. E. Wright (eds) *Despotic Dominion: property rights in British settler societies* (Vancouver, 2004), pp. 1–9; C. Wilson, *A New Lease on Life: landlords, tenants and immigrants in Ireland and Canada* (Montreal, 1994), pp. 3, 6–7, 38.

144 I. Ross Robertson (ed.), *The Prince Edward Island Land Commission of 1860* (Fredericton, 1988), pp. ix–xxvii; Bitterman, Upholding, p. 3; J. M. Bumstead, *Land, Settlement and Politics on Eighteenth Century Prince Edward Island* (Montreal, 1987), pp. ix–x; I. R. Robertson, Highlanders, Irishmen and the land question in nineteenth century Prince Edward Island, in L. M. Cullen and T. C. Smout (eds), *Comparative Aspects of Scottish and Irish Economic and Social History, 1600–1900* (Edinburgh, 1977), pp. 227–9.
145 PRONI, D1071, H/H/2/1a, ff. 34, Kimberley to Dufferin, 24 Dec. 1872; Bitterman, Upholding, pp. 8, 10; F. Mackinnon, *The Government of Prince Edward Island* (Toronto, 1951), pp. 105, 107, 109, 116, 139; I. R. Robertson, *The Tenant League of Prince Edward Island, 1864–1867* (Toronto, 1996), pp. 271, 273, 276–84.
146 Lyall, *Life of Dufferin*, p. 244; Black, *Dufferin and Ava*, p. 100; Bitterman, Upholding, pp. 3–4, 7–8; F. W. P. Bolger, *Prince Edward Island and Confederation, 1863–1873* (Charlottetown, 1964), pp. 238, 254.
147 Bodleian Library, Kimberley papers, MS.C.4087, ff. 18, Dufferin to Kimberley, 27 Nov. 1872; Blackwood, *Canadian Journal*, p. 75.
148 PRONI, D1071, H/H/2/1b, ff. 52, Dufferin to Kimberley, 23 Jul. 1873.
149 Bitterman, Upholding, pp. 4–5; R. Bitterman with M. McCallum, When private rights become public wrongs: property and the state in Prince Edward Island in the 1830s, in J. McLaren, A. R. Buck, and N. E. Wright (eds), *Despotic Dominion: property rights in British settler societies* (Vancouver, 2004), pp. 144–62.
150 PRONI, D1071, H/H9/10, speech by Lord Dufferin to members of the Toronto Club, 2 Sept. 1874.
151 PRONI, D1071, H/H/6/2, ff. 51, Dufferin to Holland, 9 Jun. 1874; Weaver, *Great Land Rush*, pp. 264–310.
152 As his initial response that he would not approve the bill demonstrates: PRONI, D1071, H/H/3/2, ff. 204, Dufferin to Mackenzie, 19 Nov. 1874.
153 See PRONI, D1071, H/H/6/3, ff. 21, Dufferin to Lord Cairns, 29 May 1878; H/H/7/41, ff. 6 and ff. 6, Dufferin to Holland, 2 May 1874; 25 Jun. 1874.
154 See, for example, his correspondence with Disraeli on land reform in Ireland at this time: PRONI, D1071, H/H/6/2, ff. 30, Dufferin to Disraeli, 22 May 1874.
155 PRONI, D1071, H/H/7/41, ff. 6, Dufferin to Holland, 2 May 1874; British Library, Carnarvon Papers, Add MS 60797, Vol. XLI (ff.1–141, 142–246), ff. 31, Dufferin to Carnarvon, 10 May 1877.
156 Bitterman, Upholding, pp. 14–15.
157 PRONI, D1071, H/H/6/2, ff. 51, Dufferin to Holland, 9 Jun. 1874. On the other hand, the PEI government was under pressure not to pay an inflated price: Bitterman, Upholding, p. 12.
158 PRONI, D1071, H/H/3/3, ff. 75, Dufferin to Mackenzie, 1 Apr. 1876.
159 PRONI, D1071, H/H/7/14, ff. 4, Dufferin to Childers, C.O., 4 Sept. 1874; Bitterman, Upholding, pp. 18–20.
160 PRONI, D1071, H/H/1/2, Dufferin to Carnarvon, 29 May 1874.
161 PRONI, D1071, H/H/2/1a, ff. 34, Kimberley to Dufferin, 24 Dec. 1872.
162 PRONI, D1071, H/H/7/77, ff. 2, Robinson to Dufferin, 16 Nov. 1872.
163 PRONI, D1071, H/H/2/3, ff. 19, Hicks Beach to Dufferin, 15 Oct. 1878; see also Queen Victoria to Dufferin, 12 Dec. 1874; Gailey, *Lost Imperialist*, p. 147.
164 Kirk-Greene argues that, along with Tweedsmuir, Dufferin was the 'most gifted' of the governors-general: The Governors-General of Canada, p. 52.
165 Inveraray Castle, Argyll estate archives, NRAS1206, 9th Duke's Canadian papers: outbook, 1878–83, ff. 3, Dufferin to Lorne, 12 Aug. 1878; Marquis of Lorne, *Memories of Canada and Scotland: speeches and verses* (London, 1884), pp. 11, 185; W. S. MacNutt, *Days of Lorne: impressions of a governor-general* (Fredericton, 1955), p. 156.

140 *Remits of power*

166 PRONI, D1071, H/H/4/1b, ff. 76, Macdonald to Sir Stafford Northcote, 1 May 1878; Lyall, *Life of Dufferin*, p. 259.
167 PRONI, D1071, H/H/1/2, Dufferin to Carnarvon, 18 Mar. 1874; Gailey, *Lost Imperialist*, pp. 143–6; O. Gust, The perilous territory of not belonging: exile and empire in Sir James Mackintosh's letters from early nineteenth century Bombay, *History Workshop Journal*, 86 (2018), pp. 1–2, 14–17.
168 Messamore, *Canada's Governors General*, p. 213; Messamore, The line, p. 455.
169 Knox, Carnarvon, pp. 60–1.
170 PRONI, D1071, H/H/1/1, Dufferin to Kimberley, 4 Dec. 1873.

6 Man on the spot
Dufferin as imperial problem solver

But there is no need to imagine that what has been must always continue even in the unchanging East, or that a race, some branches of which have evinced considerable energy as conquerors and colonists, as well as an intelligent appreciation of art and literature should prove eternally impervious to the teachings of civic morality and the instincts of patriotism, or incapable of apprehending those common axioms of government which the consensus of civilised mankind has recognised as essential to the welfare of a community.[1]

Character and the 'official mind'

At the very beginning of his public career, and at its height, Dufferin was parachuted into two short-term appointments to manage sensitive situations where British imperial strategic objectives were entwined with European geo-politics. These appointments are of interest because they sat outwith the normal processes of patronage and appointment and highlight the nature of aristocratic governance and decision-making in highly pressurised contexts.[2] These were, first, the aftermath of sectarian massacres in Syria in 1860, where complex tensions involving inter-religious hatreds and challenges to Ottoman power and French interests were at play. Second, while Dufferin was serving as ambassador to the Ottoman Porte, he was sent to Egypt in the wake of the 'Urabi rebellion to recommend measures to secure political stability, again balancing Egyptian, Ottoman, British and French interests while doing so. Both missions lasted only a few months and he was chosen for these difficult tasks because of his experience and growing reputation as a safe pair of hands that could be trusted to follow orders from Westminster. This trust stemmed from assumptions around the strength of aristocratic character, as a paternalistic and responsible elite.[3] Dufferin, as a landed aristocrat, was equipped with the correct background and character: monarchical, hierarchical, based upon a rural, landed and heritable heritage.[4] This was a specifically British and aristocratic form of political socialisation, and a highly influential one. Although separated by two decades, during which his thinking evolved considerably, by splicing together these two episodes, we can judge how effective the mechanisms underpinning aristocratic governance were in the challenging circumstances of imperial crisis. Although Dufferin had considerably more experience under his belt by the 1880s, the challenges he faced in the 1860s were similar and he met them with the same tactics. The danger to both London's and his own personal reputation was acute in both cases: there needed to be the appearance of action but, at the same time, no change to the delicate balance of power and interests at stake. Dufferin's whiggish liberalism made him a good candidate; he would not be too severe or reactionary but, instead, work with an emphasis on the art of the possible. Indeed, he was the ultimate imperial fixer, adept at creating a simulacrum of representative democracy, but never really delivering (or even intending to) any actual change. This meant he could be placed into difficult circumstances by the government, safe in the knowledge that he could be trusted to do his duty, shield London from any reputational damage and maintain autocratic power, whether that was embodied in an aristocratic elite, British imperialism or Ottoman autocracy.[5]

He also had some practical experience to offer; when he was sent to Syria by Lord John Russell he had only recently returned from a visit to the Levant and Egypt, travelling to see ancient sites, with a particular interest in Old Testament locations.[6] Additionally, as an Ulsterman, he was regarded by Westminster's grandees as having particular insight into the knotty complexities of sectarian and communal tensions, a specialist skill that was assumed to be globally translatable. Despite having had no diplomatic or imperial experience before going to Syria, he was regarded as a good appointment to the international commission gathering there in 1860. Lord John Russell was using the crisis as a diplomatic testing ground for Dufferin, who was regarded as a serious and dedicated young man and a possible rising star in the party. Looking back forty years later, Dufferin was struck by the 'accidental' nature of his appointment: 'had it not been for the accident of my going in a yacht to the Mediterranean, Lord Russell probably never would have dreamt of sending me as Commissioner to Syria, and if it had not been for that lucky accident I may never have entered the public service'.[7] Of course, Dufferin's elite landed background meant that his appointment was far from accidental. His Egyptian service in the 1880s was also prefaced by travel: he had spent time travelling in Egypt, principally in the late 1850s, collecting antiquities, digging up ancient sites and sailing on the Nile. By the time he went to Cairo in an official capacity in 1883, he had over twenty years of overseas diplomatic and administrative experience under his belt. He had a reputation by then of a skilled diplomat, able to secure British interests with honour, as defined by notions of gentlemanly character. Dufferin's experience was also seen to equip him with the necessary understanding of 'those infirmities' of 'oriental' character, enabling him to make the right kinds of recommendations as to the constitutional and social future of both Egypt and Syria.[8]

There were many tensions between the nature of British imperial 'character' and the pressures arising between the agency of the man on the spot and metropolitan strategic objectives.[9] The role played by Dufferin as that man on the spot was far from ornamental; it consisted of the exercise of significant power with long-lasting consequences for both polities. It was also an expression of the belief in 'good' governance that could only be provided by the British for 'inferior' peoples. The sectarian violence unleashed in Syria in 1860 and the rebellion in Egypt in the early 1880s were seen to demonstrate the universal truth that these were peoples historically, racially and socially unfit to rule themselves. British perception was that it had to shoulder that burden while protecting its relations with other European powers, principally France. In both cases, there was an added layer of tension consisting of the ailing Ottoman empire, propped up for various reasons by Britain, despite also regarding it as a polity demonstrably unfit to rule.[10] Good governance meant active governance, and Dufferin was the instrument to establish and execute it on the spot.

The nineteenth-century man on the spot has the reputation of being a driver of imperial expansion, often at a far faster pace than Westminster was always happy about.[11] This expansion risked political conflict which, in turn, forced the British hand to protect gains made but not approved, for reasons of prestige or strategy. Tensions blossomed between the men on the spot who wished to extend British power and those in the metropole who did not want to add further burdens to the long list of interests they had to protect. Egypt was certainly one such territory. Dufferin was well aware of these tensions and, although he was a committed imperialist, while the man on the spot he sought a path of consolidation and caution, not expansion. It was a difficult balancing act; on the one hand, Britain was politically, economically and strategically invested in these territories and they had to be protected.[12] On the other hand, there were vocal critics in Britain who argued that they were not worth the candle. Dufferin was not of this view and, in both Syria and Egypt, he found the balancing act between his vision of future British engagement and the political realities imposed by Westminster a difficult task. His approach was that of an aristocratic man on the spot.[13] There were a number of strands to this approach that developed over the twenty-three years that separated his service in Syria and Egypt. The overriding aristocratic concern expressed by Dufferin in both domestic and imperial contexts was the requirement of any government to protect both persons and property, whether from disorder, rebellion or the 'bad' governance of – in Syria and Egypt – the Ottoman empire. This was seen as the most important function of government; perhaps not surprisingly, given that landed aristocrats had the most to lose in this regard. The example of the French Revolution always loomed large, with politically motivated confiscation of property the greatest concern, but one closely followed by worries as to collateral damage from other types of disorder, such as sectarian violence. Harder to quantify was the 'governing passion'; an aristocratic commitment to political and constitutional structures and administration, the protection of property and the rule of law. These included liberal political institutions, such as parliamentary government and the disciplined administration of taxation and state finance. This was especially the case for those deemed unable to govern themselves, whether they be sectarian rioters in Belfast or Egyptian rebels. It was this political leadership that men on the spot such as Dufferin regarded as the single greatest justification for British dominion overseas.[14]

The aristocratic approach also incorporated assumptions about regions and their histories, peoples and governance, which when pulled together constituted an aristocratic vision of imperial opportunities and restrictions. In the cases of Syria and Egypt, a number of strands converged to constitute aristocratic understandings of the Middle East as a region, and Syria and Egypt as individual polities under Ottoman control. The first of these centred around religion, stressing the central place these geographies played in understandings of the Christian past, particularly the Old Testament. This was part of the historicist perspective on the region as one where ancient history was as well-known – if not better-known – as recent events, emphasised at the great public schools and the Oxbridge colleges. These were the Holy Lands, site of many of the best-known episodes from the Bible and of informal pilgrimage. Dufferin had travelled around the principal sites in the late 1850s in company with Cyril Graham, a native of Bangor, County Down, and his private secretary in Syria.[15] Egypt was seen in the same historicist light, although the emphasis was on its ancient, imperial past. Dufferin was captivated by Egyptology and spent a number of months in 1858 sailing the Nile, studying hieroglyphs, undertaking archaeological digs, to later display his finds at Clandeboye and indulge in 'the shooting of crocodiles and strange birds'.[16] There was a sense that, for both Syria and Egypt, their great days were past and they had long been in the grip of decline and decay, their governance totally corrupted and without political, financial or – most importantly – moral backbone. In Dufferin's view, this degeneracy had been precipitated by Ottoman rule, for religious as well as racial reasons. As inherently inferior peoples, Syrians and Egyptians were regarded as child-like, helplessly subject to the passing fads and rages of immature youth and therefore not able to govern themselves with justice or peace. Dufferin and his peers consistently referred to the use of a 'firm hand' when governing 'oriental' peoples, in much the same way as they thought of 'Celtic' peoples.[17] Dufferin's historicist perspective told him that these were places that could not independently redeem themselves; they could only do so through the agency of British example and power.[18]

The aristocratic approach can also be delineated in the nature and conduct of diplomacy, in which Dufferin would become a recognised expert. Although it is Dufferin's imperial career that is under primary analysis here, his contemporaries also knew him as one of the leading diplomatists of the age, appointed to almost all of the main embassies in Europe, including those of France, Russia, Italy and the Ottoman Porte.[19] The nature of his diplomacy and the ways in which it was intertwined with aristocratic understandings of British power and imperialism informed how we went about fixing emergencies as they arose.[20] In both Syria and Egypt, Dufferin had to manage a range of international interests and align them to the maintenance of British prestige and status. As a landed, elite, aristocrat – with experience of the management of land, power and people on the 'Celtic fringe' – Dufferin could be trusted to adhere to the assumptions underpinning the foreign policy devised at Westminster.[21] The political differences that dominated Westminster faded somewhat in the imperial context, as even radical Liberals agreed that Britain could not afford to lose face, or allow other European powers to take the lead, even if the price was long-term and unremunerated British commitment. Dufferin tried to secure British preferences while maintaining – for the most part – good relations with competing European powers. He could also be trusted – usually – not to overstep the boundaries of his instructions; although in both cases explored in this chapter, he did range somewhat from the tight geo-political leash imposed by his masters. Taken together, we can identify both an aristocratic intellectual framework for the diagnosis of imperial problems, as well as their proposed cures.

Syria – 'chronic blood-feuds and periodical massacres'[22]

> It is to be remembered that this is a country of vendettas; that in the war carried on between the barbarian tribes which inhabit it, usages prevail as horrible as those which disgraced the Middle Ages of Europe … In fact beneath the full blaze of modern civilisation we find in Syria habits of thought and practices prevailing for which the only historical parallel can be found in the books of Moses.[23]

Dufferin turned thirty-four in 1860, the year he was sent to Syria on his first diplomatic mission, a position obtained principally through the patronage of his uncle, Sir James Graham, with the support of Lord John Russell, although the fact that he had recently returned from touring the region was also a point in his favour.[24] A further feather in his cap was his Ulster heritage, which accorded him a certain amount of expertise in sectarian conflict, or so his English and Scottish colleagues assumed. Lastly, Dufferin's charming manners and social ease qualified him for this sensitive diplomatic position. This aspect of his personality should not be dismissed as superficial; indeed, affable and urbane manners were central to aristocratic self-understandings of the benefits they conferred on both domestic and imperial society. Manners were the overriding component of any gentlemanly education, whether public or private, taking years to develop and reinforce through family relationships and friendship networks. They were the most important indicator of gentlemanly status and, as such, were central to aristocratic identity.[25] Many contemporaries described Dufferin's manners and carriage as particularly affable and attractive, if rather off-putting at first. Dufferin had a slight figure, was short, spoke with a lisp that observers noted as being quite pronounced and was fond of wearing a monocle.[26] All of this gave people the initial impression of affectation but, on further acquaintance, his conversation and manners generated universal approval for being quick to put people at their ease, kindly and humorous. Dufferin was adept at finding the humour in most situations, something his contemporaries attributed to his Irish 'blarney', and while he took matters of protocol very seriously, this reflected his commitment to the maintenance of British – rather than his own – prestige.[27] His colleague in the Government of India Sir Henry Durand pinpointed the importance of 'the dignity of his manners' as being 'useful to him in dealing with native chiefs, and indeed with all Orientals'. Indeed, as he went on, 'there was something Oriental in his stately graveness and respect for ceremonial'.[28] He was noted as being particularly at his ease among people of a lower social station than himself, while being able to hold up British prestige by virtue of his personal rank. Sir James Graham wrote to Dufferin's mother on his appointment to the Syrian Commission, highlighting these strengths:

> I am confident he will do well. The task is a difficult one … [but] the sweetness of Dufferin's manners, combined with the firmness of his good sense will triumph over every difficulty. While he conciliates, he will not be hood-winked … He is so unassuming that he never gives offence; he is so true, that a Frenchman would scruple to deceive him, and this is my *beau ideal* of an English diplomatist.[29]

Good manners were expected by British aristocrats in their counterparts from other nations; Dufferin was pleased to note that the powerful Ottoman official he dealt with most in Syria, Fuad Pasha, was, in his words, 'one of the most remarkable public men in Europe – middle-aged, tall and handsome, speaking French in perfection, with the most charming manners and a kind and amiable character'.[30] Nevertheless, despite the assumptions of aristocratic rule by the best and his experience of managing his Irish estate, the complexities and pressures facing Dufferin in Syria were a serious matter. This may have contributed to Lord John Russell's decision to send him: it was thought that his relative inexperience would make it less likely that he would overreach himself and commit Britain to any agreement beyond its somewhat limited strategic interests. Russell made it clear that the first priority was to prevent too much pressure from other powers being applied to the tottering Ottoman empire, which Britain sought to protect.[31]

The fact that he was recently returned from a trip to the region was also a point in his favour. This tour, a somewhat exotic extension of the traditional route of the Grand Tour, had been a historical, religious and cultural experience for Dufferin. He was an enthusiastic subscriber to Romantic stereotypes of the Levant, as a place that fascinatingly combined the holy sites of Christianity with the excitements of 'oriental' barbarism. It was the Walter Scott version of Middle Eastern history, and he found his preconceptions and assumptions confirmed rather than challenged by his visit. This fed into his view of the various peoples of the region as child-like at best; at worst, barbaric and cruel, in thrall to blood feuds, disorder, and inter-religious and communal violence as a way of life.[32] These views had a concrete impact on his diplomacy and shaped the recommendations he made while commissioner in Syria, when he argued that the people were only, 'acting in accordance with a barbarous custom, uninterruptedly practiced throughout the country since the time of Moses'.[33] The Ottoman empire to his mind – and most of British political and public opinion – was the political symbol of the moral failures of its people. Corruption, superstition and weakness were the primary elements of 'oriental' governance, in sharp contrast to the rule of law and liberal parliamentary system of Britain, led by its heritable aristocracy. These were the competing and sometimes contradictory assumptions brought by Dufferin to Syria, a formative experience in his imperial and diplomatic career, and one from which we can trace elements of his later imperial governance. A key example was the balancing act he undertook between the requirements and interests of British power in relation to European neighbours; Dufferin would see this repeated again in nearly every imperial and diplomatic posting in his career. Imperial aristocrats such as Dufferin had to be as well aware of the shifting sands of European power as local conditions and pressures.

Syria in 1860 is an excellent case in point, as the context of Dufferin's appointment demonstrates. The sectarian conflict that brought him to the region consisted of an extreme outburst of murderous violence between the Maronites, an ancient Christian population of the northern part of the Lebanon and the Druses, who were a minority Muslim sect.[34] The Maronites had been under the nominal protection of the French from medieval times, with Napoleon Bonaparte claiming that they had been 'French citizens from time immemorial'.[35] However, it was the Ottoman Turks who claimed overall sovereignty of the Lebanon and Syria, although four European powers maintained some oversight to protect the 'laws, liberty and privileges' of the Christian inhabitants.[36] Contemporaries regarded Ottoman rule to be weak and corrupt, with a heavy reliance on the tactics of divide and rule, encouraging sectarian and community division in order to maintain overall control. This was certainly the diagnosis of Syrian tensions, which boiled over in May 1860 and raged on into the summer. The Maronite community came under attack from the Druses until, in July, the violence spread to Damascus, resulting in the whole Christian quarter of the city being burnt with great loss of life.[37] Dufferin estimated the dead at approximately 5000 persons, with thousands more missing and the economic loss at 'between 300,000 and 400,000 p equivalent to £1.250.000 to £1.500.000'.[38] The scale and extent of the violence and loss of control was frightening, as was the fact that local Ottoman officials and army officers failed either to prevent or to stop the violence once it had begun, either deliberately or because they lacked any real control.[39]

As reports of the violence began to circulate in the European capitals, the French immediately sprang into action, to the disconcertment of the British, who disapproved of the violence but did not want the episode to further weaken Ottoman power. Two measures were demanded by the French:

first, that the direct perpetrators of the violence should be captured and punished, and, second, any complicity of Ottoman officials and the army in the atrocities had to be exposed and punished.[40] The French were up in arms, demanding that an international commission be appointed to oversee the Turkish response, accompanied by troops to concentrate their minds. They were vigorously supported by Russia and the Prussians concurred. The British were more reluctant but, eventually, Lord Palmerston agreed to French troops landing at Beirut. To the commission representing the four European nations the Ottomans added Fuad Pasha, the high commissioner deputed by the Sultan to belatedly restore order in the province.[41] These were the ingredients Dufferin – the British representative on the commission – found in his pot; from this confused and sensitive context, he would go on to extract both what Britain wanted to achieve and a settlement that would eventually meet the approval of his European colleagues on the Syrian commission.[42] It would be the successful expression of his character as man on the spot that secured this outcome.

Dufferin's aims were to ensure that any official Ottoman complicity in the massacres was exposed and punished, without threatening their overall sovereignty in the region, and to prevent the French from gaining a permanent military foothold.[43] In the words of Lord John Russell, 'seek to gain no political influence yourself in Syria, nor allow any other nation to get any'.[44] On his arrival Dufferin met with Pasha, who assured him that the Turkish officials responsible had been tried and sentenced to death, but that he wished Dufferin to support a policy of commuting those sentences, who included powerful and high-status colleagues.[45] Dufferin refused to do so and Pasha was forced to oversee the full capital sentences carried out.[46] Dufferin also made sure that no Druse chiefs were used as scapegoats for Ottoman complicity, although he was strongly resisted in this by the French commissioner.[47] Most important were the measures to be agreed and implemented to prevent such an occurrence from happening again, and this was where Dufferin's vision began to depart from agreed British policy boundaries.[48] Essentially, the British were not overly concerned about the details of sectarian conflict in Syria; their chief aim was to manage the process by which justice was seen to be done without damaging Ottoman authority too much. Dufferin, in private correspondence with London, suggested a much more ambitious plan, one to create a new semi-independent Syrian polity within the Ottoman empire, to be called 'Greater Syria'.[49] In his seventeen-point plan, Dufferin outlined the structure of this new province, stressing two key points: that it should enjoy some measure of self-government; and that it should be overseen by a governor-general or viceroy – who would, of course, need to demonstrate the correct 'character' to govern.[50] This plan appeared fundamentally at odds with British strategic aims, but Dufferin argued that, by establishing such a structure, Ottoman rule would be strengthened not weakened.[51] In his view, problems in Syria had arisen due to the fundamental moral and political corruption of Ottoman rule. He proposed to put in place 'good' governance by creating a viceregal post, which would be filled by a man of 'talent and integrity'.[52] The pattern that we can trace throughout Dufferin's career, of an unshakeable belief in the power of elite, aristocratic men to govern well, can be seen in these recommendations, but in this case the outcome would not be all he desired.

At first, the British government gave some consideration to the plan, but the Ottoman government, alarmed by the prospect of another viceroyalty on the Egyptian model, was strongly opposed and so it was withdrawn. Dufferin was disappointed, but perhaps this failure benefitted his diplomatic education in the long term, highlighting both the limitations of the man on the spot and the *realpolitik* of British policy in relation to the Ottoman empire.[53] After the rejection of his plan, Dufferin worked on finding a compromise with the other European powers, particularly the French, who had to be persuaded very energetically to withdraw the troops they had landed in Syria.[54] This was eventually achieved and, overall, Dufferin's mission was regarded as a success, notwithstanding the failure of his own personal blueprint for the better governance of the region. Lord John Russell congratulated him in May 1861 as he prepared to return to Britain for, 'the ability and judgement which you displayed ... the temper and conciliatory spirit which you uniformly maintained in your intercourse with your colleagues, and the zeal with which, while caring for the exigencies of public justice, you endeavoured to consult the claims of humanity'.[55]

Even at this early stage in his imperial career, Dufferin's perspectives on what constituted good or bad governance were already secure. This is because they were an integral part of his socialisation as a landed aristocrat, including a strong adherence to the view that individual 'character' was at the root of good governance. The most important qualification for diplomatic service in the view of elites was aristocratic status; it conferred authority, and assumed gentlemanly integrity and honesty of conduct.[56] When Dufferin went to Syria, he did so first and foremost as an aristocratic gentleman with an amateur ethos, and he expected to work with men of an equivalent status representing other powers. Hierarchy conferred power as well as access to the powerful of other nations. In the diplomatic and imperial context, gentlemanly conduct further translated into skills of patience, firmness and the authority to speak on behalf of national interests. What is interesting about Dufferin's conduct of negotiations in Syria is that, with his plan for a 'Greater Syria', he stepped beyond the wishes of the 'official mind' he was there to represent. This demonstrates that even within the cultural boundaries of aristocratic rule by the best, tensions and disagreements were to be expected, as differing diagnoses and solutions to international problems came into conflict. In Syria, interpretations diverged; the conflict was between local conditions and British geopolitical aims, and Dufferin was forced to concede to the latter. He argued hard that his plan in fact supported British security in the region, as he believed it would better prop up Ottoman power. In his view, weak or corrupt rule could be demolished by introducing an executive office held by one elite, aristocratic official, who could be trusted to deliver good governance by virtue of their social status. He made exactly the same argument in Canada twelve years later, arguing that the governorship should be promoted to a viceroyalty, to match those of Ireland and India.[57] In other words, his vision was hierarchical and monarchical; from the heritable principle came his essential vision of imperial governance. Dufferin was also informed – as he was in Ireland and India – by popular historicist and orientalist scholarship, and travel literature. In the case of Syria, most of his historicist inspiration came from its connection to the Old Testament, something he was encouraged in through his friendship at this time with a number of Ulster and American Presbyterian missionaries who had been active in Syria since the 1820s.[58] This informed his urge to protect Christian minorities in what was the historical heartland of the faith. This was not an aim shared – at least publicly – with the British government; when all was said and done, they were prepared to sacrifice those interests to protect Ottoman power. Seventeen years later, he reflected back on the episode in correspondence with Gladstone, in a somewhat more cynical tone, as the Eastern Question flared up once again in European politics:

> I don't think it ought to be such an insoluble problem to secure a decent government for the Christian or the semi-Christian Provinces of Turkey. There was no part of the Turkish empire so rife with perennial disturbance as the Lebanon, but the European Commission framed a Constitution for its mixed population in which the principal representative institutions were largely introduced, and we crowned the edifice with a Christian governor, and ever since the Mountain has been the most prosperous and peaceable of any district in the Sultan's Dominions. It is true we began by making Fuad Pasha shoot a Governor General, a commander in chief and two or three colonels. I do not say this satisfactory state of things is made to last forever, but a respite of seventeen years from the Pandemonium which prevailed there is always something.[59]

Dufferin had to engage all of his diplomatic *nous* to manage French expectations and come to a compromise, particularly tricky in what was a non-imperial (for the British) setting. Overall, the Syrian mission acted as something of a proving process for Dufferin, and one in which the influences of his aristocratic and landed philosophies on imperial governance were already clear.

Egypt – 'limited and controlled modernisation'[60]

> It is true that from the commencement of the historical era the Valley of the Nile has been ruled by foreigners, and its inhabitants domineered over by alien races. Nor do its annals indicate an epoch when the 'justice' of the country was not corrupt, its administration oppressive, and the indigenous population emotional, obsequious and submissive. But

Man on the spot 151

there is no need to imagine that what has been must always continue ... or that a race ... should prove eternally impervious to the teachings of civic morality and the instincts of patriotism, or incapable of apprehending those common axioms of government which the consensus of civilised mankind has recognised as essential to the welfare of a community.[61]

Twenty-three years after Dufferin left Syria, he was parachuted back into the region to deal with remarkably similar issues, this time in Egypt.[62] He arrived in Cairo in the dying days of 1882, having been commissioned by the British government to temporarily leave his post as ambassador to the Sublime Porte and go to Egypt in the wake of the 'Urabi Rebellion.[63] His role was to gain a thorough grounding in both Egyptian problems and the objectives of the French, and to report to the government with recommendations to promote immediate stability and on what Britain's role should be in that process.[64] There were a number of echoes of Dufferin's Syrian mission twenty years before. First, the political context was as – if not more – complex. Egypt was under overall Ottoman sovereignty, but day-to-day control had long been left to the office of the Khedive, under which financial and political mismanagement had escalated, and in which British and French imperial and financial interests were hopelessly entangled.[65] Dufferin found himself again in the position of having to conciliate and manage relations between Egyptian political elites, the Ottoman empire, and French mistrust and suspicion. His later biographer put it bluntly: 'Lord Dufferin was now for a second time called in to rescue an Eastern province from a condition of intolerable misgovernment, to repair dilapidations, to proscribe remedies, and to provide against relapse.'[66] On top of this, the steer from the British government was nowhere near as clear as it had been in Syria. There, British aims had been at least consistent even if Dufferin had placed his own interpretation on their execution. In 1882–83, both political and public opinion was divided on the extent Britain to which should be involved in Egypt and for how long. Egypt also created tension within the Liberal party, emphasising the distance between radical and Whig elements in the party.[67] Gladstone had been highly critical of Disraelian activity in Egypt, including the purchase of shares in the Suez Canal.[68] By 1883, Egyptian policy satisfied no one and Gladstone, in particular, only tolerated it by supposing it would be a temporary commitment: the key British aim was evacuation as soon as economically and administratively possible.[69] Gladstone was acutely aware of the dangers inherent in the occupation of Egypt – principally, the damage it would do to Britain's moral reputation and, practically, by overstretching their imperial commitments and costs.[70] He demanded a morally defensible Christian imperial policy: he could accept an empire that promoted a civilising mission, but not the kind of bombastic imperialism he saw Disraeli and the Tories promoting.[71] The Liberals had no desire to make the Egyptian occupation permanent; instead, they wanted to secure tranquillity so that no internal disturbances could threaten Britain's strategic route to the East or its financial investments.[72] Kimberley made the position clear to Dufferin in his usual bracing manner: 'our position in regard to Egyptian affairs is, if possible, more embarrassing than ever. We are making no progress with the financial settlement, and ... in short, as long as we are in Egypt, we have a millstone tied around our necks, and no one sees how or when we are to get rid of it. A pleasant prospect!'[73] Dufferin was of the same view, as he reflected much later: 'from a political point of view, I have never thought that Egypt was of much benefit to us. In peacetime we have absolutely no political interest in being there, and in wartime my conviction is that the Canal would become more or less impossible for vessels.'[74] Dufferin had the unenviable task of balancing this ambivalent British attitude with French and Ottoman suspicions, and his aristocratic views as to good governance and the 'benefits' of British rule. He had to ensure that British involvement was not going to be permanent while, at the same time, putting in place structures that would maintain law and order, and the protection of European property and interests, and demonstrate British fitness to act as international and imperial policeman, all within as short a time frame as possible.[75] As Kimberley put it privately in his diary: 'Dufferin is our *deus ex machina* and we must hope he may drag the coach out of the rut.'[76] The context in Egypt made this a very tall order indeed. His first priority was the re-establishment of law and order, stabilising the country after a period of violent revolt and occupation. This was necessary to restore European confidence in Egypt as a location for investment, as well as Ottoman sovereignty.[77] British public opinion was mixed on this front; there was some sympathy for 'Urabi's aims – after all, as Dufferin knew very well, the government of the Khedive and the Ottomans was riddled with mismanagement and corruption.[78] Politically, Dufferin grappled with the legacy of a society that had known nothing but autocratic rule; the question was whether and how to introduce any measure of representative government, particularly when both the British and French governments were not interested in the niceties of the eventual settlement, as long as it did not impose long-term responsibilities and secured their financial interests.[79]

Dufferin arrived in Egypt and was thrown into a maelstrom of work: meetings, reading and an extensive correspondence. The immediate priority was agreeing a fate for 'Urabi and his fellow conspirators, who were in prison and under penalty of death.[80] The Khedive wished to impose the full penalty, but Dufferin, acting under the pressure of political and public opinion in Britain that saw 'Urabi as a sincere patriot, compelled a compromise whereby the death penalty was commuted to lifetime exile.[81] For securing this alone, Dufferin was flooded with congratulations, with the outcome becoming known as the *coup Dufferin*. Charlie Beresford wrote to picture the joy of the cabinet, '[they] danced a "can can" which was led off by Mr Gladstone and ended by Lord Granville'.[82] Dealing with the aftermath of the revolt was only the first step, however; Dufferin now had to turn to the future. The cabinet was still divided as to what the British commitment should be, and so the foreign secretary, Lord Granville, gave

Dufferin a wide remit, within the limits of shoring up the Khedive's authority.[83] Dufferin sought to understand Egypt's 'traditions' and history before making recommendations that were eventually presented in the Dufferin Report of 1883.[84] The Report covered almost all aspects of Egyptian governance, while sidestepping the Gordian knot of national finance, which he rightly diagnosed as an international issue.[85] Almost all other aspects of government were covered, from policing and military institutions, to agriculture, agricultural credit, education, communications infrastructure, the future place of the Sudan in Egyptian affairs, taxation and the reduction of foreign influence in all branches of the administration.[86] For a temporary British intervention, the Dufferin Report outlines a strikingly permanent vision. There are also clear resonances of the imperial mission inculcated into Dufferin and his peers, itself an echo of ancient Roman imperialism, with its emphasis on technology, education and enlightenment.[87] Of interest to us here are just two of those proposals: first, those dealing with local representative institutions, and, second, recommendations for economic and infrastructure development.

Before discussing these in detail, it is worth considering the spirit in which Dufferin constructed his proposals, put forth in his introduction to the report in the literary style typical to his official as well as unofficial correspondence, and reflective of his aristocratic education and perspective. That is, the language he used is as significant as the concrete recommendations he made.[88] His chief recommendation – met with hearty agreement in Britain – was that Egypt could not be ruled direct from London.[89] The reasons he put forward in his report did not touch directly on British wishes, however, but on the nature of Egypt and the consequences of European influences there:

> The metamorphic spirit of the age, as evoked by the inventions of science, intercourse with European countries and other invigorating influences, has already done something to inspire the fellahin with the rudiments of self-respect, and a dim conception of hitherto unimagined possibilities. Nor, like his own Memnon, has he remained irresponsive to the beams of the new dawn ... and in many indirect and half-conscious ways he has shown himself not only equal to the discharge of some of those functions of which none but members of the most civilised communities were thought capable, but unexpectedly appreciative of his legitimate political interests and moral rights.[90]

This literary flair was not allowed to pass without comment in the British press; the *Pall Mall Gazette* noting that, 'Lord Dufferin's despatch is almost too eloquent for a despatch; and sometimes the rhetorician is more visible than the diplomatist.'[91] Dufferin was framing the recommendations contained in his report – some of which he knew would be controversial – by elucidating his view of existing conditions in Egypt, as well as reinforcing the hierarchy of nations, at the top of which stood Britain, the best guide for Egypt through a process of moderate reform to ensure stability and prevent further violent outbursts.[92] This, in turn, reflected wider British assumptions as to hierarchy, their superiority and fitness to rule, through which they would govern those unable to govern themselves.[93] As the *Saturday Review* noted, 'The general nature of the scheme proposed by Lord Dufferin for the guidance of Egypt is easy to understand. A crushed, backward, childish nation is to be made independent, prosperous and civilised.'[94] As Dufferin's later involvement in Afghanistan and Burma also show, for the British, Egypt was fundamentally a strategic – not a political and economic – asset and the recommendations in his report reflect that British priority.[95] Like Afghanistan, Egypt was not annexed by the British; instead, a puppet ruler remained in place, in part to appease the Porte, but also to keep it at arm's length in terms of British commitment.[96] As in every other imperial context, Dufferin diagnosed Egyptian society as not being advanced enough – not yet having the required 'character' – to carry the weight of full representative government; 'a long enslaved nation instinctively craves for the strong hand of a master rather than for a lax constitutional regime', as he noted in his report.[97] Dufferin had been in correspondence with the viceroy of India, Lord Ripon (who he would succeed in 1884) as to the introduction of local self-government in Egypt, then a major political issue in India. The correspondence highlights the transnational exchange of ideas of imperial governance, as well as the aristocratic nature of its application, flavoured by a commitment to 'good' governance, as described by Ripon:

> I imagine that Egypt is a much more homogenous country than India and that therefore a uniform system would be more suitable there than here. I am very anxious wherever possible to found any system of local government upon indigenous native institutions and to suit it to native wants and feelings … I do not know if anything of the kind is to be now found in Egypt. If it is I should strongly recommend you to avail yourself of it as much as possible. European ideas imported *en bloc* into Egypt are not likely to flourish in that oriental soil, though according to my belief the broad principles of good government are equally applicable everywhere – the problem is, and it is by no means an easy one – how to apply those principles in the manner most suitable to the peculiarities of social and political conditions, which exist in the country with which we are dealing.[98]

Like Ripon, Dufferin regarded it as Britain's responsibility to plant in Egypt the seed of representative government, starting at the communal level through village constituencies, which would vote for members of Provincial Councils, from which would be elected the majority of members of a Legislative Council. The powers of these two Councils were to be limited to a consultative role with no veto powers; they offered the appearance – rather than the exercise – of power, which is no doubt why they were eventually approved and constituted.[99] *The Observer* for one did not blame Dufferin for this, noting that the British government had essentially tasked him, 'to make bricks without straw'.[100] As such, Dufferin's constitutional proposals were regarded by most of British political and public opinion as a success; they gave the flavour of British liberal benefits of rule by the best, without actually passing any real power into democratic hands.[101]

The other aspect of the Dufferin Report that highlights aristocratic conceptions of imperial improvement and their role in it was his proposal regarding the economic and infrastructural development of Egypt. Dufferin made no recommendations as to state finance as it was outwith his remit, but he had plenty to say about agricultural finance and debt, and the necessity of a significant programme of road, bridge and railway building, as well as irrigation and dam projects, all to lay the groundwork for future Egyptian economic security.[102] Dufferin recognised that one of the causes of the 'Urabi revolt was peasant indebtedness and dissatisfaction, and he drew upon his Irish experiences when he recommended that rural standards of living had to be improved and the chronic corruption, heavy taxation and unjust judicial system must be reformed to secure Egypt from a future revolt.[103] It was not just Ireland that he took his ideas from, however; India was also a source of both structures and personnel.[104] Dufferin recommended in his report that engineers with Indian experience be transferred to Egypt to establish an infrastructure programme, a recommendation that was followed through when the prominent Indian civil engineer Colin Scott-Moncrieff was drafted across.[105] This is a good example of the intra-imperial exchange of both ideas and people that was a key marker of British conceptions of the benefits of their overseas rule.[106] Tried and tested models and means of governance were transferred across geographies and, crucially, in the age of personalised, often aristocratic, governance, this transfer was managed through people such as Dufferin and their networks.[107]

As with Syria in 1860, when Dufferin left Egypt in 1883 he was showered with praise (as well as a Grand Cross of the Bath and the Vice-Admiralty of Ulster and the maritime ports thereof).[108] On its own somewhat limited terms, the report was a success; it struck a balance between basic administrative modernisation and the refurbishment of traditional Egyptian institutions, as understood through British eyes.[109] Later commentators on Egypt noted that, while it was one thing to write a set of recommendations, it was quite another to put them into practice.[110] This task was left primarily to the 'masterful hand' of an India veteran, Sir Evelyn Baring (later Lord Cromer) of the Baring banking dynasty and a leading financial expert.[111] This, more than any praise for the liberal recommendations made by Dufferin, illustrates the true nature of British aims in Egypt: the security of British financial and strategic interests.[112] Nevertheless, reflecting twenty years after Dufferin submitted his report, Cromer considered that, 'Lord Dufferin's main design was wisely conceived'.[113] Certainly, it was regarded as a successful outcome in terms of the balancing act between competing local, imperial and international interests, as had been the case in Syria. As Dufferin put it to his uncle Brin: 'I have every reason I think to be grateful for the indulgence with which my Report has been received, though it has pleased nobody altogether. I had a very multifarious audience to address in France, Europe, the Sultan, the Egyptians, the people who wanted to take Egypt altogether, those who wished to let her "stew", my own government, the Radicals and lastly, the "British Lion."'[114]

One aspect of the Egyptian question that was not satisfactorily resolved in Dufferin's view, or for British interests more broadly, was 'the prospect of the prolongation of our Egyptian entanglements' in the Sudan.[115] Officially, the British had no role in the ill-fated mission of General Hicks in the Sudan or, later, that of General Charles Gordon at Khartoum, all questions relating to the management of the Sudan having been laid at the door of the Khedive. Dufferin had been in correspondence with both men and was in sympathy with them both.[116] He acted quickly to defend his own reputation after their deaths, however, particularly that of Hicks in 1883, writing to Lansdowne that, 'fortunately as far as my own credit is concerned I put on record before I left Egypt a strong opinion that the Egyptian government should not attempt to extend their dominion ... had they done this all would have been well'.[117] It was a sour note after the relative success of Dufferin's mission to Egypt.[118] His tone when discussing the episode is of a parent taking to task an errant child that had been given the best advice but had wilfully chosen to ignore it. Implicit in this language is a perceived clash between inherent 'national characters', as it was in all of Dufferin's thinking on Egypt, as in Syria, Ireland, India and all of the imperial contexts within which he worked.[119] It was this expression of his aristocratic, historicist and racially infused view that characterised Egyptian governance well into the twentieth century.

'A new era of prosperity and contentment'?[120]

> It was upon this mission that Lord Dufferin first proved that kind of high political and diplomatic capacity which is always in great demand for the foreign service of the British empire, with its manifold interests and responsibilities, its possessions, protectorates and spheres of influence in so many parts of the world.[121]

> As an essay in romantic politics, the Despatch is beyond reproach; it fails only when the test of calm analysis is applied.[122]

What does Dufferin's experience of Syria and Egypt tell us more broadly about the character expected of the man on the spot and British imperial power?[123] In other words, what implications are there for the British and Irish aristocracy that a key part of their identity was connected to ruling others?[124] Certainly, they both illuminate the essentially aristocratic nature of both imperial thinking and action. It is this that lies behind Dufferin's appointments to both Syria and Egypt: as an aristocratic, landed gentleman, he had the requisite status and experience to operate in the world of international and imperial diplomacy, and was a trusted pair of safe hands. This was about as far from an ornamental role as can be imagined; in both cases, Dufferin was given explicit instructions and there was a good deal of clarity on overall British aims, but there was still room for both the interpretation of those aims and the manner in which they were to be achieved. Dufferin made good use of this space, according to his own definitions and those of his class more broadly, promoting his view of honourable British rule and the benefits it ought to bring, and protecting his own and Britain's reputation in the process. Central to this was the point that ideological issues mattered just as much as practical ones.[125] This generated the fundamental requirement of good governance: the protection of both persons and property, without resorting to the outright repression of personal or political liberties. It was a fine line and was reflected in the nature of these particular diplomatic episodes: delicate balancing acts between British, Ottoman, local and European interests.[126] This was underpinned by received colonial knowledge on 'oriental' peoples, constructions that informed the recommendations Dufferin made as to the future governance in not only Syria and Egypt, but also in Ireland and India. Both the form and content of imperial diplomacy was aristocratic in character; as such, the question is not really whether Dufferin carried out the wishes of the 'official mind' but, rather, to what extent was aristocratic thinking *itself* the official mind? Arguably it was, to a significant degree, although it was always under pressure from both the British and the local imperial contexts, which is why men such as Dufferin were continually articulating what it meant, and claiming that it was one and the same as Britain's interests. A significant part of that thinking was the pressure to demonstrate in concrete fashion the benefits of British imperial governance, or 'guidance', depending on the requirements of British policy. This could range from the settlement of political institutions – as in both Syria and Egypt – to the construction of railways, irrigation systems and other economic infrastructure, as in the case of Egypt. In both cases, the physical incarnation of perceived British superiority and dominion through the transnational movement of people and ideas was on display.[127]

Notes

1 General Report by the Earl of Dufferin respecting reorganisation in Egypt, 1883 [hereafter Dufferin Report], p. 1.
2 J. A. Mangan, *Making Imperial Mentalities: socialisation and British imperialism* (Manchester 1990), pp. 1–3; L. Fawaz, *An Occasion for War: civil conflict in Lebanon and Damascus in 1860* (London, 1994).
3 Z. Laidlaw, Richard Bourke: Irish liberalism tempered by empire, in D. Lambert and A. Lester (eds), *Colonial Lives Across the British Empire* (Cambridge, 2006), pp. 120–2.
4 P. J. Cain, Character and Imperialism: the British financial administration of Egypt, 1878–1914, *Journal of Imperial and Commonwealth History*, 34:2 (2006), p. 177; Mangan, *Making Imperial Mentalities*, p. 2; D. Castronovo, *The English Gentleman: images and ideals in literature and society* (1987), pp. 75–7.
5 A. L. Stoler, *Along the ArchivalGgrain: epistemic anxieties and colonial common sense* (Princeton, NJ, 2008), pp. 64–9.

158 *Man on the spot*

6 Public Record Office of Northern Ireland [hereafter PRONI], D1071, H/H/B/B/449, ff. 21, Dufferin to Lady Anna Dufferin (his aunt), 2 Dec. 1859; The National Archives, Kew [hereafter TNA], PRO 30/22/94, correspondence between Lords Dufferin and John Russell, 1860–1; A. Gailey, *The Lost Imperialist: Lord Dufferin, memory and mythmaking in an age of celebrity* (London, 2015), pp. 75–9.
7 Clandeboye House, Dufferin to Lord Basil (his son), 1 Jun. 1900; Gailey, *Lost Imperialist*, pp. 82–5, 185–92; J. Parry, *The rise and fall of Liberal government in Victorian Britain* (New Haven, 1993), pp. 182–3.
8 Dufferin Report, p. 3; Cain, Character and imperialism, pp. 177–8.
9 D. Cannadine, *Ornamentalism: how the British saw their empire* (London, 2001), pp. 123–8; Castronovo, *English Gentleman*, pp. 78, 88; B. Porter, *The Absent-Minded Imperialists: empire, society and culture in Britain* (Oxford, 2004), pp. 227–31.
10 Dufferin Report, p. 1–3; M. Kovic, *Disraeli and the Eastern Question* (Oxford, 2011); A. G. Hopkins, Back to the future: from national history to imperial history, *Past and Present*, 164 (1999), pp. 209–10, 222–3; J. Epstein, Taking class notes on the empire, in S. Rose and C. Hall (eds), *At Home with the Empire: metropolitan culture and the imperial world* (Cambridge, 2006), pp. 253–5; D. R. Khoury and D. K. Kennedy, Comparing empires: the Ottoman domains and the British Raj, *Comparative Studies of South Asia, Africa and the Middle East*, 27:2 (2007), pp. 234, 236–7, 241.
11 See, for example, B. Porter, Gladstone and imperialism, in M. E. Daly and K. T. Hoppen (eds), *Gladstone, Ireland and Beyond* (Dublin, 2011), pp. 170–2; R. D. Long (ed.), *The Man on the Spot: essays on British empire history* (Connecticut, 1995); M. Lynn, Consul and kings: British policy, 'the man on the spot', and the seizure of Lagos, 1851, *Journal of Imperial and Commonwealth History*, 10:2 (1982), pp. 150–67.
12 R. A. Atkins, The Conservatives and Egypt, 1875–80, *Journal of Imperial and Commonwealth History*, 2:2 (1974), p. 190.
13 B. Blakely, *The Colonial Office, 1868–1892* (Durham, USA, 1972), pp. vii–x.
14 See, for example, Dufferin Report, pp. 7–10.
15 TNA, PRO/30/22/94, ff. 4, Dufferin to Lord John Russell, 3 Aug. 1860; PRONI, D1071, H/H/B/449, ff. 21, Dufferin to Lady Anna Dufferin, 2 Dec. 1859. Carnarvon also travelled out to see the issues for himself and met Dufferin there: Sir A. Hardinge, *The Life of Henry Howard Molyneux Herbert, Fourth Earl of Carnarvon, 1831–1890*, vol. 1 (Oxford, 1925), p. 168; Gailey, *Lost Imperialist*, p. 83; R. Symonds, *Oxford and Empire: the last lost cause?* (Oxford, 1992), pp. 25, 35.
16 A. C. Lyall, Sir, *The Life of the Marquis of Dufferin and Ava* (London, 1905), p. 99. Dufferin's mother, Lady Helen, accompanied him on this trip, publishing a humorous book gently satirizing Lord Dufferin's *Letters from High Latitudes*: H. S. Blackwood, *Lispings from Low Latitudes* (London, 1863); Gailey, *Lost Imperialist*, pp. 75–7; M. Jasanoff, Collectors of empire: objects, conquests and imperial self-fashioning, *Past and Present*, 184 (2004), pp. 110–16.
17 See, for example, Lyall, *Life of Dufferin*, p. 566; R. L. Shukla, *Britain, India and the Turkish Empire 1853–1882* (New Delhi, 1973), pp. 213–15, 219.
18 See also the views of E. Rogers, a correspondent and long-term resident of Egypt: PRONI, D1071, K/1/3, ff. 85, E. Rogers to Dufferin, 8 Nov. 1881.
19 Lyall, *Life of Dufferin*, pp. 562–8.
20 N. Ethrington, *Theories of Imperialism: war, conquest and capital* (London, 1984), pp. 263–7, 270; Epstein, Taking class notes, pp. 256, 270.
21 Kovic, *Disraeli and the Eastern Question*, p. 307–15.
22 Lyall, *Life of Dufferin*, p. 127; PRONI, D1071, H/C/2/3, despatches from Syria, 1859–61.

23 Lyall, *Life of Dufferin*, p. 115.
24 PRONI, D1071, H/H/K/1/1, ff. 64, Lord Granville to Dufferin, 25 May 1881; Lyall gives a full overview of the Syrian episode at pp. 104–123; TNA, PRO 30/22/94, Dufferin to Russell, 2 Aug. 1860; University of Edinburgh, *Address by the Marquess of Dufferin and Ava (Lord Rector)* (Edinburgh, 1901), p. 23.
25 Castronovo, *English Gentleman*, pp. 75–83; Nicolson, *Helen's Tower*, pp. 117–22.
26 Lyall, *Life of Dufferin*, p. 563.
27 Lyall, *Life of Dufferin*, pp. 564–5; Nicolson, *Helen's Tower*, pp. 205–7.
28 Lyall, *Life of Dufferin*, p. 566; see also PRONI, D1071, H/H/B/449, ff. 21, Dufferin to Lady Anna Dufferin, 2 Dec. 1859.
29 PRONI, D1071, H/B/G/316, ff. 9, Sir James Graham to Lady Dufferin, 7 Sept. 1860; Lyall, *Life of Dufferin*, p. 109.
30 TNA, FO 78/1625, No. 3, Dufferin to Sir Henry Bulwer, 8 Sept. 1860; Lyall, *Life of Dufferin*, p. 111; Fawaz, *An Occasion for War*, pp. 194–5.
31 Dufferin spoke of his aim to promote the 'regeneration of the Turkish empire': TNA, FO 78/1625, ff. 15, Dufferin to Sir Henry Bulwer, 23 Sept. 1860.
32 Gailey, *Lost Imperialist*, pp. 83–9.
33 TNA, FO 78/1625, ff. 15, Dufferin to Sir Henry Bulwer, 23 Sept. 1860.
34 F. Zachs, 'Novice' or 'heaven-born' diplomat? Lord Dufferin and his plan for a 'Province of Syria': Beirut, 1860–61, *Middle Eastern Studies*, 36:3 (2000).
35 Lyall, *Life of Dufferin*, p. 105.
36 These were Britain, France, Prussia and Russia; Lyall, *Life of Dufferin*, p. 105.
37 TNA, FO 78/1625, ff. 13, Dufferin to Sir Henry Bulwer, 23 Sept. 1860; Zachs, Novice, pp. 161–2.
38 TNA, FO 78/1625, ff. 13, Dufferin to Sir Henry Bulwer, 23 Sept. 1860.
39 Lyall, *Life of Dufferin*, p. 108.
40 Fawaz, *An Occasion for War*, pp. 202, 203, 204.
41 TNA, FO 78/1630, Dufferin to Russell, 25 Apr. 1861.
42 TNA, FO 78/1625, ff. 3, Dufferin to Sir Henry Bulwer, 8 Sept. 1860; E. D. Steele, *Palmerston and Liberalism, 1855–1865* (Cambridge, 1991), pp. 285–7.
43 Zachs, Novice, p. 164; Kovic, *Disraeli and the Eastern Question*, pp. 307–14.
44 Cited in Lyall, *Life of Dufferin*, p. 122.
45 TNA, PRO/30/22/94, ff. 28, Dufferin to Lord John Russell, 14 Sept. 1860; Fawaz, *An Occasion for War*, pp. 195–6.
46 TNA, FO 78/1625, ff. 3, Dufferin to Sir Henry Bulwer, 8 Sept. 1860. He also donated £500 for the relief of Damascus's Christians: Lyall, *Life of Dufferin*, pp. 112–16.
47 TNA, FO 78/1625, ff. 15, Dufferin to Sir Henry Bulwer, 23 Sept. 1860; Lyall, *Life of Dufferin*, pp. 116–18.
48 TNA, PRO/30/22/94, ff. 51, Dufferin to Lord John Russell, 4 Nov. 1860, and ff. 54, 18 Nov. 1860.
49 Zachs, Novice, p. 164.
50 In other words, more of a British than a Turkish 'character'; Zachs, Novice, pp. 165–7; Fawaz, *An Occasion for War*, pp. 214–16.
51 Zachs, Novice, pp. 164–6.
52 TNA, PRO/30/22/94, ff. 54, Dufferin to Lord John Russell, 18 Nov. 1860; Lyall, *Life of Dufferin*, p. 120; D. Cannadine, *Aspects of Aristocracy: grandeur and decline in modern Britain* (New Haven, 1994), pp. 77–81.
53 TNA, PRO/30/22/94, ff. 65, Dufferin to Lord John Russell, 16 Dec. 1860 and ff. 118, 10 Mar. 1861; Lyall, *Life of Dufferin*, pp. 120–1; Zachs, Novice, p. 167–8; Fawaz, *An Occasion for War*, pp. 215–16. In the end, an arrangement whereby the Lebanon district was placed under a Christian governor nominated by the Porte, and altogether unconnected to the tribes of the region, was agreed.
54 Zachs, Novice, p. 167; Lyall, *Life of Dufferin*, p. 121.
55 Cited in Lyall, *Life of Dufferin*, p. 122.

56 See discussion in Lyall, *Life of Dufferin*, pp. 563–8.
57 PRONI, D1071, H/H/1/3, Dufferin to Carnarvon, 11 Nov. 1875; Cannadine, *Ornamentalism*, pp. 27–33; J. W. Cell, *British Colonial Administration in the Mid-Nineteenth Century: the policy-making process* (New Haven, 1970), p. viii.
58 See TNA, FO 78/1625, ff. 9, Dufferin to Sir Henry Bulwer, 23 Sept. 1860; Zachs, Novice, pp. 169–70; Kovic, *Disraeli and the Eastern Question*, p. 307; K. Tidrick, *Empire and the English Character* (London, 1990), p. 4.
59 British Library [hereafter BL], Gladstone Papers, Add MS 44151, Vol. LXVI, ff. 140, Dufferin to Gladstone, 31 Oct. 1879; M. Tusan, Britain and the Middle East: new historical perspectives on the Eastern Question, *History Compass*, 8:3 (2010), pp. 212, 214.
60 R. Tignor, *Modernisation and British Colonial Rule in Egypt, 1882–1914* (New Jersey, 1966), p. 56.
61 Dufferin Report, cited in Lyall, *Life of Dufferin*, p. 331; C. Hall, *Macaulay and Son: architects of imperial Britain* (New Haven, 2012), p. 186; A. Porter, Empires in the mind, in P. J. Marshall (ed.), *The Cambridge Illustrated History of the British Empire* (Cambridge, 1996), pp. 218–19, 223.
62 PRONI, D1071, H/H/K/1/5, ff. 38, Queen to Dufferin on his appointment, 9 Nov. 1882; Lyall, *Life of Dufferin*, p. 312; for a full overview from Lyall on Egypt, see pp. 324–52.
63 A. Scholch, *Egypt for the Egyptians! The socio-political crisis in Egypt, 1878–1882* (Reading, 1981), pp. 306, 311, 313.
64 TNA, FO 141/168, No. 1 and No. 3, Dufferin to Granville, 12 Nov. 1882. He would later write of his pleasure at the 'friendly attitude' demonstrated by the French during his mission: TNA, FO141/168, No. 143, Dufferin to Granville, 29 Apr. 1883.
65 R. Tignor, The 'Indianisation' of the Egyptian administration under British rule, *American Historical Review*, 68:3 (1963), pp. 636–7; TNA, FO141/168, No. 53, Dufferin to Granville on discussions with the French, 18 Dec. 1882.
66 Lyall, *Life of Dufferin*, p. 328; A. Colvin, *The Making of Modern Egypt* (New York, 1906), p. 28; A. Scholch, The 'men on the spot' and the English occupation of Egypt in 1882, *Historical Journal*, 19:3 (1976), pp. 784–5.
67 M. Bentley, *Politics without Democracy, 1815–1914* (Oxford, 1984), pp. 170, 172; Colvin, *Making of Modern Egypt*, p. 27.
68 Dufferin Report, p. 37; R. A. Atkins, The Conservatives and Egypt, 1875–80, *Journal of Imperial and Commonwealth History*, 2:2 (1974), p. 191; P. J. Durrans, A two-edged sword: the Liberal attack on Disraelian imperialism, *Journal of Imperial and Commonwealth History*, 10:3 (1982), pp. 262, 265; Kovic, *Disraeli and the Eastern Question*, pp. 305–9; R. Blake, *Disraeli* (London, 1966), pp. 757, 759–60.
69 Atkins, The Conservatives and Egypt, p. 190; P. Marshall, The Imperial factor in the Liberal Decline, 1880–1885, in J. Flint and G. Williams (eds), *Perspectives of Empire: presented to Gerald S. Graham* (Harlow, 1973), p. 138.
70 Porter, Gladstone and imperialism, pp. 170–2.
71 T. Koditschek, *Liberalism, Imperialism, and the Historical Imagination: nineteenth-century visions of a Greater Britain* (Cambridge, 2011), pp. 314–17.
72 BL, India Office Papers, F130/3, ff. 22, Kimberley to Dufferin, 13 Mar. 1885; Tignor, *Modernisation and British Colonial Rule in Egypt*, p. 48; Atkins, The Conservatives and Egypt, pp. 192–3.
73 BL, F130/3, ff. 5, Kimberley to Dufferin, 11 Dec. 1884; A. Hawkins and J. Powell (eds), *The Journal of John Wodehouse, First Earl of Kimberley for 1862–1902* (London, 1997), p. 333.
74 BL, Mss Eur, Papers of Mountstuart Grant Duff, F234/11, ff. 17, Dufferin to Grant Duff, 12 Jan. 1896.

Man on the spot   161

75 Colvin, *Modern Egypt*, pp. 35–7; Tignor, *Modernisation and British Colonial Rule in Egypt*, pp. 90–1. This included financial 'character' and discipline, Cain, Character and imperialism, p. 179–80; L. Mak, *The British in Egypt: community, crime and crisis, 1822–1922* (New York, 2012), pp. 1, 9–10; Scholch, The 'men on the spot', p. 784.
76 Hawkins and Powell, *The Journal of John Wodehouse*, p. 333. For an alternative perspective, see W. S. Blunt, *The Secret History of the English Occupation of Egypt* (London, 1907), pp. 349, 353, 360.
77 TNA, FO141/168, No. 10, Dufferin to Granville, 20 Nov. 1882.
78 Letter to Sir William Gregory, cited in Lyall, *Life of Dufferin*, pp. 330–1.
79 Back to the 'Palmerstonian politics' utilised in 1860s Syria; Cain, Character and imperialism, p. 191; Atkins, The Conservatives and Egypt, p. 190.
80 TNA, FO141/168, No. 4, Dufferin to Granville, 16 Nov. 1882, on options for dealing with 'Urabi; PRONI, D1071, H/H/K/1/5, ff. 33, Lord Northbrook to Dufferin, 3 Nov. 1882.
81 PRONI, D1071, H/H/K/1/5, ff. 131, Lord Northbrook to Dufferin, 6 Dec. 1882; Tignor, *Modernisation and British Colonial Rule in Egypt*, pp. 67–8; Cain, Character and imperialism, pp. 185–6; Gailey, *Lost Imperialist*, p. 186.
82 PRONI, D1071, H/H/K/1/6, ff. 1, Sir Charles Beresford to Dufferin, 1 Jan. 1883; see also ff. 77, Lord Granville to Dufferin with the official congratulations, 15 Mar. 1883.
83 TNA, FO141/168, No. 6, Dufferin to Granville on the army and security, 18 Nov. 1882; Dufferin Report, pp. 3–6; Tignor, *Modernisation and British Colonial Rule in Egypt*, pp. 52–3.
84 'I am already nearly dead with all the work I have on hand', he wrote privately to Granville; cited in Lyall, *Life of Dufferin*, p. 330.
85 Atkins, The Conservatives and Egypt, p. 201.
86 Dufferin Report, 1883, pp. 1–41; TNA, FO141/168, No. 7, Dufferin to Granville, 18 Nov. 1882.
87 M. Bradley, Tacitus' *Agricola* and the conquest of Britain: representations of empire in Victorian and Edwardian Britain, in M. Bradley (ed.), *Classics and Imperialism in the British Empire* (Oxford, 2010), pp. 134, 157; J. W. Cell, *Hailey: a study in British Imperialism* (Cambridge, 1992), p. 3.
88 It was not met with universal enthusiasm in the British press, however: see *The Standard*, 20 Mar. 1883; *The Observer*, 1 Apr. 1883; *Saturday Review*, 24 Mar. 1883.
89 Dufferin Report, pp. 1–3.
90 Dufferin Report, p. 3, and see Dufferin's amused recollection of this passage in his *Address delivered at St Andrews University April 6, 1891 by the Marquess of Dufferin and Ava, Lord Rector* (Edinburgh, 1891), pp. 33–4.
91 *Pall Mall Gazette*, 21 Mar. 1883; see also *The Standard*, 20 Mar. 1883, for a further roasting of his report.
92 Dufferin Report, p. 1–2; Tignor, The 'Indianisation' of the Egyptian administration under British rule, p. 651. See similar views of his contemporaries: PRONI, D1071, H/H/B/35, ff. 3, Sir Samuel Baker to Dufferin, 22 Apr. 1883.
93 PRONI, D1071, H/H/K/1/6, ff. 118, Dufferin to Cherif Pasha, 29 Apr. 1883.
94 *Saturday Review*, 24 Mar. 1883.
95 Tignor, *Modernisation*, pp. 48–9; A. G. Hopkins, Back to the future: from national history to imperial history, *Past and Present*, 164 (1999), pp. 222–3.
96 Dufferin Report, p. 3; Porter, Gladstone and imperialism, p. 173.
97 Dufferin Report, p. 1; Lyall, *Life of Dufferin*, p. 334; see also TNA, FO141/168, No. 7, Dufferin to Granville, 18 Nov. 1882; Cain, Character and imperialism, p. 191; M. Bentley, *Lord Salisbury's World: Conservative environments in late-Victorian Britain* (Cambridge, 2001), pp. 221–4.

162 *Man on the spot*

98 PRONI, D1071, H/H/K/5, ff. 128, Ripon to Dufferin, 5 Dec. 1882; see also H/H/K/1/6, ff. 16, Ripon to Dufferin, 16 Jan. 1883; Tignor, Indianisation, p. 659, 661.
99 Lyall, *Life of Dufferin*, pp. 334–5; PRONI, D1071/K/1/6, ff. 16, Ripon to Dufferin, 16 Jan. 1883; TNA, FO141/168, No. 7, Dufferin to Granville, 18 Nov. 1882; No. 36, Dufferin to Granville, 26 Jan. 1883.
100 *Observer*, 1 Apr. 1883.
101 U. S. Mehta, *Liberalism and Empire: a study in nineteenth century British Liberal thought* (Chicago, 1999), pp. 1–2, 4, 7, 30.
102 Dufferin Report, pp. 18–28.
103 Tignor, *Modernisation*, p. 91. His ideas on this point were laid out in the 1860s in Dufferin, *Contributions to an Inquiry into the State of Ireland* (London, 1866); Dufferin, *The Case of the Irish tenant, as stated sixteen years ago by the Rt. Hon. Lord Dufferin, in a speech delivered to the House of Lords, February 28, 1854* (London, 1870); Gailey, *Lost Imperialist*, pp. 171–7.
104 TNA, FO141/168, No. 16, Dufferin to Granville, 27 Nov. 1882; Tignor, Indianisation, pp. 636–8.
105 PRONI, D1071, H/H/B/C/529, ff. 9, Sir Auckland Colvin, 15 May 1883.
106 Including concerns about the impact of rebellion in one imperial context on others; see Sir Alfred Lyall's correspondence with Dufferin on the impact of unrest in Egypt on India: BL, India Office Records, Mss Eur IOR Neg 4325–4370, ff. 71, Lyall to Dufferin, 14 Feb. 1885; Tignor, *Modernisation*, pp. 57, 63–9; E. Delaney and C. O'Niall (eds), Beyond the nation: transnational Ireland, *Eire–Ireland*, 51:1–2 (2016).
107 See, for example, the 3rd Duke of Sutherland's correspondence with Dufferin as to Egyptian railway investment; PRONI, D1071, H/H/L, ff. 22, Duke of Sutherland to Dufferin, 26 Nov. 1882; and ff. 21, memorandum from the British India Steam Navigation Co., n.d. [1882].
108 PRONI, D1071, H/H/K/1/7, ff. 1, Gladstone to Dufferin, 1 Jun. 1883; Lyall, *Life of Dufferin*, pp. 340–50.
109 Tignor, *Modernisation*, p. 55.
110 A. Milner, *England in Egypt* (London, 1892); Lyall, *Life of Dufferin*, p. 336; Tignor, *Modernisation*, p. 55.
111 Dufferin Report, p. 43; Cain, Character and imperialism, pp. 181–3.
112 This included Dufferin's own interests; like many wealthy Britons he had investments tied up in Egypt. See correspondence in PRONI, D1071, H/H/B/C/144, ff. 6 and ff. 7, Sir Walter Campbell to Dufferin, 20 Jun. 1881 and 29 Jun. 1881; Tignor, *Modernisation*, pp. 73–9.
113 Cited in Lyall, *Life of Dufferin*, p. 338. See also Dufferin's retrospective views in correspondence with Cromer, PRONI, D1071, H/H/B/106, ff. 19, Dufferin to Cromer, 12 Apr. 1892.
114 PRONI, D1071, H/H/B/S/251B, ff. 8, Dufferin to Brin, 6 Apr. 1883; Dufferin Report, p. 44; S. T. Buzpinar, The repercussions of the British occupation of Egypt on Syria, 1882–3, *Middle Eastern Studies*, 36:1 (2006), pp. 82–5, 89.
115 Dufferin Report, pp. 30–1; BL, IOR, F130, reel 4351, ff. 5a, Dufferin to the Queen, 16 Feb. 1886; BL, Mss Eur, Papers of Arthur Godley, Lord Kilbracken, F102/10, ff. 10, Dufferin to Kilbracken, 16 Mar. 1885; Tignor, *Modernisation*, p. 66.
116 'Was there ever such a tragedy?', he wrote to Argyll when news of the death of Gordon filtered out in 1885: PRONI, D1071, K/1/9, ff. 7, General Charles Gordon to Dufferin from Khartoum, 11 Mar. 1884; PRONI, D1071, H/H/B/C/95, ff. 114, Dufferin to Argyll, 23 Mar. 1885; PRONI, D1071, H/H/B/C/529, ff. 9, Sir Auckland Colvin to Dufferin, 15 May 1883.
117 PRONI, D1071, H/H/B/F/175, ff. 13, Dufferin to Lansdowne, 28 Nov. 1883; Lyall, *Life of Dufferin*, p. 345.

118 BL, Gladstone Papers, Add MS 44151, Vol. LXVI Gladstone, ff. 231, Dufferin to Gladstone, 5 Aug. 1883.
119 Cain, Character and imperialism, pp. 177–8.
120 Queen to Dufferin, cited in Lyall, *Life of Dufferin*, p. 341.
121 Lyall, *Life of Dufferin*, p. 123.
122 *The Standard*, 20 Mar. 1883.
123 Dufferin summarised the place of his service in Syria to Gladstone as part of his elevation in the peerage: BL, Gladstone Papers, Add MS 44151, Vol. LXVI, ff. 102, Dufferin to Gladstone, 13 Sept. 1871.
124 Hall, *Macaulay and Son*, p. xiii.
125 C. A. Bayly, *The Birth of the Modern World, 1780–1914: global connections and comparisons* (Oxford, 2004), p. 298.
126 Hansard, HL Debates, 9 Jun. 1884, vol. 288, cc. 1724–31.
127 For example, Evelyn Baring; Tignor, *Modernisation*, pp. 63–9; Lyall described the Ottoman empire as having 'obliterated and put back for centuries the civilisation of south-eastern Europe and of Asia Minor': *Life of Dufferin*, pp. 301–2.

7 Ornamental empire?
Dufferin as viceroy

The days when great reputations are to be made in India are, happily perhaps, as completely past as those in which great fortunes were accumulated. Famous Indian Pro-Consuls are no longer required by their superiors or compelled by circumstances to startle their countrymen by the annexation of provinces, the overthrow of dynasties, the revolutionising of established systems and all those dramatic performances which invariably characterise the founding and consolidation of newborn empires. Their successors must be content with the less ambitious and more homely, but equally important and beneficent work of justifying the splendid achievements of those who have gone before them.[1]

Famous last words

Throughout his imperial career, Dufferin often claimed that he would be well-pleased if his tenures were peaceful and uncontroversial; he regarded the days of the chaotic expansion of empire on the Indian subcontinent, in particular, as over and his role as consolidating the 'British connection'.[2] Despite the fact that his two most important imperial governorships – Canada and India – had long been part of British imperial life, they were not without their challenges. Before leaving for Calcutta, Dufferin gave a speech at a dinner in his honour, noting that for him there would be no annexations, no 'revolutionising' and yet, that is exactly what did happen while he was viceroy. Burma was annexed at significant military, financial and reputational cost, the sitting dynasty overthrown.[3] Established systems of land tenure and local government were reformed and, most importantly, the Indian National Congress was established in 1885, with which Dufferin had a complicated and sometimes acrimonious relationship. In both the internal and external spheres, Dufferin's was an active viceroyalty, if somewhat less controversial among Anglo-Indian and British public opinion than that of his predecessor, Lord Ripon.[4]

But how far was this activity really driven by Dufferin and his fellow aristocratic viceroys, and how much of it was the result of the administrative machinery of British rule in India, for which he provided the figurehead? Perhaps India was the colony where the aristocratic nature of British

Ornamental empire? 165

imperial governance found its apogee. With its alignment to hierarchy, monarchy and sovereignty, much of British political culture in India chimed with aristocratic values.[5] Dufferin's tenure as viceroy was in part ornamental in nature, but this should not be understood as being passive; instead, it was an active ornamentalism, underpinned by a set of well-understood intellectual, political, economic and constitutional purposes.[6] Dufferin knew very well that landed and aristocratic elites such as himself had to demonstrate that they had not lost their will to rule in order to remain in positions of power.[7] The components of the aristocratic governing culture of British India, as well as the opportunities and restrictions it offered British security on the subcontinent, will be examined through Dufferin's experiences. The forty years from 1860 have been seen as Britain's golden age in India and, despite the challenges, India's problems were perceived in Britain as far less controversial than those in Ireland or Egypt during the same period.[8] This somewhat rosy picture was regularly disrupted, however, and, as such, the nature of aristocratic governance in India was never static. India's challenges

Figure 7.1 Official portrait of Lord Dufferin as viceroy of India, c. 1885. Photo by Bourne and Shepherd of Calcutta. Nineteenth-century albumen print. The original uploader was Fawcett5 at English Wikipedia/Public domain.

coalesced around familiar issues for Dufferin: land, finance and the extent to which colonised peoples should govern themselves. But the historical precedents were unique to India and it was part of the perceived responsibility of men such as Dufferin to grasp those differences, while maintaining a certain level of consistency across Britain, Ireland and the empire. This consistency was rooted in the identity and purpose of British rule: constitutional monarchy and aristocracy, stability through firm and 'just' governance over those many peoples who the British regarded as being unable to govern themselves. As one of his Indian colleagues said of Dufferin, he was, 'full of patriotism and pride in his country. He believed that Englishmen were at least the equals of any people in the world; the interests and the honour of England, or rather of Great Britain – for he always corrected me when I spoke of England and the English – were very dear to him.'[9]

The transnational web of British thinking about the nature of their imperial governance has since been reflected in the historiography.[10] There is a flourishing literature on the connections between and the transmission of ideas about race, governance, nationalism, famine, gender, class and professional cohorts between and within Britain and its empire, which examines its effect on the imperial territories and on the culture and identities of the metropole, within a four nations context.[11] This has been particularly the case with studies that highlight the connections between Ireland and India, including the intellectual and personal connections between nationalists in the later nineteenth century, as well as exchanges within British policy on issues that affected each, such as famine, coercion and violence, and 'improvement'.[12] Critical to this analysis is the work that examines how ideas and policies were translated through the medium of people: civil servants, military personnel, the professional and merchant classes, missionaries, doctors and many others.[13] The group that is often missing from these studies has been the aristocratic governor, an omission even more surprising when we consider the numerical influence of Anglo-Irish aristocrats in India (and elsewhere, as we have seen). Along with their Scottish peers, Irish landowners made a substantial contribution to the top ranks of governance in India, as well as in the larger cohorts of military servicemen, civil servants and other professions.[14] These aristocratic governors provided a distinctive mode of governance, as both insiders and outsiders of the elite metropolitan world and drawing on the distinctly aristocratic traditions and historical precedents of British governance. The aristocracy were motivated by their heritable status and the justification of their status and privileges. Part of their inheritance was a will to provide 'rule by the best'. Their fitness to govern was conferred by lineage and history, and in their contemporary modes of education, including the cultivation of gentlemanly conduct. As such, they embodied a high level of class cohesiveness across the four nations of the British and Irish Isles and the empire. But the past was also a source of weakness. History, after all, was a matter of interpretation; one Anglo-Irish aristocratic family might look back and see a glorious tradition of upholding British rule – and thereby civilisation – in Ireland; an Irish nationalist might see that past very differently, as one of oppression, coercion and terror.[15] Competing interpretations of the past, once the stable bedrock of aristocratic privilege, would become one of the greatest challenges to their social, economic and political power in Dufferin's lifetime.

Did the aristocratic nature of British rule in India weaken or strengthen British dominion on the subcontinent overall? The answer depends a great deal on the chronological perspective taken. Dufferin died in 1902: he did not live to see the gradual but eventual dismantling of British imperial dominion throughout the early twentieth century and in the wake of World War II.[16] He did see enough of the growing nationalist movement in India to concern him about the colony's long-term future, but he did not regard Britain's imperial dominion as being in any true danger. For Dufferin and other aristocratic men of his generation, the maintenance of a British rule infused with aristocracy was the key aim; this was what made it unique in their view – both in the world around them and in the long histories of the ancient empires they spent so much time studying at the public schools and Oxford.[17] For Dufferin, the fact that the empire was led on the spot and at home by a hereditary, landed (and therefore invested) class gave the empire its strength. If we broaden our perspective, however, we can see that aristocratic imperial governance constituted a fragile façade and directly contributed to the weakening of British imperial power. In the context of British society shifting from a rural and agricultural to industrial and urban dominance with a burgeoning middle class, it is not surprising that there were growing challenges to the hereditary nature of aristocratic rule, traditionally underpinned by the ownership of agricultural acres in rural locations. Ireland's trajectory in the nineteenth century was different and it did not industrialise or urbanise to anything like the same extent as Britain. However, the association of its Ascendancy class with British rule in Ireland acted as its essential weakness.[18] In both cases, the argument that the aristocracy represented the majority of the people was breaking down. The empire represented a context in which aristocrats were able to escape the challenges of democracy in the metropole, and to perform their traditional functions and identities for longer.[19] Imperial governance was even more aristocratic in terms of its cultural and governing identity nature than that in Britain and Ireland.[20] On this basis, this chapter will explore two themes: first, it will diagnose what was aristocratic about British rule in India, unpicking four aspects in detail: sovereignty and autocracy; land and property; bureaucracy; and terror. It will then discuss the challenges and opportunities the aristocratic nature of British rule presented, focusing on Dufferin's viceroyalty, 1884–1888. It will discuss whether the aristocratic nature of British rule was a strategic strength or weakness, and examine the relationship between the challenges being made to aristocratic hegemony in Britain and Ireland and British imperial rule in India. Lastly, it examines the translation of aristocratic intellectual and institutional frameworks, and how successful that transnational exchange was – for the aristocratic class and for British imperial control. Dufferin's career demonstrates that those linkages were part of a much wider web of activity. From Russia to Egypt, Prince Edward Island to Syria, transnational aristocratic exchange was integral to the translation of understandings of British power. The weaknesses of this mode of autocratic, hereditary governance were translated into British imperial culture, with consequences that Dufferin would not live to see, but his descendants would.

'More trains, more troops, more dust' – aristocratic rule in India[21]

> I opened an Institution for sick cattle. Having pulled the doors of a cowshed asunder amidst the cheers of the people, a gentleman advanced, bearing in his hand a tray filled with fruits and vegetables, cocoa-nuts and bottles of variously coloured unguents. The eggs he dashed upon the ground, to the great detriment of the ladies' dresses. He broke the cocoa-nuts and sprinkled the milk around. He then smeared the lintels of the door-post with his red and yellow-coloured ointments, and finally strewed the rest of the contents of his basket on the ground. It was like seeing a chapter of Leviticus in action.[22]

Dufferin's comparison of this ceremony – one of hundreds in which he would take part – to the Old Testament echoes his experience of Syria in 1860. More importantly, it demonstrates the aristocratic nature of day-to-day British governance in India. So many of the assumptions of colonial knowledge, historicist thinking and the self-appointed position of aristocrats is exposed in this everyday viceregal episode. It illuminates what was aristocratic about the nature of British rule in India; the layering of cultural symbolism in the opening of this animal hospital demonstrates this very clearly, not least in the ordering and choreography. First was the viceroy, with the 'official' opening, followed by a colonial practitioner of 'superstitious' religious practice, adding the local flavour that would be reported as an amusing anecdote to friends at home. For Dufferin, the 'native' aspects of these ceremonies represented the past being played out in the present, representing the inferiority – historical, racial, cultural, religious – of the people he had been sent to govern, to be led by the most advanced nation on earth and its history, represented by its aristocratic governing classes.[23]

Of course, British rule was under constant challenge. Much of the historiography for the later nineteenth century has focused on the rise of Indian nationalism and how it responded to the impact of British rule on all aspects of Indian society, including political reform, caste, gender, the economy and infrastructure.[24] The debate also questions whether British rule was as secure as the Raj appeared, or whether it was always fundamentally chaotic and weak. These challenges were in part predicated on the transnational exchange of ideas of nationalism and socialism, between India and Ireland in particular, but also other colonial territories such as Egypt and South Africa, too.[25] The nature of British bureaucracy in India has been scrutinised, including detailed studies of the recruitment to and ethnic make-up of the Indian Civil Service and the armed forces.[26] The focus has primarily been on the middle and professional classes; but without a consideration of the aristocratic figureheads, both in India and Westminster, we cannot fully understand the nature of British rule in the subcontinent. Looking at the failures of British colonial rule – the famines, oppression (of all types), racism, economic stagnation and decline, communal and sectarian division and violence – we can recognise echoes of debates over the role of the landlord in the welfare of their tenantry in rural Britain and Ireland.[27] Lastly, we can question whether the aristocratic contribution was purely ornamental or not, an expression of their declining power and influence writ large across the empire. Dufferin's career could be interpreted in such a way, but this chapter suggests, instead, that his career was actively aristocratic and consisted of real power as well as ornamental polish.[28] By defining British rule in India (as elsewhere in the empire) as aristocratic, conclusions can be drawn as to the wider purpose and function of British rule and the impact it had. This aristocratic rule can be understood in four interrelated ways: sovereignty, property and land, bureaucracy and autocratic terror.

Sovereignty was at the heart of aristocratic rule in India and, in the absence of the physical presence of the Queen-Empress Victoria, the aristocratic viceroys, their wives and families performed it.[29] With the exception of Sir John Lawrence, every nineteenth-century Indian viceroy was titled and regularly received an elevation in the peerage as a result of their Indian service. This was the purest expression of British understanding of their authority over India. Power came and went according to challenge and disruption, most infamously in 1857–58: sovereignty was the constant.[30] By placing the Queen at the head of British India as Empress in 1877, the British were enforcing their sovereignty in India, enacted on a daily basis through the person of the viceroy. This was the performance of status and prestige on a grand scale, and it took a number of different forms, all of which aristocrats such as Dufferin were educated to perform with aplomb while never losing sight of the *realpolitik* that sat behind them.

Dufferin's imperial life was an unending swirl of official functions, ceremonies, *durbars*, visits, soirees, openings, levees and receptions, peppered with the acceptance and donation of honours, addresses, prizes and awards. This had been the case in Canada, but there Dufferin had established this activity, finding that this aspect of the role had not been prioritised by his immediate predecessors.[31] He had worked hard to make the glittering expression of sovereignty visible once more. On arrival in India, he found that this would constitute the backbone of his role, with much of the daily and annual progress of the viceroy, his wife, family and entourage following set patterns of travel (winters in Calcutta; summers at Simla), including a series of viceregal tours, literally making sovereignty visible outside of the main presidency and provincial capitals.[32] In order for this to work, the viceroy had to embody the requisite inherited status by being a landed aristocrat himself. Of course, it also helped that Dufferin revelled in this aspect of his duties, ably supported by his wife and his, by now, mature children, who took a leading role in managing the social whirl. Once again, the Dufferins took a holistic approach to the viceroyalty, as the ultimate imperial family. Perhaps the best example of this were the efforts of Lady Dufferin in establishing the Lady Dufferin Fund in 1885, a charity sponsored by Queen Victoria that promoted women's health care by providing scholarships for women to be educated in the medical field as doctors, hospital assistants, nurses, and midwives. It also financed the construction of female hospitals, dispensaries, and female only wards in pre-existing hospitals. Although once established there was criticism of the Fund and its workings, it was broadly successful in terms of geographic spread and impact, with many of the original Lady Dufferin hospitals still in operation. It was a classic expression of the aristocratic benevolence expected from elite women, both on their landed estates at home and in the empire.

Dufferin was a stickler for protocol and the correct conduct of himself and others while carrying out heavy programmes of official events in India. This was because, although he found them personally somewhat ridiculous, he understood their meaning and what they represented to British and Indian observers and participants.[33] It was the expression of British sovereignty and, as such, was not a laughing matter or simple vanity. This is not to say he was stiff or severe; indeed, he was popular exactly because he was expert at putting people at their ease during cumbrous formal events, for smoothing down feathers, and otherwise applying his charm and 'Sheridan sparkle' to ease the passage of dull gatherings. His colleague in India, Sir Henry Mortimer Durand, would later recall that:

> There was something of the Oriental in his [Dufferin's] stately graveness and respect for ceremonial. He was at his very best on occasions of Durbars, investitures and the like. He saw the humour of them as much as anyone, but he held that such things if done should be well done, and he enjoyed doing them. It irritated him to see men giggling or jeering instead of acting their parts properly, and he disliked anything that savoured of want of self-respect. He never affected a contempt for decorations. It gave him real pleasure, I think, to wear the close-fitting red uniform which showed off his figure so well, the breast festooned with collars and stars carefully arranged to hang in the most graceful and effective manner.[34]

The performance of sovereignty was adapted to the place; in Canada, Dufferin hosted tobogganing and curling tournaments; in India it was polo, entering *durbars* by elephant and tiger shooting holidays in the Terai. The setting was critical, too, and Dufferin led the building of a brand new viceregal lodge in Simla, at great expense to the government. His justification for this expenditure was that the viceroy and his family required, as a matter of urgency, a suitable backdrop against which social and political duties could be carried out and subjects awed by the power on display.[35] Some of this gloss was taken directly from the traditions of the Indian princely states and Mughal empire and grafted onto a peculiarly British performance of status: the protocols around order of entry into and out of rooms, seating arrangements and similar expressions of rank.[36] The co-opting of Indian princes into these pageants of sovereignty was crucial, too; wherever the British went, they looked around them to establish points of familiarity in the structures of other societies.[37] This was what sat behind Dufferin's arguments about 'native' aristocracies, in India, Canada and elsewhere. They were seeking their reflection in the colonial mirror and this was expressed most strongly in India. The British believed that, if they could secure the loyalty of the princely families, aristocracy and landowners, they could regard the loyalty of all Indian subjects as secure. As such, a new order – the Star of India – was created specifically to enable the reward of high-status Indians without polluting existing British honours, and they were incorporated into the imperial pageantry of the Raj.[38]

Other hierarchies were observed, too, and although Dufferin as viceroy was the pinnacle in India, he and the Government of India operated under the surveillance of the India Office, the India Council and the Secretary of State in London. Dufferin was not the type of man to seek to flex his political or military muscles; he was by nature cautious and, after the tumultuous tenure of Lord Ripon, he understood his main task to be a calming influence on both the Indian intelligentsia and Anglo-Indian community. His correspondence with the Secretaries of State expresses a consistent anxiety to be seen to be following instructions, requesting permission and ensuring relations between the Government of India and the India Office were good. Any hint that acrimony or disagreement was seeping in generated a flurry of correspondence, seeking to patch up any differences, demanding to know 'what is amiss?' He wrote in such a tone to each of the Secretaries of State he served under, as well as Arthur Godley, later Lord Kilbracken, permanent secretary of the India Office. Dufferin summarised his philosophy to Kilbracken: 'It has always been my desire and endeavour in every situation I have occupied to transact business with my employers in a deferential and sympathetic spirit.'[39] Dufferin's choice of language – employers, masters – to describe the India Office highlights that, as well as being alive to the symbolic importance of hierarchy within the Indian system, he was equally alert to his place within the British imperial world.

The primacy of sovereignty and the ways in which it was expressed was one aspect of the aristocratic nature of British rule in India. Linked to that was an overriding concern about land and property in the Indian context. Land was one of the great transnational issues of the age, even in urbanising and industrialising Britain, whose political and constitutional culture was still, to a large degree, led by landed aristocrats. India was, even so, something of an exceptional case in this regard, with all issues pertaining to land – including the conduct of landlord–tenant relations, agricultural improvement and taxation – remaining central to the purpose of British rule and generating constant controversy from the eighteenth to the twentieth centuries. This was, in part, because it represented the application of the liberal ideology of improvement being applied in a global imperial context.[40] During Dufferin's tenure as viceroy, these issues were crystallised in two important land reform bills: the Bengal Tenancy Act (1885) and the Oudh Rent Act (1886). The Bengal Tenancy bill had been initiated by his predecessor, Lord Ripon, and Dufferin was obliged to tackle this complex and acrimonious question almost as soon as he arrived. He was 'full of misgivings about it', and feared that it would generate 'the same disastrous results as have accrued in Ireland' if it were passed in the form in which he initially found it.[41] As in Ireland and Canada, the reform of land tenures was a vital political and economic issue in India. Although they had global resonance, they were also intensely local questions, governed by a multitude of customs overlaid with previous colonial interventions.[42] Many interests were at stake: first, those of the occupiers themselves, who struggled with disadvantageous contractual conditions or customs, as well as climatic vagaries and lack of infrastructure, and difficult market conditions. Second, were the interests of the landowners, of varying size and political importance, whom any legislation would directly affect. Last were the interests of the British Government of India: their interests were twofold and often in contradiction with each other. First, they had to demonstrate their good and beneficent governance through legislation of exactly this type, but for every step taken to alleviate the conditions of occupiers of the land, privileges enjoyed by the landowning classes would have to be curtailed, upsetting the delicate balance of loyalty.[43]

Dufferin was in an unusually authoritative position on these questions, given his experiences on his own estates in Ireland, the Prince Edward Island land purchase measures passed while he was governor-general of Canada and during his period as undersecretary of state for India in the 1860s.[44] By the early 1880s, he was fully behind a policy of land purchase for Ireland, writing to Sir Randolph Churchill a few years later that, if 'the sale to the tenantry of the remnants of the Irish Landlords' proprietary rights' might be facilitated, the tenantry would 'become as Conservative as that of France'.[45] The question of mediating between the interests of ownership and occupancy in rural society was a critical aspect of Dufferin's Indian experience and his transnational aristocratic world.[46] It would also dash the hopes expressed by Indian reformers on his arrival that he would be Ripon's liberal heir. The bill as originally drafted aimed to amend the definition of the occupancy right to land of the ryot (tenant), which stood at twelve continuous years of occupation.[47] The disadvantage of this to the ryot had been that the zemindars (their landlords), on the approach of twelve years, forced their tenants to move either by directly evicting them, or by raising their rents to force them to give up their occupation.[48] The ryots had not taken this cynical land tenure management peacefully, and rioting and other agrarian disturbances – often compared to those of Ireland – had become a serious issue from 1873. This agitation formed the background of the bill, which sought to protect the rights of ryots by giving them stronger occupancy tenure and rent controls. This had whipped up significant controversy, which Dufferin faced on his arrival.[49]

His initial, and perhaps unsurprising, reaction was to attempt to neutralise the bill, and he instructed his staff to strip out a number of clauses that undermined traditional zemindar privileges. Dufferin wrote in unguarded tone to Argyll describing his outrage, calling the first draft of the bill, 'one of the most unjust pieces of legislation you could imagine', putting this down to the fact that Augustus Rivers Thompson, the Lieutenant Governor of Bengal who had made the initial recommendations to Ripon, was, 'a well-meaning but pretty weak and incapable man, who is virtually in the hands of a parcel of wild Irishmen'.[50] To Dufferin's surprise, this 'weak' man stuck as far as possible to his original draft, refusing to yield on the rent enhancement clauses that he felt the ryot interest deserved.[51] Dufferin was forced to support these clauses in order to get the bill passed, an early experience of the necessity for compromise, even on dearly held principles of land tenures and property rights, particularly, 'any interference with private contract'.[52] Although a very different governing context, the experience of the Bengal Tenancy Act for Dufferin was politically almost an exact replay of the land purchase legislation he had been obliged to approve for Prince Edward Island and the land reform legislation he had faced in Ireland. His initial resistance to these acts was eventually overcome in the face of political realities and the necessity to demonstrate 'good' governance in the colonies.[53]

After putting the Bengal Act to bed, Dufferin was faced with another controversial land question in Oudh.[54] The Oudh Act had been prompted by a particular and controversial case that had generated much publicity and, as a result, in 1882 Lord Ripon had appointed an enquiry into the condition of the Oudh tenants, a year before an enquiry with an identical remit was appointed by Gladstone for the Scottish Highlands and Islands.[55] Sir Alfred Lyall undertook the investigation, Dufferin noting confidently that, 'I do not think he will land us in any difficulty', and he submitted a report recommending that powers of 'capricious' eviction should be removed from the armoury of the landed classes in Oudh, the Talukdars.[56] The Talukdars were large and often titled landowners, a powerful group that neither the Government of India nor the India Office wished to alienate if they could help it.[57] Despite this, Dufferin eventually, 'resolved that Lord Ripon's policy was right', and that the law should be changed to give the occupier in Oudh basic tenancy protections.[58] The echoes of the Irish land question can be heard in Dufferin's response to the controversy the bill engendered, reviving debates about whose duty it was to fund and encourage agricultural improvement and that if tenants did – as they usually did in Ireland – then they must have some security over their value. This was a relatively moderate position to take and Dufferin had reconciled himself to it for Ireland for at least ten years. His support of these measures for Oudh gradually overcame the opposition of the Talukdars and the Oudh Rent Act was passed in 1886.[59] As he noted to Churchill, 'as an Irish landlord dealt with under the Act of 1880 [1881], you need have no doubt of my fully taking into account the deep bitterness engendered in a man's mind by unjust land legislation, and that I shall not overlook the political dangers likely to be created by any error on our part in that direction'.[60] In the case of both the Bengal and Oudh Acts, Dufferin arrived on a scene that had been set by his predecessor, and was required to step in and engineer compromises to see the legislation through, whatever his personal objections to the reduction of the rights of property. In the case of the Bengal Act, his initial response was to attempt to water down some of the less palatable clauses, informed by a desire to protect the rights of property, wherever he might find them, in keeping with his long held views of land legislation. Dufferin embodied a link between Ireland, Canada and India of aristocratic principles being subordinated to the political realities on the ground and the necessity of visibly providing material benefits to colonised peoples.[61]

Compromises aside, British rule in India was straightforwardly autocratic in structure and nature, with no pretence in the way of representative governance. The nature of this autocracy can be split into two key areas; autocracy reinforced by bureaucracy, and autocracy reinforced by violence. British rule in India represented an empire of paper: rule and regulations, layers of civil and military bureaucracy, the councils, presidencies and governance structures that Dufferin headed as viceroy, all constructed to maintain British dominion and sovereignty.[62] The reams of reports, despatches, telegrams, memoranda and minutes illuminate the nature of British rule in India, of bureaucracy as a political activity, investigating, recording and planning all aspects of the imperial mission on the subcontinent. Dufferin was personally not a man for administrative detail; instead, he was careful to reserve his efforts for the most important issues, such as the controversies of land reform, Afghanistan, or Burma, leaving his subordinates to manage the details. In other words, his style of governance was monarchical, providing overall direction and responsibility for the Government of India. As he put it, 'every act of the Indian government, and every characteristic of its policy, is regarded as the outcome and the product of the Viceroy's personal initiative and will … it is the viceroy and the viceroy alone, who is properly held answerable by his countrymen, whether things go well or whether they go ill; nor, in the event of their going ill, have I ever heard of the principle being disputed'.[63] He also took seriously the meetings of the Viceroy's Council, acting as referee and pushing for resolution and compromise as required. He was well-known for the quickness of his perception and readiness of mind; he was able to grasp the essentials of a question rapidly, although was more reluctant to go into the details. Details, however, were the bread and butter of the Indian Civil Service. Sir Henry Durand remembered the frustration engendered by Dufferin's approach: 'I sometimes tried in vain to get him to look into cases which seemed to me rather important. "My dear fellow", he used to say, "I really cannot go into that. Life is too short."'[64] It was this tendency that led some later commentators and historians to regard Dufferin as lazy; his viceroyalty came after the tumultuous years under Lytton and Ripon and, as he noted in his

Ornamental empire? 175

farewell speech to Belfast's citizens, he actively hoped for a quiet term.[65] This was quite different to laziness though, and, as in his record in Syria, Canada and Egypt shows, Dufferin was far from lazy. A more useful way of looking at his style is as aristocratic; after all, why should be personally be involved in the detail of every question? That was what subordinates were for. When it was required, when dealing with great issues of state – such as the annexation of Burma, or reform of local self-government, or relations with Afghanistan – Dufferin stepped forward, mobilising his status and authority to secure the outcome best for British interests. It was this, as well as taking ultimate responsibility, that Dufferin saw as his main contribution. It was vital therefore that his colleagues were trustworthy and of the best possible quality. Across the course of his career he was well-supported by a series of agents on the Clandeboye estate and private secretaries while overseas. Most notable of these was Donald Mackenzie Wallace, a very able journalist for *The Times* and Dufferin's right-hand man in India.[66] Dufferin prided himself on being a shrewd judge of character – another aristocratic trait. Being able to judge quality and gentlemanly status was part of elite culture – male and female – and maintained its integrity.[67] There was a delicate balance to be struck here between Dufferin's personal leadership as viceroy and the necessity for a large staff to undertake the actual day-to-day work of governing. It was this element of aristocratic governing style that most closely overlapped with contemporary practice in diplomacy, of which Dufferin was also a leading practitioner and at which he was perhaps more successful than the rough and tumble of colonial governance. This was certainly the view of the toughest of his friends in the cabinet, Lord Kimberley, who, on Dufferin's appointment to the viceroyalty, noted in his diary that, 'He [Dufferin] is an admirable diplomatist; it is not so certain that he possesses the qualities necessary to govern.'[68] This was quite possibly an assessment with which Dufferin would have agreed and introduces an interesting strand of tension into his appointment. Kimberley also expressed his surprise at the positive public reaction to the news of Dufferin's appointment, contrasting this with, 'the opinion of the "inner" political world. Gladstone was reluctant to appoint him.'[69] Kimberley was concerned that Dufferin lacked the backbone to be unpopular and to push through controversial measures, particularly as, in Kimberley's view, the most important issues facing the Government of India lay outwith its borders.[70] Military action, due to its human and financial cost, was unpopular with Indian political opinion, but Kimberley would find that between his urgency and the more opportunistic forwardism of his successor, Lord Randolph Churchill, Dufferin was willing to use force.[71]

This other side of autocracy seemed about as far away from gentlemanly pedigree and aristocratic veneer as it was possible to be: violence and terror, imposed by the British military and police state at all levels of Indian society from local policemen to the massed ranks of the Indian Army. What lay behind this? The subterranean river of terror that constituted one of the legacies of the 1857 Rebellion was one important factor. The Rebellion was one of the most significant events of the nineteenth century for Britain and its imperial project. Dufferin, like many of his class and era, saw in it the defining test of British character and the nature of its governance over inferior peoples. In 1857, he suggested in private correspondence that the nature of the East India Company's rule was at least in part to blame for the Rebellion; like many, he saw it as a justification for the British state to promote the good governance he championed all his career. These liberal principles aside, Dufferin was as filled with feelings of betrayal, rage and vengeance as the next British person, claiming that, 'If it were not for my mother, I would set off tomorrow in order to have a share in avenging those poor ladies ... But how an event of this kind, which I suppose great sagacity and thoughtfulness might have guarded against, makes one feel what a solemn charge they undertake who make politics their profession.'[72] His great friend the 8th Duke of Argyll reflected on these issues in an essay on India, published the year before Dufferin took up the Under Secretaryship for India.[73] With the benefit of five years distance, 'the violent reactions of feeling and opinion which arose out of the Great Indian Mutiny are now beginning to subside', he noted, attempting to inject some patrician rationality.[74] For Argyll, the rapid rate of annexations made by the Company in the subcontinent before 1857, although widely criticised, had been the correct policy: 'there is no need to defend that acquisition in point of right, and as little need now to support it in respect to policy. The right never has admitted, and never could admit, of rational doubt.'[75] He further asserted that much of the discontent of India in the 1850s was a result of the oppressive regimes not of the Company, but of native landowners; indeed, the Talukdars of Oudh were singled out for especial opprobrium.[76] The violence with which the Rebellion was suppressed is not given much room in Argyll's analysis. Instead, it is simply the means to a better end: the establishment of a secure enough arena for the benefits of good British government to be applied. This was certainly Dufferin's view, and one that was fairly orthodox amongst India hands and officials. Military force – or the threat of it – was the bedrock of British dominion in India and, as long as it was applied according to the accepted rules of the day, it was regarded as perfectly reasonable, with controversies arising only when cost in lives or finance seemed abnormally high. Dufferin spent time during his Indian perambulations visiting the scenes of the bitter fighting that had taken place thirty years previously, noting in Delhi that, 'the breaches made in the walls by our cannon are left in exactly the same state as they were on the day of the assault ... one has to come to the spot to realise the nature of the achievement'.[77]

Under Dufferin's tenure as viceroy one such abnormal episode did take place and the role of the press as well as political and public opinion, and Dufferin's responses to these, serve to highlight the ways in which the iron fist operated within a velvet glove. This was the invasion, occupation and annexation of Burma from late 1885. Burma is interesting in relation to the utilisation of terror as part of the of the aristocratic governing culture of the Government of India because it is both an example of a fairly standard and straightforward military invasion and conquest and, once the military occupation became bogged down in reprisals, torture and village burnings, it exposed the underbelly of paramilitary violence and coercive control of British rule. Tracking this, and Dufferin's horrified responses to these 'un-British' actions, give an insight into the nature of British violence and terror in the colonial context.[78]

Once Dufferin signed off the order for the military invasion in November 1885, a force of 10,000 men under General Prendergast swiftly moved into Upper Burma and secured Mandalay and the Burmese royal family in less than a month.[79] The ease – in terms of speed and minimal loss of British life – by which this took place led to a free flow of medals, honours and praise in the British press, all of which Dufferin revelled in, sensing the opportunity to shape his legacy and reputation.[80] This quickly turned sour in the face of a guerrilla resistance and the expensive necessity of many more additional troops, military police and a communications infrastructure to crush it.[81] Before the situation began to unravel, Dufferin visited Burma in person with Lady Dufferin, accompanied by the Commander-in-Chief, Lord Roberts, Donald Mackenzie Wallace and their eldest son, Lord Archie, arriving in Mandalay in February 1886. This visit highlights the management of violence and autocracy, and the aristocratic nature of colonial governance extremely clearly, not least the treatment of the Burmese royal family, the racially infused discussions of the Burmese people and the ways in which the loot was recorded and divided up.[82] It was a tense visit for Dufferin, who was as yet undecided on annexation as Burma's future and on whose shoulders rested Churchill's expectation of, 'the better order and stability which I know will be the result of your visit'.[83] These military and constitutional worries were reflected in the choreography of his visit: within a few days, he and Lady Dufferin began laying on a programme of events – a levee, a visit to the military hospitals, a party for the wives and daughters of Burmese officials, a dinner for the officers.[84] The ceremonial nature of their role was once again put to the fore, designed to support the morale of the troops and civilian officials to and emphasise the symbolic power of a regime putting in place its social and cultural norms almost immediately after a military conquest.[85] Every aspect of their visit was choreographed to enhance the legitimacy of British power, from their installation in the Mandalay palace's throne room after the evacuation of King Thibaw and Queen Supayalat, to the allocation of the loot, carefully listed and tagged against the recipients in order of importance, beginning with the Queen, followed by Dufferin and so on down the social order. This was the official loot, but there were unofficial opportunities for collecting also, as there had been throughout Dufferin's life of travel and service. His wife noted that during a visit to see the great bell at Mengdoon, 'lying in the jungle we found some carved wooden ladies, who were shouldered by the sailors and carried off with a view to their taking up position some day in the hall at Clandeboye'.[86]

Most striking were Dufferin's descriptions and characterisations of the Burmese 'character', which were highly racialised. His descriptions emphasise the perceived child-like qualities of the Burmese: he describes them as, 'full of fun, jollity and light-heartedness', reinforcing his view that Burma would never make a reliable buffer state due to its 'pulpy' nature.[87] These descriptions make an interesting contrast to the serious and very un-pulpy nature of Burmese resistance which, by the early months of 1886, was just becoming evident and which would remain an expensive – financially and reputationally – thorn in the side of the Government of India well after Dufferin resigned as viceroy.[88] This was crystallised in the controversy over extra-judicial executions of Burmese prisoners carried out by British troops, exposed to the full glare of British public opinion by the despatches by E. K. Moylan, a *Times* journalist.[89] Dufferin was concerned both with British security in Burma and with the reputational damage the scandal might inflict on his viceroyalty.[90] 'I cannot tell you how much annoyed I have been by the accounts of these executions in Burmah. The one thing I had impressed … was that our operations were to be conducted with exceptional humanity … At the same time, I asked him [Prendergast] whether such severe punishment need be inflicted upon flying bands of dacoits … for I felt that too great leniency sometimes only leads eventually to greater effusion of blood.'[91] How did Dufferin reconcile his liberal principles with the application of autocracy and terror on this scale? He was able to do so because the maintenance of British sovereignty overruled any other priorities, personal, political or collective. As in Ireland (but not Canada), this was his overriding priority, and disruptions such as the Indian Rebellion – like the Fenian movement – were formative and invited a coercive response to avoid a further spread of revolt against British power.[92] The collective group-think displayed is what is important here; Dufferin's views expressed in his private and public papers reflected this collective view.[93]

Dufferin's performance as viceroy was situated within the framework of a particular aristocratic identity. Aristocratic rule in India was part of Britain's assumed colonial knowledge of the subcontinent, grafted onto assumptions around race, religion, property and governance.[94] Although expressed by the British Raj at all levels, the nature of British rule was heavily influenced by aristocratic and monarchical ideals: a particular vision of themselves and of India.[95] Dufferin took this aspect of his role very seriously; indeed, he was irritated when others failed to do so. It was central to British rule on the subcontinent, in its conduct as well as its expression.[96] It was in many ways what was distinctive about British rule: the symbolism, the ceremony, the monarchical, hierarchical vision, were all expressed through and by aristocratic men and their wives and families.[97] Rather than ornamental froth, they were central to the definition and workings of British colonial governance in India.

'We are in a fearful mess' – challenges to aristocratic rule

> Through the mysterious decrees of Providence, the British nation and its rulers have been called upon to undertake the supreme government of this mighty empire; to vindicate its honour, to defend its territories, and to maintain its authority inviolate; to rule justly and impartially a congeries of communities, many of them widely differing from each other in race, language, religion, social customs and material interests; to preserve intact and unimpaired the dignity, rights and privileges of a large number of feudatory princes; to provide for the welfare of a population nearly as numerous as that of Europe, and presenting every type of civilisation known to history from the very highest to the very lowest; to safeguard and develop the enormous moral and material British interests which have become inextricably implicated with those of the natives of the soil.[98]

The nature of aristocratic British rule outlined in the previous section can be discerned best when backlit by pressures, tensions and challenges that were often transnational in nature. As Dufferin noted, the autocratic nature of Indian governance meant that the immediate consequence of any challenge – such as the rise of Indian nationalism – was quickly magnified, drawing in similar concerns from Ireland, or Egypt, or Canada. In other words, the sinews of power had to be upheld in the present to prevent a worse future everywhere. This was Dufferin's 'germ theory' at play: his terminology for the transnational shift of (usually bad) ideas, which unsurprisingly led to a great deal of aristocratic paranoia.[99] After all, in Ireland the collapse of hard aristocratic power was eventually achieved and Dufferin's view was that, whatever the future held for Ireland, it would be the result of the nature of 'English' rule:

> Of course I am a Unionist, no Ulsterman could be otherwise, and I fully believe now that we shall win, though I quite agree with you in thinking that the present condition of Ireland is our own fault, and the fault of English statesmen, and of that intolerable and vulgar brutality which the strong English race always manifests towards inferior and more sensitive populations. We are irritating the natives out here in exactly the same manner as for hundreds of years we have been irritating the Irish, and now they are beginning to borrow Irish methods of political agitation.[100]

This section will examine these questions by focusing on two areas: first, the rise of Indian nationalism and demands for measures of self-government in the 1880s and, second, Indian imperial finance, the hard costs of British rule.[101] Aside from policy dealing with Burma and Afghanistan, and land reform, these were the two issues that exercised Dufferin most during his tenure as viceroy.[102] The rise of Indian nationalism, fuelled by the growing numbers of educated middle and professional classes of India, was a fairly obvious concern to patrician governors such as Dufferin, given an added *frisson* due to his Irish roots. Questions of Indian finance appear to be a less pressing issue but, in fact, underwrote a growing sense of insecurity – both practically and of the ideological mission – of the British in India, and Dufferin's responses highlight his aristocratic sense of financial management and consequences.[103]

The financial performance of the Government of India was perhaps one of the most challenging aspects of Dufferin's viceroyalty.[104] The rapidly darkening outlook for India's finances, a combination of heavy expenditure and the declining value of silver (on which Indian currency was based) in relation to gold (on which sterling was based) dogged Dufferin's tenure: 'the silver question is becoming frightfully serious', he repeatedly reported to London.[105] It also provides a somewhat melancholy echo of his experiences with Irish estate finance: declining income, increasing burden and cost of debt, apparently very little room for manoeuvre, with the only options for retrenchment being deeply politically and socially unpopular, as well as threatening the social contract between the people and their aristocratic leaders.[106] There are three main aspects to Dufferin's struggles with Indian finance, the first of which was the cost of 'improvement' and the alleged benefits of empire, channelled through the public works programme.[107] Expensive capital projects in irrigation, railways, road building and other communications infrastructure were barrelling ahead during Dufferin's term and were lauded as important – and visible – proof of British rule moving the subcontinent along the road of progress towards material prosperity.[108] The government's Public Works Office was a high-spending area and there were many reasons why this was tolerated internally.[109] In most cases, these programmes of 'public' works generated very clear benefits for British rule and its security across the subcontinent. The building of roads, railways, bridges and telegraph systems increased British military capacity, and major agricultural improvements such as the implementation of irrigation systems, planting schemes and the establishment of new agricultural sectors such as tea and indigo generated increased taxation and land revenues.[110] There are very clear parallels here with Dufferin's rhetoric as a young landowner in the 1840s and 1850s, pouring capital into major improvements across his estates, expressing the identity of the benevolent landlord and committing to a long-term vision of future generations reaping the benefits of investment made in the present. In both cases, these investments, although on vastly differing scales, were as much expressions of aristocratic governance as hard economics. They speak to the long-term vision of the purpose of both aristocratic power and imperial dominion. This vision could only work if the economic context were favourable and, by the last quarter of the nineteenth century, in both the domestic landed and agricultural context and in the unbalanced structures of imperial economics, this was not the case.[111] Aristocratic governors of India such as Dufferin recognised the economic challenges, but had yet to adjust their behaviour, leading to significant financial issues for both their landed estates and the Indian economy.[112]

Ornamental empire? 181

These macro issues aside, Dufferin's tenure was not exactly noted for financial restraint. The costs of his foreign policy, including the management of their eastern 'buffer' Afghanistan but, much more expensively, the occupation and annexation of Burma ('can we afford it?' asked Kimberley, only semi-facetiously) are two of the most striking examples of this.[113] Burma, in particular, was an unexpected and expensive acquisition.[114] There were the costs of the military operation as already noted, but there followed the spiralling costs of setting up an apparatus of civil government and administration. The initial estimates for the invasion of Burma were quickly exceeded as the occupation became bogged down in grappling with the guerrilla campaign waged intermittently in the rural and remote provinces of that country. The cost of Burma aroused the ire of Indian and British public opinion, adding another layer of distress for Dufferin, who wrote lengthy public and private minutes, memoranda and justifications of these costs, but to little avail. In Britain, Burma became another example of a reckless forward policy that added territories to an already heavy imperial burden with little hope of immediate or even long-term economic return. In India, it was painted as a return to the bad old days of annexations, the costs of which were forced upon the Indian – not the British – taxpayer, investment that would be better spend on famine relief or tax cuts.[115] Accusations revolved around 'bad' governance – poor decision-making and planning, bad principles, reckless and selfish rule – the opposite of the principles of good governance that Dufferin and his fellow aristocratic governors claimed to be leading. Dufferin, of course, rejected these criticisms:

> But even did she [Britain] so desire, it is now too late for this country to disinherit herself of the destiny with which I firmly believe she has been endowed by Providence. The same hidden hand which planted the tree of constitutional liberty within her border, which called upon her to become the mother of Parliaments, has sent her people forth to possess and fructify the waste places of the earth's surface.[116]

What made the situation worse was the fact that the annexation of Burma took place against a general economic background of declining revenues and increasing costs. As the Indian press and nationalist leaders pointed out with increasing bitterness, the cost of military adventures and public works projects was being forced onto the shoulders of an already overburdened Indian peasantry in the form of increased taxation on essentials for life such as salt and land.[117] In other words, the mythical benefits of British dominion were scarce to be seen by the average Indian who, instead, faced increasing taxation and, in many areas, recurrent famine and food shortages. This mirrors the situation in Ireland, another imperial territory with a dire economic record, including stunted industrialisation, and a recent and deadly famine. Accusations over Britain's role in generating the conditions for the sometimes catastrophic economic performances of both countries were made by Indian and Irish nationalists in this period.[118]

One of the reasons taxation was increased was the declining value of silver against gold, which fatally undermined the rupee's value and presented a huge challenge to the Government of India's financial resources. This had been an issue in India since 1873 and would continue to be so well after Dufferin sailed back to Europe in 1888, but the convergence of the problems with silver and the costs of the Burma campaign concentrated minds in the mid-1880s. One of the inescapable conclusions drawn by Dufferin was that, behind all the rhetoric of good governance and beneficent British rule, when it came to brass tacks there was no appetite in London to re-set the rules of the game so that India was on anything like a level playing field with Britain. The hopes of the Indian government rested on a proposed bimetallist agreement, whereby the relative values of gold and silver would be agreed upon and set internationally, thereby removing some of the financial challenges India faced: this never came to pass, not least because it was met with opposition and apathy amongst British statesmen.[119] The entrenched opposition to accepting any kind of shift against their interests in relation to those of India – or indeed Ireland – was a longstanding criticism of what nationalists perceived to be the hypocritical, cynical and selfish economic policies of the British.

The economic management of India in the 1880s was a significant political question although Dufferin was by no means solely responsible for it. Much of the detail was left to his finance minister, to be fought out with the India Office and Secretary of State in London.[120] But for Dufferin personally, it must have revived the spectre of financial problems that had dogged him his whole life; from Clandeboye to Canada, debt, declining capital liquidity and stagnating income would overshadow his steps and constrain his options, as they did for many other landowning and imperial aristocrats. This is not to argue that being bad at handling finance was an aristocratic characteristic, whether in personal terms or in relation to the economies of imperial territories. Instead, it was a result of changing macro level economic circumstances globally, and the consequence of these individuals and their families having a great deal of personal and landed wealth to begin with. These two factors came into collision in the second half of the nineteenth century for Dufferin and the decline became stark: personally, in Ireland and for India's public finances. In both contexts, significant political repercussions would be the result.

Debate about the balance between British autocracy and colonial self-government were a constant across Dufferin's imperial career and in Ireland. At the crux of this was Dufferin's belief in the unique fitness of Britain's traditional governing class to rule, in Ireland, Britain and the empire. This would be challenged in both Ireland and India and, for Dufferin, the two were linked both conceptually and by radical individuals and organisations. There was a series of flash point issues that highlighted for Dufferin the interconnectedness of the two, including the controversy over the Ilbert Bill, which was still raging when he arrived in 1884; the Indian volunteer and provincial councils questions; the establishment in 1885 of the Indian

Ornamental empire? 183

National Congress; and, more broadly, the often highly critical stance of the Indian press towards British policy.[121] All of these issues touched, with varying degrees of directness, upon questions about the extent of Indian involvement in government, the professions and in military service. Dufferin related these issues to Ireland, certain that his home country was setting a dangerous example for India. 'I cannot help having a strong suspicion that the course of events at home in regard to Ireland has produced a very considerable effect upon the minds of the intelligent and educated sections of our own [Indian] native community', he warned Kimberley.[122] This was foremost in his mind, as evidenced in his personal correspondence with fellow aristocrats and politicians, cabinet ministers and statesmen. He was much more forthright in this private correspondence than he dared to be in his official despatches as viceroy; he also knew that, in most cases, his correspondents would be in general agreement but required some spine-stiffening to face off the bitter realities in parliament before it was too late. The private correspondence Dufferin received in India was dominated by Irish, not Indian, affairs. This lobbying, influencing and emphasis on who-you-know, adding up to an 'almighty writing-machine', was the predictable aristocratic response.[123] It was also indicative of an awareness of the insecurity of British (and aristocratic) rule in both Ireland and the subcontinent, and underlay the seesawing between principles of benevolent imperial rule and the coercion and violence that kept it in place.[124] Dufferin was well aware of the contradictions: 'I cannot help asking myself how long an autocratic Government like that of India – and a Government which everyone will admit for many a long year to come must in its main features remain autocratic – will be able to stand the strain implied by the importation *en bloc* from England, or rather from Ireland, of the perfected machinery of modern democratic agitation.'[125] Of course, Dufferin's colleagues were also very aware of the contradictions. Kimberley took a similar line:

> I have no faith in a mere repressive policy … the English democracy will never allow such a policy to be firmly and continuously pursued. This democracy in fact constitutes one of the main difficulties in maintaining our Indian empire. We are, who are all in the end responsible to a House of Commons, swayed by the opinions of nearly the whole mass of our male adult population, have to govern near one-sixth of the human race in India, an immense congeries of people in a wholly different stage of civilisation from that of their masters.[126]

Two further underlying frameworks, administrative and racial, informed Dufferin's responses to challenges to supremacy in India and Ireland. In India, Dufferin was working within a fixed administrative and constitutional framework that presented him with a series of constraints and opportunities to which he was hyper-sensitive.[127] These included the structures of the Government of India itself and those of the India Office, the Indian Council and the Secretary of State for India in London. Beyond that was wider political and public opinion to which he was equally sensitive. Like the principles – allegedly sacrosanct – of property, the administrative structures Dufferin operated within in India, despite their 'illusion of permanence', were in fact open to often acrimonious negotiation. This is what underwrote Dufferin's term as viceroy: the challenge to and negotiation of power structures in India, part of which was aristocratic power.[128] The other was attitudes of racial superiority and how they connected into more nebulous definitions of status. Three racial and social stereotypes had the greatest impact on Dufferin's thinking: the Bengali '*baboo*', the Irish radical and the British gentleman. Each played a role in how Dufferin understood the challenge to British and aristocratic fitness to rule in both Ireland and India. 'Upon Ireland I dare not venture to speak, the subject makes me so angry and indignant', he wrote to James Fitzjames Stephen in 1886:

> But apart from what I feel as an Irishman, what is now happening occasions me even greater anxiety as Viceroy, for people must not suppose that such things can be said and done at home without their having their effect in this country. Already associations after the fashion of O'Connell's have sprung into existence, the Caucus has been naturalised and all the arts of a Radical agitation are coming into use in India. A Celtic Parliament is not likely to prove the home of either wisdom, justice or moderation, but imagine a Baboo Parliament![129]

Before Dufferin arrived in India in 1884, he knew he would have to tackle the raging controversy surrounding the Criminal Procedure Amendment Bill, popularly known as the Ilbert Bill, which proposed to give Indians with responsible positions in the Covenanted Judicial service the same rights as their British colleagues to try Europeans in criminal cases.[130] Although just one element in a much wider reform programme introduced by Ripon, it was this proposal that whipped Anglo-Indian opinion into a furious and paranoid frenzy, and Dufferin was tasked to moderate and calm 'the little social storm', as he called it.[131] Ripon made the compromise necessary, by granting Europeans special jury privileges denied to Indians, but the bad feeling generated by the controversy had far-reaching consequences. One of these was an active curb on Ripon's reform programme by the then-Secretary of State, Lord Kimberley, who wished to avoid 'strife' and agitation – whether within the Indian or Anglo-Indian community – and pull the Government of India back into a less controversial tack. This shift in direction had led to Dufferin's appointment to the viceroyalty; he was explicitly tasked with smoothing the feathers ruffled by Ripon's policies. Kimberley made it clear that Dufferin's first task was to restore domestic tranquillity in India to enable the government to focus on the far more important (in Kimberley's view) external challenges facing the colony. In consequence, Dufferin was coached to see the domestic questions as secondary to foreign policy, and would quickly prove himself to be a disappointment to the Indian intelligentsia, despite some liberal-sounding speeches.[132]

A consequence was the realisation on the part of the educated Indian community that, however sympathetic any future viceroy might be, it was not enough to establish permanent change in India and they would have to organise more effectively on their own terms, which they did with the establishment of the Indian National Congress in 1885. Dufferin was, at first, not overly concerned; indeed, he responded fairly positively to the group.[133] 'My own inclination', he wrote to Kimberley, 'would be to examine carefully and seriously the demands which are the outcome of these various movements, to give quickly and with good grace whatever it may be possible or desirable to accord, to announce that these concessions must be accepted as a final settlement of the Indian system for the next ten or fifteen years, and to forbid mass meetings and incendiary speechifying.'[134] In other words, the classic Whig-Liberal tactic of gracious but controlled reform.[135] This is surprising given that, at their first meeting, the Congress passed a resolution formally opposing Dufferin's administration, and another to activate a nationwide political movement in order to revive the political reforms initiated by Ripon.[136] These focused onto three key areas; first, the reform of the framework of government to allow for greater Indian participation; second, a reform of civil rights and, third, finance.[137] All three of these areas mapped onto Dufferin's concerns as viceroy but, unsurprisingly, he did not act on any of them. They were, after all, effectively revolutionary in that they sought to overturn the autocratic basis on which British power in India rested. Echoes of Ireland were here, not least in Dufferin's horrified realisation that radical members of Anglo-Indian society – and worse, the Indian Civil Service – were encouraging the Congress and other Indian reform movements. The most prominent example, and one who would become a bitter enemy, 'a mischievous busy-body', was a Scot, Allan Octavian Hume.[138]

Dufferin could not ignore the Congress, however, and he eventually gave a controversial speech in Calcutta in which he gave his view of it in public for the first time, just as he was preparing to leave his post in November 1888.[139] While agreeing that a few thousand men could not continue to rule the destinies of '200 millions' forever, he refuted the claim that the Congress in any way represented the interests of those millions, evidenced by their choice of supporting a programme of political reform over the more pressing requirement for social reform. Dufferin painted the Congress as selfishly pursuing its own political ends, rather than performing the true duties of good governance, which the 'august impartiality of English rule' already provided: they were unrepresentative, disloyal and tactically foolish.[140] Instead, he called upon the Indian nobility and aristocracy to take up this mantle, placing faith in a social and political model in which only the elite were fit to rule. The speech generated a furore, not only in the Indian and Anglo-Indian press, but also amongst Dufferin's friends, colleagues and leading imperial figures. Sir Samuel Baker wrote to Dufferin to praise his 'forcible and beautiful' speech, further noting that, 'we already possess a terrible example in Ireland of the ruin that must result from the agitation stirred up by professional disturbers', reserving especial venom for those 'professionals' from England and Ireland who, 'although of no weight at home, they act as pebbles thrown into still water, which disturb the surface'.[141]

Two issues crystallised the principles at stake and the new kinds of demands being made: first, the question of Indian volunteers in the Indian Army and, second, the extent to which Indians might participate in local government through provincial legislative councils.[142] The question of volunteering had come to the fore in 1885, driven by Dufferin's foreign policy in Burma, which required an increasing number of troops, further heightened by expectations of another Afghan war.[143] Volunteering had, until this period, been the privileged bastion of the Anglo-Indian community, so although there was no legal barrier to Indian volunteering, in practice Anglo-Indian prejudice meant only they were admitted into the volunteer companies.[144] Emotions ran high over the issue: practically, the Government of India needed more volunteers than could be supplied by the Anglo-Indian community alone, but the controversies recently whipped up by the Ilbert Bill made this politically very difficult.[145] Dufferin was acutely aware of the requirement to bolster manpower but, in a speech in Calcutta in February 1885, he called on the existing corps to create volunteer reserves while omitting all mention of 'native' volunteers. For Dufferin, the issue was a dead letter and it might have remained so if not for an accidental incident in Madras city the next month, whereby a call for new volunteers that failed explicitly to debar Indian volunteers was released. Four Indians promptly signed up and were accepted, leading to elation amongst Indian reformers and renewed demands from other parts of India, notably Bengal, for similar privileges. Dufferin was absorbed in difficult negotiations with the Amir of Afghanistan at Rawalpindi at the moment the crisis broke and his initial reaction was to play down its significance, advising the Madras presidency to prevent it from spiralling beyond a 'minor incident'.[146] But the horse had bolted: S. Banerjea wrote a memorial to Dufferin, declaring that Indians wished to volunteer out of a sense of duty to Queen and empire, and that if they continued to be debarred from doing so, their loyalty was in doubt and they were being treated as aliens, 'unworthy of the confidence of their rulers'.[147] Dufferin issued a statement that expressed how thankful the government was for their loyalty, now the immediate crisis in Afghanistan had passed, the requirement for extra volunteers was no longer necessary – knowing, of course, that this was hardly the point. In private, his tone was very different: he wrote to Kimberley that, 'the instinctive desire which now possesses them is to ape the tactics and organisation of the Irish Revolutionists. With this object they denounce the whole Indian Administration and its various services as brutally inimical to native interests.'[148] Indian reformers added this episode to their list of other disappointments in Dufferin.[149] Allan Octavian Hume was not to be put on the back foot, however, and, after discussions in Bombay, Madras and Allahabad, met with Dufferin in Simla with a proposed plan for Indian

Ornamental empire? 187

volunteering. Dufferin was wary of Hume, but their meetings did lead to some initial areas of agreement. Although the focus of these meetings was the volunteer question, Hume also outlined details for a national organisation whereby grievances could be discussed by Indians and represented to the government: this was a long way from true representation but was framed as a step towards it.[150] Dufferin gave these plans his private blessing, but denied official recognition to the Congress.[151] Indeed, as letters against reform poured in from the presidencies and his Council members, Dufferin retreated to a more cautious position and refrained from making any decision at all on the matter.[152] His way out of the situation presented itself unexpectedly in March 1885 with Kimberley's strong support for another set of proposals to reform the British Indian Army by establishing a reserve with 'Native officers and non-commissioned officers', with an emphasis on, 'the higher classes of Native gentlemen', from 'noble and respectable families'.[153] Moving forward on this basis was the perfect solution: it had a good chance of finding support in Britain, would demonstrate the government's confidence in Indian loyalty as demanded by Banerjea's memorial, and would avoid the spectre of a separate Indian volunteer corps full of 'hot-headed students'.[154] He utilised a classic stalling tactic by sending out the proposals for consultation to the provincial governments in June 1885, asking them to assess how far the desire for volunteering was evident in their jurisdictions and for their general view on the proposals. Indian newspapers and reformers finally gave up hope in him as a reforming viceroy.[155]

Linking all of these hotly contested issues was the Indian newspaper press and how the British authorities wished to see it managed. This highlights some similarities with Dufferin's earlier engagement with the Irish and Canadian press, but also how the much more autocratic nature of British rule in India opened other possibilities, such as limits on a free press and other forms of censorship. Although in theory these options were available to Dufferin, politically it would have been very difficult for him to apply them, even setting aside his liberal principles of rule by the best. He feared the kind of hostile controversy the Vernacular Press Act had generated for Lord Lytton in the 1870s.[156] Ripon had repealed this legislation in 1882 and, as well as sharing Ripon's liberal views on the press, Dufferin did not want to be the viceroy who rolled it back out, no matter the level of press hostility to his policies. There was no escaping the fact that it would look like a sign of weakness to have to impose censorship.[157] However, he was regularly infuriated by the accusations and criticisms of him and his policies, and kept a private tally of 'occasions of which the "Indian Mirror" has lied without the slightest authority', among other titles.[158]

It was a similar story with the proposed reform of the Indian Civil Service and Indian demands to have a greater access to its more senior levels. Dufferin's initial view was one of cautious acceptance, whereby:

> personally I should feel it both a relief and an assistance if in the settlement of many Indian administrative questions affecting the interests

of millions of Her Majesty's subjects I could rely to a larger extent than at present upon the experience and counsels of Indian coadjutors. Amongst the natives I have met there are a considerable number who are both able and sensible, and upon whose loyal cooperation one could undoubtedly rely. The fact of their supporting the government would popularise many of its acts.[159]

A Commission of Inquiry on the subject was established that reported in Dufferin's last year as viceroy; based on their report, Dufferin developed some 'very liberal', proposals to admit Indians into the higher grades of the Indian Civil Service.[160] His support for these reforms was grounded in the belief that a measure of decentralisation of power in India should be the government's guiding principle. He wished to see the provincial legislatures strengthened so that their diverse requirements could be more easily met and public opinion acknowledged. As such, Dufferin aimed to enlarge the number of councils but also their powers, both of which policies were eventually brought into operation by his successor Lansdowne in 1890. In this, Dufferin was influenced by his experiences in both Ireland and Canada. As in Ireland, his views of strengthening local involvement in government was a long way away from 'home rule', or accepting that British rule was on an equal plane to any structure of 'native' government, 'for evidently India is not a country in which the machinery of European democratic agitation can be applied with impunity'.[161] But he recognised in a practical sense that some reform was necessary to prevent future agitation and to act on the liberal principles underpinning his entire career. As he said to Cross, who was getting cold feet: 'Of course as an autocratic power, with an army of more than 200,000 men at our disposal, we can afford for a time to ignore their demands, but only for a time.'[162] It was an impossible position: on the one hand, reform meant the British would start to, 'saw the branch on which we are sitting', but failure to demonstrate their much-vaunted good governance would equally undermine their position.[163] In the Indian case this was given expression in the widespread criticisms of Russian autocracy and territorial ambitions in Central Asia, as opposed to the liberal 'democracy' evident in Britain.[164] This argument fell down with just the briefest glance at the nature of British rule in India. This contradiction exercised Dufferin throughout his period as viceroy and in relation to his views on the constitutional future of Ireland.[165] For Dufferin, Ireland was an integral part of the British state and could not be judged in the same way as a colony such as India, or even a dominion such as Canada. He put it in stark terms to Sir Thomas MacKnight, editor of the *Northern Whig*, at the end of his career: 'The thing [Home Rule] cannot in my opinion by done unless the Government are prepared to contemplate the almost inevitable contingency of sacrificing not only the unity of the Kingdom but the breaking up of the British Empire. This is my deep conviction and nothing can alter it.'[166] Social unity, not social equality, was the aim.[167] But the most important element in his analysis was his adherence to the fitness of rule by the best, the duty of the

Ornamental empire? 189

traditional ruling classes, landed and aristocratic, even if, as he wrote in 1887, 'by the time I get back to England I expect to find my Irish estate ... whittled down to nothing'.[168]

'A very critical undertaking'[169]

I'm old. I followed Power to the last,
Gave her my best, and power followed Me.
It's worth it – on my soul I'm speaking plain,
Here by the claret glasses! – worth it all.
I gave – no matter what I gave – I win.
I know I win. Mine's work, good work that lives!
A country twice the size of France – the North
Safeguarded. That's my record: sink the rest
And better if you can.[170]

In India, Dufferin operated the most untrammelled expression of his notion of aristocratic rule by the best. It was embedded in the constitutional structures of Indian governance, expressed and embodied by the figurehead of the viceroy. Dufferin's dusty tours of the presidencies, the triumphal visit to Burma ('the conqueror of millions and the absorber of new territories', as Argyll hailed him) and the annual treks to Simla were all part of this.[171] The investitures, ceremonies, dinners and *durbars* were not a garnish resting on the real operation of power: they were the truest expression of that power, as Dufferin understood very well from his experiences in Canada and the courts of Europe. In many ways, the viceroyalty was the apogee both of Dufferin's career and of how he understood his role in British imperial dominion itself. In a way that was under attack in Britain and Ireland, he was able to express aristocratic rule by the best, unshackled by the demands of democracy and, instead, free to govern in a way that expressed his identity as an Irish Whig-Liberal, an identity that had changed in ways both subtle and clearly evident since his domestic political engagements of the 1860s.[172] It was all a question of perspective, of course: when he was visited in Rome by Rudyard Kipling, he discussed this quality of power with the young writer: 'I had seen administrative machinery from beneath, all stripped and overheated. This was the first time I had listened to one who had handled it from above. And unlike the generality of Viceroys, Lord Dufferin *knew*.'[173] But even in autocratic India, Dufferin found this position challenged on many fronts: by the various land reform agendas, the volunteering question, the reform of legislative provincial councils and, of course, the establishment of the Indian National Congress.[174] Despite these challenges, the governing culture of India, led by men such as Dufferin, remained resolutely aristocratic in nature, attempting to appeal to India's princely, noble and landowning classes, with varying degrees of success.[175]

But how successful was aristocratic governance in India? Dufferin and his peers worked hard to maintain both the power structures and the ornamental gloss of aristocratic rule, but it would prove to be inherently flawed. The problems generated by the hierarchical and aristocratic nature of British rule, most importantly its focus on sovereignty over power, were stored up for a future Dufferin would not live to see, but one against which he did warn. It generated paranoia and crackdowns by the British, weakening the supposed moral basis for their rule. There are complexities, however, and it would be wrong to dogmatise. In Dufferin's case, his liberal principles were ruffled on his arrival in India: before his departure, he had read all of Ripon's despatches and, in principle, approved of his reforming programme, despite being explicitly charged with repressing the controversies generated by them when in India. He was uncomfortable with the autocratic nature of British power in India and, when first presented with reforming proposals for Indian volunteering and engagement in the higher ranks of the Indian Civil Service, or even the idea of the Indian National Congress, he was initially cautiously supportive – partly on idealistic grounds, but also on the more practical grounds that some reform was desirable to balance the interests in India to maintain peace. His outlook was fundamentally hierarchical, however, and the structure of his daily life in India only entrenched that view. He regarded the behaviour of the more radical elements of the Congress as disloyal and ungrateful, although his greatest censure was reserved for those British and Irish personnel who supported the aims of the Congress, however much they protested that their activities were in British interests.[176] Dufferin's Irish experiences taught him that loyalty had to be earned by good governance, which for him was aristocratic rule by the best. This was a question that was bigger than Dufferin, however; as his colleague and biographer Sir Alfred Lyall pointed out in his assessment of Dufferin's tenure, 'while England is at home growing more and more democratic, in India she continues raising higher and higher the fabric of a huge semi-barbaric empire'.[177] This was the tension at the heart of Dufferin's experience in India, an echo of that in Ireland.

On his departure from India in late 1888, he wrote extensively to friends and statesmen, reflecting on his legacy, as was his somewhat anxious habit. Broadly speaking, this was complacent in tone. To Lord Cross, he summarised:

> Indeed, without self-flattery, I think I can say that I shall have handed over the country to Lansdowne in a satisfactory condition. There is not a cloud on the horizon, and we have succeeded in all our undertakings. Even our financial position Sir David Barbour considers as free from anxiety; the princes of India are certainly friendly to us; and as for our domestic politicians, they will be easily dealt with, as their machinations are, after all, but a storm in a tea-cup and will be dissipated by a little wise and sympathetic management. When I consider the many dangers we have run, and the innumerable mischances

which might have overtaken us, even without any fault of our own, I am truly grateful to be able to escape out of India under these tolerable conditions and without any very deep scratches on my credit and reputation.[178]

This summary exposes many of Dufferin's underlying anxieties and reflects those of both his class and the British in general. The calm of Dufferin's tenure was superficial and he was astute enough to recognise the challenges that lay close to the surface, even if he personally escaped the requirement to deal with them. This may be why Curzon was rather critical of Dufferin in his later analysis of the viceroys of India for being too cautious, too lazy, to act on the shifting political challenges in India that would, with the benefit of hindsight, be easily recognisable as the beginning of a 'new India'. Curzon's analysis was that Dufferin, 'exhibited a curious mixture of application and indifference', and that his administration was, 'in reality a monument to the saving grace of tact'.[179] This was meant as a barb, but was of course one of Dufferin's priorities when he left for Calcutta in 1884. One of his chief motivations was the protection of his 'credit and reputation', a strongly aristocratic trait and one that highlights the centrality of personal rule to Dufferin. He occupied a position of immense privilege and, in return, felt all his life the pressure of the personal responsibility he carried, cranked up to an almost unbearable level in India due to the truly autocratic nature of the imperial structures there. Unlike in Canada, there was no negotiation with politicians who did the actual governing; in India, Dufferin was faced with the consequences of a truly monarchical structure. His innate caution came to the fore and much of his energy was taken up in managing his Council, the Government of India's relations with the India Office and Secretary of State, and the social duties of the viceroy, depleting his capacity for engaging in the complex political questions being asked with increasing urgency. As he said, he did 'escape' India with his reputation intact, but he also left unanswered many questions on the future nature and composition of British rule.[180]

Notes

1 Dufferin, speech made in Belfast, 15 Oct. 1884; cited in A. Lyall, *The Life of the Marquis of Dufferin and Ava* (London, 1905), p. 355.
2 As he saw his role in Canada: C. W. De Kiewiet and F. H. Underhill (eds), *Dufferin–Carnarvon Correspondence, 1874–1878* (Toronto, 1955), p. xii; B. Messamore, *Canada's Governors General, 1847–1878: biography and constitutional evolution* (Toronto, 2006), pp. 179–80; A. Gailey, *The Lost Imperialist: Lord Dufferin, memory and mythmaking in an age of celebrity* (London, 2015), pp. 195, 197, 199–200.
3 A. T. Q. Stewart, *The Pagoda War* (Newton Abbot, 1974); A. Lyall, The Conquest of Burma, *Edinburgh Review*, 165 (1887), pp. 489, 494.
4 C. E. D. Black, *The Marquess of Dufferin and Ava* (London, 1903), p. 215; A. Denholm, *Lord Ripon, 1827–1909: a political biography* (London, 1982), pp. 139–61.

5 With the possible exception of Ireland. 'The viceroy of India still represents in his person a distinct ruling force', as Donald Mackenzie Wallace would put it: D. M. Wallace, India under the Marquis of Dufferin, *Edinburgh Review*, 169 (1889), pp. 1–2; J. Wilson, *India Conquered: Britain's Raj and the chaos of empire* (London, 2016), pp. 494–5; *Civil and Military Gazetteer*, 23 Jan. 1885.
6 D. Cannadine, *Ornamentalism: how the British saw their empire* (London, 2001) pp. 46–51.
7 F. Harcourt, Disraeli's imperialism, 1866–68: a question of timing, *Historical Journal*, 23:1 (1980), p. 92.
8 D. Omissi, A most arduous but a most noble duty: Gladstone and the British Raj, in M. E. Daly and K. T. Hoppen (eds), *Gladstone, Ireland and Beyond* (Dublin, 2011), p. 180.
9 Lyall, *Life of Dufferin*, pp. 566–7; Gailey, *Lost Imperialist*, pp. 200, 207–11.
10 E. Delaney, Our island story? Towards a transnational history of late modern Ireland, *Irish Historical Studies*, 37 (2011), pp. 599–600, 612; N. Whelehan (ed.), *Transnational Perspectives on Modern Irish History* (London, 2015), pp. 1–23.
11 C. A. Bayly, Ireland, India and the Empire: 1780–1914, *Transactions of the Royal Historical Society*, 6th ser., 10 (2000), pp. 377–89, 391–3; D. Fitzpatrick, Ireland and the empire, in A. Porter (ed.), *Oxford History of the British Empire: vol. III, The Nineteenth Century* (Oxford, 1999), pp. 494–520.
12 M. Holmes, The Irish and India: imperialism, nationalism and internationalism, *Past and Present*, 164 (1999), pp. 199–243; J. Bender, The imperial politics of famine: the 1873–4 Bengal Famine and Irish parliamentary nationalism, *Eire–Ireland*, 42:1 and 2 (2007), pp. 132–51; M. Matikkala, William Digby and the Indian question, *Journal of Liberal History*, 58 (2008), pp. 12–19; S. Niyogi, *India in the British Parliament, 1865–84: Henry Fawcett's struggle against British colonialism in India* (Calcutta, 1986).
13 J. W. Cell, *British Colonial Administration in the Mid-Nineteenth Century: the policy-making process* (London, 1970), pp. vii–xi; A. Kirk-Greene, *Britain's Imperial Administrators, 1858–1966* (London, 2000), pp. 206–14; C. Boylan, Victorian ideologies of improvement: Sir Charles Trevelyan in India and Ireland, in T. Foley and M. O'Connor (eds), *Ireland and India: colonies, culture and empire* (Dublin, 2006), pp. 1–4.
14 S. Howe, *Ireland and Empire: colonial legacies in Irish history and culture* (Oxford, 2002), pp. 142–64.
15 Ironically, this was Dufferin's – and Argyll's – great criticism of Gladstone's land reform legislation from 1870 onwards, that its basis on a shaky historical interpretation fatally undermined its integrity: J. W. Mason, The Duke of Argyll and the land question in late nineteenth century Britain, *Victorian Studies*, 21 (1978).
16 Although his sons would, one of whom died in the Boer War, one in the First World War, and a grandson who died – ironically enough – in Burma during World War II: Gailey, *Lost Imperialist*, epilogue.
17 G. Shrosebree, *Public Schools and Private Education* (1988); H. B. Gray, *Public Schools and Empire* (London, 1913); J. Gathorne-Hardy, *The Public School Phenomenon* (London, 1977).
18 T. Dooley, *The Decline of the Big House in Ireland: a study of Irish landed families, 1860–1960* (Dublin, 2001), pp. 9–11, 79; O. Purdue, *The Big House in the North of Ireland: land, power and social elites, 1878–1960* (Dublin, 2009), pp. 1–5; J. C. Beckett, *The Anglo-Irish Tradition* (Belfast, 1976), pp. 85–7, 91–6; L. P. Curtis, The Anglo-Irish predicament, *Twentieth Century Studies*, 4 (1970), pp. 37–43, 61.
19 Cannadine, *Ornamentalism*, pp. 1–13; F. M. L. Thompson, English landed society in the twentieth century: III: self-help and outdoor relief, *Transactions of the Royal Historical Society*, 6th series, 2 (1992).

20 A. M. Burton, *At the Heart of the Empire: Indians and the colonial encounter in late-Victorian Britain* (Berkeley, 1998), pp. 1–19; Gailey, *Lost Imperialist*, pp. 289–90; J. Ridden, Britishness as an imperial and diasporic identity: Irish elite perspectives, c. 1820–70s, in P. Gray (ed.), *Victoria's Ireland? Irishness and Britishness, 1837–1901* (Dublin, 2004), pp. 88–104.
21 Kipling, One Viceroy Resigns (1888).
22 Dufferin to Lady Dartrey, 13 Jan. 1885, cited in Lyall, *Life of Dufferin*, p. 361; *Times of India*, 9 Dec. 1884.
23 B. Martin, The viceroyalty of Lord Dufferin, part II, *History Today*, 11:1 (1961), pp. 62–3; D. Cannadine, *Aspects of Aristocracy: grandeur and decline in modern Britain* (New Haven, 1994), pp. 77–8, 83–4.
24 D. Gilmour, *The Ruling Caste: imperial lives in the Victorian Raj* (London, 2005), pp. 18, 54–5.
25 Wilson, *India Conquered*, pp. 128, 169, 296, 309–11, 480–1.
26 B. Crosbie, *Irish Imperial Networks: migration, social communication and exchange in nineteenth-century India* (Cambridge, 2012), pp. 1–23; S. B. Cook, *Imperial Affinities: nineteenth century analogies and exchanges between India and Ireland* (New Delhi, 1993), pp. 9–37; S. B. Cook, The Irish Raj: social origins and careers of Irishmen in the Indian Civil Service, 1855–1914, *Journal of Social History*, 20:3 (1987), pp. 507–22.
27 See, for example, Public Record Office of Northern Ireland [hereafter PRONI], D1071, H/H/M/13/7, Review of reports on the condition of the lower classes of the agricultural population and of measures for the relief of densely populated tracts, Oct. 1888.
28 Cannadine, *Ornamentalism*, pp. 57, 95.
29 P. J. Durrans, A two-edged sword: the Liberal attack on Disraelian imperialism, *Journal of Imperial and Commonwealth History*, 10:3 (1982), pp. 263, 268.
30 F. Mount, *Tears of the Rajas: mutiny, money and marriage in India, 1805–1905* (London, 2015), pp. 285, 615–17.
31 Gailey, *Lost Imperialist*, pp. 261, 294–6; Cannadine, *Ornamentalism*, pp. 85, 95–8.
32 Nicolson, *Helen's Tower*, pp. 194–5; M., Bence-Jones, *The Viceroys of India* (London, 1982).
33 Lyall comments on this: *Life of Dufferin*, pp. 562–3, 566.
34 Lyall, *Life of Dufferin*, p. 566; see a similar analysis from Wallace: D. M. Wallace, India under the Marquis of Dufferin, *Edinburgh Review*, 169 (1889), pp. 3, 34, 41.
35 P. Kanwar, *Imperial Simla: the political culture of the Raj* (Oxford, 1990), pp. 49, 52–3; Bence-Jones, *Viceroys of India*, p. 142–3.
36 Much of this detail was handled by Lady Dufferin, and she meticulously recorded it in her journals, later published: Marchioness of Dufferin, *Our Viceregal Life in India: selections from my journal, 1884–88* (London, 1890); J. Lennon, *Irish Orientalism: a literary and intellectual history* (Syracuse, 2004), pp. xv–xxxi, 162–72, 193–5; J. M. Wright, *Ireland, India and Nationalism in Nineteenth Century Literature* (Cambridge, 2007), pp. 1–25.
37 P. J. Cain, Character and imperialism: the British financial administration of Egypt, 1878–1914, *Journal of Imperial and Commonwealth History*, 34:2 (2006), p. 177.
38 Cannadine, *Ornamentalism*, pp. 45, 47, 85, 95–7; A. Kirk-Greene, *Britain's Imperial Administrators, 1858–1966* (London, 2000), p. 235.
39 BL, India Office Papers, Mss Eur F102/10, ff. 42, Dufferin to Kilbracken, 27 May 1887; Gailey, *Lost Imperialist*, p. 224.
40 C. Dewey, Images of the village community: a study in Anglo-Indian ideology, *Modern Asian Studies*, 6 (1972), pp. 291–327; T. R. Metcalfe, *Forging the Raj: essay on British India in the heyday of empire* (Oxford, 2005), pp. 41–9; C. A. Bayly, *The Birth of the Modern World, 1780–1914: global connections and*

194 *Ornamental empire?*

comparisons (Oxford, 2004), pp. 295–6, 298; Cannadine, *Ornamentalism*, p. 42; S. Den Otter, Thinking in communities: late nineteenth century Liberals, idealists and the retrieval of community, in E. H. H. Green (ed.), *An Age of Transition: British Politics, 1880–1914* (Edinburgh, 1997), pp. 67–84; P. J. Cain and A. G. Hopkins, *British Imperialism, I: Innovation and Expansion; II, Crisis and Deconstruction* (London, 1993), p. 14.
41 BL, India Office Papers, F130/2, ff. 3, Dufferin to Kimberley, 23 Dec. 1884; A. Denholm, *Lord Ripon, 1827–1909: a political biography* (London, 1982), p. 150; S. Gopal, *The Viceroyalty of Lord Ripon, 1880–1884* (Oxford, 1953), pp. 186–96; Gailey, *Lost Imperialist*, pp. 212–13, 223.
42 G. Campbell, The tenure of land in India, in *Systems of Land Tenure in Various Countries: a series of essays published under the sanction of the Cobden Club* (London, 1870), pp. 127–30; O. MacDonagh, *States of Mind: a study of Anglo-Irish conflict 1780–1980* (London, 1983), pp. 34, 37–9.
43 C. Dewey, The influence of Sir Henry Maine on agrarian policy in India, in A. Diamond (ed.), *The Victorian Achievement of Sir Henry Maine: a centennial reappraisal* (Cambridge, 1991), pp. 353–74.
44 A. Lyall, The Indian administration of Lord Dufferin, *Edinburgh Review*, Jan. 1889, pp. 3–7; F. Mackinnon, *The Government of Prince Edward Island* (Toronto, 1951), pp. 105–7, 116.
45 BL, India Office Papers, F130/2, ff. 119, Dufferin to Churchill, 30 Jul. 1885. See the contrasting views of G. Campbell, Land legislation for Ireland, *Fortnightly Review*, 19 (1881), pp. 18–19, 29.
46 Lyall, *Life of Dufferin*, pp. 362–6; T. R. Metcalfe, The influence of the mutiny of 1857 on land policy in India, *Historical Journal*, 4 (1961), pp. 152–63.
47 B. Martin, *New India 1885* (Berkley, 1969), pp. 31–2; D. Rothermund, *Government, Landlord and Peasant in India: agrarian relations under British rule, 1865–1935* (Wiesbaden, 1978), pp. 101–3.
48 Campbell, Tenure of land in India, pp. 144–55.
49 'There will of course be any amount of the three Fs in their fullest and most rasping form', wrote one outraged Anglo-Indian: R. Lethbridge, *The Mischief threatened by the Bengal Tenancy Bill (The Bengal Tenancy Bill: report of proceedings of a meeting held at St James's Hall, 25 June 1884)*, (London, 1884), pp. 3–6.
50 That was, Irish-born Indian Civil Service personnel: PRONI, D1071, H/H/C/95, ff. 114, Dufferin to Argyll, 23 Mar. 1885 and to Kimberley, BL, India Office Papers, F130/2, ff. 3, 23 Dec. 1884; Gilmour, *The Ruling Caste*, pp. 113, 141; I. M. Cumpston, Some early Indian nationalists and their allies in the British parliament, 1851–1906, *English Historical Review*, 76 (1961), pp. 284–6; H. V. Brasted, Irish home rule politics and India, 1873–1886: Frank Hugh O'Donnell and other Irish 'Friends of India', unpublished PhD thesis (University of Edinburgh, 1974), pp. xiv, 1–4.
51 Martin, *New India*, p. 32.
52 BL, India Office Papers, F130/2, ff. 46, Dufferin to Kimberley, 10 Mar. 1885; Wallace, India under the Marquis of Dufferin, pp. 4–5; BL, India Office Papers, F130/2, ff. 7, Dufferin to Kimberley, 6 Jan. 1885; and for a full review of the debate in Council, ff. 15, Dufferin to Kimberley, 20 Jan. 1885.
53 Lethbridge, *The Mischief threatened by the Bengal Tenancy Bill*, p. 60.
54 Campbell, Tenure of land in India, pp. 156–64, 184–90; E. D. Steele, Ireland and the Empire: imperial precedents for Gladstone's first Irish Land Act, *Historical Journal*, 11:1 (1968), pp. 66–7, 72–6.
55 BL, India Office Papers, F130/2, ff. 111, Dufferin to Churchill, 17 Jul. 1885; Lyall, *Life of Dufferin*, p. 366; 8th Duke of Argyll, A model land law: a reply to Arthur Williams MP, *Fortnightly Review*, 41 (1887), pp. 764, 784.
56 BL, India Office Papers, F130/2, ff. 154, Dufferin to Churchill, 12 Oct. 1885; F130/42e, ff. 30, Lyall to Dufferin, 12 Sept. 1886; PRONI, D1071, H/H/M/17/1,

Viceroy's Notebook, ff. 267, Talukdars of Oudh, n.d. [Mar. 1885?] and Memorandum by Sir A. Lyall, Mar. 1886.
57 BL, India Office Papers, F130/3, ff. 72, Churchill to Dufferin, 16 Sept. 1885; D. Cannadine, *Aspects of Aristocracy: grandeur and decline in modern Britain* (New Haven, 1994), p. 109; B. Porter, *The Absent-Minded Imperialists: empire, society and culture in Britain* (Oxford, 2004), pp. 228–31.
58 Lyall, *Life of Dufferin*, p. 367.
59 D. M. Wallace (ed.), *Speeches delivered in India, 1884–1888, by the Marquis of Dufferin and Ava* (London, 1890), speech by Dufferin, Simla, 9 Jun. 1886, p. 118; Rothermund, *Government, Landlord and Peasant*, pp. 128,130–6.
60 BL, India Office Papers, F130/2, ff. 154, Dufferin to Churchill, 12 Oct. 1885; see also in comparison, G. R. G. Hambly, Richard Temple and the Punjab Tenancy Act of 1868, *English Historical Review* (1964), pp. 47–66.
61 Gailey, *Lost Imperialist*, pp. 211–12; Lyall, *Life of Dufferin*, p. 363; I. Ali, *The Punjab under Imperialism, 1885–1947* (Princeton, 1988), p. 4.
62 J. W. Cell, *Hailey: a study in British imperialism* (Cambridge, 1992), pp. 1–4; N. Ethrington, *Theories of Imperialism: war, conquest and capital* (London, 1984), pp. 263–4, 270.
63 Wallace, *Speeches delivered in India*, Dufferin to the Mansion House, London, 29 May 1888, p. 263.
64 Lyall, *Life of Dufferin*, p. 565.
65 Marquis of Curzon, *British Government in India: the story of the viceroys and government houses*, 2 vols (London, 1925), pp. 246–9; Nicolson, *Helen's Tower*, pp. 193–4; Gailey, *Lost Imperialist*, pp. 209, 292.
66 L. Stanley, The epistolarium: on theorising letters and correspondences, *Auto/Biography*, 12 (2004), pp. 202–9, 223; Bence-Jones, *The Viceroys of India*, p. 133; Gailey, *Lost Imperialist*, pp. 209, 228, 294.
67 See Lyall, *Life of Dufferin*, p. 564, for a description of Dufferin's judgement of character; A. L. Stoler, *Along the Archival Grain: epistemic anxieties and colonial common sense* (New Jersey, 2008), pp. 64–6, 101.
68 A. Hawkins and J. Powell (eds) *The Journal of John Wodehouse, First Earl of Kimberley for 1862–1902* (London, 1997), 14 Aug. 1884, p. 345.
69 Hawkins and Powell, *Journal of John Wodehouse*, 8 Oct. 1884, p. 346; B. Martin, The viceroyalty of Lord Dufferin, *History Today*, 10 (1960), pp. 821–2.
70 Principally Afghanistan and Burma: A. Preston, Sir Charles MacGregor and the defence of India, 1857–1887, *Historical Journal*, 12:1 (1969), pp. 58–68, 76–7.
71 Lord Kilbracken, *Reminiscences, 1847–1916* (London, 1931), p. 121; M. P. Callahan, *Making Enemies: war and state-building in Burma* (Ithaca, 2005), pp. 24–31; Gailey, *Lost Imperialist*, pp. 227–31.
72 Cited in Lyall, *Life of Dufferin*, p. 98; R. C. Black, Economic policy in Ireland and India in the time of J.S. Mill, *Economic History Review*, 21:2 (1968), pp. 327–8.
73 R. J. Moore, *Liberalism and Indian Politics, 1872–1922* (London, 1966), pp. 42–4.
74 8th Duke of Argyll, India under Dalhousie and Canning, (reprinted from the *Edinburgh Review*, Jan. and Apr. 1863; Edinburgh, 1865).
75 Argyll, India, p. 4.
76 Argyll, India, pp. 72, 107.
77 PRONI, D1071, H/H/B/S/251B, ff. 11, Dufferin to Brinsley Sheridan, 3 Dec. 1885.
78 See C. A. Bayly, *Empire and Information: intelligence gathering and social communication in India, 1780–1870* (Cambridge, 1996), pp. 1–9, 338; A. G. Hopkins, Back to the future: from national history to imperial history, *Past and Present*, 164 (1999), pp. 222–3; J. Epstein, Taking class notes on empire, in S. Rose and C. Hall (eds), *At Home with the Empire: metropolitan culture and the imperial world* (Cambridge, 2006), pp. 255–6.
79 'We breakfasted at 8 o'clock. At a quarter past the Viceroy signed the declaration of war with Burmah', recorded his wife: Dufferin, *Our Viceregal Life*, p. 192; Lyall, *Life of Dufferin*, pp. 400–1; Martin, *New India*, p. 253.

196 *Ornamental empire?*

80 'Nor, I am happy to think, will our military expedition ... prove a very expensive one', he boldly claimed: BL, India Office Papers, F130/2, ff. 157, Dufferin to Churchill, 19 Oct. 1885; Gailey, *Lost Imperialist*, p. 230.
81 PRONI, D1071, H/H/M/10/6/10, Memorandum by Dufferin to the Military Department, asking for details as to British casualties, 1886; H/H/M/17/1, Viceroy's notebook, ff. 385, Memorandum on officering Upper Burma, 25 Jan. 1886; H/H/M/17/4, Viceroy's notebook, Burmese troop numbers, Nov. 1886; Black, *Dufferin and Ava*, pp. 255–8; Callahan, *Making Enemies*, p. 25.
82 'Funny people the Burmans', wrote Field Marshall Sir George White in a typical judgement: H. M. Durand, *Life of Field Marshall Sir George White, V.C.*, vol. 1 (Edinburgh, 1915), p. 341. See also the division of Burmese loot, listed in PRONI, D1071, H/H/M/17/4, Viceroy's notebook, 10 Dec. 1886; Gailey, *Lost Imperialist*, pp. 233–5, 241.
83 BL, India Office Papers, F130/6, ff. 2, Churchill to Dufferin, 22 Jan. 1886; Wallace, *Speeches delivered in India*, Speech to Sir Frederick Roberts and the troops, Mandalay, 17 Feb. 1886, p. 98; R. Foster, *Lord Randolph Churchill: a political life* (Oxford, 1981), pp. 206–10; D. P. Singhal, *British Diplomacy and the Annexation of Upper Burma* (New Delhi, 1981), pp. 72–107; Stewart, *The Pagoda War*, pp. 132–9; Moore, *Liberalism and Indian Politics*, pp. 45–9.
84 Stewart, *Pagoda War*, p. 138.
85 Thant Myint-U, *The Making of Modern Burma* (Cambridge, 2001), pp. 196–7.
86 Dufferin, *Our Viceregal Life*, p. 315.
87 Lyall, *Life of Dufferin*, p. 402; Black, *Dufferin and Ava*, p. 233; see in contrast contemporary views of the 'martial' race of Afghanistan: BL, Mss Eur, D727, Papers of Sir Henry Durand, D727/9, ff. 69, Durand to Dufferin, 21 Apr. 1888.
88 BL, India Office Papers, F130/13, No. 461, Churchill to Dufferin, 25 Dec. 1885; PRONI, D1071, H/H/M/13/2/5, Report by Maj. Gen. Sir George White, 6 Jul. 1888; PRONI, D1071, H/H/M/17/1, Viceroy's notebook, Report: Consolidation of British power in Upper Burma, 30 Jul. 1886; C. E. Crothswaite, *The Pacification of Burma* (London 1912), pp. 5–17, 102; D. Woodman, *The Making of Burma* (London, 1962), p. 228.
89 Dufferin described Moylan as, 'a man of such perverse and brutal temper and so unprincipled': BL, India Office Papers, F130/5, ff. 75, Dufferin to Kimberley, 9 Jul. 1886; F130/6, ff. 12, Kimberley to Dufferin, 25 Mar. 1886; F130/13, No. 504, Churchill to Dufferin, 22 Jan. 1886; and as, 'an Irish lawyer, excitable, inaccurate and prone to exaggeration', in F130/13, No. 452, to Churchill, 15 Feb. 1886; see also F130/42g, ff. 44, J. C. Macdonald, *Times* to Wallace, 19 Nov. 1886; Myint-U, *The Making of Modern Burma*, p. 201; Stewart, *Pagoda War*, pp. 119–30; I. Sheehy, The view from Fleet Street: Irish nationalist journalists in London and their attitudes towards empire, 1892–1898, in S. J. Potter (ed.), *Newspapers and Empire in Ireland and Britain* (Dublin, 2004), pp. 143–6.
90 See, for example, Dufferin requesting Kimberley's help in putting across the difficulties he faced in Burma in the House of Lords: BL, India Office Papers, F130/5, ff. 120, 20 Sept. 1886.
91 BL, India Office Papers, F130/5, ff.5, Dufferin to Churchill, 26 Jan. 1886; Martin, The viceroyalty of Lord Dufferin, p. 830; Gailey, *Lost Imperialist*, pp. 236–9, 241.
92 P. Marshall, The imperial factor in the Liberal decline, 1880–1885, in J. Flint and G. Williams (eds), *Perspectives of Empire: presented to Gerald S. Graham* (Harlow, 1973), pp. 136–7.
93 For example, BL, India Office Papers, F130/39, ff. 24, Dufferin to Bernard, 3 Nov. 1885; ff. 33, Dufferin to Prendergast, 29 Nov. 1885.

94 See, for example, BL, India Office Papers, F130/2, ff. 83, Dufferin to Kimberley, 5 May 1885, on those who have 'black blood in their veins'; J. A. Mangan, *Making Imperial Mentalities: socialisation and British imperialism* (Manchester 1990), pp. 1–3; R. Romani, British views on Irish national character, 1800–1846: an intellectual history, *History of European Ideas*, 23:5–6 (1997), pp. 193–4, 201, 207–8.
95 Much of this was also expressed through Dufferin's correspondence with the Queen; see BL, India Office Papers, F130/20, ff. 1, Dufferin to Queen, 16 Feb. 1885.
96 Hatfield House, Papers of the 3rd Marquess of Salisbury, Dufferin to Salisbury, ff. 13, 6 Aug. 1885; BL, India Office Papers, F130/20, ff. 31, Dufferin to Sir Henry Ponsonby, 9 Nov. 1885; M. Bentley, *Lord Salisbury's World: Conservative environments in late-Victorian Britain* (Cambridge, 2001), pp. 220–1, 232–43.
97 This activity also cost a great deal: PRONI, D1071, H/H/M/14/6, viceregal household accounts, 1884–8; Kirk-Greene, *Britain's Imperial Administrators*, pp. 222–4.
98 Cited in Lyall, *Life of Dufferin*, p. 433; speech by Dufferin on the occasion of the Queen's Jubilee celebrations in Calcutta, 16 Feb. 1887.
99 Stoler, *Along the Archival Grain*, pp. 94, 98.
100 BL, India Office Papers, F130/29a, ff. 28, Dufferin to Sir Henry Verney, 6 Jan. 1888; N. C. Fleming, The landed elite, power and Ulster unionism, in D. G. Boyce and A. O'Day (eds), *The Ulster Crisis, 1885–1921* (Basingstoke, 2005), pp. 88–9.
101 J. Darwin, *The Empire Project: the rise and fall of the British World system, 1830–1970* (Cambridge, 2009), p. 184.
102 M. Yasin, *India's Foreign Policy: the Dufferin years* (New Delhi, 1994), pp. 8–11, 21, 39.
103 BL, India Office Papers, F130/8a, ff. 40, Dufferin to Cross, 1 Sept. 1887, for a full description of the looming financial disaster; Bodleian Library, Kimberley Papers, MS 4234, ff. 36, Wallace to Kimberley, 26 Mar. 1886.
104 He was writing to the Secretary of State about his worries on this front almost as soon as he arrived in India; for example, BL, India Office Papers, F130/2, ff. 86, Dufferin to Kimberley, 11 May 1885; Cain and Hopkins, *British Imperialism, I: Innovation and Expansion*, pp. 341–50; Gailey, *Lost Imperialist*, pp. 274.
105 BL, India Office Papers, F130/11a, ff. 24, Dufferin to Cross, 25 May 1888; Wallace, India under the Marquis of Dufferin, p. 30; Wallace, *Speeches delivered in India*, Calcutta, 27 Jan. 1888, p. 181.
106 BL, India Office Papers, F130/2, ff. 33, Dufferin to Kimberley, 24 Feb. 1885; F130/39, ff. 20, Dufferin to Colvin, 1 Nov. 1885.
107 BL, India Office Papers, F130/5, ff. 87, Dufferin to Lord Warrington, 13 Aug. 1886; A. Seal, Imperialism and nationalism in India, in J. Gallagher, G. Johnson and A. Seal (eds), *Locality, Province and Nation: essays on Indian politics, 1870–1940* (Cambridge, 1973), pp. 8–11.
108 Wallace, *Speeches delivered in India*, Address from the Municipal Corporation of Bombay, 8 Dec. 1884, p. 23; Black, *Dufferin and Ava*, pp. 284–9; Omissi, A most arduous, p. 186.
109 See, for example, BL, India Office Papers, F130/2, ff. 127, Dufferin to Churchill, 14 Aug. 1885; F130/6, ff. 49, Lord Cross to Dufferin, 26 Aug. 1886.
110 This work is summarised in PRONI, D1071, H/H/M/13/7, Summary of the principal measures of the viceroyalty of the Marquess of Dufferin and Ava in the department of revenue and agriculture, Dec. 1888, especially ff. 8 for famine relief and ff. 27 on agricultural improvement; J. Bender, The imperial politics of famine: the 1873–4 Bengal Famine and Irish parliamentary nationalism, *Eire–Ireland*, 42:1 and 2 (2007), pp. 132–5.

198 Ornamental empire?

111 Lyall, The Indian administration of Lord Dufferin, pp. 28–30.
112 See, for example, BL, India Office Papers, F130/2, ff. 29, Dufferin to Kimberley, 13 Feb. 1885; ff. 98, Dufferin to Kimberley, 19 Jun. 1885.
113 BL, India Office Papers, F130/6, ff. 27, Kimberley to Dufferin, 28 May 1886; P. Hopkirk, *The Great Game: on secret service in high Asia* (London, 1990), pp. 6, 409, 434–7; R. L. Shukla, *Britain, India and the Turkish empire, 1853–1882* (New Delhi, 1973), pp. 213–15, 219.
114 PRONI, D1071, H/H/M/17/1, Viceroy's notebook, Railway to Mandalay, 10 Jun. 1886; BL, India Office Papers, F130/2, ff. 3, Dufferin to Kimberley, 23 Dec. 1884; ff. 18, Dufferin to Kimberley, 27 Jan. 1885; Moore, *Liberalism and Indian Politics*, pp. 43–4.
115 See, for instance, Cross's irate correspondence with Dufferin on these questions: BL, India Office Papers, F130/12, ff. 1, 5 Jan. 1888; ff. 2, 12 Jan. 1888; ff. 3, 19 Jan. 1888; ff. 7, 10 Feb. 1888.
116 Wallace, *Speeches delivered in India*, Empire Club, London, 1883, p. 3.
117 Hatfield House, Papers of the 3rd Marquess of Salisbury, Dufferin to Salisbury, ff. 35, 17 Sept. 1888.
118 And Irish nationalists in Canada: D. Wilson (ed.), *Irish Nationalism in Canada* (Toronto, 2009), pp. 20–1; B. Chandra, *The Rise and Growth of Economic Nationalism in India: economic policies of Indian national leadership, 1880–1905* (New Delhi, 1966), pp. 1–3, 13–14, 21.
119 Chandra, *Economic Nationalism in India*, pp. 272–5, 287.
120 PRONI, D1071, H/H/M/17/3, Viceroy's Notebook, Memorandum to Colvin [Finance minister] on financial matters, 31 May 1887; BL, Mss Eur, F102, Kilbracken Papers, F102/10, ff. 24, Dufferin to Kilbracken, 10 Apr. 1887.
121 Omissi, A most arduous, p. 192; B. Martin, Lord Dufferin and the Indian National Congress, 1885–88, *Journal of British Studies*, 7:1 (1967), pp. 72–3; Moore, *Liberalism and Indian Politics*, p. 53.
122 BL, India Office Papers, F130/5, ff. 25, Dufferin to Kimberley, 21 Mar. 1886.
123 See, for example, BL, India Office Papers, F130/20, ff. 61, Lansdowne to Dufferin, 2 Dec. 1885: 'if you are not too busy with Burmese and other complications, could you not write a little good advice to Salisbury?'; Stoler, *Along the Archival Grain*, pp. 1–15; 57–60; D. A. Roberts, Merely birds of passage: Lady Hariot Dufferin's travel writings and medical work in India, 1884–88, *Women's History Review*, 15:3 (2006), pp. 447–9.
124 PRONI, D1071, H/H/M/17/1, Viceroy's Notebook, Note on Political associations now existent in the Bombay Presidency, n.d. [late 1884/early 1885?]; H/H/M/17/4, Viceroy's notebook, memo on The 'Pioneer' on Upper Burma administration, 21 Dec. 1885.
125 BL, India Office Papers, F130/5, ff. 25, Dufferin to Kimberley, 21 Mar. 1886; Gailey, *Lost Imperialist*, pp. 276–86.
126 BL, India Office Papers, F130/6, ff. 20, Kimberley to Dufferin, 22 Apr. 1886.
127 See his anxious correspondence with Arthur Godley, Lord Kilbracken, at the India Office, BL, Mss Eur, F102/10; A. P. Kaminsky, The India Office in the late nineteenth century, in R. Crane and N. G. Barrier (eds), *British Imperial Policy in India and Sri Lanka, 1858–1912* (New Delhi, 1981), pp. 28–30, 40, 46.
128 Nicolson, *Helen's Tower*, pp. 194–5.
129 BL, India Office Papers, F130/20, ff. 29, Dufferin to James Fitzjames Stephen, 6 Mar. 1886; L. Stephen, *The Life of James Fitzjames Stephen* (London, 1895), pp. 284–8; G. Peatling, Race and empire in nineteenth century British intellectual life: James Fitzjames Stephen, James Anthony Froude, Ireland, and India, *Eire-Ireland*, 42 (2007), pp. 157–60, 163, 168; Gailey, *Lost Imperialist*, pp. 262–3; A. Porter, Empires in the mind, pp. 218–19, 223.
130 Martin, *New India*, p. 13; A. Tripathi and A. Tripathi, *Indian National Congress and the struggle for freedom, 1885–1947* (Oxford, 2014), pp. 21–8; L. P. Curtis,

Anglo-Saxons and Celts: a study of anti-Irish prejudice in Victorian England (Bridgeport, 1968), pp. 74–80, 85.
131 PRONI, D1071, H/H/F/175, ff.14, Dufferin to Lansdowne, 30 Jan. 1885.
132 BL, Mss Eur F130/2, ff. 1, Dufferin to Kimberley, 15 Dec. 1884.
133 See, for instance, BL, Mss Eur, F130/8a, ff. 1, Dufferin to Cross, 4 Jan. 1887; and his speech marking the Queen's jubilee, Calcutta: Wallace, *Speeches delivered in India*, p. 156, 17 Feb. 1887.
134 BL, Mss Eur, f130/5, ff. 45, Dufferin to Kimberley, 26 Apr. 1886; Gailey, *Lost Imperialist*, pp. 275–8, 280–3, 285–9; B. Chandra, *India's Struggle for Independence, 1857–1947* (New Delhi, 1988), pp. 61, 70–4.
135 BL, Mss Eur, F130/5, ff. 56, Dufferin to Kimberley, 17 May 1886; U. S. Mehta, *Liberalism and Empire: a study in nineteenth century British liberal thought* (Chicago, 1999), pp. 2, 4, 11–15, 30.
136 Martin, New India, p. 299.
137 Martin, New India, p. 300; S. Checkland, *The Elgins, 1766–1917: a tale of aristocrats, proconsuls and their wives* (Aberdeen, 1988), pp. 216, 227.
138 BL, India Office Papers, F130/5, ff. 66, Dufferin to Kimberley, reporting on Hume's visit, 11 Jun. 1886; F130/20, ff. 43, Dufferin to Ripon, 9 Jul. 1886; F130/41b, ff. 18, Dufferin to Sir Henry Maine, 9 May 1886; Gailey, *Lost Imperialist*, pp. 282, 285–6; Bayly, Maine and change in nineteenth century India, pp. 389–96; Martin, Lord Dufferin and the Indian National Congress, pp. 74–7.
139 Wallace, *Speeches delivered in India*, 30 Nov. 1888, pp. 229–48; Martin, *New India*, pp. 333–4; BL, India Office Papers, F130/55, ff. 31, Dufferin's copy of his speech, November 1888; Martin, Lord Dufferin and the Indian National Congress, pp. 95–6.
140 Wallace, *Speeches delivered in India*, 30 Nov. 1888, p. 231.
141 PRONI, D1071, H/B/B/35, ff. 6, Sir Samuel Baker to Dufferin, 14 Dec. 1888. Dufferin sent copies of this speech to key political figures such as Gladstone: BL, Gladstone Papers, Add MS 44151, ff. 269, Dufferin to Gladstone, 3 Dec. 1888; Omissi, A most arduous, p. 193.
142 BL, India Office Papers, F130/40a, ff. 1, Lyall to Dufferin, 13 May 1885; Yasin, *India's Foreign Policy*, pp. 231–44.
143 PRONI, D1071, H/H/M/17/1, tables of troops numbers in the Indian provinces, n.d. [late 1885?].
144 Martin, *New India*, pp. 103–4.
145 Martin, *New India*, p. 105.
146 BL, India Office Papers, F130/2, ff. 54, Dufferin to Kimberley, 30 Mar. 1885 and ff. 56, 5 Apr. 1885; ff. 64, 11 Apr. 1885 all from Rawalpindi; Martin, *New India*, p. 107; see also Dufferin's later reflections, character and views of the Amir, in PRONI, D1071,H/H/M/17/1, ff. 309, 31 Mar. 1885; Gailey, *Lost Imperialist*, pp. 218–22.
147 Martin, *New India*, p. 111; BL, India Office Papers, F130/20, ff. 36, Dufferin to Kimberley, 21 Mar. 1886.
148 BL, India Office Papers, F130/20, ff. 74, Dufferin to Kimberley, 26 Apr. 1886.
149 T. Koditschek, *Liberalism, Imperialism and the Historical Imagination: nineteenth-century visions of a Greater Britain* (Cambridge, 2011), p. 325.
150 Martin, Lord Dufferin and the Indian National Congress, pp. 76–8; A. Parel, Hume, Dufferin and the origins of the Indian National Congress, *Journal of Indian History* (Dec. 1964), pp. 707, 715–16.
151 See long report of these meetings: BL, India Office Papers, F130/55, ff. 13, Colvin to Hume, 8 Oct. 1888; Wallace, *Speeches delivered in India*, 30 Nov. 1888, p. 242; Martin, *New India*, pp. 118–19.
152 For all of these letters, see BL, India Office Papers, F130/40a, ff. 406, 421, 422, 426b, 431, Jun. 1885.

153 Army commissions to native gentlemen, 22 Jan. 1885, cited in Martin, *New India*, p. 123.
154 Martin, *New India*, p. 124; Martin, Lord Dufferin and the Indian National Congress, pp. 83–4.
155 Martin, Lord Dufferin and the Indian National Congress, pp. 83.
156 BL, India Office Papers, F130/5, ff. 25, Dufferin to Kimberley, 21 Mar. 1886; F130/6, ff. 51, Cross to Dufferin, 8 Sept. 1886; F130/41a, ff. 45, Dufferin to Hon. Mr Mitter, 14 Mar. 1886; Bayly, *Empire and Information*, pp. 340–3.
157 Martin, *New India*, p. 13; C. Kaul, *Reporting the Raj: the British press and India, c. 1880–1922* (Manchester, 2003), pp. 6–21.
158 PRONI, D1071, H/H/M/17/2, Viceroy's notebooks, ff. 33, n.d.; and BL, India Office Papers, F130/43a, ff. 1, Dufferin to Geo. Allen, 1 Jan. 1887.
159 BL, India Office Papers, F130/20, ff. 67, Dufferin to Northbrook, 16 Oct. 1886; Lyall, *Life of Dufferin*, p. 427; and see BL, India Office Papers, F130/8a, ff. 5, Dufferin to Cross, 1 Feb. 1887.
160 BL, India Office Papers, F130/6, ff. 30, Kimberley to Dufferin, 11 Jun. 1886; Lyall, *Life of Dufferin*, pp. 429–31; Black, *Dufferin and Ava*, pp. 290–4; Bentley, *Lord Salisbury's World*, p. 234.
161 Cited in Lyall, *Life of Dufferin*, p. 427; see B. Porter, Gladstone and imperialism, in M. E. Daly and K. T. Hoppen (eds), *Gladstone, Ireland and Beyond* (Dublin, 2011), pp. 172, 174; H. Brasted, Indian nationalist development and the influence of Irish Home Rule, 1870–1886, *Modern Asian Studies*, 14:1 (1980), pp. 37–63.
162 BL, India Office Papers, F130/8a, ff. 11, Dufferin to Cross, 20 Mar. 1887; Moore, *Liberalism and Indian Politics*, pp. 56, 60.
163 PRONI, D1071, H/H/B/D/252, ff. 19, Mountstuart Grant Duff to Dufferin, 19 Apr. 1890; and see Sir Henry Maine's views in support on this, BL, India Office Papers, F130/20, ff. 114, Maine to Dufferin, 2 Jun. 1886; G. Johnson, India and Henry Maine, in A. Diamond (ed.), *The Victorian Achievement of Sir Henry Maine: a centennial reappraisal* (Cambridge, 1991), pp. 376–88; J. Pitts, *A Turn to Empire: the rise of imperial liberalism in Britain and France* (Princeton, 2005), pp. 133, 146–9.
164 PRONI, D1071, H/H/M/17/4, Memorandum regarding a secret report by a foreign agent on the viceroy's tour in India, 1 Mar. 1887.
165 K. Tidrick, *Empire and the English Character* (London, 1990), pp. 1–4.
166 PRONI, D1071, H/H/B/M/236, ff. 60, Dufferin to MacKnight, 23 Mar. 1896.
167 Lyall, The Indian administration of Lord Dufferin, p. 2; A. B. Cooke and J. B. Vincent, *The Governing Passion: cabinet government and party politics in Britain, 1885–6* (Brighton, 1974), pp. 8, 17, 19; Bayly, *Empire and Information*, p. 360.
168 BL, India Office Papers, F130/26b, ff. 15. Dufferin to Henry Reeve, 15 May 1887.
169 BL, India Office Papers, F130/8a, ff. 12, Dufferin to Cross, 10 Apr. 1887.
170 Kipling, One viceroy resigns (1888); this poem is written as a fictional soliloquy in Dufferin's voice, handing over the viceroyalty to Lansdowne; L. D. Wurgraft, *The Imperial Imagination: magic and myth in Kipling's India* (Middleton, CN, 1983), pp. 2–14; C. Allen, *Kipling Sahib* (London, 2007), pp. 175–85, 239; Gilmour, *The Ruling Caste*, p. 232; Gailey, *Lost Imperialist*, pp. 288–9.
171 'Was it really on the dull side?', asked Nicolson of Dufferin's Indian tenure. 'I have a suspicion that it was': Nicolson, *Helen's Tower*, p. 129; Black, *Dufferin and Ava*, pp. 312–21; PRONI, D1071, H/H/C/95, ff. 115, Argyll to Dufferin, 19 Feb. 1889; P. Kanwar, *Imperial Simla: the political culture of the Raj* (Oxford, 1990), pp. 49–53, 74.

172 See, as a comparison, Z. Laidlaw, Richard Bourke: Irish liberalism tempered by empire, in D. Lambert and A. Lester (eds), *Colonial Lives Across the British Empire* (Cambridge, 2006), pp. 113–16.
173 R. Kipling, *Something of Myself: for my friends known and unknown* (London, 1937: this edn. Cambridge, 2013), pp. 56–7.
174 Martin, Lord Dufferin and the Indian National Congress, pp. 72–3.
175 D. R. Khoury and D. K. Kennedy, Comparing empires: the Ottoman domains and the British Raj, *Comparative Studies of South Asia, Africa and the Middle East*, 27:2 (2007), pp. 234, 236–7, 240–1.
176 J. L. Hill, A. P. Macdonnell and the changing nature of British rule in India, 1885–1901, in R. Crane and N. G. Barrier (eds), *British Imperial Policy in India and Sri Lanka, 1858–1912* (New Delhi, 1981), pp. 57–9, 62; Gailey, *Lost Imperialist*, pp. 202–8, 298; Cook, The Irish Raj, p. 519; M. L. Brillman, An uncommon under-secretary: Sir Anthony Macdonnell, India and Ireland, in T. Foley and M. O'Connor (eds), *Ireland and India: colonies, culture and empire* (Dublin, 2006), pp. 179, 182, 187.
177 Lyall, The Indian administration of Lord Dufferin, p. 32; C. Dewey, *Anglo-Indian Attitudes: the mind of the Indian Civil Service* (1993), pp. 5–8; T. Ballantyne, The sinews of empire: Ireland, India and the construction of British colonial knowledge, in T. MacDonagh (ed.), *Was Ireland a Colony? Economics, Politics and Culture in NineteenthCcentury Ireland* (Dublin, 2005), pp. 147–9, 151, 156–8; E. Sullivan, Liberalism and imperialism: John Stuart Mill's defence of the British Empire, *Journal of the History of Ideas*, 44 (1983), pp. 599, 606–11.
178 Cited in Lyall, *Life of Dufferin*, pp. 472–3; Gailey, *Lost Imperialist*, pp. 289–98.
179 Curzon, *British Government in India*, p. 246.
180 BL, India Office Papers, F130/29g, ff. 25, Dufferin to Salisbury, 17 Sept. 1888; Martin, The viceroyalty of Lord Dufferin, pp. 824–5.

Conclusion
Decline and fall

And so, you see, there can be no room for good intentions in one's work.[1]

Clouds across the evening skies

Dufferin returned to Clandeboye from his final appointment as ambassador to France in 1896 to a further shower of honours, speeches and dinners.[2] This was his final return, but the symbolism and ceremony of empire remained. He had addresses to receive and to make, club dinners to attend, the Cinque Ports to oversee, and he found himself elected as rector at both St Andrews and Edinburgh universities.[3] There were compensations; in contrast to his experience in 1847, he returned to an Ireland that was significantly more economically prosperous, even if the politics were not going in his direction. His vision for Clandeboye seemed at last to be coming to fruition, however: 'I am so delighted with everything at Clandeboye', he wrote to his daughter, 'I am at last beginning to reap the fruits of my life long labours, for my plantations and all my schemes are now producing the effect I originally contemplated.'[4] Of course, he also came back to an estate shorn of the bulk of its tenanted acres, long since sold off. In his years of retirement, he was finally able to enjoy Clandeboye, the house and demesne maturing into the vision he first laid out fifty years before. One of the advantages of his land sales was that he had fewer of the worries of estate management or the tangled and bitter politics of land to face. Work began on refreshing the house and its interiors, too: it was becoming the Clandeboye later memorialised so affectionately by Harold Nicolson in *Helen's Tower*.[5] The fine libraries, the house's museum and the relics on display everywhere of the places, cultures and scholarship Dufferin had engaged with across his life all came into focus in the late 1890s.[6] As he had hoped when leaving India early, he and his wife were able to manage the careers and marriages of their seven children, and the honourable retirement of a prestigious and popular imperial proconsul and diplomat seemed set. There were gathering clouds on the horizon, however; the stress and scandal of the collapse of the London and Globe Company inflicted a heavy punishment – both financial and reputational – on Dufferin.[7] In its later obituary, *Country Life* blamed national parsimony: the man who had empty honours heaped upon him was left, 'to live as best he might on a beggarly pension of £1,700 a year – less than we give a retired Common Law judge – with the additional encumbrance of an Irish estate'.[8] Far worse was to come with the death of their eldest son Archie, Lord Ava, in South Africa while on active service fighting the Boers. With his growing deafness and increasing ill-health, after a broadly sunny life and career, Dufferin's last two years were sadly overshadowed.[9]

In these years of retirement, Dufferin had many opportunities to reflect, publicly and privately, on his life and experiences as an Irish landlord, and as colonial governor and diplomat. He and Lady Hariot had created and equipped an ideal imperial family, and he was ready to assist his children and relations into imperial positions, securing the next generation. Dufferin's experience of immersion in Irish questions and then pivoting to the empire was one his son-in-law Lord Ronald Munro Ferguson could well understand, coming from minor Scottish gentry stock but hoping to make his name in the empire. Of course, both Dufferin and Lord Ronald were unaware that they were moving from one declining concern – landownership – to another: empire. Dufferin in retirement glossed over any concerns, writing to Lord Ronald that, 'the life of a Colonial Governor is a very agreeable one. The climates are almost always excellent, the work is extremely easy, the position very honourable and the interest attaching to it very great.'[10] His diagnosis of the work as 'easy' is interesting when we consider that he had, in fact, generally worked very hard. His sons also required direction and placement, with Terence and Basil both going into diplomatic and official service. Dufferin was pleased overall, as an opening to what might hopefully be, 'an interesting and distinguished career', for his boys, for which he certainly felt he had been, 'well rewarded'.[11] He steadfastly resisted the notion that he had followed any specific philosophy or system of governance during his own career, regarding himself as a pragmatist. He did not offer the kind of ideological vision that later proconsuls such as George Curzon or Alfred Milner stressed; British imperial rule for men of his generation emphasised character over ideology. It was this point that Dufferin chose to dwell on when giving some of his final speeches and addresses, including those to the next generation; the students of St Andrews and Edinburgh.[12] His rectorial address in Edinburgh was, in fact, his last public appearance: he had already been seriously unwell but insisted on travelling from Clandeboye to give his speech with Lady Dufferin in support. He was able to travel home but died a few weeks later surrounded by his family at Clandeboye, where he was buried in the Campo Santo, the family plot in the demesne.[13]

Rule by the best?

Aristocratic and landed men evolved a particular governing mentality that drew on the history of their class, and emphasised good character and will to rule.[14] It was both an ornamental and pragmatic style of governance, relatively free from ideology or even party politics. It was a type of rule that could not be learned, but could only be born into, bolstered by the right kind of education and socialisation. It was a serious business and was strictly policed; its heart lay in the London metropole, but it found its most explicit expression in the empire, including Ireland.[15] After 1880, its most serious threat was aristocratic and landed decline, a trend most pronounced in Ireland, as Dufferin found.[16] These pressures led to a greater openness about how the aristocratic classes viewed their rights and responsibilities in a period of tumult and existential challenge. For them, class was less a diagnostic category and more of an outlook, tinged with romanticism but driven by a hard-headed pragmatism and belief in their right to rule.

For Dufferin, this was complicated by his Irishness: although undoubtedly elite and aristocratic, the anguished nature of the Irish questions he faced throughout his life destabilised his aristocratic identity in the British context, pushing him into the liminal position of both insider and outsider among elite circles.[17] This led to life-long anxiety about reputation and he developed a particular stance on his own identity; pride in both his Scottish Blackwood and Irish Sheridan forebears; an insistence that he was Irish, not Anglo-Irish; and increasing frustration towards those who rejected his claim to that Irishness as the parameters hardened in the later nineteenth century.[18] From the point of his entry into Westminster he defended his class, consistently arguing that Ireland's problems were not solely due to the failure of its landed classes. He attempted to put this into practice by instituting major improvements on his estate and then going on to become a distinguished colonial governor and diplomat, showing by example what rule by the best should be. Critically, he was demonstrating that the Irish landed elite were as much part of that world as their British peers.[19]

Aristocracy was what defined Dufferin, and what defined aristocracy was land.[20] Property was much more than debates over contract, landlord–tenant relations or improvement: it was at the heart of how the aristocratic classes saw themselves both retrospectively into the distant past and prospectively down future generations.[21] The delicious irony of Dufferin's life is that although land defined aristocratic power, he struggled throughout his life with the disadvantage of Irish land and then the eventual sale of much of it. In many ways, he demonstrates the point that aristocrats were no longer born to rule because the world was increasingly a place where landownership mattered less and less. His entanglement with the London Globe and Finance Company – although disastrous for him and its shareholders – actually pointed to the future more accurately than endless debates over property. It was not land but finance that would constitute the future security of Britain and Ireland's social elites. Even where conscientious landowners such as Dufferin poured their efforts into setting a good example on their estates – attempting to govern well – it was not enough. Dufferin sank tens of thousands of pounds into improvements on his estates in the 1840s and 1850s, only to be forced to sell most of them off in the face of unserviceable levels of debt and a declining income. The economic fate of his tenantry was better than on many Irish estates throughout the nineteenth century, but this was no longer enough for them or for a wider society changing under Dufferin's feet. He and his peers were unable to maintain their traditional status, or to offer enough benefit for their tenants, and this was the root of their decline and fall as a group. These changes were also expressed in the various iterations of legislative land reform and state intervention in Ireland faced by Dufferin across his lifetime, and explains why passions ran so high on the issue. In his view, Ireland's problems could only be solved by emigration and modern agriculture married to industrial development and diversification; historicist land reform, based on shaky – at best – interpretations of Ireland's turbulent past was anathema to him.[22] But a bigger principle still was at stake: state intervention into private property represented a fundamental attack on aristocratic understandings of their duties and privileges.

But land was not the only arena for aristocrats of Dufferin's generation. Their will to rule was increasingly exercised across the British empire, into which they infused a particular kind of aristocratic ethos.[23] There were two aspects to this aristocratic spirit: first, the maintenance of visual displays of rank and power, the pomp and circumstance of imperial rule.[24] The soirees, levees, drawing rooms and drums, the uniforms, honours and addresses that soaked up so much time and effort was not hollow display; it was rich in the meaning and symbolism of aristocratic rule by the best.[25] This was a philosophy of rule that emphasised the right of those aristocratic men, born into the best families, educated at the right institutions, and experienced in the management of land and people on their estates, to rule those 'backward' peoples and societies – from Ireland to India, Egypt to Syria – who were not yet fit to govern themselves.[26] This was a long-standing expectation of the aristocracy in Ireland ('England's garrison'), but one that came under enormous challenge.[27] The rise of a new urban and industrial society all put pressure on the domestic power of the landed elite and was translated into the imperial context.[28] Dufferin carried these concerns across the empire; in Canada, for example, where owner-occupancy was the norm, his attentions focused on where there were tenants and landlords, the unusual case of Prince Edward Island. He could not let the aristocratic system go and tried to uphold it wherever he went, even though his own experiences demonstrated that it was not working. He was, by the expectations of the time, excellent at carrying out his duties, but the imperial and aristocratic systems he believed in were flawed and, although at their height during his lifetime, within a few years of his death would become horribly exposed. Although born to rule, Dufferin and his peers were really imperial managers, and managing increasingly less well. Dufferin observed working self-government in Canada, and saw the development of democratic ideas and governing experience in India: the writing was on the wall.

The story of the family and the Clandeboye estate after his death follows a pattern familiar to many landed families in twentieth-century Ireland and Britain. The estate and title were inherited by Dufferin's second son, Lord

Terence, in 1902, with significantly reduced assets in land or cash to support the operation of family, house and estate. Worse was to come with the Great War: Lord Basil was killed in action in 1917 and Terence died the following year of pneumonia. Lord Frederick (Freddie) inherited at a period widely regarded as one of the nadirs in the fortunes of the aristocracy in Europe. Something like one-quarter of the land in England changed hands in the immediate post-World War I years, and the situation was worse in Ireland, where war, partition, radical land legislation and the direct targeting of Big Houses and their families served as a sombre warning to those more fortunate families in Ulster.[29] Lord Freddie faced an even more dire financial situation than his brother, brutally captured for posterity in Lady Caroline Blackwood's novel *Great Granny Webster*, with its descriptions of the once grand house in a state of chronic decline, the inhabitants wearing wellingtons indoors and the persistent Irish rain leaking into the house, soaking the libraries and imperial collections.[30] After his early death in an aeroplane accident in 1930, Freddie was succeeded by his son, Lord Basil (or Ava to his friends), the fourth marquis in as many decades. He, too, would die young, aged just 40, fighting the Japanese outside Ava in Burma, leading to another early inheritance by his son Sheridan, the 5th Marquis of Dufferin and Ava. As for many landed families, the immediate wake of World War II was a very difficult period both politically and financially. The Dufferins were assisted through two fortunate marriages, both into the Guinness banking and brewing family. Lord Basil left his widow, Lady Maureen Guinness, with three children and she would later apply some of her wealth in clearing Clandeboye's debts. Her son, the 5th Marquis, would marry another Guinness, Lindy, Lady Dufferin, and together they restored the house, the demesne and the collections, repurposing them to align with new values, away from the shadow of colonialism and deference that the memory of the 1st Marquis cast over later generations of his family.[31]

Dufferin's experience clearly captures the contradictions faced by his class: his upbringing, education and personality brought many riches – a fine landed estate, a serious political engagement, and a distinguished imperial and diplomatic career. But he also inherited many difficulties and lived through turbulent times: his estates delivered complex political and financial difficulties as the landlord–tenant relationship came under pressure, and the economy stagnated and atrophied.[32] He sold large parcels of land to ensure the financial survival of his family, and a significant aspect of his motivation in taking up imperial and diplomatic service was the opportunity to support a suitable style of living while carrying out the traditional leadership expected of the aristocracy. Dufferin's life and career certainly encapsulated decline – certainly of acres and wealth – but also robust resistance: of diversification of thinking about the traditional role played by his class and its context. Dufferin's life was one of struggle and decline, but also of purpose, activity and happiness.[33] He died before seeing the real beginning of the end of either his class or the empire, and was able to 'suck his paws in peace' at Clandeboye, cultivating the legacy that would long outlive him and enjoying the company of his wife and children, that most imperial of families.

Notes

1 Dufferin to Rudyard Kipling, 1891 cited in R. Kipling, *Something of Myself and other Autobiographical Writings* (ed.), T. Pinney (Cambridge, 1990), pp. 56–7; L. D. Wurgraft, *The Imperial Imagination: magic and myth in Kipling's India* (Middleton, 1983), pp. 2–14; C. Allen, *Kipling Sahib* (London, 2007), pp. 175–80; A. Gailey, *The Lost Imperialist: Lord Dufferin, memory and mythmaking in an age of celebrity* (London, 2015), pp. 288–9.
2 H. Nicolson, *Helen's Tower* (London, 1937), pp. 245, 255.
3 A. C. Lyall, *The Life of the Marquis of Dufferin and Ava* (London, 1905), pp. 548–53; Gailey, *Lost Imperialist*, pp. 304–8.
4 Clandeboye house, Dufferin to Lady Helen, 25 Sept. 1894.
5 Nicolson, *Helen's Tower*, see especially pp. 75–8.
6 Nicolson, *Helen's Tower*, pp. 75, 97.
7 D. Kynaston, *The City of London, vol. II: The Golden Years, 1890–1914* (London, 1995), pp. 138–40, 173–4, 180–1, 217–18; Gailey, *Lost Imperialist*, pp. 335–9.
8 *Country Life*, 22 February 1902, obituary of Lord Dufferin.
9 Nicolson, *Helen's Tower*, pp. 264–6; Gailey, *Lost Imperialist*, p. 335; Lyall, *Life of Dufferin*, p. 554.
10 Clandeboye house, Dufferin to Lord Ronald, 4 Aug. 1893.
11 Clandeboye house, Dufferin to Lord Basil, 1 Jun. 1900.
12 P. J. Cain, Character and imperialism: the British financial administration of Egypt, 1878–1914, *Journal of Imperial and Commonwealth History*, 34:2 (2006), pp. 177–9; *Address delivered at St Andrews University April 6, 1891 by the Marquess of Dufferin and Ava, Lord Rector* (Edinburgh, 1891); Gailey, *Lost Imperialist*, p. 343; University of Edinburgh, *Address by the Marquess of Dufferin and Ava (Lord Rector)* (Edinburgh, 1901).
13 Lyall, *Life of Dufferin*, pp. 559–61; Gailey, *Lost Imperialist*, p. 354.
14 C. Dewey, *Anglo-Indian Attitudes: the mind of the Indian Civil Service* (London, 1993), pp. 3–6; B. Porter, *The Absent-Minded Imperialists: empire, society and culture in Britain* (Oxford, 2004), pp. 228–9.
15 M. Bence-Jones, *The Viceroys of India* (New York, 1982), pp. 142, 148; D. Cannadine, *Aspects of Aristocracy: grandeur and decline in modern Britain* (New Haven, 1994), pp. 77–8; C. C. Eldridge, *England's Mission: the imperial idea in the age of Gladstone and Disraeli* (London, 1973), pp. 53–6, 86; S. Howe, *Ireland and Empire: colonial legacies in Irish history and culture* (Oxford, 2002), pp. 65–8, 72–3.
16 M. Bence-Jones, *Twilight of the Ascendancy* (London, 1987), pp. 65, 71.
17 P. Gray, Introduction: Irishness and Britishness, in P. Gray (ed.), *Victoria's Ireland? Irishness and Britishness, 1837–1901* (Dublin, 2004), pp. 9–13; Gailey, *Lost Imperialist*, p. 350; F. Campbell, *The Irish Establishment 1879–1914* (Oxford, 2009), pp. 7–17.
18 S. B. Cook, The Irish Raj: social origins and careers of Irishmen in the Indian Civil Service, 1855–1914, *Journal of Social History*, 20:3 (1987), pp. 507–8, 522.
19 L. P. Curtis, Landlord responses to the Irish Land War, 1879–1987, *Eire–Ireland*, Fall–Winter (2003); O. MacDonagh, *States of Mind: a study of Anglo-Irish conflict 1780–1980* (London, 1983), pp. 34–8, 49; E. Heggs, Whig politics and the 3rd Duke of Leinster (1791–1874), in P. Cosgrove, T. Dooley and K. Mullaney-Dignam (eds), *Aspects of Irish Aristocratic Life* (Dublin, 2014), pp. 169, 171–5; J. Loughlin, *Gladstone, Home Rule and the Ulster Question, 1882–93* (Dublin, 1986), pp. 172, 251–5.

20 T. Dooley, Landlords and the land question, 1879–1909, in C. King (ed.), *Famine, Land and Culture in Ireland* (Dublin, 2001), pp. 116–22, 124–7; P. Readman, *Land and Nation in England: patriotism, national identity and the politics of land, 1880–1914* (Woodbridge, 2008), pp. 137–40; A. Jackson, *Colonel Edward Saunderson: land and loyalty in Victorian Ireland* (Oxford, 1995), pp. 181–3.
21 M. Bentley, *Lord Salisbury's World: Conservative environments in late-Victorian Britain* (Cambridge, 2001), pp. 94–100.
22 C. Dewey, Celtic agrarian legislation and the Celtic revival: historicist implications of Gladstone's Irish and Scottish Land Acts, *Past and Present*, lxiv (1974); J. W. Mason, The Duke of Argyll and the land question in late nineteenth century Britain, *Victorian Studies*, 21 (1978); Gailey, *Lost Imperialist*, pp. 161–3; K. T. Hoppen, *Governing Hibernia: British politicians and Ireland 1800–1921* (Oxford, 2016), pp. 179–83, 193.
23 A. Kirk-Greene, *Britain's Imperial Administrators, 1858–1966* (London, 2000), pp. 1–2, 9, 237; U. S. Mehta, *Liberalism and Empire: a study in nineteenth century British Liberal thought* (Chicago, 1999), pp. 1–7, 11, 29–30; P. J. Cain and A. G. Hopkins, *British Imperialism, I: Innovation and Expansion* (London, 1993), pp. 330–2; D. Fitzpatrick, Ireland and the empire, in A. Porter (ed.), *Oxford History of the British Empire: vol. III, The Nineteenth Century* (Oxford, 1999), pp. 494–9; C. A. Bayly, *The Birth of the Modern World, 1780–1914: global connections and comparisons* (Oxford, 2004), pp. 295–9.
24 D. Cannadine, *Ornamentalism: how the British saw their empire* (London, 2001), pp. 21–2, 95; Z. Laidlaw, Richard Bourke: Irish liberalism tempered by empire, in D. Lambert and A. Lester (eds), *Colonial Lives Across the British Empire* (Cambridge, 2006), pp. 113–16, 143–4.
25 G. Bolton, The idea of a colonial gentry, *Historical Studies*, 13 (1968), pp. 308–16.
26 T. R. Metcalfe, *Forging the Raj: essay on British India in the heyday of empire* (Oxford, 2005), pp. 41–4; Bentley, *Lord Salisbury's World*, pp. 221–7.
27 J. C. Beckett, *The Anglo-Irish Tradition* (Belfast, 1976), pp. 85–96; J. A. Mangan, *Making Imperial Mentalities: socialisation and British imperialism* (Manchester, 1990), pp. 1–3.
28 A. Taylor, *Lords of Misrule: hostility to aristocracy in late nineteenth and early twentieth century Britain* (Basingstoke, 2004), pp. 1–15; J. Ridden, Making good citizens: national identity, religion and liberalism among the Irish elite, c. 1800–1850, unpublished PhD thesis (King's College London, 1998), pp. 7–9, 12–13, 15–18.
29 D. Cannadine, *The Decline and Fall of the British Aristocracy* (London, 1990), pp. 1–23.
30 Gailey, *Lost Imperialist*, pp. 354–8; C. Blackwood, *Great Granny Webster* (London, 1977), especially pp. 66–70.
31 Gailey, *Lost Imperialist*, pp. 354–8.
32 L. P. Curtis, The Anglo-Irish predicament, *Twentieth Century Studies*, 4 (1970), pp. 37–42, 61.
33 Nicolson, *Helen's Tower*, p. 276; Gailey, *Lost Imperialist*, pp. 351–3.

General bibliography and sources

Archival and primary sources – an introduction

A major benefit of working on the lives, estates and careers of the landed and aristocratic classes is the extent to which they were both publicly and privately documented. Dufferin is no exception to this, and an understanding of the opportunities and restrictions of the archival record underpinning this study, and how that has affected the focus of this book, is essential.[1] Like many aristocratic families, the Blackwoods generated a very extensive archive related to their landed estates, through which is woven their personal and family papers. One of the interesting aspects of working on landed elites are the ways in which the personal is intertwined with the more professional aspects of running an estate with diverse economic, social and political interests. For the Blackwoods, this included the traditional economic landscape of rented farms and smallholdings, tree plantations, gardens and the demesne, home farm management, small-scale commercial mining, buildings and other improvements, including the Big House, a railway, the development of the seaside town of Helen's Bay, the financial management of liquid assets combined with the personal diaries, correspondences between family members, photographs, paintings, other mementoes and keepsakes.

The archive spans over four hundred years, although by far the physical majority of the archive was generated in the nineteenth and early twentieth centuries, as is usual for landed estates. The professionalisation of estate management, combined in Ireland with the necessity of dealing with new state agencies such as the Encumbered Estates Court, as well as Dufferin's personal requirement to leave the day-to-day management of his estates in the hands of his agents while he was overseas, resulted in an enormous paper archive detailing almost every aspect of life on the land and well beyond it.[2] The archive also offers the reader an additional temporal dimension; that is, either Dufferin or his agents reflecting widely back in time and into the future when assessing a situation or making a decision. Dufferin saw his estates not simply as a financial, political and social platform, but as the defining aspect of his identity. That he had inherited the estate on trust from his father, grandfather and so on back through the generations, and that it was a heavy burden in terms of keeping it intact for future generations, was an explicit and defining element of his existence. Understanding this temporal element of the archive illuminates critical themes explored in this book.

The majority of the Dufferin and Ava archive is deposited at the Public Record Office of Northern Ireland, Belfast [PRONI].[3] The centre of gravity of the archive is the 1st Marquess, subject of this book, but it covers much more besides, including: the papers of Lady Hariot, his wife, his seven children and his heirs, the 2nd, 3rd and 4th Marquesses, his mother and other Blackwood relations, as well as older material relating to the development of the estate, its legal foundations, mapping and charters. The elements relating to the 1st Marquess are a fascinating if confusing blend of the official and public, the personal and private. Aside from the public business of the estate and financial records, we find his official and professional archive: self-contained runs of material relating to his appointments in Syria, Canada, India, and his diplomatic postings in Russia, Turkey, France and Italy. Adjacent to these is the personal and private correspondence carried on throughout his life with his family and friends, drafts and copies of his various publications, and his personal diaries. One of the aims of this study has been to reintegrate the personal with the official, the private with the professional, as Dufferin would himself have viewed it: archival procedures having separated these out, they now need to be put back together again to provide the basis for a holistic study of the aristocratic mindset and will to rule that is the subject of this book.

Due to Dufferin's wide-ranging official career, other archival repositories were critical to this study. When Dufferin finished a post, he would receive a full set of his papers and, in addition, they were also archived by the relevant government department or office; so, The National Archives is the repository for material on Dufferin's postings to Syria in 1860, Canada in 1872, Russia in 1879, Turkey in 1881, Italy in 1888 and France in 1892, spread across the archives of the Foreign Office, Colonial Office and War Office.[4] For his term as viceroy of India, the British Library India Office Papers hold the official record of his activities, an almost embarrassingly voluminous archive, illustrating the truth of Karl Marx's verdict on the nineteenth-century British Raj as 'one immense writing machine'.[5] Also in the India Office Papers are the collections of many of Dufferin's colleagues in India, including his first biographer Sir Alfred Lyall, the India Office tsar Arthur Godley, Lord Kilbracken, his generals and military subordinates in Burma and many more besides.[6] Before Dufferin embarked on his overseas career, he was a leading figure in Westminster and Liberal politics, leaving a trail of material in Hansard and other parliamentary papers, including his chairmanship of and evidence given to a number of royal commissions and enquiries on Irish matters.[7] Much of this was reported in the newspapers, in which he was also extensively published. In nearly all of these cases, the published columns were carefully cut out and compiled into scrapbooks, arranged next to his independently published pamphlets, now cared for by

PRONI. The emphasis of this material is on Ireland, Canada and India, and on the major political issues of the day, especially land reform and emigration. These 'mini-archives' were preserved and structured at the point of their creation, which indicates to the historian the importance with which it was viewed by Dufferin. One of the largest and best catalogued is Dufferin's personal correspondence, covering hundreds of individuals who corresponded with him over his lifetime. 'Personal' is something of a misnomer; much of the material is personal in nature but, in the way of the period, his friends were very often highly placed politicians, statesmen, fellow aristocrats, diplomats and imperial officials, and they commented freely on the politics of the day as well as the health of their children, or the latest gossip. This is both a rich and a grey area for the historian, allowing an examination of the ways in which the official and unofficial intertwined, the latter both reinforcing and contradicting the former. Some of this material is of direct interest to the official perspective; correspondence with figures such as William Gladstone, and Lords Salisbury, Kimberley and Argyll, for instance.[8] The Argyll correspondence is of particular interest in this regard; they were political allies and best friends, and their archive, spanning the late 1840s to the turn of the twentieth century, is one of the great political and personal exchanges of the period.[9]

Notes

1 Literature drawn on to frame this discussion includes: L. Stanley, The epistolarium: on theorising letters and correspondences, *Auto/Biography*, 12 (2004), p. 202–12; A. L. Stoler, *Along the Archival Grain: Epistemic Anxieties and Colonial Common Sense* (New Haven, 2008), pp. 1–15; 64–6; O. Gust, The perilous territory of not belonging: exile and empire in Sir James Mackintosh's letters from early nineteenth century Bombay, *History Workshop Journal*, 86 (2018), pp. 1–17.
2 For an overview, see L. A. Rees, C. Reilly and A. Tindley (eds), *The Land Agent, 1700–1920* (Edinburgh, 2018).
3 A full summary of the archive can be found at: https://apps.proni.gov.uk/eCatNI_IE/ResultDetails.aspx [accessed 20 Nov. 2019].
4 The National Archives, Kew: Foreign Office [FO], FO 27, FO 65, FO 84, FO 141, FO 181, FO 78, for the collections relevant to Dufferin.
5 K. Marx, The government of India, *New York Daily Tribune*, 20 July 1853; British Library, India Office Papers, Mss Eur. F130, Papers of Lord Dufferin as Viceroy.
6 Including: British Library, Papers of Lord Avebury, Add MS 49668, Vol. XXXI; British Library, Cross Papers Add MS 51269, Vol. VII (ff. 260) correspondence with Lord Dufferin; British Library, India Office Papers, Lord Curzon as Viceroy (1898–1905), Mss Eur F111/219: Letters received while viceroy; British Library, India Office Papers, Papers of Sir Henry Durand, Mss Eur D727; British Library, India Office Papers, Papers of Sir Mountstuart Elphinstone Grant Duff, Mss Eur F234; British Library, India Office Papers, Kilbracken Papers, Mss Eur F102; British Library, India Office Papers, Mss Eur F132, Papers of Sir Alfred Lyall; British Library, India Office Papers, Mss Eur F108, Papers of Field Marshall Sir George White; British Library, India Office Papers, Papers of Col. Sir Edward Sladen, Mss Eur E290.

212 *General bibliography and sources*

7 For instance: British Library, Carnarvon Papers, Add MS 60797, Vol. XLI (ff.1–141, 142–246) Correspondence about and with Lord Dufferin; British Library, Gladstone Papers Add MS 44151, Vol. LXVI (ff.304) correspondence with Lord Dufferin; Hatfield House, Papers of the 3rd Marquess of Salisbury, Dufferin correspondence, ff. 1–41, 1879–1889.
8 Bodleian Library, Kimberley Papers, MSS Eng C., 4086–4093; British Library, Gladstone Papers, Add MS 44151, Vol. LXVI (ff.304) Correspondence with Lord Dufferin; Hatfield House, Papers of Lord Salisbury, 3rd Marquess.
9 PRONI, D1071, H/B/C/95/1-195.

Bibliography

Archival sources

Public Record Office of Northern Ireland, Belfast
 D1071, Dufferin and Ava Papers.
The British Library, London
  British Library, Papers of Lord Avebury, Add MS 49668, Vol. XXXI.
  British Library, Papers of Lord Carnarvon, Add MS 60797, Vol. XLI, correspondence about and with Frederick Hamilton Temple Blackwood, Lord Dufferin.
  British Library, Papers of Lord Cross, Add MS 51269, Vol. VII (ff. 260) correspondence with Frederick Temple Blackwood, Lord Dufferin.
  British Library, Papers of William Ewart Gladstone, Add MS 44151, Vol. LXVI, correspondence with Frederick Temple Hamilton Blackwood, Lord Dufferin.
  India Office Papers, Papers of Col. Sir Edward Sladen, Mss Eur E290.
  India Office Papers, Papers of Field Marshall Sir George White, Mss Eur F108.
  India Office Papers, Papers of Lord Curzon as Viceroy, Mss Eur F111.
  India Office Papers, Papers of Lord Dufferin as Viceroy, Mss Eur F130.
  India Office Papers, Papers of Sir Alfred Lyall, Mss Eur F132.
  India Office Papers, Papers of Sir Arthur Godley, 1st Baron Kilbracken, Mss Eur F102.
  India Office Papers, Papers of Sir Henry Durand, Mss Eur D727.
  India Office Papers, Papers of Sir Mountstuart Elphinstone Grant Duff, Mss Eur F234.

The National Archives, London
 Foreign Office Papers [FO]:

  FO 27, FO 65, FO 84, FO 141, FO 181, FO 78.

The Bodleian Library, Oxford

  Kimberley Papers, MSS Eng C., 4086–4093.

Inveraray Castle, Argyll

   Papers of the 8th and 9th Dukes of Argyll.

Hatfield House, Hertfordshire

   Papers of Lord Salisbury, 3rd Marquess.

Printed primary sources

Address by the Marquess of Dufferin and Ava (Lord Rector), at the University of Edinburgh (Edinburgh, 1901).
Address delivered at St Andrews University April 6, 1891 by the Marquess of Dufferin and Ava, Lord Rector (Edinburgh, 1891).
Argyll, 8th Duke of, India under Lord Canning, *Edinburgh Review*, 240 (1863).
Argyll, 8th Duke of, India under Lord Dalhousie, *Edinburgh Review*, 239 (1863).
Argyll, 8th Duke of, Agricultural Holdings Act of 1875, *Contemporary Review*, 27 (1876).
Argyll, 8th Duke of, New Irish Land Bill, *Nineteenth Century*, 9 (1881).
Argyll, 8th Duke of, *Crofts and Farms in the Hebrides: Being an Account of the Management of an Island Estate for 130 Years* (Edinburgh, 1883).
Argyll, 8th Duke of, A corrected picture of the Highlands, *Nineteenth Century*, 16 (1884).
Argyll, 8th Duke of, Land Reformers, *Contemporary Review*, 48 (1885).
Argyll, 8th Duke of, A model land law: a reply to Arthur Williams MP, *Fortnightly Review*, 41 (1887).
Argyll, 8th Duke of, *Irish Nationalism: An Appeal to History* (London, 1893).
Argyll, 8th Duke of, *Autobiography and Memoirs*, 3 vols (London, 1906).
Baillie, Sir A., Cazalet, Captain V., Dufferin et al., *India from a Back Bench* (London, 1934).
Bence-Jones, W., *The Life's Work in Ireland of a Landlord Who Tried to Do His Duty* (London, 1880).
Bernard, Sir C. (ed.), *George Campbell, Memoirs of my Indian Career* (London, 1893).
Black, C. E. D., *The Marquess of Dufferin and Ava* (London, 1903).
Blunt, W. S., *The Secret History of the English Occupation of Egypt* (London, 1907).
Bosworth Smith, R., *Life of John Lawrence* (London, 1883).
Browne, E. C., *The Coming of the Great Queen: A Narrative of the Acquisition of Burma* (London, 1888).
Caird, J., *The Irish Land Question* (London, 1869).
Campbell, G., *The Irish Land* (London, 1869).
Campbell, G., The tenure of land in India, in *Systems of Land Tenure in Various Countries: A Series of Essays Published under the Sanction of the Cobden Club* (London, 1870).
Campbell, G., Land legislation for Ireland, *Fortnightly Review*, 19 (1881).
Chamberlain, J., *Home Rule and the Irish Question: A Collection of Speeches Delivered between 1881 and 1887* (London, 1887).
Childers, E. S. E., *The Life and Correspondence of the Right Hon. Hugh C. E. Childers, 1827–1872* (London, 1901).

Colvin, A., *The Making of Modern Egypt* (New York, 1906).
Crothswaite, C. E., *The Pacification of Burma* (London, 1912).
Curzon, G., *British Government in India: The Story of the Viceroys and Government Houses*, 2 vols (London, 1925).
Davitt, M., *Speech delivered by Michael Davitt in Defence of the Land League* (London, 1890).
Davitt, M., *The Fall of Feudalism in Ireland* (London, 1904).
De Kiewiet, C. W. and Underhill, F. H. (eds), *Dufferin–Carnarvon Correspondence, 1874–1878* (Toronto, 1955).
Dent, J. C., *The Last Forty Years: Canada since the Union of 1841*, 2 vols (Toronto, 1881).
Dufferin, Marchioness of, *Our Viceregal Life in India: Selections from my Journal, 1884–88* (London, 1890).
Dufferin, Marchioness of, *My Canadian Journal 1872–78* (London, 1891).
Dufferin, Marquess of, *Contributions to an Inquiry into the State of Ireland* (London, 1866).
Dufferin, Marquess of, *Mr Mill's Plan for the Pacification of Ireland Examined* (London, 1868).
Dufferin, Marquess of, *Irish Emigration and the Tenure of Land in Ireland* (Dublin, 1870).
Dufferin, Marquess of, *The Case of the Irish Tenant, as Stated Sixteen Years Ago by the Rt. Hon. Lord Dufferin, in a speech delivered to the House of Lords, February 28, 1854* (London, 1870).
Dufferin, Marquess of, *Lord Dufferin in Manitoba: Testimony of the Settler Shipment of Manitoban Wheat to Europe* (Liverpool, 1878).
Dufferin, Marquess of, *Speeches of the Earl of Dufferin*, Ed. H. Milton (Toronto, 1878).
Dufferin, Marquess of, *Helen's Tower* (London, 1884).
Dufferin, Marquess of, *Songs, Poems and Verses by Helen, Lady Dufferin (Countess of Gifford)* (London, 1894).
Dufferin, Marquess of and the Hon. G. F. Boyle, *Narrative of a Journey from Oxford to Skibbereen during the Year of the Irish Famine* (Oxford, 1847).
Durand, H. M., *Life of Sir Alfred Lyall* (London, 1913).
Durand, H. M., *Life of Field Marshall Sir George White, V.C.*, vol. 1 (Edinburgh, 1915).
Fitzgibbon, G., *The Land Difficulty of Ireland with an Effort to Solve It* (London, 1869).
Gladstone, W. E., Notes and queries on the Irish Demand, *Nineteenth Century*, 21 (1887).
Godley, A., *Reminiscences* (London, 1931).
Gower, Lord Ronald, *My Reminiscences* (London, 1883).
Gray, H. B., *Public Schools and Empire* (London, 1913).
Hamilton, Lord George, *Parliamentary Reminiscences and Reflections*, 2 vols, 1868–1885; 1886–1906 (London, 1917, 1922).
Hardinge, Sir A., *The Life of Henry Howard Molyneux Herbert, Fourth Earl of Carnarvon, 1831–1890*, 3 vols (Oxford, 1925).
Hawkins, A. and Powell, J. (eds), *The Journal of John Wodehouse, First Earl of Kimberley for 1862–1902* (London, 1997).
Hunter, W., *A Life of the Earl of Mayo, Fourth Viceroy of India* (London, 1876).
Kipling, R., *Something of Myself: For my Friends Known and Unknown* (London, 1937).

Lang, A., *Life, Letters and Diaries of Sir Stafford Northcote, First Earl of Iddlesleigh* (London, 1891).
Leggo, W., *The History of the Administration of the Rt. Hon Frederick Temple, Earl of Dufferin, late Governor General of Canada* (Montreal, 1878).
Lethbridge, E., *The Mischief Threatened by the Bengal Tenancy Bill: the Bengal Tenancy Bill: Report of Proceedings of a meeting held at St James's Hall, 25 June 1884* (London, 1884).
Lorne, Marquis of, *Memories of Canada and Scotland: Speeches and Verses* (London, 1884).
Lyall, A. C., The Conquest of Burma, *Edinburgh Review*, 165 (1887).
Lyall, A. C., The Indian administration of Lord Dufferin, *Edinburgh Review*, 167 (1889).
Lyall, A. C., *The Life of the Marquis of Dufferin and Ava* (London, 1905).
Mackenzie, A., Ireland and the Irish Land Act from the Highland point of view, *Celtic Magazine*, 10 (1884–5).
MacKnight, T., *Ulster as It Is: Or Thirty Years' Experience as an Irish Editor* (London, 1896).
MacNutt, W. S., *Days of Lorne: Impressions of a Governor-General* (Fredericton, 1955).
Marx, K., Irish tenant right, in J. Ledbetter (ed.), *Dispatches for the New York Tribune: Selected Journalism of Karl Marx* (London, 2007).
Marx, K. and Engels, F., *Ireland and the Irish Question* (this edn. Moscow, 1972).
Matthew, H. C. G., *The Gladstone Diaries* (Oxford, 1978).
Matthew, H. C. G., *Gladstone, 1809–1898* (Oxford, 1999).
Mill, J. S., *England and Ireland* (London, 1868).
Milner, A., *England in Egypt* (London, 1892).
Montgomery, J. F., *An Experiment in Communism and Its Results: A Letter to the Right Honourable the Earl of Carnarvon, Secretary of State for the Colonies, on the Prince Edward Island Land Commission* (Charlottetown, 1875).
Napier, Lord Francis, The Highland crofters: a vindication of the report of the Crofters Commission, *Nineteenth Century*, 17 (1885).
Nicolson, H. G., *Helen's Tower* (London, 1937).
O'Dwyer, M., *India as I Knew It, 1885–1925* (London, 1925).
Pope, J., *Memoirs of the Rt Hon Sir John Alexander Macdonald*, 2 vols (Ottawa, 1894).
Ramm, A. (ed.), *The Political Correspondence of Mr Gladstone and Lord Granville 1876–1886, Vol. II: 1883–1886* (Oxford, 1962).
Russell, W. T., *Ireland and the Empire: A Review* (London, 1901).
St John, F. E. M., *The Sea of Mountains: An Account of Lord Dufferin's Tour through British Columbia in 1876*, 2 vols (London, 1877).
Stephen, L., *The Life of James Fitzjames Stephen* (London, 1895).
Stewart, G., *Canada under the Administration of the Earl of Dufferin* (Toronto, 1878).
Todd, A., *Parliamentary Government in the British Colonies* (London, 1894).
Trench, G. F., *Are the Landlords Worth Preserving? Or, Forty Years' Management of an Irish Estate* (London and Dublin, 1881).
Wallace, D. M., India under the Marquis of Dufferin, *Edinburgh Review*, 169 (1889).
Wallace, D. M. (ed.), *Speeches delivered in India, 1884–1888, by the Marquis of Dufferin and Ava* (London, 1890).
Young, J., *Public Men and Public Life in Canada*, 2 vols. (Toronto, 1912).

Secondary sources

Aalen, F. H. A., Constructive unionism and the shaping of rural Ireland, c. 1880–1921, *Rural History*, 4:2 (1993).

Ali, I., *The Punjab under Imperialism, 1885–1947* (Princeton, 1988).

Allen, C., *Kipling Sahib* (London, 2007).

Alston, R., Dialogues in imperialism: Rome, Britain and India, in E. Hall and P. Vasunia (eds), *India, Greece and Rome, 1757–2007* (London, 2010).

Ansell, R., Educational travel in Protestant families from post-Restoration Ireland, *Historical Journal*, 58:4 (2015).

Atkins, R. A., The Conservatives and Egypt, 1875–80, *Journal of Imperial and Commonwealth History*, 2:2 (1974).

Ballantyne, T., The sinews of empire: Ireland, India and the construction of British colonial knowledge, in MacDonagh, T. (ed.), *Was Ireland a Colony? Economics, Politics and Culture in Nineteenth Century Ireland* (Dublin, 2005).

Ballhatchet, K., *Caste, Class and Catholicism in India, 1789–1914* (London, 1998).

Barczewski, S., Country houses and the distinctiveness of the Irish imperial experience, in McMahon, T. G. (ed.), *Ireland in an Imperial World* (Cambridge, 2017).

Barr, C., Imperium in imperio: Irish episcopal imperialism in the nineteenth century, *English Historical Review*, 502 (2008).

Bayly, C. A., *The Raj: India and the British 1600–1947* (London, 1991).

Bayly, C. A., *Empire and Information: Intelligence Gathering and Social Communication in India, 1780–1870* (Cambridge, 1996).

Bayly, C. A., Ireland, India and the Empire: 1780–1914, *Transactions of the Royal Historical Society*, 6th series, 10 (2000).

Bayly, C. A., *The Birth of the Modern World, 1780–1914: Global Connections and Comparisons* (Oxford, 2004).

Bayly, C. A., *Recovering Liberties: Indian Thought in the Age of Liberalism and Empire* (Cambridge, 2012).

Bayly, C. A., Beckhert, S., Connolly, M., Hoffmeyr, I., Kozol, W., Seed, P., AHR conversation: on transnational history, *American Historical Review*, 111:5 (2006).

Beaumont, P. and Beaumont, R., *Imperial Divas: The Vicereines of India* (London, 2010).

Beckett, J. C., *The Anglo-Irish Tradition* (Belfast, 1976).

Behm, A., Settler historicism and anticolonial rebuttal in the British World, 1880–1920, *Journal of World History*, 26:4 (2015).

Bence-Jones, M., *The Viceroys of India* (New York, 1982).

Bence-Jones, M., *Twilight of the Ascendancy* (London, 1987).

Bender, J., Mutiny or freedom fight? The 1857 Indian Mutiny and the Irish press, in Potter, S. J. (ed.), *Newspapers and Empire in Ireland and Britain: Reporting the British Empire, c. 1857–1921* (Dublin, 2004).

Bender, J., The imperial politics of famine: the 1873–4 Bengal Famine and Irish parliamentary nationalism, *Eire–Ireland*, 42:1–2 (2007).

Bentley, M., *Politics without Democracy, 1815–1914* (Oxford, 1984).

Bentley, M., *Lord Salisbury's World: Conservative Environments in late-Victorian Britain* (Cambridge, 2001).

Bew, J., *Castlereagh: Enlightenment, War and Tyranny* (London, 2011).

Bew, P., *C. S. Parnell* (Dublin, 1980).

Bew, P., *Conflict and Conciliation in Ireland, 1890–1910: Parnellites and Radical Agrarians* (Oxford, 1987).

Bew, P., *Enigma: A New Life of Charles Stewart Parnell* (London, 2011).
Biagini, E. F., *Liberty, Retrenchment and Reform: Popular Liberalism in the Age of Gladstone, 1860–1880* (Cambridge, 1992).
Bielenberg, A. (ed.), *The Irish Diaspora* (Harlow, 2000).
Bigelow, G., *Fiction, Famine and the Rise of Economics in Victorian Britain and Ireland* (Cambridge, 2003).
Bitterman, R., *Rural Protest on Prince Edward Island: From British Colonization to the Escheat Movement* (Toronto, 2006).
Bitterman, R. (with Dr Margaret McCallum), When private rights become public wrongs: property and the state in Prince Edward Island in the 1830s, in McLaren, J. Buck, A. R. and Wright, N. E. (eds), *Despotic Dominion: Property Rights in British Settler Societies* (Vancouver, 2004).
Bitterman, R. (with Dr Margaret McCallum), Upholding the land legislation of a communistic and socialist sssembly: the benefits of confederation for Prince Edward Island, *Canadian Historical Review*, 87:1 (2006).
Bitterman, R. (with Dr Margaret McCallum), *Lady Landlords of Prince Edward Island: Imperial Dreams and the Defense of Property* (Montreal and Kingston, 2008).
Black, R. C. D., *Economic Thought and the Irish Question, 1817–1870* (Cambridge, 1960).
Black, R. C. D., Economic policy in Ireland and India in the time of J. S. Mill, *Economic History Review*, 21:2 (1968).
Blake, K., *Pleasures of Benthamism: Victorian Literature, Utility, Political Economy* (Oxford, 2009).
Blake, R., *Disraeli* (London, 1966).
Blakely, B., *The Colonial Office, 1868–1892* (Durham, 1972).
Bolger, F. W. P., *Prince Edward Island and Confederation, 1863–1873* (Charlottetown, 1964).
Bolger, F. W. P., *Canada's Smallest Province: A History of Prince Edward Island* (Charlottetown, 1973).
Bolton, G., The idea of a colonial gentry, *Historical Studies*, 13 (1968).
Bouton, C. W., John Stuart Mill on liberty and history, in Eisenach, E. J. (ed.), *Mill and the Moral Character of Liberalism* (Pennsylvania, 1999).
Boyce, D. G., *Nationalism in Ireland* (London, 2005).
Boylan, T. A. and Foley, T. P., *Political Economy and Colonial Ireland: The Propaganda and Ideological Function of Economic Discourse in the Nineteenth Century* (London, 1992).
Bradley, M., Tacitus' *Agricola* and the conquest of Britain: representations of empire in Victorian and Edwardian Britain, in Bradley, M. (ed.), *Classics and Imperialism in the British Empire* (Oxford, 2010).
Brasted, H., Indian nationalist development and the influence of Irish Home Rule, 1870–1886, *Modern Asian Studies*, 14:1 (1980).
Brundage, D., *Irish Nationalists in America: The Politics of Exile, 1798–1998* (Oxford, 2016).
Bull, P., *Land, Politics and Nationalism: A Study of the Irish land Question* (Dublin, 1996).
Bumstead, J. M., *Land, Settlement and Politics on Eighteenth Century Prince Edward Island* (Montreal, 1987).
Burn, W. L., Free trade in land: an aspect of the Irish Question, *Transactions of the Royal Historical Society*, 4th series, 31 (1949).

218 General bibliography and sources

Burroughs, P. and Stockwell, A. J. (eds), *Managing the Business of Empire: Essays in Honour of David Fieldhouse* (London, 1998).

Burrow, J. W., *A Liberal Descent: Victorian Historians and the English Past* (Cambridge, 1981).

Burton, A. M., *At the Heart of the Empire: Indians and the Colonial Encounter in late-Victorian Britain* (Berkeley, 1998).

Buzpinar, S. T., The repercussions of the British occupation of Egypt on Syria, 1882–3, *Middle Eastern Studies*, 36:1 (2006).

Cain, P. J., Character and imperialism: the British financial administration of Egypt, 1878–1914, *Journal of Imperial and Commonwealth History*, 34:2 (2006).

Cain, P. J., Capitalism, aristocracy and empire: some 'classical' theories of imperialism revisited, *Journal of Imperial and Commonwealth History*, 35:1 (2007).

Cain, P. J. and Hopkins, A. G., *British Imperialism, I: Innovation and Expansion; II, Crisis and Deconstruction* (London, 1993).

Callahan, M. P., *Making Enemies: War and State-Building in Burma* (Ithaca, 2005).

Callan, H. and Ardener, S. (eds), *The Incorporated Wife* (Croom Helm, 1984).

Campbell, F., *The Irish Establishment 1879–1914* (Oxford, 2009).

Cannadine, D., *The Decline and Fall of the British Aristocracy* (London, 1990).

Cannadine, D., *Aspects of Aristocracy: Grandeur and Decline in Modern Britain* (New Haven, 1994).

Cannadine, D., *Ornamentalism: How the British Saw Their Empire* (London, 2001).

Capaldi, N., *John Stuart Mill: A Biography* (Cambridge, 2004).

Castronovo, D., *The English Gentleman: Images and Ideals in Literature and Society* (London, 1987).

Cell, J. W., *British Colonial Administration in the mid-Nineteenth Century: The Policy-Making Process* (London, 1970).

Cell, J. W., *Hailey: A Study in British Imperialism* (Cambridge, 1992).

Chadwick, M., The role of redistribution in the making of the Third Reform Act, *Historical Journal*, 19:3 (1976).

Chandra, B., *The Rise and Growth of Economic Nationalism in India: Economic Policies of Indian National Leadership, 1880–1905* (New Delhi, 1966).

Chandra, B., *India's Struggle for Independence, 1857–1947* (New Delhi, 1988).

Checkland, S., *The Elgins, 1766–1917: A Tale of Aristocrats, Proconsuls and Their Wives* (Aberdeen, 1988).

Chew, E., The fall of the Burmese kingdom in 1885: review and reconsideration, *Journal of Southeast Asian Studies*, 10:2 (1979).

Clark, S. and Donnelly, J. S. (eds), *Irish Peasants: Violence and Political Unrest, 1780–1914* (Manchester, 1983).

Coates, C. M. (ed.), *Majesty in Canada: Essays on the Role of Royalty* (Toronto, 2006).

Cohn, B., Representing authority in Victorian India, in E. Hobsbawm and T. Ranger (eds), *The Invention of Tradition* (Cambridge, 1983).

Colley, L., What is imperial history now? in D. Cannadine (ed.), *What Is History Now?* (Basingstoke, 2002).

Cook, S. B., The Irish Raj: social origins and careers of Irishmen in the Indian Civil Service, 1855–1914, *Journal of Social History*, 20:3 (1987).

Cook, S. B., *Imperial Affinities: Nineteenth Century Analogies and Exchanges between India and Ireland* (New Delhi, 1993).

Cooke, A. B. and Vincent, J. B., *The Governing Passion: Cabinet Government and Party Politics in Britain, 1885–6* (Brighton, 1974).

Cowan, J., *Canada's Governors General: Lord Monck to General Vanier* (Toronto, 1965).
Cragoe, M. and Readman, P. (eds), *The Land Question in Britain, 1750–1950* (Basingstoke, 2010).
Crane, R. and Barrier, N. G. (eds), *British Imperial Policy in India and Sri Lanka, 1858–1912* (New Delhi, 1981).
Crawford, W. H., Landlord–tenant relations in Ulster, 1609–1820, *Irish Economic and Social History*, 2 (1975).
Creighton, D., The Victorians and empire, *Canadian Historical Review*, 19 (1938).
Creighton, D., *John A. Macdonald*, 2 vols, (Toronto, 1952, 1955).
Crosbie, B., *Irish Imperial Networks: Migration, Social Communication and Exchange in Nineteenth-Century India* (Cambridge, 2012).
Cumpston, I. M., Some early Indian nationalists and their allies in the British parliament, 1851–1906, *English Historical Review*, 76 (1961).
Curtis, L. P. *Coercion and Conciliation in Ireland, 1880–92: A Study in Conservative Unionism* (Princeton, 1963).
Curtis, L. P., *Anglo-Saxons and Celts: A Study of Anti-Irish Prejudice in Victorian England* (Bridgeport, 1968).
Curtis, L. P., The Anglo-Irish predicament, *Twentieth Century Studies*, 4 (1970).
Curtis, L. P., Incumbered wealth: landed indebtedness in post-famine Ireland, *American Historical Review*, 85 (1980).
Curtis, L. P., Landlord responses to the Irish Land War, 1879–1987, *Eire–Ireland*, 38 (2003).
Curtis, L. P., *The Depiction of Eviction in Ireland, 1845–1910* (Dublin, 2011).
Daly, M. E. and Hoppen, K. T., *Gladstone, Ireland and Beyond* (Dublin, 2011).
Darwin, J., *The Empire Project: The Rise and Fall of the British World System, 1830–1970* (Cambridge, 2009).
Davis, P., The liberal unionist party and the Irish policy of Lord Salisbury's government, 1886–1892, *Historical Journal*, 18:1 (1975).
Dawson, N. M., Letters from Inveraray: the eighth duke of Argyll's correspondence with the first marquess of Dufferin and Ava, with particular reference to Gladstone's Irish Land Acts, in H. MacQueen (ed.), *Miscellany Seven* (Stair Society, Edinburgh, 2015).
Delaney, E., Our island story? Towards a transnational history of late modern Ireland, *Irish Historical Studies*, 37 (2011).
Delaney, E. and O'Niall, C. (eds), Beyond the nation: transnational Ireland, *Eire–Ireland*, 51:1–2 (2016).
Denholm, A., *Lord Ripon, 1827–1909: A Political Biography* (London, 1982).
Dewey, C., Images of the village community: a study in Anglo-Indian ideology, *Modern Asian Studies*, 6 (1972).
Dewey, C., Cambridge idealism: Utilitarian revisionists in late nineteenth Cambridge, *Historical Journal*, 17 (1974).
Dewey, C., Celtic agrarian legislation and the celtic revival: historicist implications of Gladstone's Irish and Scottish Land Acts, *Past and Present*, 64 (1974).
Dewey, C., The rehabilitation of the peasant proprietor in nineteenth century economic thought, *History of Political Economy*, 6:1 (1974).
Dewey, C., *Anglo-Indian Attitudes: The Mind of the Indian Civil Service* (1993).
Diamond, A. (ed.), *The Victorian Achievement of Sir Henry Maine: A Centennial Reappraisal* (Cambridge, 1991).
Donnelly, J. S., *The Land and the People of Nineteenth Century Cork* (London, 1975).

220 General bibliography and sources

Donnelly, J. S., The Irish Agricultural Depression of 1859–64, *Irish Economic and Social History*, (1976).

Dooley, T., *The Decline of the Big House in Ireland: A Study of Irish Landed Families, 1860–1960* (Dublin, 2001).

Dooley, T., Landlords and the land question, 1879–1909, in C. King (ed.), *Famine, Land and Culture in Ireland* (Dublin, 2001).

Dooley, T., *The Big Houses and Landed Estates of Ireland: A Research Guide* (Dublin, 2007).

Dooley, T., *The Decline and Fall of the Dukes of Leinster, 1872–1948* (Dublin, 2014).

Dowling, M. W., *Tenant Right and Agrarian Society in Ulster, 1600–1870* (Dublin, 1999).

Duffy, P. J., The evolution of estate properties in south Ulster 1600–1900, in Smyth, W. J. and Whelan, K. (eds), *Common Ground: Essays in the Historical Geography of Ireland* (Cork, 1988).

Dunae, P., *Gentlemen Emigrants: From the British Public Schools to the Canadian Frontier* (Toronto, 1981).

Durrans, P. J., A two-edged sword: the Liberal attack on Disraelian imperialism, *Journal of Imperial and Commonwealth History*, 10:3 (1982).

Dwyer, P. and Ryan, L., Reflections on genocide and settler-colonial violence, *History Australia*, 13:3 (2016).

Eisenach, E. J., *Mill and the Moral Character of Liberalism* (Pennsylvania, 1999).

Eldridge, C. C., *England's Mission: The Imperial Idea in the Age of Gladstone and Disraeli* (London, 1973).

Ethrington, N., *Theories of Imperialism: War, Conquest and Capital* (London, 1984).

Evatt, H. V., *The King and His Dominion Governors* (London, 1967).

Farr, D. M. L., *The Colonial Office and Canada, 1867–1887* (Toronto, 1955).

Fawaz, L., *An Occasion for War: Civil Conflict in Lebanon and Damascus in 1860* (London, 1994).

Fitzpatrick, D., The geography of Irish nationalism, 1910–21, *Past and Present*, 78 (1978).

Fitzpatrick, D., Ireland and the empire, in Porter, A. (ed.), *Oxford History of the British Empire, Vol. III: The Nineteenth Century* (Oxford, 1999).

Fleming, N. C., The landed elite, power and Ulster unionism, in Boyce, D. G. and O'Day, A. (eds), *The Ulster Crisis 1885–1921* (Basingstoke, 2005).

Foley, T. and O'Connor, M. (eds), *Ireland and India: Colonies, Culture and Empire* (Dublin, 2006).

Forsey, E., The role of the Crown in Canada since confederation, *Parliamentarian*, 60 (1979).

Foster, R., *Lord Randolph Churchill: A Political Life* (Oxford, 1981).

Foster, R., *Paddy and Mr Punch: Connections in Irish and English History* (London, 1993).

Francis, M., *Governors and Settlers: Images of Authority in the British Colonies, 1820–60* (Basingstoke, 1992).

Frie, E. and Neuheiser, J., Introduction: noble ways and democratic means, *Journal of Modern European History*, 11:4 (2013).

Gailey, A., *Ireland and the Death of Kindness: The Experience of Constructive Unionism, 1890–1905* (Cork, 1987).

Gailey, A., *The Lost Imperialist: Lord Dufferin, Memory and Mythmaking in an Age of Celebrity* (London, 2015).
Gallagher, J., Johnson, G. and Seal, A. (eds), *Locality, Province and Nation: Essays on Indian Politics 1870–1940* (London, 1973).
Gash, N., *Aristocracy and People: Britain 1815–1865* (London, 1979).
Gathorne-Hardy, J., *The Public School Phenomenon* (London, 1977).
Gavin, R. J., The Bartle Frere mission to Zanzibar, 1873, *Historical Journal*, 5 (1962).
Geary, L. M., *The Plan of Campaign, 1886–1891* (Cork, 1986).
Gibson, R. and Blinkhorn, M. (eds), *Landownership and Power in Modern Europe* (London, 1991).
Gibson, S. K. and Milnes, A. (eds), *Canada Transformed: The Speeches of Sir John A. Macdonald – A Bicentennial Celebration* (Toronto, 2014).
Gilley, S., Catholicism, Ireland and the Irish diaspora, in Gilley, S. and Stanley, B. (eds), *The Cambridge History of Christianity: World Christianities, c. 1815–c. 1914* (Cambridge, 2006).
Gilmour, D., *The Ruling Caste: Imperial Lives in the Victorian Raj* (London, 2005).
Gopal, S., *The Viceroyalty of Lord Ripon, 1880–1884* (Oxford, 1953).
Gopal, S., *British Policy in India, 1858–1905* (Cambridge, 1965).
Gray, P., *Famine, Land and Politics: British Government and Irish Society, 1843–50* (Dublin, 1999).
Gray, P. (ed.), *Victoria's Ireland? Irishness and Britishness, 1837–1901* (Dublin, 2004).
Green, E. H. H., *An Age of Transition: British Politics, 1880–1914* (Edinburgh, 1997).
Guinnane, T. W. and Miller, R. I., Bonds without bondsmen: Tenant-Right in nineteenth century Ireland, *Journal of Economic History*, 56:1 (1996).
Guinnane, T. W. and Miller, R. I., The limits to land reform: the land acts in Ireland, 1870–1909, *Economic Development and Cultural Change*, 45 (1997).
Gust, O., The perilous territory of not belonging: exile and empire in Sir James Mackintosh's letters from early nineteenth century Bombay, *History Workshop Journal*, 86 (2018).
Hall, C., *Cultures of Empire: A Reader: Colonizers in Britain and the Empire in the Nineteenth and Twentieth Centuries* (London, 2000).
Hall, C., *Macaulay and Son: architects of Imperial Britain* (New Haven, 2012).
Hall, C. and Rose, S. O. (eds), *At Home with the Empire: Metropolitan Culture and the Imperial World* (Cambridge, 2015).
Hambly, G. R. G., Richard Temple and the Punjab Tenancy Act of 1868, *English Historical Review*, 79:310 (1964).
Hamer, D. A., The Irish question and liberal politics, 1886–1894, *Historical Journal*, 12:3 (1969).
Hansson, H., The gentleman's north: Lord Dufferin and the beginnings of Arctic tourism, *Studies in Travel Writing*, 13:1 (2009).
Harcourt, F., Disraeli's imperialism, 1866–68: a question of timing, *Historical Journal*, 23:1 (1980).
Harris, C. (ed.), *The Resettlement of British Columbia: Essays on Colonialism and Geographical Change* (Vancouver, 1997).
Harvie, C., Ideology and Home Rule: James Bryce, A. V. Dicey and Ireland, 1880–7, *English Historical Review*, 91 (1976).
Hawkins, A, 'Parliamentary Government' and victorian political parties, c. 1830–c. 1880, *English Historical Review*, 104:412 (1989).

General bibliography and sources

Heard, A., *Canadian Constitutional Conventions: The Marriage of Law and Politics* (Oxford, 1991).

Heggs, E., Whig politics and the 3rd Duke of Leinster (1791–1874), in Cosgrove, P. Dooley, T. and Mullaney-Dignam, K. (eds), *Aspects of Irish Aristocratic Life* (Dublin, 2014).

Holmes, M., The Irish and India: imperialism, nationalism and internationalism, *Past and Present*, 164 (1999).

Hopkirk, P., *The Great Game: On Secret Service in High Asia* (London, 1990).

Hoppen, K. Theodore, *Governing Hibernia: British Politicians and Ireland, 1800–1921* (Oxford, 2016).

Hoppen, K. T., Landlords, society and electoral politics in mid-nineteenth century Ireland, *Past and Present*, 75 (1977).

Howe, S., *Ireland and Empire: Colonial Legacies in Irish History and Culture* (Oxford, 2002).

Howe, S. (ed.), *The New Imperial Histories Reader* (London, 2010).

Howell, D., The land question in nineteenth century Wales, Ireland and Scotland: a comparative study, *Agricultural History Review*, 61:1 (2013).

Hubbard, R. H., *Rideau Hall: An Illustrated History* (Montreal, 1977).

Hutchins, F., *The Illusion of Permanence: British Imperialism in India* (Princeton, 1967).

Hyam, R. and Martin, G. (eds), *Reappraisals in British Imperial History* (London, 1975).

Jackson, A., *The Ulster Party: Irish Unionists in the House of Commons, 1884–1911* (Oxford, 1984).

Jackson, A., *Colonel Edward Saunderson: Land and Loyalty in Victorian Ireland* (Oxford, 1995).

Jackson, A., *Ireland 1798–1998: Politics and War* (Oxford, 1999).

Jackson, A., *Home Rule: An Irish History, 1800–2000* (Oxford, 2004).

Jackson, A., Foreword – Ireland and Finland: Mr Gladstone, national and transnational historiographies, *Irish Historical Studies*, 41:160 (2017).

James, H., The assassination of Lord Mayo: the 'first' jihad? *International Journal of Asian Pacific Studies*, 5:2 (2009).

Jasanoff, M., Collectors of empire: objects, conquests and imperial self-fashioning, *Past and Present*, 184 (2004).

Jenkyns, R., *The Victorians and Ancient Greece* (Oxford, 1980).

Jones, A. and Jones, B., The Welsh world and the British empire, c. 1851–1939: an exploration, *Journal of Imperial and Commonwealth History*, 31:2 (2003).

Kanwar, P., *Imperial Simla: The Political Culture of the Raj* (Oxford, 1990).

Kaul, C., *Reporting the Raj: The British Press and India, c. 1880–1922* (Manchester, 2003).

Keck, S., Involuntary sightseeing: soldiers as travel writers and the construction of colonial Burma, *Victorian Literature and Culture*, 43:2 (2015).

Kehoe, K., Catholic identity in the diaspora: nineteenth century Ontario, in Bueltmann, T., Hinson, A. and Morton, G. (eds), *Ties of Bluid, Kin and Countrie: Scottish Associational Culture in the Diaspora* (Guelph, 2009).

Kennedy, D., Imperial history and post-colonial theory, *Journal of Imperial and Commonwealth History*, 24 (1996).

Kennedy, L. and Ollerenshaw, P. (eds), *An Economic History of Ulster 1820–1940* (Manchester, 1985).

Khoury, D. R. and Kennedy, D. K., Comparing empires: the Ottoman domains and the British Raj, *Comparative Studies of South Asia, Africa and the Middle East*, 27:2 (2007).
Kinzer, B., J. S. Mill and Irish land: a reassessment, *Historical Journal*, 27:1 (1984).
Kinzer, B. L. (ed.), *The Gladstonian Turn of Mind: Essays Presented to J. B. Conacher* (Toronto, 1985).
Kinzer, B. L., *England's Disgrace? J. S. Mill and the Irish Question* (Toronto, 2001).
Kirk-Greene, A., The Governors-General of Canada, 1867–1952: a collective profile, *Journal of Canadian Studies*, 12 (1977).
Kirk-Greene, A., *Britain's Imperial Administrators, 1858–1966* (London, 2000).
Knightley, P., *The First Casualty from the Crimea to Vietnam: The War Correspondent as Hero, Propagandist and Myth-Maker* (New York, 1975).
Knox, B., Conservative imperialism 1858–1874: Bulwer Lytton, Lord Carnarvon and Canadian confederation, *International History Review*, 4 (1984).
Knox, B., The Earl of Carnarvon, empire and imperialism, 1855–90, *Journal of Imperial and Commonwealth History*, 26 (1998).
Koditschek, T., *Liberalism, Imperialism, and the Historical Imagination: Nineteenth-Century Visions of a Greater Britain* (Cambridge, 2011).
Kovic, M., *Disraeli and the Eastern Question* (Oxford, 2011).
Kynaston, D., *The City of London, Vol. II: The Golden Years, 1890–1914* (London, 1995).
Laidlaw, Z., *Colonial Connections 1815–45: Patronage, the Information Revolution and Colonial Government* (Manchester, 2005).
Laidlaw, Z., Richard Bourke: Irish liberalism tempered by empire, in D. Lambert and A. Lester (eds), *Colonial Lives across the British Empire* (Cambridge, 2006).
Laidlaw, Z. and Lester, A. (eds), *Indigenous Communities and Settler Colonialism: Land Holding, Loss and Survival in an Interconnected World* (Basingstoke, 2015).
Large, D., The wealth of the greater Irish landowners, 1750–1815, *Irish Historical Studies*, 15 (1966).
Lee, J., *The Modernisation of Irish Society, 1848–1918* (Dublin, 1973).
Lee, J. J., The Irish diaspora in the nineteenth century, in Geary, L. M. and Kelleher, M. (eds), *Nineteenth Century Ireland: A Guide to Recent Research* (Dublin, 2005).
Lennon, J., *Irish Orientalism: A Literary and Intellectual History* (Syracuse, 2004).
Long, R. D. (ed.), *The Man on the Spot: Essays on British Empire History* (Connecticut, 1995).
Loughlin, J., *Gladstone, Home Rule and the Ulster Question, 1882–93* (Dublin, 1986).
Lynch, N., Defining Irish nationalist anti-imperialism: Thomas Davis and John Mitchel, *Eire–Ireland*, 42 (2007).
Lynn, M., Consul and kings: British policy, 'the man on the spot', and the seizure of Lagos, 1851, *Journal of Imperial and Commonwealth History*, 10:2 (1982).
Lynn, S., Before the Fenians: 1848 and the Irish plot to invade Canada, *Eire–Ireland*, 51:1–2 (2016).
Mac Suibhne, B., Spirit, spectre, shade: a true story of an Irish haunting: or, troublesome pasts in the political culture of North-West Ulster, *Field Day Review*, 9 (2013).
Mac Suibhne, B., *The End of Outrage: Post-Famine Adjustment in Rural Ireland* (Oxford, 2017).
MacDonagh, O., *States of Mind: A Study of Anglo-Irish Conflict, 1780–1980* (London, 1983).

Macdonald, N., *Canada: Immigration and Colonisation, 1841–1903* (Toronto, 1966).

Mackenzie, J. M., Irish, Scottish, Welsh and English worlds? A four-nation approach to the history of the British empire, *History Compass*, 6:5 (2008).

Mackillop, A., *More Fruitful Than the Soil: Army, Empire and the Scottish Highlands, 1715–1815* (East Linton, 2000).

Mackinnon, F., *The Government of Prince Edward Island* (Toronto, 1951).

Maguire, W. A., *The Downshire Estates in Ireland, 1801–1845* (Oxford, 1972).

Mak, L., *The British in Egypt: Community, Crime and Crisis, 1822–1922* (New York, 2012).

Mangan, J. A., *Making Imperial Mentalities: Socialisation and British Imperialism* (Manchester, 1990).

Mangan, J. A., *The Imperial Curriculum: Racial Images and Education in the British Colonial Experience* (London, 1993).

Mantena, R. S., Imperial ideology and the uses of Rome in discourses on Britain's Indian empire, in Bradley, M. (ed.), *Classics and Imperialism in the British Empire* (Oxford, 2010).

Marshall, P., The imperial factor in the Liberal decline, 1880–1885, in Flint, J. and Williams, G. (eds), *Perspectives of Empire: Presented to Gerald S. Graham* (Harlow, 1973).

Martin, B., The viceroyalty of Lord Dufferin, *History Today*, 10 (1960).

Martin, B., Lord Dufferin and the Indian National Congress, 1885–88, *Journal of British Studies*, 7:1 (1967).

Martin, B., *New India, 1885: British Official Policy and the Emergence of the Indian National Congress* (Berkeley, 1969).

Martin, G., *Britain and the Origins of Canadian Confederation, 1837–1867* (Vancouver, 1995).

Masefield, R., *Be Careful, Don't Rush: Celebrating 150 Years of Train Travel between Bangor and Holywood* (Newtownards, 2015).

Mason, J. W., The Duke of Argyll and the land question in late nineteenth century Britain, *Victorian Studies*, 21 (1978).

Mason, J. W., Political economy and the response to socialism in Britain, 1870–1914, *Historical Journal*, 23:3 (1980).

Matikkala, M., William Digby and the Indian question, *Journal of Liberal History*, 58 (2008).

Maung Htin, A., *Lord Randolph Churchill and the Dancing Peacock: British Conquest of Burma, 1885* (New Delhi, 1990).

Maxwell, J. A., Lord Dufferin and the difficulties with British Columbia, 1874–7, *Canadian Historical Review*, 12 (1931).

Mayer, A. J., *The Persistence of the Old Regime: Europe to the Great War* (1981).

Mc Mahon, R. and Newby, A., Introduction – Ireland and Finland, 1860–1930: comparative and transnational histories, *Irish Historical Studies*, 41:160 (2017).

McDowell, R. B., *The Irish Administration, 1801–1914* (London, 1964).

McLaren, J., Buck, A. R. and Wright, N. E. (eds), *Despotic Dominion: Property Rights in British Settler Societies* (Vancouver, 2004).

McMinn, J. R. B., Liberalism in north Antrim, 1900–1914, *Irish Historical Studies*, 23:89 (1982).

Mehta, U. S., *Liberalism and Empire: A Study in Nineteenth Century British Liberal Thought* (Chicago, 1999).

Messamore, B., The line over which he must not pass: defining the office of Governor General, 1878, *Canadian Historical Review*, 86:3 (2005).
Messamore, B., *Canada's Governors General, 1847–1878: Biography and Constitutional Evolution* (Toronto, 2006).
Metcalfe, T. R., The influence of the Mutiny of 1857 on land policy in India, *Historical Journal*, 4 (1961).
Metcalfe, T. R., *Land, Landlords, and the British Raj: Northern India in the Nineteenth Century* (Berkeley, 1979).
Metcalfe, T. R., *Forging the Raj: Essay on British India in the Heyday of Empire* (Oxford, 2005).
Moir, J., MacKirdy, K. A. and Zoltvany, Y. F. (eds), *Changing Perspectives in Canadian History: Selected Problems* (Ontario, 1971).
Moir, J. S., *Church and State in Canada, 1627–1867* (Toronto, 1967).
Moore, R. J., *Liberalism and Indian Politics, 1872–1922* (London, 1966).
Morrell, W. P., *British Colonial Policy in the mid-Victorian Age* (Oxford, 1969).
Moss, M., The high price of Heaven: the 6th Earl of Glasgow and the College of the Holy Spirit on the Isle of Cumbrae, *Architectural Heritage*, 22 (2011).
Mount, F., *Tears of the Rajas: Mutiny, Money and Marriage in India, 1805–1905* (London, 2015).
Murphy, T. and Stortz, G. (eds), *Creed and Culture: The Place of English-Speaking Catholics in Canadian Society, 1750–1930* (Montreal, 1993).
Nettlebeck, A., Colonial protection and the intimacies of indigenous governance, *History Australia*, 14:1 (2017).
Newby, A., Black spots on the map of Europe: Ireland and Finland as oppressed nationalities, c. 1860–1910, *Irish Historical Studies*, 41:160 (2017).
Ni Bheacháin, C., Seeing ghosts: gothic discourses and state formation, *Eire–Ireland*, 47:3–4 (2012).
Niyogi, S., *India in the British Parliament, 1865–84: Henry Fawcett's Struggle against British Colonialism in India* (Calcutta, 1986).
O'Grada, C., The investment behaviour of Irish landlords, 1850–75, *Agricultural History Review*, 23 (1975).
O'Grada, C., Irish agricultural history: recent research, *Agricultural History Review*, 38:2 (1990).
Ormsby, M., Prime Minister Mackenzie, the Liberal party and the bargain with British Columbia, *Canadian Historical Review*, 26 (1945).
Parel, A., Hume, Dufferin and the origins of the Indian National Congress, *Journal of Indian History*, 42 (1964).
Parry, J., *Democracy and Religion: Gladstone and the Liberal Party, 1867–1875* (Cambridge, 1986).
Parry, J., *The Rise and Fall of Liberal Government in Victorian Britain* (New Haven, 1993).
Peatling, G., Race and empire in nineteenth century British intellectual life: James Fitzjames Stephen, James Anthony Froude, Ireland and India, *Eire–Ireland*, 42 (2007).
Perin, R., *Rome in Canada: The Vatican and Canadian Affairs in the late Victorian Age* (Toronto, 1990).
Perren, R., The landlord and agricultural transformation, 1870–1900, *Agricultural History Review*, 18 (1970).
Perry, A., *On the Edge of Empire: Gender, Race and the Making of British Columbia* (Toronto, 2001).

Pitts, J., *A Turn to Empire: The Rise of Imperial Liberalism in Britain and France* (Princeton, 2005).
Pollak, O., *Empires in Collision: Anglo-Burmese Relations in the mid-Nineteenth Century* (Westport, 1979).
Porter, A., Empires in the mind, in Marshall, P. J. (ed.), *The Cambridge Illustrated History of the British Empire* (Cambridge, 1996).
Porter, B., *The Absent-Minded Imperialists: Empire, Society and Culture in Britain* (Oxford, 2004).
Preston, A., Sir Charles MacGregor and the defence of India, 1857–1887, *Historical Journal*, 12:1 (1969).
Proudfoot, L., The management of a great estate: patronage, income and expenditure on the Duke of Devonshire's Irish property, c. 1816–1891, *Irish Economic and Social History*, 13 (1986).
Purdue, O., *The Big House in the North of Ireland: Land, Power and Social Elites, 1878–1960* (Dublin, 2009).
Readman, P., *Land and Nation in England: Patriotism, National Identity and the Politics of Land, 1880–1914* (Woodbridge, 2008).
Reeves, R., *John Stuart Mill: Victorian Firebrand* (London, 2007).
Rendle, M., Conservatism and revolution: the all-Russian union of landowners, 1916–18, *Slavonic and East European Review*, 84:3 (2006).
Robb, P., *Ancient Rights and Future Comfort: Bihar, the Bengal Tenancy Act of 1885 and British Rule in India* (Surrey, 1997).
Roberts, D. A., Merely birds of passage: Lady Hariot Dufferin's travel writings and medical work in India, 1884–88, *Women's History Review*, 15:3 (2006).
Romani, R., British views on Irish national character, 1800–1846: an intellectual history, *History of European Ideas*, 23:5–6 (1997).
Rosenberg, J. D., *Carlyle and the Burden of History* (Oxford, 1985).
Ross Robertson, I., Political alignment in pre-confederation Prince Edward Island, 1863–1870, *Acadiensis*, 15:1 (1985).
Ross Robertson, I. (ed.), *The Prince Edward Island Land Commission of 1860* (Fredericton, 1988).
Ross Robertson, I., *The Tenant League of Prince Edward Island, 1864–1867* (Toronto, 1996).
Roszman, J. R., Ireland as a weapon of warfare: Whigs, Tories and the problem of Irish outrages, 1835 to 1839, *Historical Journal*, 60:4 (2017).
Rothermund, D., *Government, Landlord and Peasant in India: Agrarian Relations under British Rule, 1865–1935* (Wiesbaden, 1978).
Rubinstein, W. D., *Men of Property: The Very Wealthy in Britain since the Industrial Revolution* (Brunswick, 1981).
Sandwell, R. W., Dreaming of the princess: love, subversion and the rituals of empire in British Columbia, 1882, in Coates, C. M. (ed.), *Majesty in Canada: Essays on the Role of Royalty* (Toronto, 2006).
Scheltema, J. F., *The Lebanon in Turmoil: Syria and the Powers in 1860* (New Haven, 1920).
Scholch, A., The 'men on the spot' and the English occupation of Egypt in 1882, *Historical Journal*, 19:3 (1976).
Scholch, A., *Egypt for the Egyptians! The Socio-Political Crisis in Egypt, 1878–1882* (Reading, 1981).
Schull, J., *Edward Blake: The Man of the Other Way, 1833–1882* (Toronto, 1985).

Seal, A., *The Emergence of Indian Nationalism: Competition and Collaboration in the Later Nineteenth Century* (Cambridge, 1968).
Seal, A., Imperialism and nationalism in India, in Gallagher, J., Johnsonand, G., Seal, A. (eds), *Locality, Province and Nation: Essays on Indian Politics, 1870–1940* (Cambridge, 1973).
Sehrawat, S., The foundation of the Lady Hardinge Medical College and Hospital for Women at Delhi: issues in women's medical education and imperial governance, in Kak, S. and Pati, B. (eds), *Exploring Gender Equations: Colonial and Post-Colonial India* (New Delhi, 2005).
Sehrawat, S., Feminising empire: the Association of Medical Women in India and the campaign to found a women's medical service, *Social Scientist*, 41:5–6 (2013).
Sellar, W. C. and Yeatman, R. J., *1066 and All That* (London, 1930).
Senior, H., *The Fenians and Canada* (Toronto, 1978).
Senior, H., *The Last Invasion of Canada: The Fenian Raids, 1866–1870* (Toronto, 1991).
Shanks, A., *Rural Aristocracy in Northern Ireland* (Aldershot, 1988).
Sheehy, I., The view from Fleet Street: Irish nationalist journalists in London and their attitudes towards empire, 1892–1898, in Potter, S. J. (ed.), *Newspapers and Empire in Ireland and Britain* (Dublin, 2004).
Shrosbree, G., *Public Schools and Private Education* (Manchester, 1988).
Shukla, R. L., *Britain, India and the Turkish Empire, 1853–1882* (New Delhi, 1973).
Silvestri, M., *Ireland and India: Nationalism, Empire and Memory* (Basingstoke, 2009).
Singh, Hera Lal, *Problems and Policies of the British in India, 1885–1898* (Bombay, 1963).
Singhal, D. P., *British Diplomacy and the Annexation of Upper Burma* (New Delhi, 1981).
Smith, C., Second slavery, second landlordism and modernity: a comparison of antebellum Mississippi and nineteenth century Ireland, *Journal of the Civil War Era*, 5:2 (2015).
Smyth, W. J., *Toronto, the Belfast of Canada: The Orange Order and the Shaping of Municipal Culture* (Toronto, 2015).
Soldon, N., Laissez-faire as dogma: the Liberty and Property Defence League, 1882–1914, in Brown, K. D. (ed.), *Essays in Anti-Labour History* (London, 1974).
Solow, B., *The Land Question and the Irish Economy, 1870–1903* (Massachusetts, 1971).
Spurr, D., *The Rhetoric of Empire: Colonial Discourse in Journalism, Travel-Writing and Imperial Administration* (Durham, 1993).
Stanley, L., The epistolarium: on theorising letters and correspondences, *Auto/Biography*, 12 (2004).
Steele, E. D., Ireland and the empire: imperial precedents for Gladstone's first Irish Land Act, *Historical Journal*, 11:1 (1968).
Steele, E. D., J. S. Mill and the Irish question: the principles of political economy, 1848–1865, *Historical Journal*, 13:2 (1970).
Steele, E. D., J. S. Mill and the Irish question: reform and the integrity of empire, 1865–70, *Historical Journal*, 13:3 (1970).
Steele, E. D., *Irish Land and British Politics: Tenant-Right and Nationality, 1865–1870* (Cambridge, 1974).
Steele, E. D., *Palmerston and Liberalism, 1855–1865* (Cambridge, 1991).

Steven, A., Lord Dufferin: a tennis-playing diplomat, administrator and statesman, *Ulster Folklife*, 47 (2001).
Stevenson, G., *Ex Uno Plures: Federal-Provincial Relations in Canada, 1867–1896* (Montreal, 1993).
Stewart, A. T. Q., *The Ulster Crisis* (London, 1967).
Stewart, A. T. Q., *The Pagoda War* (Newton Abbot, 1974).
Stokes, E., *The English Utilitarians and India* (Oxford, 1959).
Stoler, A. L., *Along the Archival Grain: Epistemic Anxieties and Colonial Common Sense* (Princeton, 2008).
Sullivan, E., Liberalism and imperialism: John Stuart Mill's defence of the British empire, *Journal of the History of Ideas*, 44 (1983).
Swinfen, D. B., *Imperial Control of Colonial Legislation, 1813–1865* (Oxford, 1970).
Swinfen, D. B., *Imperial Appeal: The Debate on the Appeal to the Privy Council, 1833–1986* (Manchester, 1987).
Symonds, R., *Oxford and Empire: The Last Lost Cause?* (Oxford, 1992).
Taylor, A., *Lords of Misrule: Hostility to Aristocracy in late Nineteenth and Early Twentieth Century Britain* (Basingstoke, 2004).
Thant Myint-U., *The Making of Modern Burma* (Cambridge, 2001).
Thompson, F., Attitudes to reform: political parties in Ulster and the Irish Land bill of 1881, *Irish Historical Studies*, 24 (1985).
Thompson, F., The landed classes, the Orange Order and the anti-league campaign in Ulster, 1880–81, *Eire–Ireland*, 20 (1987).
Thompson, F., *The End of Liberal Ulster: Land Agitation and Land Reform, 1868–1866* (Belfast, 2001).
Thomson, D., *Alexander Mackenzie: Clear Grit* (Toronto, 1960).
Thornley, D., The Irish Conservatives and home rule, 1869–73, *Irish Historical Studies*, 11:43 (1959).
Thornley, D., *Isaac Butt and Home Rule* (London, 1964).
Tidrick, K., *Empire and the English Character* (London, 1990).
Tignor, R., The 'Indianisation' of the Egyptian administration under British rule, *American Historical Review*, 68:3 (1963).
Tignor, R. L., *Modernisation and British Colonial Rule in Egypt, 1882–1914* (Princeton, 1966).
Toner, P., The green ghost: Canada's Fenians and the Raids, *Eire–Ireland*, 16:4 (1981).
Townend, P., *The Road to Home Rule: Anti-Imperialism and the Irish National Movement* (Wisconsin, 2016).
Townshend, C., *Political Violence in Ireland: Government and Resistance since 1848* (Oxford, 1984).
Tripathi, A. and Tripathi, A., *The Indian National Congress and the Struggle for Freedom, 1885–1947* (Oxford, 2014).
Tusan, M., Britain and the Middle East: new historical perspectives on the Eastern question, *History Compass*, 8:3 (2010).
Vaughan, W. E., Landlord and tenant relations in Ireland between the famine and the land war, 1850–1878, in Cullen, L. M. and Smout, T. C. (eds), *Comparative Aspects of Scottish and Irish Economic and Social History, 1600–1900* (Edinburgh, 1977).
Vaughan, W. E., An assessment of the economic performance of Irish landlords, 1851–81, in Lyons, F. S. L. and Hawkins, R. A. J. (eds), *Ireland under the Union: Varieties of Tension* (Oxford, 1980).

Vaughan, W. E., *Landlords and Tenants in mid-Victorian Ireland* (Oxford, 1994).
Vaughan, W. E. (ed.), *A New History of Ireland, Vol. 6: Ireland under Union, 1801–1921, II, 1870–1921* (Oxford, 2010).
Vincent, J. R., *Disraeli, Derby and the Conservative Party: The Political Journals of Lord Stanley, 1849–69* (Hassocks, 1978).
Warren, A., Gladstone, land and social reconstruction in Ireland, 1881–1887, *Parliamentary History*, 2 (1983).
Weaver, J. C., *The Great Land Rush and the Making of the Modern World, 1650–1900* (Montreal, 2003).
Whelehan, N., *The Dynamiters: Irish Nationalism and Political Violence in the Wider World, 1867–1900* (Cambridge, 2012).
Whelehan, N. (ed.), *Transnational Perspectives on Modern Irish History* (London, 2015).
Whyte, J. H., Landlord influence at elections in Ireland, 1760–1855, *English Historical Review*, 80:317 (1965).
Williams, D., *The India Office, 1858–1869* (Hoshiarpur, 1983).
Wilson, C., *A New Lease on Life: Landlords, Tenants and Immigrants in Ireland and Canada* (Montreal, 1994).
Wilson, D. (ed.), *Irish Nationalism in Canada* (Toronto, 2009).
Wilson, D. A., *The Orange Order in Canada* (Dublin, 2007).
Wolfreys, J., *Victorian Hauntings: Spectrality, Gothic, the Uncanny and Literature* (Basingstoke, 2001).
Woodman, D., *The Making of Burma* (London, 1962).
Wright, J. M., *Ireland, India and Nationalism in Nineteenth Century Literature* (Cambridge, 2007).
Wurgraft, L. D., *The Imperial Imagination: Magic and Myth in Kipling's India* (Middleton, 1983).
Yasin, M., *India's Foreign Policy: The Dufferin Years* (New Delhi, 1994).
Zachs, F., 'Novice' or 'heaven-born' diplomat? Lord Dufferin and his plan for a 'Province of Syria': Beirut, 1860–61, *Middle Eastern Studies*, 36:3 (2000).
Zastoupil, L., Moral government: J. S. Mill on Ireland, *Historical Journal*, 26:3 (1983).

Unpublished works

Brasted, H. V., Irish home rule politics and India, 1873–1886: Frank Hugh O'Donnell and other Irish 'Friends of India', unpublished PhD thesis (University of Edinburgh, 1974).
Harrison, A. T., The first Marquess of Dufferin and Ava: Whig, Ulster landlord and Imperial statesman, unpublished DPhil thesis (New University of Ulster, Colerain, 1983).
McHugh, D. M., Family, leisure and the arts: aspects of the culture of the aristocracy of Ulster, 1870–1925, unpublished PhD thesis (University of Edinburgh, 2011).
Ridden, J., Making good citizens: national identity, religion and liberalism among the Irish elite, c.1800–1850, unpublished PhD thesis (King's College London, 1998).

Index

absenteeism 60, 61, 115, 126, 127–128
Act of Union (1801) 17, 19, 53–54
Afghanistan 13, 87, 89, 99, 102–103, 154, 175, 181, 186
agitation, *see* political agitation, *see* tenant agitation
agricultural depression 28, 38, 40, 41
agriculture 2, 28, 30, 32, 34, 38, 55–59, 69, 119, 124, 126, 153, 155, 167, 180, 205
Albert, Prince Consort 96, 115
Allan, Sir Hugh 119
American Civil War 117, 122, 123
Anglo-Burmese Wars 99–101
Anglo-Indian community 99, 164, 171, 184–186
Anglo-Irish Ascendancy 6, 17, 27–28, 44, 54, 60, 72, 101, 166–167
Anglo-Irish identity 17, 27–28, 44
Anglo-Saxonism 70–71
annexation 13, 18, 94–95, 99–101, 114, 119, 123, 164, 175–178, 181
anti-intellectualism 84, 88
arbitration 59, 121, 128–129
Argyll, George Douglas Campbell, 8th Duke 11–13, 34–35, 41, 55, 58, 62–66, 68, 94, 124, 173, 176, 189
armed forces, *see* military
Australia 14, 127
autocracy 18–20, 70, 72, 87, 93–94, 97–99, 142, 152, 167–169, 174–179, 182–191

Baker, Sir Samuel 69, 185–186
Banerjea, Surendranath 186, 187
barbarism 11, 55, 58, 89, 145–147
Barbour, Sir David 190
Baring, Sir Evelyn 155
Belfast 4, 33, 36, 38, 69, 91, 125, 175

Bengal Tenancy Act (1885) 68, 172–173, 174
Beresford, Charles Sir 152
Bessborough Commission 67–68, 129
Big Houses 5, 36, 206
Black, Charles Drummond 16
Blackwood, Lady Caroline 206
Blackwood, Lady Helen 1, 9–10, 15, 16, 35, 37
Blackwood, Price 9
Blackwood, W. J. 31
Blake, Edward 116, 118, 120–122
Boer War 14, 203
Bombay 12, 186
Bombay Burma Trading Company 99
borders 13, 87–89, 99, 102
Boyle, George F., 1
Breakfast Club 95
British Columbia 113, 116, 118–121, 124, 126
British identity 17, 84
buffer policy 87, 99, 102, 178, 181
bureaucracy 167–169, 174–175
Burma 6, 13, 18, 87, 94–95, 99–102, 154, 164, 175–178, 181, 186, 189, 206
Butt, Isaac 60, 64

Caird, Sir James 61
Cairo 142, 151
Calcutta 70, 104, 164, 169, 185, 186, 191
Cambridge University 89, 144
Campbell, Sir George 61
Canada: confederation 13, 18, 112, 113, 116–124, 127, 129, 130; corruption 13, 93, 118–119; Dufferin's service in 12–13, 15–16, 18–19, 32, 56, 58, 63–65, 86, 91,

Index 231

93–97, 112–131, 150, 170, 172–173, 175, 205; economic depression 116, 117; emigration to 115, 122, 124–125, 127–128; Fenian raids 56, 124; French Canada 116, 124–125; indigenous peoples 114, 117, 125–126; infrastructure 13, 32, 116, 119–122, 129, 130; Irish diaspora 56, 114–115, 124–125; land reform 114, 126–129, 172, 173, 205; and loyalty 97, 113–115, 122–126, 130; national identity 129; Pacific Scandal 13, 118–122; railways 13, 32, 116, 119–122, 129, 130; rebellions 63, 116–117; relations with the US 6, 93, 114, 115, 117, 119, 122–124; sectarianism 56, 117, 124–125; self-government 13, 18, 19, 93, 112–131, 205
Canadian identity 129
Canadian Pacific Railway 32, 116, 119–122, 129, 130
Cannadine, David 19, 29
Carnarvon, Henry Herbert, 4th Earl 65, 89, 117, 120–121, 123, 126
Castle Rackrent (Edgeworth) 43
Catholicism 27, 37, 44, 53, 63, 90, 117, 124–125
censorship 187
ceremony 7, 15, 19–20, 71, 84, 86, 96–97, 102–103, 146, 168–171, 177–178, 189, 202, 205
Chamberlain, Joseph 103
character 7, 17–18, 85, 92, 141–143, 148–149, 154, 175, 203
charity 1, 12, 42, 43, 55, 60, 170
China 87
Churchill, Lord Randolph 69, 99–100, 172–174, 175, 177
Cinque Ports 14, 202
civil rights 185
civilisation 70, 85–86, 89, 94, 102–103, 145, 154, 166
Clandeboye estate: collection of artefacts for 94, 142, 144, 177; Dufferin inherits 1, 7, 9, 16; Dufferin retires to 202–203; estate debt 10, 13, 29, 35, 38–42, 180, 182, 206; location 4; management of 2, 7, 10, 16–17, 19, 29–44, 53, 55, 57, 63–66, 68, 72, 175, 180, 182, 202, 204; passed down through Dufferin's descendants 205–206; sale of parts of 13, 19, 29, 35, 38–42, 54, 64, 68, 128, 202, 204, 206

classical education 10, 32, 55, 85, 89
clubs 10, 35, 36, 95
coercion 8, 12, 53, 60, 67, 70, 95, 101, 166–167, 177–178, 183
Colonial Office 84, 96, 113, 117–120, 127, 130
communications infrastructure 36, 153, 177, 180
compensation (for improvements) 56–57, 59, 67
confederation 13, 112, 113, 116–124, 127, 129, 130
conquest 28, 60, 94, 177; *see also* annexation
Conservative party (Britain) 63, 65, 71, 90, 99, 117, 151
Conservative party (Canada) 118–120
Constantinople 68, 91
constitutional reform 70, 93–94, 154–155
contract 7, 28, 114, 172, 173, 204
corruption 13, 93, 118–119, 144, 147–150, 152, 155
Country Life 202–203
Crofters Holdings (Scotland) Act (1886) 68
Cross, R. A. 1st Viscount 69, 89, 188, 190
Curtis L. P., 35, 38, 56
Curzon, George, 1st Marquis 97, 99, 103, 191, 203

Damascus 147
Davitt, Michael 61
debt 10, 13, 29, 35, 38–42, 65, 72, 155, 180, 182
deference 8, 19, 43, 171
Delhi 91, 176
democracy 70, 72, 93, 142, 155, 167, 183, 188, 189, 205
diplomacy 2, 4, 6, 10–12, 17, 19–20, 44, 57–58, 71, 123, 141–157, 175
disestablishment 53
Disraeli, Benjamin 37, 151
diversification 2, 19, 38, 59, 205
dominion, *see* economic dominion, *see* political dominion
Dooley, Terence 29
Druse 147, 148
dual ownership 68, 129
Dublin 36, 56
Dufferin, Basil Hamilton-Temple-Blackwood, 4th Marquis 206
Dufferin, Frederick Hamilton-Temple-Blackwood, 1st Marquis: biographies

232 Index

of 13, 15–16, 41–42, 90; in Canada 12–13, 15–16, 18–19, 32, 56, 58, 63–65, 86, 91, 93–97, 112–131, 150, 170, 172–173, 175, 205; charitable donations 1, 55; death 14, 203; diplomatic and imperial career 2, 6, 11–14, 17–20, 37, 40, 44, 63–65, 69–71, 83–104, 112–131, 141–157, 164–191, 204–206; education 9–10, 44, 53, 55, 89, 153, 206; in Egypt 13, 17–18, 20, 58, 93–94, 98, 141–145, 150–157, 175; family background 9; finances 9, 10, 13, 14, 29, 31, 33–42, 55, 58, 63–64, 112–113, 180, 182, 203, 206; in France 13, 85, 144; in India 13, 15–16, 18, 20, 32, 58, 60, 68–71, 86, 89, 91–94, 96–104, 127, 150, 164–191; in Italy 13, 103, 144; literary career 1–2, 9, 11, 15, 17, 63, 94; management of Clandeboye estate 2, 7, 16–17, 19, 29–44, 53, 55, 57, 63–66, 68, 72, 175, 180, 182, 202, 204; manners 145–146, 170; obituaries 202–203; peerage granted to 11, 57; pictured 8, 14, 114, 165; political career 2, 11, 12, 53–54, 57–64, 94; relationship with mother 9–10, 12, 15–16; reputation 14–16, 39–40, 42, 57, 65–66, 94–95, 99, 100–101, 117, 119–120, 130, 142, 156–157, 177–178, 191, 202, 204; retirement 202–203; in Russia 13, 67, 68, 91, 94, 144; sale of lands and properties 13, 19, 29, 35, 38–42, 54, 64, 68, 128, 202, 204, 206; sensitivity to criticism 12, 15, 34, 65, 100, 187; in Syria 11, 17, 19–20, 141–150, 156–157, 175; travel 10, 11, 35, 94, 125, 142, 146; visit to Skibbereen 1–2, 33, 55; wife and children 11–15, 36, 63, 113, 115, 169–170, 177, 202–203, 205–207

Dufferin, Frederick Hamilton-Temple-Blackwood, 3rd Marquis 206
Dufferin, Hariot Rowan Hamilton, Lady 11–12, 36, 63, 113, 115, 130, 169–170, 177, 202–203
Dufferin, Lindy Guinness, Lady 206
Dufferin, Sheridan Hamilton-Temple-Blackwood, 5th Marquis 206
Dufferin, Terence Hamilton-Temple-Blackwood, 2nd Marquis 203, 205–206
Dufferin House 35
Dufferin Lodge 35
Dufferin Monument 4, 5
Dufferin Report 153–156
Durand, Sir Henry 86, 146, 170, 174
duty 1, 15, 17, 19, 29–32, 41, 53, 55–57, 84–85, 88, 91, 94–95, 120, 186, 205; *see also* responsibilities

East India Company 176
economic depression 39, 64–65, 116, 117, 206
economic development 32, 36, 60, 129, 153, 155, 157
economic dominion 19, 87, 94
Edinburgh University 14, 202, 203
education 2, 53, 85, 89, 91, 92, 144, 145, 153, 166, 167, 204
Egypt 13, 17–18, 20, 58, 93–94, 98, 141–145, 150–157, 168, 175
Egyptology 94, 142, 144
1848 revolutions 55
1857 Rebellion 175–176, 178
emigration 2, 17, 44, 53–56, 59, 115, 122, 124–125, 127–128, 205
employment 30, 33, 43, 55, 60
Encumbered Estates Act 39
England and Ireland (Mill) 61
estate management 2, 5, 7, 17, 28–38, 43–44, 53, 55–59, 65–66, 85, 87, 91, 180, 202, 204
Eton College 7, 9, 31, 89
evictions 28, 33, 56, 64, 65, 97, 172, 173
evolutionism 60
exile 13, 30, 85, 88, 94, 130
extra-judicial executions 100–101, 178

Faeroes 11
famine 1–2, 7, 15–17, 28–31, 33, 38, 41, 43–44, 54–56, 60, 64–65, 72, 91, 97, 98, 166, 169, 181
Fenian movement 56, 60, 69, 124, 178
Ferguson, Lord Ronald Munro 203
First World War 206
fitness to rule 18, 55, 71, 93, 101, 143, 154, 166, 182, 184–185, 188–189, 205
fixity of tenure 61
France 6, 10, 13, 17, 85, 99, 141, 143, 144, 147–152, 156
franchise 7, 53
French Canada 116, 124–125
French Revolution 143
Fuad Pasha 146, 148, 150

Gailey, Andrew 16
generosity 9, 33–34, 40, 43

gentlemanly conduct 7, 18, 95, 142, 145, 149, 166
germ theory 69, 124, 179
Gladstone, William Ewart 6, 12, 18, 53–54, 58, 61–71, 90, 93, 95, 101, 150, 152, 173, 175
good governance: of estates 33–34, 58; of imperial territories 8, 17–19, 29, 60, 62, 71, 83, 87, 94, 97–98, 101, 103, 116, 118, 120–122, 125–127, 130, 143, 148–150, 152, 154, 157, 173, 176, 181–182, 188, 190
Gordon, Charles 156
governing culture 83–85, 89, 96, 118, 165, 176–177, 189
governing passion 44, 143–144
Government of India 100, 101, 146, 171, 176–178, 180, 182–184, 186, 191
Graham, Cyril 144
Graham, Sir James 1, 10, 11, 31, 57, 145, 146
Granville, Granville Leveson-Gower, 2nd Earl 86, 152–153
Great Famine 1–2, 7, 15–17, 28–31, 33, 38, 41, 43–44, 54–56, 60, 64–65, 72, 91, 97, 181
Great Game 6
Great Granny Webster (Blackwood) 206
Guinness, Lady Maureen 206

Hamilton-Temple-Blackwood, Basil 203, 206
Hamilton-Temple-Blackwood, Archie, Lord Ava 14, 177, 203
healthcare 12, 170
Helen's Bay 33, 36
Helen's Tower 33
Helen's Tower (Nicolson) 16, 202
Hicks, William 156
hierarchy 7–8, 71, 85, 87, 96, 101–103, 115, 126, 141, 149–150, 153–154, 165, 171, 178, 190
historicism 7, 58, 60, 94, 144, 150, 156, 168, 205
Home Rule 6, 11, 18, 19, 28, 44, 53, 68–72, 188
House of Commons 57, 96, 183
House of Lords 2, 11, 57–58, 60, 62–63, 96
housing 2, 33, 36
Howe, John 31, 37, 65–66, 68
Hume, Allan Octavian 185, 186–187
Hume, David 92

Iceland 11
identity, *see* Anglo-Irish identity, *see* British identity, *see* Canadian identity, *see* Irish identity, *see* landed identity
Ilbert Bill 182, 184, 186
imperial expansion 18, 88, 99, 143, 164
imperial justification 18, 54, 60, 72, 87, 88, 101, 144, 164
imperial mission 87, 88, 90, 92, 103–104, 153
imperial purpose 18, 54, 72, 88, 90–91, 103–104, 166, 180
improvement 2, 7, 8, 17, 29–44, 56–57, 67, 91, 98, 155, 166, 171–173, 180, 204
India: Anglo-Indian community 99, 164, 171, 184–186; annexation of Burma 13, 18, 94–95, 99–102, 164, 175–178, 181, 186, 189; army 100, 102, 169, 175–177, 182, 186–187, 189, 190; autocratic government 18, 20, 70–71, 97–99, 167–169, 174–179, 182–191; bureaucracy 167–169, 174–175; Civil Service 169, 174, 185, 187–188, 190; Dufferin's service in 13, 15–16, 18, 20, 32, 58, 60, 68–71, 86, 89, 91–94, 96–104, 127, 150, 164–191; 1857 Rebellion 175–176, 178; famines 98, 166, 169, 181; finances 102, 166, 179–182, 185, 190; Government of India 100, 101, 146, 171, 176–178, 180, 182–184, 186, 191; healthcare 12, 170; indigenous nobility and aristocracy 96, 103, 171, 185, 189, 190; infrastructure 32, 168, 172, 180; Indian National Congress 13, 15, 89, 164, 182–183, 185–186, 187, 189, 190; land reform 13, 68, 127, 164, 171–174, 189; local government 164, 175, 182, 186, 188, 189; and loyalty 97, 98, 103, 171–172, 186–187, 190; military volunteers 182, 186–187, 189, 190; nationalism 18, 70–71, 98, 126, 166–168, 179–180, 181; political agitation 69–71, 92–93, 98–99, 179, 183–190; political reform 168, 184–190; and self-government 70–71, 93, 154, 166, 175, 179, 182–190; terror 167, 169, 175–178, 183
India Office 69, 84, 96, 99, 102, 171, 173, 182, 183, 191
Indian Army 100, 102, 169, 175–177, 182, 186–187, 189, 190

234 *Index*

Indian Civil Service 169, 174, 185, 187–188, 190
Indian Council 171, 183, 191
Indian Mutiny, *see* 1857 Rebellion
Indian National Congress 13, 15, 89, 164, 182–183, 185–187, 189, 190
Indian nationalism 18, 70, 71, 98, 126, 166–168, 179–181
Indian reservations 126
indigenous peoples 114, 117, 125–126
Industrial Revolution 55
industry 7, 30, 33, 38, 43, 55, 59, 69, 88, 92, 167, 171, 181, 205
infrastructure 8, 32, 36, 100, 119–122, 129, 153, 155, 157, 168, 172, 180; *see also* public works programmes; railways; roads
inheritance 2, 5, 9, 19, 31–32, 43, 85, 90, 95, 126, 166
insider/outsider status 7, 15, 84, 90, 117, 130, 166, 204
interest costs 35, 38–39
Irish diaspora 56, 114–115, 124–125
Irish identity 6–7, 16, 17, 28, 42, 44, 53, 70, 90, 204
Irish Land Act (1870) 17, 56, 62–63, 66, 67, 69, 93
Irish Land Act (1881) 17, 42, 54, 65–69, 129, 173
Irish Land Question (Caird) 61
Irish nationalism 6, 7, 15, 17, 19, 28–29, 54, 64, 69–71, 98, 124–126, 166–168, 179, 181
irrigation 155, 157, 180
Italy 13, 103, 144

judicial systems 155, 184

Khartoum 156
Kilbracken, Arthur Godley, 1st Baron 101, 171
Kimberley, John Wodehouse, 1st Earl 9, 15, 30, 62, 69–71, 89, 93, 113, 116–120, 125, 127, 129, 152, 175, 181, 183–187
Kipling, Rudyard 103, 189

Lady Dufferin Fund 12, 170
land agents 29, 31, 34, 37–38, 63–66, 68, 175
Land League 42, 68, 69
land lotteries 127
land purchase 42, 44, 61, 67, 68, 72, 127–129, 172, 173

land reform 2, 6–8, 13, 17–19, 32, 44, 53, 57–70, 72, 126–129, 164, 171–174, 189, 205, 206
land tenure 7, 8, 17, 53, 56–61, 114, 126–129, 164, 172–174
Land Wars 15, 16, 28, 54, 64–65, 68
landed classes, *see* aristocracy
landed identity 7, 9, 28, 34, 41–42, 44, 61, 64, 71–72, 117
landlord–tenant relations 2, 32–34, 42, 55, 57–68, 91, 97, 171–174, 204–206
landlordism 6, 15, 17, 19, 27–30, 32–33, 42–43, 55–70, 88, 127–128
Lansdowne, Henry Petty-Fitzmaurice, 5th Marquis 15, 30, 156, 188, 190
Lawrence, Sir John 169
laziness 53, 84, 86, 97, 174–175
leases 2, 56–57, 63, 65
Lebanon 150
legal reform 91, 184
Lepine, Ambroise-Dydime 117
Letters from High Latitudes (Dufferin) 11, 125
Liberal party (Britain) 2, 6, 11, 12, 28, 32, 34, 53–54, 58–71, 92, 117, 129, 145, 151–152, 189
Liberal party (Canada) 116, 118–122, 124
local government 91, 154, 164, 175, 182, 186, 188, 189
London 11, 35, 36, 85, 95, 127, 204
London and Globe Finance Corporation 14, 42, 202, 204
loneliness 94
looting 177
Lorne, John Campbell, Lord 113, 130
loyalty 19, 34, 44, 58, 71–72, 87, 96–103, 113–115, 122–126, 130, 171–172, 186–187, 190
Lyall, Sir Alfred 13, 16, 85, 89, 91, 173, 190
Lytton, Robert Bulwer-Lytton, 1st Earl 174

Macaulay, Thomas 92
Macdonald, Sir John A. 118–119, 130
Mackenzie, Alexander 116, 118, 120–122
MacKnight, Thomas 188
Madras 186
'man on the spot' 19–20, 62, 84, 87, 94, 95–103, 117, 141–157
Mandalay 99, 100, 177
manners 2, 10, 37, 145–146, 170

Index 235

market economy 55, 60
Maronite Christianity 147
Mayo, Richard Bourke, 6th Earl 15, 30
meritocracy 6, 7, 88
middle classes 7, 18, 33, 59, 83–84, 85, 88, 102, 116, 167, 169, 179–180
military: aristocratic military service 7, 9, 85, 92, 166; costs of 100–101, 181; decision-making on military action 94, 175; French Army 148, 149; Indian Army 100, 102, 169, 175–177, 182, 186–187, 189, 190; Indian volunteers in 182, 186–187, 189, 190; military classes 18, 84, 85; military conquest 94, 99–101, 164, 176–178; military oppression 94, 125, 175–176
Mill, John Stuart 60, 61, 88
Milner, Alfred 203
modernisation 35, 155
monarchy 86, 89–90, 92, 96, 126, 141, 150, 165, 166, 178
Montreal 56, 116, 123, 125
Moylan, E. K. 100–101, 178
Mughal empire 171
Mulholland, John 38, 39
Murray, John 12

nation-building 114
nationalism, *see* Indian nationalism, *see* Irish nationalism
Newfoundland 130
newspapers, *see* press
Nicolas II, Tsar of Russia 13
Nicolson, Harold 16, 28, 58, 202
Northbrook, Thomas Baring, 1st Earl 101
Northern Star 63
Northern Whig 188
Norton, Caroline 9

Observer 154–155
O'Connell, Daniel 184
Old Testament 142, 144, 145, 150, 168
oppression 44, 61, 94, 104, 167, 169, 176
Orange Order 7, 56, 117, 124, 125
order 91–92, 96, 152, 177
Orientalism 94, 146–147, 150, 157
ornamentalism 30, 84, 86, 165, 169, 190, 203–204
Ottoman empire 6, 11, 13, 141–150
Ottowa 39, 65, 113
Oudh Rent Act (1886) 68, 172–174
Oxford Union 10

Oxford University 1, 7, 9–10, 31, 43, 53, 55, 89, 144, 167

Pacific Scandal 13, 118–122
Pall Mall Gazette 153
Palmerston, Henry John Temple, Lord 37, 53, 148
Panjdeh 102
Paris 10, 85
Parnell, Charles Stewart 65
partition 206
paternalism 28, 43, 61, 87, 98, 115, 116, 141
patronage 37, 66, 90, 94, 141
Peace Preservation bill 62
peasantry 2, 11, 55, 58, 94, 155, 181
petitions 42, 65–66
plantations 60, 89, 114
police 93, 100, 125, 175, 177
political agitation 58, 69–71, 92, 93, 97–99, 104, 124, 179, 183–190
political dominion 8, 13, 18, 20, 83, 87, 94, 101, 167
political economy 17, 32, 42, 53, 55–64, 71–72
political reform 88, 104, 168, 184–190
potatoes 10, 33, 34, 55, 56
poverty 2, 28, 33, 55–56, 67
power 6–8, 18–19, 43, 69–71, 84–90, 97, 103, 117–118, 141–150, 167, 169, 184, 189–190, 205
pragmatism 36, 37, 85, 203–204
Prendergast, Harry 177, 178
Presbyterianism 37, 44, 150
press 42, 57, 63–66, 95, 100–101, 113, 118–119, 130, 153–155, 177–178, 181, 183, 185, 187
Prince Edward Island 64, 116, 127–129, 172, 173, 205
privilege 15, 18, 27, 32, 44, 61, 84, 89, 91–92, 95, 128, 166–167, 190, 205
professional classes 7, 18, 83–85, 102, 166, 169, 179–180
progress 19, 87, 88, 90–95, 101, 104, 126, 180
property rights 7, 17, 28, 30, 62, 72, 114, 126–129, 143, 171–174, 205
Protestantism 27–28, 40, 44, 53, 63, 117, 124–125
provincial councils 154, 182, 186–188, 189
Prussia 61, 148
public opinion 30, 43, 60, 94–95, 115, 118, 124, 147, 151–152, 155, 164, 178, 181, 184, 188

Index

public schools 7, 9, 31, 86, 89, 144, 167
Public Works Office 180
public works programmes 32, 180–181
Purdue, Olwen 29, 44
Pythic club 9, 10

Quebec 2, 63, 112, 125

racial hierarchies 67, 70–71, 87, 91, 104, 125–126, 143–144, 153–154, 168, 184
racialisation 11, 18, 70, 122, 124, 125, 178
rack-renting 28, 43
railways 4, 13, 32, 36, 116, 119–122, 127, 129, 130, 155, 157, 180
Rawalpindi 102, 186
Read, Arthur 31
rebellion 8, 33, 54, 65–66, 92, 116–117, 141, 143, 151–152, 155, 175–176
Reciprocity Treaty 117
Red River Rising 116–117
reform, *see* constitutional reform, *see* land reform, *see* legal reform, *see* political reform, *see* social reform
religion 10, 29, 43–44, 54–55, 72, 91, 117, 124–125, 141, 144, 147–148, 150, 168; *see also* Catholicism; Maronite Christianity; Protestantism; Presbyterianism; sectarianism
rent arrears 29, 31, 33, 34, 39, 128
rent strikes 64–65, 127
rents 8, 33–35, 42, 43, 55, 57, 65, 67, 172–173
reputation: of Britain and the empire 56, 84, 102, 126, 142, 151, 157; Dufferin's personal reputation 14–16, 39–40, 42, 57, 65–66, 94–95, 99, 100–101, 117, 119–120, 130, 142, 156–157, 177–178, 191, 202, 204; of landlords generally 43, 64
responsibilities: of imperial office 30, 84, 86, 87, 94, 166, 174–175, 191; of landownership 7, 17, 28–31, 37, 43, 54–55, 57, 66, 68, 72, 91, 97, 128, 204; of the state 54, 68; *see also* duty
revolution 54, 55, 143
Rhodes, Cecil 103
Rideau Hall 112–113
Riel, Louis 63, 116–117
right to rule 18, 30, 61, 92, 122, 204, 205

rights 7, 17, 28–31, 37, 57, 68, 125, 128, 204; *see also* property rights
Ripon, George Robinson, 1st Marquis 30, 90, 102, 154, 164, 171–174, 184, 190
roads 33, 155, 180
Roberts, Sir Frederick 177
Roman empire 55, 85, 89, 94, 153
Romanticism 43, 146
romanticism 57, 63, 70, 72, 125, 204
royal commissions 127
royal courts 4, 7, 11, 15, 28, 43, 189
ruby mining 6, 99
'rule by the best' 5, 7, 19, 53, 92, 146, 149, 155, 166, 187–190, 203–204
rule of law 91, 125, 126, 143–144, 147, 152
Russell, Lady Frances 33
Russell, Lord John 11, 37, 142, 145, 146, 148, 149
Russia 13, 61, 67–68, 87, 89, 91, 94, 99, 102, 144, 148, 188

St Andrews University 14, 202, 203
St Petersburg 68, 91
Salisbury, Robert Gascoyne-Cecil, 3rd Marquis 9, 15, 65, 71, 89, 94, 101
Saturday Review 154
Scotland 6, 32, 35, 55, 61, 68, 173
Scott, Sir Walter 6, 43, 72, 146
Scott-Moncrieff, Colin 155
Second World War 206
Secretary of State for India 62, 89, 99, 171, 182–184, 190
sectarianism 11, 17, 44, 54, 61, 63, 91–92, 117, 124–125, 141–143, 145–148, 169
security 8, 18, 54–55, 66, 70, 88, 94, 97, 99, 101, 149, 165, 178
self-government 18–19, 29, 54, 68–72, 92–93, 112–131, 148, 154, 166, 175, 179, 182–190, 205
service aristocracy 30, 53, 85, 88, 92, 94, 103, 113
1798 Rebellion 33, 63
Sheridan, Richard Brinsley 9, 28, 204
silver 180, 182
Simla 169, 170–171, 186–187, 189
Skibbereen 1–2, 33, 55
slavery 89, 92
social reform 85, 185
socialism 168
Somerset, Edward Seymour, 12th Duke 11

Somerset, Georgiana Seymour, Duchess 9
South Africa 14, 168, 203
sovereignty 91, 97–101, 148, 152, 165, 167, 169–171, 178, 190
Star of India order 171
state, the 54, 66, 68, 96–98, 205
state violence 19, 87, 95, 98–102, 125–126, 166, 174–178, 183
Stephen, James Fitzjames 184
stereotyping 11, 18, 28, 43, 122, 125, 146, 178, 184
Sublime Porte 13, 141, 144, 151, 154; *see also* Ottoman empire
Sudan 153, 156
Suez Canal 13, 151–152
'surplus' population 35, 54, 55–56, 59
Sutherland, George Sutherland-Leveson-Gower, 3rd Duke 55
Svalbard 11
Syria 11, 17, 19–20, 141–150, 156–157, 175

tariffs 6
taxation 31, 129, 144, 153, 155, 171, 180–182
tenant agitation 28, 40, 54, 58, 64–65, 68–71, 91–92, 127–128, 172–173
tenure, *see* land tenure
Tenure and Improvment of Land (Ireland) Act (1860) 59
terror 19, 87, 167, 169, 175–178
textile industry 33, 38
Thibaw 99–100, 177
Thompson, Augustus Rivers 173
Thomson, Mortimer 34, 37–40, 63–64
Three Fs (fair rent, freedom from eviction, free sale) 67–68
Times 95, 100–101, 175, 178

Tone, Theobald Wolfe 63
tours 86, 96, 103, 115, 130, 169, 189
tradition 17, 19, 43, 67, 85, 94, 153, 166, 170–171
transnational exchange 17, 87, 154, 155, 157, 166, 167–168
travel 10, 11, 35, 91, 94, 125, 142, 146

Ulster Tenant Right 17, 39, 54, 56–63, 67
unionism 69, 70–71, 104, 179
United States 6, 14, 56, 114, 115, 117, 119, 122–124
unity 19, 69, 87, 113–114, 117–122, 188
'Urabi Revolt 13, 17, 93–94, 141, 143, 151, 152, 155
urbanisation 88, 167, 171, 205

Vaughan, W. E. 34
Verney, Sir Henry 104
Victoria, Queen 11, 33, 55, 56, 69, 91, 96, 97, 103, 115, 130, 169, 170
violence 19, 60, 64–66, 87, 92, 95, 98–102, 125–126, 143, 146–148, 152, 166, 169, 174–178, 183
visibility 96, 113, 115, 126, 169–170, 205

Wallace, Donald Mackenzie 175, 177
Walter, John 100
will to rule 7, 19, 83–88, 96, 103, 165, 203–204
working classes 85, 125
Wright, Whittaker 14
Wyndham Act 16

Young, George 68

Printed in the United States
By Bookmasters